THE ATTALID KINGDOM

A Constitutional History

THE ATTALID KINGDOM

A Constitutional History

R. E. ALLEN

CLARENDON PRESS·OXFORD
1983

Oxford University Press, Walton Street, Oxford OX2 6DP

London Glasgow New York Toronto
Delhi Bombay Calcutta Madras Karachi
Kuala Lumpur Singapore Hong Kong Tokyo
Nairobi Dar es Salaam Cape Town
Melbourne Auckland

and associated companies in
Beirut Berlin Ibadan Mexico City Nicosia

Published in the United States
by Oxford University Press, New York

British Library Cataloguing in Publication Data
Allen, R.E.
The Attalid Kingdom.
1. Pergamon - History
I. Title
939'.21 DS156.P4
ISBN 0-19-814845-3

Typeset by Fotron SA., Athens, Greece
Printed in Hong Kong

PREFACE

There has been a long-felt need for a new constitutional history of the Attalid Kingdom, that can embrace the extensive research done and reassessments made since Cardinali's *Il Regno di Pergamo*, still the basic work on the subject, was published in 1906. The present work is an attempt to meet that need. I was further aware in the course of my research that a great deal of important specialist work, above all that of Ohlemutz (1940) and Kähler (1948), had not been adequately absorbed into the more recent works on the Attalids now available, and I hope that my debt to these and to others who have studied the Attalid Kingdom will be obvious.

This book began its life as a doctoral thesis of the University of London, presented in 1972. Since then I have benefited greatly from the advice of teachers and examiners, as well as from work published in the meantime. I owe a great debt of gratitude to Mr P. M. Fraser, who first suggested a study of the Attalids to me and has advised and helped me most generously in achieving it. I am glad to have this opportunity at last of thanking him. I am also indebted to Professor A. D. Momigliano, without whose initial support my research could not have been contemplated, and to Professor H. Bengtson, under whose direction I studied for a year as a guest of the Seminar (now Institut) für Alte Geschichte of the University of Munich in 1972–3; I greatly appreciate his kindness and hospitality, as also the stimulating discussion afforded by members of the Seminar, especially Dr Wolfgang Orth.

Finally I must thank the managing committee of the British School at Athens for admitting me as a Student of the School from 1968 to 1970; the British Institute of Archaeology at Ankara for facilitating my research in Turkey, especially at Pergamon itself; Mme D. Peppa Delmousou for enabling me to study the epigraphical material relating to the Attalids in the Epigraphical Museum in Athens; and Miss E. Rohde for admitting me to the archives of the Pergamon Museum in Berlin in 1969. To all these I am most grateful.

Oxford, 1979   R . E . ALLEN

CONTENTS

ABBREVIATIONS

The following abbreviations and short titles are used of works cited frequently. Others generally follow those listed in *The Oxford Classical Dictionary* (ed. 2, 1970). In some cases further information is given in the bibliography.

Abh. Berlin	*Abhandlungen der Preussischen Akademie der Wissenschaften, Phil.-Hist. Kl.*
Abh. München	*Abhandlungen der Bayerischen Akademie der Wissenschaften, Phil.-Hist. Kl.*
AM	*Mitteilungen des Deutschen archäologischen Instituts: Athenische Abteilung*
AvP	*Altertümer von Pergamon*
Bengtson, *Strat.*	H. Bengtson, *Die Strategie in der hellenistischen Zeit*, i–iii
Bull.	J. and L. Robert, *Bulletin épigraphique* (annually in *REG*)
Cardinali, *RP*	G. Cardinali, *Il Regno di Pergamo* (1906)
CRAI	*Comptes rendues de l'Académie des inscriptions et belles-lettres*
F. Delphes	*Fouilles de Delphes*
FGrHist	F. Jacoby, *Fragmente der griechischen Historiker* (1923–)
Hansen, *Attalids*	E. V. Hansen, *The Attalids of Pergamon* (ed. 2, 1972)
Holleaux, *Études*	M. Holleaux, *Études d'épigraphie et d'histoire grecques*, i–vi
ISE	L. Moretti, *Iscrizioni storiche ellenistiche* (2 vols., Florence, 1965 and 1976)
IvM	O. Kern, *Die Inschriften von Magnesia am Meander* (Berlin, 1900)
IvP	*Inschriften von Pergamon*
IvPr	F. Hiller von Gaertringen, *Inschriften von Priene* (Berlin, 1906)
Kähler, *Gr. Fries*	H. Kähler, *Der grosse Fries von Pergamon.* (Berlin, 1948)
Magie, *Roman Rule*	D. Magie, *Roman Rule in Asia Minor* (1950)
MvP	F. von Fritze, *Die Münzen von Pergamon* (1910)

OGIS	W. Dittenberger, *Orientis Graeci Inscriptiones Selectae* (Leipzig, 1903)
Ohlemutz, *Kulte*	E. Ohlemutz, *Die Kulte und Heiligtümer der Götter in Pergamon* (1940)
ÖJh	*Jahreshefte des Österreichischen archäologischen Instituts*
RE	*Real-Encyclopädie der klassischen Altertumswissenschaft*, ed. A. Pauly, G. Wissowa, W. Kroll (1893–)
REA	*Révue des études anciennes*
REG	*Révue des études grecques*
Robert, *Ét. anat.*	L. Robert, *Études anatoliennes* (1937)
Robert, *Villes*	L. Robert, *Villes d'Asie Mineure* (ed. 2, 1962)
Rostovtzeff, *SEHHW*	M. Rostovtzeff, *The Social and Economic History of the Hellenistic World* (Oxford, 1941)
SB München	*Sitzungsberichte der Bayerischen Akademie der Wissenschaften, Phil.-Hist. Kl.*
SB Wien	*Sitzungsberichte der Österreichischen Akademie in Wien, Phil.-Hist. Kl.*
Schmitt, *Untersuchungen*	H. H. Schmitt, *Untersuchungen zur Geschichte Antiochos'des Grossen und Seiner Zeit*
StV	*Die Staatsverträge des Altertums* (ed. H. Bengtson): iii. *Die Verträge der griechisch-römischen Welt von 338 bis 200 vor Chr.* (ed. H. H. Schmitt, Munich, 1969)
Syll.[3]	W. Dittenberger, *Sylloge Inscriptionum Graecarum* (ed. 3, Leipzig, 1915)
Walbank, *Comm.*	F. W. Walbank, *A Historical Commentary on Polybius* (3 vols., Oxford, 1957, 1967, and 1979)
Welles, *RC*	C. B. Welles, *Royal Correspondence in the Hellenistic Period* (New Haven, 1934)

1. Western Asia Minor

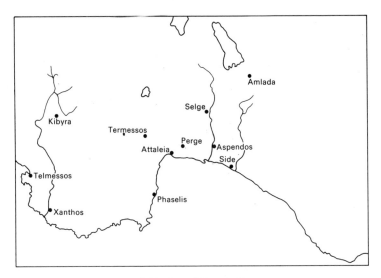

2. Lycia and Pamphylia

1

THE NATURE OF THE EVIDENCE

The history of the Attalid dynasty falls in the third and second centuries BC, the period of Hellenistic history for which the paucity of good literary source-material is most acutely felt, and the modern historian's complaint with regard to evidence about the Attalids coincides to some extent with that which may be expressed of the events and institutions of the Hellenistic kingdoms generally in these years.[1] There are, however, special problems arising in a study of the Attalids, as we shall see, and the inadequacies of the literary sources in providing information that will contribute to their solution is only partly redeemed by the admittedly copious epigraphical evidence that is now at the disposal of the historian of the Attalids. When the literary tradition is fullest and most reliable — for the reigns of Attalos I and Eumenes II — our understanding of the men and their reigns is correspondingly penetrating; when it fails they become obscure and ambiguous. This state of affairs is strikingly illustrated by the contrast between our knowledge of Attalos I and Eumenes II, who are figures of substance and true historical significance, and our knowledge of Attalos III, who continues to elude a historical perspective and understanding appropriate to his importance, although a growing body of epigraphical and other evidence has thrown valuable new light on his character and achievements as a corrective to the largely anecdotal literary tradition.[2]

We may begin by reviewing the literary evidence on which we may hope to rely in this study of the Attalid dynasty. The only extant historical narrative written at a time more or less contemporary to the events is that provided by Polybios for the reigns of Eumenes II (197–159 BC) and Attalos II (159–138 BC); it is not

[1] See now C. Préaux, *Monde hell.* i. 88–9.
[2] See the recent discussion of J. Hopp, *Untersuchungen*, 107–20.

completely preserved and it becomes increasingly fragmentary and episodic in the course of the later of these reigns. The early books of Polybios' *Histories* deal with events that occurred before his own lifetime and fall from our point of view in the reign of Attalos I (241–197 BC); because this part of his work is more completely preserved than the later parts we obtain a relatively fuller narrative for these years than we would expect from the generally contemporary theme of Polybios' work as a whole. In providing such good evidence for these important early years, and despite the shortcomings of incompleteness, Polybios' *Histories* constitute an important element in the study of Attalid Asia Minor.

Comparable in importance to the narrative evidence of Polybios is that of a different kind to be derived from Strabo's *Geographia*. Writing in the age of Augustus, Strabo refers to the Attalids at several points in the part of his work that deals with western Asia Minor, and shows a precise knowledge and authority that are all the more impressive for the support they often receive from independent evidence, chiefly epigraphical; a great deal of importance will be attached throughout this book to the testimony he provides. It is evident that Strabo had a sound and detailed knowledge both of the history of Asia Minor in general and of the Attalid dynasty in particular. Of special importance for our purposes is the summary account which Strabo inserts by way of historical background in his treatment of the city of Pergamon and its environs (xiii. 4. 623–4); this account explores family relationships and individual dynastic achievements, as well as some of the more important events of each reign: as will be seen in the next chapter, our knowledge and understanding of the reigns of the dynasts Philetairos and Eumenes I owes much to these brief but astute remarks, and the value of the epigraphical evidence is greatly enhanced by the possibility of interpreting it in the contexts that they provide.

The nature and scope of Strabo's remarks about the Attalids indicate that the sources at his disposal were sound, and it is probable that they were in many cases contemporary to the events described. The account is based largely on biographical information: lengths of rule and other chronological details are given with great precision and accuracy; there is much personal detail and anecdotal material concerning individual dynasts, especially

Philetairos, and their individual plans and achievements are stressed. It is very likely that the authority for all this information rests at least partly with the biographies of the Attalids that were compiled during the course of the dynasty, works such as those of Lysimachos, a contemporary and admirer of a King Attalos; Neanthes of Kyzikos, a city with which the Attalids established early connections; and Leschides, a contemporary of Eumenes II.[3] We may also adduce the many scholars who were attracted to Pergamon during its royal prosperity under Attalos I and more particularly at the invitation of Eumenes II, whose enlightened aspirations envisaged Pergamon as a famous centre of culture and learning in the Greek world.[4] Some of these scholars are known to have researched and written about local history and antiquities, notably Polemon of Ilion, ὁ κληθεὶς περιηγητής, whose activity is dated firmly to the reign of Eumenes II, and who is known to have been concerned in his travels with antiquities and monuments rather than with considerations of geography in the usual sense. Demetrios of Skepsis, a contemporary of Polemon who explored and wrote at length on the antiquities of the Troad, is named by Strabo as his source on a number of occasions.[5] These two names adequately represent the antiquarian research that was encouraged at Pergamon under Attalid rule and which constitutes the sound authority with which much of the evidence transmitted by Strabo may be associated.

Before passing to consider the secondary literary evidence we should pause to reflect on a danger that is inherent in the tradition so far discussed, and which arises from the fact that all the elements of this tradition are favourable to the Attalids and sympathetic to their aims and achievements. Polybios was generally very well disposed to the dynasty and to the order it represented and was invariably hostile to its enemies, especially Prusias I and II of Bithynia and Pharnakes of Pontos, these being also the

[3] *FGrHist* IIB, 170–2. Préaux, *Monde hell.* i. 86, laments the loss of these biographies but does not consider their status as sources of Strabo's information.

[4] On what follows see R. Pfeiffer, *History of Classical Scholarship* (Oxford, 1968), 246–51.

[5] See for example the references in book xiii (which will mainly concern us) at 1.27, 594; 1.43, 602; 1.44, 603 (where an unnamed work by Attalos I of Pergamon is cited, probably a geographical treatise).

enemies of Rome as long as the Senate supported Attalid interests in Asia Minor.[6] Even when the Senate became suspicious, sometimes with apparent justification, of Eumenes II's ambitions, Polybios continued to defend him.[7] Thus the picture of Attalid rule we derive from Polybios is an entirely favourable one, and very little hostile opinion of the kind that we have, for example, pertaining to Rhodian rule in the subject *Peraia* has reached our literary sources.[8] We must discount from this context the so-called Rhodian propaganda directed against Eumenes II at the time of the Roman settlement of 188 BC as amounting to nothing more than a disagreement with Eumenes over the future of the Greek cities of Asia Minor in that year.[9] Of greater substance is the propaganda recorded by Polybios (especially at xxxii.17) as being directed at Eumenes II personally by a large part of the Roman Senate in the 160s with the intention of encouraging his brother Attalos (later Attalos II) to usurp power in his place. Then there is the largely successful attempt of Perseus of Macedon to discredit Eumenes at Rome, evidence of which can be discerned in surviving extracts of Appian's *Makedonika* (notably xviii.1). None of this however, interesting though it is, has influenced the literary tradition as we know it or constituted any part of it; it is largely confined to the reign of Eumenes II and is simply the reporting of elements hostile to him, and as such it comes from predictable quarters and causes no surprise. Of reasoned opposition to Attalid rule we find no traces in the literary sources even when opportunities may be thought to arise for its inclusion. This tendency is shared by the epigraphical evidence, to be reviewed below, since this also ema-

[6] See the comment on Pharnakes of Pontos (xxvii. 17, on which see also Walbank, *Comm.* iii. 318), and, above all, the hostile assessment of Prusias II of Bithynia (xxxvi. 15; Walbank, *Comm.* iii. 46).

[7] Polyb. xxxi. 6. 6; Holleaux, *Études,* ii. 170.

[8] P. M. Fraser and G. E. Bean, *The Rhodian Peraea and Islands* (Oxford, 1954), 118–22.

[9] C. G. Starr, *C. Phil.* xxxiii (1938), 63–8, argues that mutual hostility is a continuous factor in Rhodian–Pergamene relations from early in the reign of Attalos I; but it was the issue of the Greek cities in 189 that first divided them, according to Polyb. xxi. 22. 6. We shall see in chapter 3 that Rhodes and Pergamon were brought together during the reign of Attalos I by the common need to defend the south-east Aegean against Philip V of Macedon.

nates from pro-Attalid sources, either Pergamon itself or cities and regions that were well disposed to the kings.

A second caveat needs to be entered with regard to the kind of evidence so far discussed. We have already seen that much of it lacks context and substance, especially where events of the later years of the dynasty are concerned. Thus, apart from the sketch of Attalid history that has been mentioned, much of Strabo's information is given in passing and with no attempt to offer a full background to the statements made. Strabo in the *Geographia* was not writing history and cannot be expected to answer the kinds of historical questions that we are inclined to pose. In the case of Polybios the trouble lies with the transmission of the text, which is increasingly fragmentary from book vii onwards. There is also in this connection a qualitative point to be made, that these literary sources do not always adequately meet our demand for knowledge of constitutional machinery and procedure, which are a primary concern of this study. Polybios is notoriously confusing on the occasions when he pauses to describe administrative or constitutional organization, even when he is thoroughly familiar with them: we can therefore hardly expect him to transmit a clear and consistent picture of the institutions of Attalid rule, which he knew less well and about which he was probably less concerned to inform his readers. These readers could be expected furthermore to be mostly Greeks, and therefore sufficiently familiar with the connotations of his terminology as not to require careful precision or elaboration.[10] These factors increase our difficulties in interpreting the significance of official titles and regional designations, and (even more noticeably) of institutions of taxation and financial administration.

Despite these reservations Polybios and Strabo stand as the most important literary sources at our disposal, and they are joined by Livy when he is following lost or fragmentary sections of Polybios' account. When Livy is not following Polybios we are faced with the usual problem of deciding what his source is at a particular point in the narrative and what its worth is; we will be

---

[10] F. W. Walbank, *Polybius* (Sather Classical Lectures, 42, 1972), 1–6. The institutions that Polybios explains are generally those that would be unfamiliar to Greek readers: see Walbank, loc. cit., 4, n.19.

particularly aware of this problem for instance when we come to consider Livy's evidence for the institution of the cistophoric coinage in the Attalid Kingdom. Also to be considered as an element of the extant literary tradition is the anecdotal material about the Attalid kings, usually fanciful stories that represent a kind of elaboration or variation of known historical circumstances and must be regarded as sensational and untrustworthy. These have survived in the accounts of later historians (including Justin) and in works such as the *Deipnosophistai* of Athenaios and the *Moralia* of Plutarch, whose nature and purpose provided suitable contexts for the retailing and preservation of such material. In this category belongs much of the evidence on the parentage and reign of Attalos III:[11] since in a number of significant instances this evidence will be seen to be contradicted by sounder elements in the tradition its value is correspondingly diminished; it needs to be carefully distinguished from the more reliable biographical material preserved in Strabo's writing and certainly to be treated with a greater degree of caution than is often the case in modern accounts.

Enough has been said to familiarize the reader with the problems to be expected of the literary evidence that will be adduced in this study. We turn now to consider briefly the nature of the evidence provided by inscriptions. What we know of the institutions of Attalid rule, as distinct from the historical background of their implementation, is derived very largely from epigraphical evidence, both the copious body of texts from Pergamon itself, augmented over the years since the original publications of *Inschriften von Pergamon,* and that from other parts of the Greek world in Asia Minor and on the Greek mainland. Of great importance is the material, consisting chiefly of honorary decrees in favour of members of the royal family or their officials, from cities that were in some way subject or tributary to the Attalids, since these frequently record the names and titles of officials and at times attest, explicitly or otherwise, procedures and even policies of the royal administration; in this category should be mentioned a decree from Bursa honouring the Attalid *strategos* Korrhagos,

---

[11] See Appendix i; Hopp, *Untersuchungen,* 16–26, esp. 18–19.

which is probably the most important and certainly the most discussed single item of evidence relating to Attalid procedures of regional administration after 188 BC. Another significant genre of documents that may be mentioned here is that of the royal letters written to cities of varying status; these are particularly valuable in that they are more usually dated than are other kinds of inscription, and by their nature frequently include references to and explanations of royal policy such as we would not expect to find in other sources.

Of equal importance in other ways are the texts from cities and regions not subject to the Attalids but enjoying friendly relations with them. Most notable are the records of Attalid benefactions, beginning at an early stage in the history of the dynasty, at Athens, at Delphi, and in Boiotia. Such evidence documents the history of the Attalids' external relations and in some cases further illustrates constitutional procedures and institutions, since ambassadors, members of the royal family, and other officials and representatives are occasionally designated and described. Even more important is the evidence relating to the institution of royal cults in cities which were the object of the Attalids' beneficence; worthy of special mention in this regard is the material now accumulated from Teos and Miletos.

Numismatic evidence is of less importance to constitutional matters in the case of the Attalids, but it contributes significantly to our knowledge of the dynasty's standing, both before 188 BC (the dynastic coinage)[12] and after that date, when (as will be argued) the cistophoric coinage became an institution of Attalid fiscal control throughout the newly acquired kingdom.

Finally we must consider what may be termed the monumental evidence. Of all the Hellenistic royal capitals Pergamon has provided the richest yield of monumental and architectural remains, enabling us to reconstruct with a high degree of precision not only the growth and development of the city in material terms, but also the nature and purpose of many royal and religious buildings, and the relative importance of the institutions and cults (whether royal

---

[12] See in general the remarks of Rostovtzeff, *SEHHW* ii. 1288–96; Préaux, *Monde hell.* i. 106–10, and the references given below, 24 n. 51.

or divine) that they represent. Although it will not be a part of our purpose to consider the material and artistic development of Pergamon, certain features of it will be noticed as they attest or contribute to our knowledge of the Attalids' power and standing in the Greek world. Thus the early years of the reign of Attalos I, and in particular the significance of his numerous military victories over Galatians and other enemies in western Asia Minor, can only be fully comprehended in relation to the series of monuments that he dedicated to Athena on the citadel of Pergamon; and the value of these as historical evidence is in many cases further enhanced by the presence of dedicatory inscriptions which attest both the purpose for which they were erected and the events which they were intended to celebrate. This kind of evidence is less prominent for the early years of the dynasty, but is of great importance to an assessment of the reigns and achievements of Attalos' successors, especially Eumenes II, for whom the Pergamene monuments are a true mirror of the expansion and strengthening of royal authority in Asia Minor after the Roman settlement of 188 BC.[13]

[13] An excellent historical account of the monuments of Pergamon is given by Kähler, *Gr. Fries*, 131–49 (with detailed notes).

2

PERGAMON UNDER
PHILETAIROS AND EUMENES I

Under Philetairos and Eumenes I the Attalids achieved the status of a dynasty; it is the purpose of this chapter to examine the process.[1] Philetairos' position at Pergamon dates from about 302, or shortly before the battle at Ipsos,[2] but for the twenty years' period of his allegiance to Lysimachos we have only a few literary notices, usually in late writers, and no certainly pertinent documentary evidence.[3] We do not even know the exact title or nature of the office entrusted to Philetairos by Lysimachos, although it was almost certainly a purely financial one.[4] The official foundation of the Attalid dynasty, however, was put some twenty years later in 283, when Philetairos placed himself, and the wealth he administered, at the disposal of Seleukos, whom he correctly assessed as the more likely winner in the imminent conflict with Lysimachos. This date, 283, can be reached with some precision from the chronology of the reigns of the Attalids given by Strabo

[1] For the early growth of Pergamon, see Cardinali, *RP* 4–16; Rostovtzeff, *SEHHW* i. 553–66; Bengtson, *Strat.* ii. 195–8; Magie, *Roman Rule* i. 1–33, with the well-documented notes, ii. 725–81. The second edition of Hansen's *Attalids* shows only superficial revision and is as uncritical as the first, which was well reviewed by A. Aymard, *REA* xlix (1947), 339–45. The thesis of R.B. McShane, *Foreign Policy* (Illinois, 1964), that the Attalids worked from a panhellenic ideal and on a legalistic federal basis in their relations with Greek cities, does only occasional justice to the evidence, and is hardly realistic.

[2] According to Diodoros xx. 107. 4–5, Dokimos, *strategos* of Antigonos at Synnada, took up the cause of Lysimachos in 302, and Philetairos was probably given the charge of the stronghold at Pergamon at the same time. Cf. Cardinali, *RP* 6–7; Bengtson, *Strat.* i. 199–201.

[3] For the relevance to this period of the Pergamene treaty of ἰσοπολιτεία with Temnos (*StV* iii. 555), see below, 16–17.

[4] He was probably simply γαζοφύλαξ, that is, keeper of the treasury at Pergamon (cf. Bengtson, *Strat.* ii. 195), but there is no direct evidence to this effect. His position was certainly not a military one; cf. Cardinali, *RP* 7, n. 2.

(xiii. 4. 1–2, 623–4), supplemented by other information. Strabo gives the length of each reign in years as follows: Philetairos, 20; Eumenes I, 22; Attalos I, 43; Eumenes II, 49; Attalos II, 21; and Attalos III, 5. This chronology is mistaken at two points, but each mistake is fortunately easy to account for. Firstly, the 49 years assigned to Eumenes II is evidently a slip for 39; this lower figure then fits with the rest of Strabo's dates, and an error of 10 is not difficult to explain in simple arithmetical terms.[5] Strabo meant, then, to say 39, but even this figure is not quite accurate: the death of Attalos I can be placed from the narrative of Livy (xxxiii. 2. 1–3; 21.1) in the late summer or autumn of 197,[6] and we know from Delphian documents recording Pergamene donations of the year 160/59, that Eumenes II died in the autumn of 159.[7] Thus Eumenes II ruled for a little over 38 years, which were evidently rounded upwards in Strabo's source to 39. Now Polybios, followed by Livy, assigns 44 years to Attalos I, and not 43;[8] it is therefore clear what happened to the chronology followed by Strabo: Attalos I ruled for 43½ years (= 43 in Strabo, 44 in Polybios), and

[5] K. Meischke, *Symbolae*, 12–13; Magie, *Roman Rule*, ii. 771–2, n. 75.

[6] The account of Attalos' death is missing from the fragments of Polyb. xviii. All we have is Polybios' own eulogy (xviii. 41). Livy's narrative, at this point drawn from Polybios, enables us to date the event to late summer or autumn 197; cf. Holleaux, *Études*, v. 114, n. 1. An inscription from Delphi (Appendix iv, no. 4), records the presence at Delphi, in connection with a manumission, of Dameas, ὁ παρὰ τοῦ βασιλέως Ἀττάλου ὁ ἐπὶ τῶν ἔργων τῶν βασιλικῶν, in August–September 197. On this evidence Meischke concluded (*Symbolae*, 23) that Attalos was still alive in September 197, but since Dameas' titulature will probably not have changed immediately after Attalos' death, such an exact chronological inference is hardly valid.

[7] The chronology of the death of Eumenes II was established by G. Daux, *BCH* lix (1935), 220–30; see also his *Delphes*, 502–9, on the basis of Delphian documents (*Syll.*[3] 671, now to be consulted in the edition in *F. Delphes*, iii. 3. 238–9, with the additional corrections and suggestions of Ad. Wilhelm, *Griech. Inschriften rechtlichen Inhalts*, 51–5; *Syll.*[3] 672, = Daux, *Delphes*, 682–98, C), which record donations of Eumenes II in the ninth month of the archonship of Amphistratos (160 / 59), and of Attalos II, called King, in the sixth month of the same year. These texts show, as Daux demonstrated, that Eumenes was alive in March–April 159, and that Attalos II was associated in the kingship some months before Eumenes' death, which must be placed towards the end of the year 159. The establishing of the co-regency is probably referred to in an Athenian decree, also of 160/59 (Appendix iv, no.18).

[8] Polyb. xviii. 41. 8; Livy xxxiii. 21. 1.

Eumenes II ruled for 38½ years (= 39 in Strabo).[9] In absolute terms, then, the accession of Attalos I should be dated 241, and not 240, which means, in turn, that the official beginning of Philetairos' rule was in 283, and not 282, although it remains a possibility, but an unlikely one, that the 20 years assigned to Philetairos by Strabo was a round figure, and that the beginning of Philetairos' rule was not exactly dated.[10] It seems safer, however, to leave the chronology of the reigns of the Attalids as follows:

PHILETAIROS	283–263	EUMENES II	197–159
EUMENES I	263–241	ATTALOS II	159–138
ATTALOS I	241–197	ATTALOS III	138–133.

This chronology leaves us with the year 283 as most probably that of the foundation of the Attalid dynasty. Unfortunately no chronological precision, corroborative or otherwise, can be gained from the available accounts of the events leading to the battle fought between the armies of Lysimachos and Seleukos at Corupedion, since these accounts appear in the highly dramatized narratives of later writers, but they do have some value in throwing light on the position taken by Philetairos. The two principal accounts, those of Justin and Pausanias, deal with the events which made up the final downfall of the house of Lysimachos: the conspiracy against, and murder of, his son Agathokles, widespread revolt from Lysimachos (including Philetairos' change of allegiance), and the battle at Corupedion.[11] In the narrative of Justin (xvii. 1) these disasters are related to the portent of an earthquake which hit Lysimacheia in 287/6;[12] thus chronological precision is sacrificed to the making of a dramatic point:

Per idem ferme tempus Hellesponti et Chersonesi regionibus terrae motus fuit, maxime tamen Lysimachia urbs, ante duos et XX annos a Lysimacho rege condita, eversa est. Quod portentum dira Lysimacho stirpique eius ac regni ruinam cum clade vexatarum regionum portend-

[9] Cf. Cardinali, *RP* 8, n. 3.

[10] It was K. J. Beloch's view (*Gr. Gesch.* iv.² 2. 207) that the twenty years assigned to Philetairos is a round number, but the exact figures given for the other reigns count against it.

[11] For these events, see B. Niese, *Geschichte der griechischen und Makedonischen Staaten,* i. 402–4; Beloch, *Gr. Gesch.* iv.² 1. 242–5.

[12] Beloch, *Gr. Gesch.* iv.² 1. 243, n. 1.

ebat. Nec ostentis fides defuit, nam brevi post tempore Agathoclem, filium suum, quem in successionem regni ordinaverat, per quem multa bella prospere gesserat, non solum ultra patrium, verum etiam ultra humanum morem perosus ministra Arsinoë noverca veneno interfecit. Haec illi prima mali labes, hoc initium inpendentis ruinae fuit. Nam parricidium principum secutae caedes sunt luentium supplicia, quod occisum iuvenem dolebant. Itaque et ii, qui caedibus superfuerant, et ii, qui exercitibus praeerant, certatim ad Seleucum deficiunt eumque pronum iam ex aemulatione gloriae bellum Lysimacho inferre conpellunt.

The chronology is also certainly compressed *post eventum* by Pausanias, who errs further in making Lysimachos the aggressor against Seleukos (i. 10. 3–5): καὶ Φιλέταιρος ἅμα, ᾧ τὰ χρήματα ἐπετέτραπτο Λυσιμάχου, τῇ τε ᾿Αγαθοκλέους τελευτῇ χαλεπῶς φέρων καὶ τὰ παρὰ τῆς ᾿Αρσινόης ὕποπτα ἡγούμενος καταλαμ-βάνει Πέργαμον τὴν ὑπὲρ Καΐκου, πέμψας δὲ κήρυκα τά τε χρήματα καὶ αὐτὸν ἐδίδου Σελεύκῳ. The battle at Corupedion was fought early in 281, most probably in February,[13] but the death of Agathokles cannot be dated exactly between the years 287/6 and 283, and the implication in the highly dramatized late tradition, that Lysimachos and Seleukos came to blows immediately after the desertions from Lysimachos, is not a cogent objection to the (at the most) two years interval required by the chronology argued here. These passages of Justin and Pausanias, if their relation of causes and effects can be trusted, imply that Philetairos distrusted Lysimachos and took the first opportunity to betray him. This is probably again a highly dramatized and personalized account of more sober realities; namely, that Philetairos saw Seleukos as the stronger man in the coming struggle. According to Justin, Philetairos was not alone in this opinion: *ii, qui exercitibus prae-erant* is doubtless terminologically inexact or may be an interpretation of the term *strategoi*; it was probably intended to include Philetairos, who is not specifically mentioned in the narrative.

It is then important to remember that Philetairos was not alone in deserting Lysimachos, and that the dynasty he founded was in origin only one of a number of such dynasties in Asia Minor, although none of the others shared the Attalids' spectacular suc-

---

[13] Bengtson, *Historia*, iv (1953), 113; H. Heinen, *Untersuch. zur hellenistischen Geschichte des 3. Jhdt. v. Chr.* (*Historia*, Einzelschr. 20, 1972), 20–4.

cess. They owed their positions later to the partially tentative nature of Seleukid rule in Asia Minor,[14] and sought independence and an increase of authority when this power began its slow but continuous decline after the death of Seleukos I. An example is the dynasty of Lysias and Philomelos, whose position we will be examining later in this chapter.[15] Similarly, it is likely that Philetairos' own brother Eumenes was dynast for a time at the Paphlagonian city of Amastris, although his tenure was evidently brief, and he did not establish a dynasty there.[16] It is likely that these other dynasts played an important part in the issue between Seleukos and Lysimachos, whereas Philetairos held an especially important position in view of the great wealth he controlled at Pergamon.

How Philetairos' position was changed by his transference of allegiance to Seleukos in 283 is not clear, since the nature of his rule in the service of Lysimachos is, as we have seen, so poorly attested. We may safely reckon, however, that he became something more than the simple treasurer or finance-officer he had been. It is almost certain, moreover, that he gained a good measure of freedom, although not complete independence. Strabo, whose

---

[14] On the δυνάσται as an element in the Seleukid Kingdom, in Asia Minor as well as in the East, see, in addition to the studies of Wilhelm and Holleaux, cited below, n. 39, Bengtson, *Strat.* ii. 3–8; A. H. M. Jones, *Cities of the Eastern Roman Provinces* (ed. 2, Oxford, 1971), 46–9. Note especially the decree of Smyrna (treaty of συμπολιτεία with Magnesia ad Sipylum), passed probably in 243 or shortly thereafter (*OGIS* 229, = *StV* iii. 492; on the date, W. Otto, *Beitr. z. Seleukidengesch. des 3. Jahrhunderts v. Chr.* (*Abh. München*, 34, 1928), 70; Chr. Habicht, *Gottmenschentum*, 100: 'wohl vom Frühjahr 242'), lines 10–11: ἐβεβαίω-σεν τῶι δήμωι τὴν αὐ|τονομίαν καὶ δημοκρατίαν, ἔγραψεν δὲ καὶ πρὸς τοὺς βασιλεῖς καὶ τοὺς δυνάστας καὶ τὰς πόλεις καὶ τὰ ἔθνη ἀξι|ώσας ἀποδέξασθαι τό τε ἱερὸν τῆς Στρατονικίδος Ἀφροδίτης ἄσυλον εἶναι κτλ.

[15] Cf. below, n. 39.

[16] We know from a passage of Memnon (*FGrHist* 434, ch. 9) that a dynast named Eumenes held Amastris in 279 (τοῦ κατέχοντος αὐτὴν Εὐμένους), and that he surrendered the city to the rulers of Pontos in this year. The identification of this Eumenes with the brother of Philetairos (on whom see below, Appendix i), first proposed by Droysen (*Gesch. des Hellenismus* (ed. 2, 1877) iii. 255), but with a preference for an identification with the son of this Eumenes, i.e. the future dynast (cf. Niese, ii. 75, n. 7; Cardinali, *RP* 10, n. 4), is strengthened by the fact that Philetairos' native city of Tios took part in the synoikism of Amastris in *c.* 300 BC, although it later withdrew (Strabo xii. 3.10, 544; cf. Ernst Meyer, *Die Grenzen* 109–10; L. Robert, *Ét. anat.* 262–3).

source was in all probability ultimately a biography of Philetairos, whether or not used at first hand,[17] refers to his position and to his policy; he calls him (xii. 3. 8, 543) ὁ ἀρχηγέτης τοῦ τῶν Ἀτταλικῶν βασιλέων γένους, and of his administration says (xiii 4. 1, 623) διετέλεσε γοῦν ἔτη εἴκοσι κύριος ὢν τοῦ φρουρίου καὶ τῶν χρημάτων. Thus he was not simply an official in the service of the Seleukids, as he had been in the service of Lysimachos: he was κύριος of Pergamon and of its wealth, although evidently of no more.[18] The measure of his independence is shown also by the fact that his coinage bore his own name, but continued to bear the head of Seleukos even after the accession of Antiochos I, indicating that he owed a nominal allegiance to Seleukos personally, and not a continuing one to the Seleukid dynasty as a whole. His returning to Antiochos of the ashes of Seleukos, attested by Appian, is a further indication in this direction; it need not signify, as is usually inferred, a recognition in turn of the overlordship of Antiochos.[19]

In saying that Philetairos was κύριος of Pergamon and of its wealth, Strabo clearly implies a good measure of financial independence, and this position is confirmed by other evidence. Strabo himself adds (xiii. 4. 1, 623): διεγένετο μένων ἐπὶ τοῦ ἐρύματος ὁ εὐνοῦχος καὶ πολιτευόμενος δι'ὑποσχέσεων καὶ τῆς ἄλλης θεραπείας ἀεὶ πρὸς τὸν ἰσχύοντα καὶ ἐγγὺς παρόντα. This befriending of neighbours on the part of Philetairos most often took the form of financial generosity, as is amply attested by epigraphical evidence. Kyzikos, a city whose friendship the Attalids retained and treasured throughout their history, received this kind of assistance from Philetairos during the troubled years of the 270s, to alleviate the difficulties it faced during the war of Antiochos I with

[17] See above, 2–3.
[18] Cardinali, *RP* 10, n. 5.
[19] F. Imhoof-Blumer, *Die Münzen*; cf. U. Westermark, *Das Bildnis* 20–1. For the return of Seleukos' ashes, see Appian, *Syr.* 63. I cannot agree with the view, expressed for example by Cardinali, *RP* 9–10, and P. Zancan, *Il Monarcato ellenistico nei suoi elementi federativi* (Padua, 1934), 95, that this act was necessarily meant as a token of recognition of Antiochos' suzerainty; it was surely in essence a gesture of respect to Philetairos' deceased patron. Thus the position is perhaps better expressed by Meyer, *Die Grenzen*, 97: 'wie Philetairos im Anfang sich den Seleukiden gegenüber sehr loyal verhielt.' McShane writes (*Foreign Policy*, 33) 'Philetaerus curried favour with Antiochus', which is fantasy.

Nikomedes I of Bithynia and the so-called Northern League, during the Galatian crisis which followed this war, and later.[20] In the decree of Kyzikos from which this information comes, Philetairos is honoured as an independent benefactor.[21] Similarly independent were his benefactions at Delphi, where Philetairos and his family were honoured as πρόξενοι;[22] and at Thespiai inscriptions attest his dedication of land to the Helikonian Muses.[23]

Of equal interest is Philetairos' activity in areas close to Pergamon which remained under Seleukid authority. Again Philetairos used his wealth to befriend, and perhaps influence, his neighbours, but here it emerges more clearly that, in spite of his considerable financial independence, he was conceded nothing in terms of direct authority, beyond his position at Pergamon, by his Seleukid suzerain, Antiochos I. There are, however, two aspects to be considered in relation to Philetairos' policy in this area. One, as already suggested, is his relationship to Seleukid cities arising from his own relationship to the Seleukids, that is, at the time, Antiochos I; to this aspect we will return later. A second consideration, however, stems from the fact that Philetairos' activity can also be related to an already existing esteem enjoyed by the city of Pergamon. Although the history of the city before the Attalid period is, in terms of literary evidence, almost unknown,[24] archaeological and other evidence makes it clear that the city was then far from insignificant. One item of evidence is especially noteworthy. The temple erected for the worship of Meter at

[20] *OGIS* 748. The recorded donations date from 280/79 to 276/5, according to the chronology convincingly established by Dittenberger (ad loc., n. 7), and confirmed by M. Launey, *REA* xlvi (1944), 217–36; see further below, ch. 5. The fact that in 279/8 Philetairos conceded to Kyzikos (lines 8–12) ἀτέλειαν τῆς λείας | καὶ τῶν λοιπῶν ὧν ἀπεσκεύασαν | καὶ βοῶν ὧν ἀγοράσαντες | ἐκ τῆς αὐτοῦ ἐγηγάγοντο is a further indication of his financial independence. The Φιλεταίρεα mentioned in a list of names from the gymnasium at Kyzikos (*CIG* 3660) are most probably to be associated with Philetairos' donations; cf. L. Robert, *Ét. anat.* 199–201.

[21] Lines 1–2: τάδε ἔδωκεν Φιλέταιρος | ᾿Αττάλου δωρεὰν τῶι δήμωι.

[22] M. Holleaux, *Études*, ii. 9–16 = F. *Delphes*, iii. 1. 432: Θεοί· | Δελφοὶ ἔδωκαν [Φιλεταίρωι καὶ τῶι υἱ]ῶι ᾿Αττάλωι | καὶ τῶι ἀδελφῶι [Εὐμένει Περγα]μεῦσσι προξενίαν, | προμαντείαν, πρ[οεδρίαν, προδ]ικίαν, [ἀ]συλίαν, ‖ καὶ [τὰ]λλα ὅσα καὶ τοῖς ἄλλοις] προξένοις καὶ εὐ[εργ]έτ[α]ις.

[23] P. M. Fraser, *REA* liv (1952), 233–45; Appendix iv, no. 1.

[24] See the summary given by Cardinali, *RP* 1–4.

Mamurt-Kaleh, thirty kilometres from Pergamon, which is mentioned as an important cult-centre by Strabo,[25] was, according to
its excavators, a refoundation, and not an original foundation, of
Philetairos, and the altar built by him was, like the structure as a
whole, an enlargement of an existing foundation.[26] A bronze coinage associated with this cult, with examples from Adramyttion,
Gambreion, Pitane, Aigai, Elaia, Sardis, Thyateira, and Kyzikos,
nearly all of which are known to have had strong connections with
Pergamon in the Attalid period, extends from the fourth century BC
to the fifth century after Christ.[27] It was in this area, as will be seen,
that Philetairos exercised a strong influence as dynast of Pergamon; striking too is the appearance in the list of Kyzikos, a firm
friend of the Attalids during the entire period of their rule at
Pergamon. We see that the area in which Pergamon was influential
early in the Attalid period already had contacts with this city, as
subscribers to the cult of Meter, in an earlier period of its history.
This fact underlines the importance of Philetairos' work in rebuilding the cult centre, now in his control, on a larger scale; and to
this work he could add his personal dedication to the goddess:
Φιλέταιρος Ἀττάλου μητρὶ θεῶν.[28] This was clearly one aspect of
Strabo's description of Philetairos: κύριος τοῦ φρουρίου καὶ τῶν
χρημάτων.

It has already been indicated, however, that this influence,
considerable though it may have been, did not extend to direct
authority. On the contrary, his influence seems to have owed
something to the at least nominal suzerainty of Antiochos which he
had to acknowledge; this is indicated by the appearance of
Seleukid cities among those which Philetairos befriended. The
area in which the cities of Aigai and Temnos were situated provides the most striking evidence of this situation. A treaty of
ἰσοπολιτεία concluded between Pergamon and Temnos is to be
dated, according to the letters, to the beginning of the third century
BC, and it is unlikely that the stone was inscribed later than the

[25] xiii. 2. 6, 619: τὸ ἱερὸν τό ἐνταῦθα τῆς μητρὸς τῶν θεῶν Ἀσπορηνῆς.
[26] A. Conze and P. Schazmann, *Mamurt-Kaleh,* 43; Ohlemutz, *Kulte,* 174 ff.
[27] *Mamurt-Kaleh,* 42–3.
[28] *Mamurt-Kaleh,* 10.

period in which Philetairos paid allegiance to Lysimachos, although it may have been earlier.[29] In any event, it points to early, and possibly pre-Attalid contacts between the two cities. In the same area, two dedications of land to Apollo made by Philetairos further attest these early contacts; both are from the temple of Apollo situated between Kyme and Myrina, and belonging to Aigai. One reads Ἀπόλλωνι Χρηστηρίωι | Φιλέταιρος Ἀττάλου;[30] the other [Φιλέταιρος] | Ἀττάλου | Ἀπόλλωνι | Χρηστηρίῳ ‖ τὰν χώραν ἀνέθηκε | ὡς αἱ στᾶλ|λαι ὁρίσζοισι.[31] We can be sure, however, that Aigai and Temnos, and therefore the territory embraced by these cities, as well as Myrina (see below, n. 43), remained under Seleukid control as late as the reign of Antiochos II. The treaty of ἰσοπολιτεία does not in itself imply the subjection of Temnos to Pergamon, but rather suggests an equal status, that is, Temnos' independence of Pergamon, and this is confirmed by a decree found on the site of the acropolis of Temnos and dated to the third century BC, which shows this city acting independently of

---

[29] I have been unable to locate the stone *IvP* 5 (*OGIS* 265, *StV* iii. 555) either in Bergama or in the Pergamon Museum in Berlin, and have therefore to base my conclusions on Fränkel's facsimiles, which throughout *IvP* are invariably accurate. Γ and Φ are decisive letters, whereas Ϟ, which is found as late as the reign of Attalos III (*IvP* 248, = *OGIS* 331, Welles, *RC* 65–7), is clearly not. Sigma, like alpha, is an unreliable letter for dating Pergamene inscriptions, 'early' forms occurring late, and 'late' forms appearing already in the time of Eumenes I (e.g. in *IvP* 13, = *OGIS* 266, *StV* iii. 481; cf. below, n. 47). Γ is found regularly from the reign of Attalos I (*IvP* 47, 51, 52, 53, 58), although *IvP* 40, which I have studied in Berlin, has the much later form Ͱ (this text is ascribed to Attalos I by Welles, *RC* 24; I am inclined to prefer Eumenes II: see below, 173–4). The alpha with a distinctly broken cross-bar in *IvP* 5 constitutes a major difficulty to an early third century date. I know of no other Pergamene example before the reign of Attalos I, and even then it is not common, the earlier forms being still much in evidence: compare *IvP* 43–5. Attalos' victory dedications have Α almost exclusively (*IvP* 21–9; note however Α in [Ἐπι]γόνου ἔργα in *IvP* 29). Alpha with a curved cross-bar occurs rarely under Eumenes I (*IvP* 13) and occasionally as a monogram on coins of his reign (*MvP* ii. 2, 3, 7), but this is an artistic device and has no bearing on the letter-forms of inscriptions. In inscriptions Α is not found at Pergamon before the reign of Eumenes I. See the remarks of C. Paepcke, *de Pergamenorum litteratura* (1906), 9–10; Holleaux, *Études*, ii. 76, n. 3; and on the difficulties attached to this letter in the Hellenistic period, P. M. Fraser and T. Rönne, *Boeotian and West Greek Tombstones* (Lund, 1957), 82–4. See also Bonn and Schuchhardt, *Altertümer von Aigai, JDAI Ergänzungsheft*, ii (1889), 64.

[30] *OGIS* 312.

[31] G. E. Bean, *Belleten*, xxx (1966), 525–8; J. and L. Robert, *Bull.* 1968, no. 446.

Pergamon.[32] The text is a reply to a decree of Smyrna which honoured three Temnitans for rescuing some citizens of Smyrna from brigands. The decree reflects a more than casual connection between the two cities, a fact of significance in that Smyrna was at that time a Seleukid city.[33] The evidence for Aigai is more positive, and we see that this city remained Seleukid at least until the time of Eumenes I of Pergamon, and probably later. This is clearly shown by its coinage, which was Seleukid under Antiochos II (i.e. 261–246),[34] and by a group of stones fixing the boundary between Aigai and Myrina; two from the mountain country north-west of Manisa, inscribed ὅροι Αἰγαέων,[35] and a third, more recently discovered, recording the actual settlement:[36] συντάξαν|τος βασιλέως | Ἀντιόχου ὅροι |τῆς Αἰγαΐδος |οἱ τεθέντες ὑ|πὸ Ἀπελλέους | τοῦ Μητροδῶ|[ρου]. The lettering indicates a date in the middle of the third century BC, and the king is therefore most probably Antiochos II; and since the formula used in the inscription denotes a settlement imposed by a suzerain rather than an arbitration,[37] Seleukid authority over this city is clearly indicated. It is possible that Eumenes I acquired suzerainty over Aigai and Temnos later in his reign, as he did earlier over Pitane (to be discussed below), but the first tangible evidence of a more positive Pergamene control in this area dates from the reign of Attalos I, as we will see in the next chapter. In any event, when Philetairos dedicated land to Apollo, the city of Aigai was firmly under Seleukid control, and Philetairos' contact in this area is thus seen

[32] L. Robert, *Ét. anat.* 90–6.

[33] L. Robert, *REA* xxxviii (1936), 23–8; *Ét. anat.* 92. On the Antiocheia in honour of Antiochos II, and other Seleukid cults at Smyrna, see Habicht, *Gottmenschentum,* 99–102: W. Orth, *Königlicher Machtanspruch und städtische Freiheit (Münchener Beiträge zur Papyrusforschung und antiken Rechtsgeschichte,* 71, Munich, 1977), 163–4. *St V* iii. 492 (cf. above, n. 14) records the confirmation by Seleukos II of the city's αὐτονομία καὶ δημοκρατία, which were therefore already guaranteed by Antiochos II. We also know that the city's coinage was independent in the third century: J. G. Milne, *Num. Chron.* iii (1923), 1 ff.; A. Heuss, *Stadt und Herrscher des Hellenismus (Klio,* Beiheft xxxix (1937)), 197.

[34] E. T. Newell, *The Coinage of the Western Seleucid Mints* (American Numismatic Society, *Numismatic Studies,* iv, 1941), 306 ff.

[35] J. Keil and A. von Premerstein, *Bericht über eine Reise in Lydien,* nos. 204–5.

[36] P. Herrmann, *Denkschr. Wien. Akad.* lxxvii 1 (1959), 4–6, no. 2.

[37] As noted by J. and L. Robert, *Bull.* 1960, no. 340.

to exlude any kind of direct authority. The same is true of his relations with Pitane, a city on the coast of the Elaitic Gulf to the south-west of Pergamon, as is shown by a Pergamene document of a later date, which records the settlement of a land dispute between Pitane and Mytilene.[38] This document refers to donations of Philetairos to Pitane, which enabled the city to purchase an amount of land (the land later in dispute) from Antiochos I; the amount of the donation has not survived in the text (lines 135–6): δόντος [εἰς τ]αῦτα Πιταναίοις καὶ Φιλεταίρου τ[άλαντα - - - - -]‖ κοντα. It is clear, once more, that Antiochos was the city's suzerain, and Philetairos its benefactor. We have then another example of Philetairos extending his influence, by financial means, in the direction of cities which remained under Seleukid authority, and this evidence fits well with Strabo's description of Philetairos' authority and its implied limits: διετέλεσε. . . κύριος ὢν τοῦ φρουρίου καὶ τῶν χρημάτων.

Philetairos, then, based his influence on three factors: the influence already enjoyed by the city of Pergamon in connection with the nearby cult of Meter; his Seleukid patronage, whereby he was able to enjoy closer contacts with Seleukid cities; and his financial independence, which enabled him to exploit these advantages. It is worth noting that in respect of Philetairos' generosity to independent cities and cult centres, the same policy can be ascribed, as far as the limited evidence allows, to the Phrygian Philomelid dynasty mentioned earlier. This dynasty, which evidently retained the semi-independent and undefined position in relation to the Seleukids that we can reasonably attribute to Philetairos, without, however, achieving the status of a kingdom, is known to have developed the friendship of important religious centres, such as Delphi and Didyma. The Philomelid dynasty can, like the Attalid, be traced back to the early third century BC, although we have no

---

[38] *IG* xii Suppl. p. 48, no. 142 (*IvP* 245, *OGIS* 335) incorporating suggestions of L. Robert, *BCH* xlix (1925), 219–21; *BCH* l (1926), 469, n. 1 (*SEG* iv. 680); *REA* xxxvi (1934), 523; *Ét. anat.* 114, n. 1. A new edition of this text is promised by Robert in *Villes*, 413, n. 1. On the topography involved in the dispute, see Meyer, *Die Grenzen*, 106–7.

direct record of its foundation.[39] If we knew more about such dynasties in Asia Minor, we would probably find other features reminiscent of the policies of the early Attalids.

Philetairos was, as Strabo says, master of Pergamon and its wealth, but he acquired no further measure of direct authority from his Seleukid suzerains. We therefore cannot expect to define an area of Pergamene authority under his rule, since such a concept would be meaningless. The position changes entirely in this respect, however, under his successor, Eumenes I. Eumenes, as we know from Strabo (xiii. 4. 2, 624), met and defeated Antiochos I in a battle near Sardis:[40] ὅσπερ καὶ διεδέξατο τὸ Πέργαμον, καὶ ἦν ἤδη δυνάστης τῶν κύκλῳ χωρίων, ὥστε καὶ περὶ Σάρδεις ἐνίκησε μάχῃ συμβαλὼν ᾿Αντίοχον τὸν Σελεύκου. Several points emerge clearly from this statement: firstly, Eumenes is called 'dynast of the surrounding country' whereas Philetairos had been simply 'master of Pergamon and its wealth'; secondly, this position was achieved before the battle, since Strabo states clearly that it was a factor which led to the battle: ἦν ἤδη δυνάστης ... ὥστε .... On the other hand, Strabo does not allude to or imply an increase in territory achieved by Eumenes; this is consistent with the picture we have drawn of the nature of Philetairos' position at Pergamon. It is not to the extent of Eumenes' authority, as compared with Philetairos', that Strabo refers in this passage, but to the nature of this authority. Where Philetairos had exercised an influence, Eumenes claimed a definite *dynasteia*. Since the battle was fought between 263, the year of Eumenes' accession, and 261, the year of

---

[39] The chronology and genealogy of the Philomelid dynasty were clarified by Ad. Wilhelm, *Neue Beiträge zur griech. Inschriftenkunde* (*SB Wien* clxvi (1911), I. 11, 48–63). See also the important additional conclusions of Holleaux, *Études,* iii, 357–63 (from *REA* 1915); Robert, *Villes,* 156, n. 2; Bengtson, *Strat.* ii. 5–6, and his remarks in *Die Inschr. von Labranda* (*SB München,* 1971, 3), 14–16. Donations at Delphi: *SGDI* 2736 (242 BC); at Didyma: A. Rehm, *Didyma,* ii. 272, no. 458 (second century BC). At Didyma, a Philomelos gave ten pairs of mules and five drivers to the temple. This reminds us of a gift of Attalos (probably II) to the temple of Athena in Ilion (L. Robert, *BCH* liv (1930), 348–51; Welles, *RC* 62).

[40] *IvP* 15 is possibly an epigram celebrating this victory: Beloch, *Gr. Gesch.* iv.[2] 1. 593, n. 4; Magie, *Roman Rule,* ii. 733, n.16.

the death of his opponent,[41] this claim must have been made at the very beginning of Eumenes' reign, which is also the natural place to put it. Some indications of the significance and implications of this change of authority can be deduced from other evidence.

Of first importance in this regard is the inscription already mentioned, relating to the land dispute between Pitane and Mytilene. Here, as we have seen, Philetairos is shown to be an independent benefactor to Pitane, while the city remained under Seleukid authority; under Eumenes, however, this authority in itself passed to the dynast, as is clear from the statement in the text (lines 141–2):[42] [κ]αὶ ὡς Εὐμένης παραλαβὼν τὰ πράγ[ματα παρὰ Σε]λεύκου [ἔγ-ραψεν ἐ]πιστολὴν π[ρὸς | Πι]ταναίους κτλ. This assumption of direct authority by Eumenes is to be dated most plausibly early in his reign, before the accession of Antiochos II, to whom there is no reference in the document among the line of successive suzerains at Pitane; the suzerainty therefore passed directly to Eumenes. This evidence adds meaning to the statement of Strabo, that Eumenes was 'dynast of the surrounding country'; he was in this respect suzerain of Pitane. In view of the chronological indications already argued, it is most probable that Eumenes acquired, or more probably usurped authority over Pitane before the battle at Sardis, as one aspect of his aspiration to *dynasteia*. An acquisition of new territory would perhaps be more understandable after the defeat of Antiochos, but such acquisition does not come into question here;[43] a declaration of independent authority, with

---

[41] The death of Antiochos I is dated in the Babylonian King-list published by A. J. Sachs and D. J. Wiseman, *Iraq,* xvi (1954), 206, to year 51 (Seleukid era), (month) II, (day) 16, namely June 1st or 2nd, 261 BC. Cf. R. A. Parker and W. H. Dubberstein, *Babylonian Chronology 626 B. C. – A. D. 75,* Brown University Studies, vol. xix (Providence, R.I., 1956), 21.

[42] I give the restorations of L. Robert, as followed in *IG* xii Suppl. p. 48, no. 142 (see above, n. 38).

[43] The attempt has too often been made to see an increase in Pergamene territory, implying an existing Pergamene authority under Philetairos, as a result of the battle at Sardis; e.g. Meyer, *Die Grenzen,* 98, speaks of 'dieser grosse Landgewinn'. It was a 'Landgewinn', in my view, only in the sense that Philetairos had had no direct authority in the area. It was, as I have stressed, the nature and not the extent of the authority that changed with Eumenes I. This does not mean that Eumenes' claim was necessarily implemented fully and immediately: we see Myrina, which lay within the area embraced by Philetaireia and Attaleia and the ὅροι Περγαμηνῶν, remaining under Seleukid authority until later. On Gryneion, see below, n. 52.

which we are concerned, is a tangible motive for the battle.

A few words need to be said at this point on the position of Eumenes in relation to Antiochos' opponents, especially Ptolemy II of Egypt, in the so-called Second Syrian War.[44] It is not known whether Eumenes had any contact with these other enemies of Antiochos. It has been supposed (one can hardly say argued) that in opposing Antiochos Eumenes was acting in collusion with, or even in alliance with Ptolemy, enabling the latter to pursue more easily the war at sea, and to make a number of specific gains, including Ephesos, which was evidently under Ptolemaic control for a while in the 250s.[45] For this supposition there is not a shred of evidence, direct or otherwise. The fact that Eumenes established contacts with Delos does not mean that he was bound to follow Ptolemaic policy, and still less that he was Ptolemy's formal ally.[46] It is possible that Eumenes was shrewd enough to take account of the threat to Antiochos in Koile Syria in making his own attack, and that his success at Sardis in turn provided Ptolemy with an opportunity for more vigorous action against Antiochos' successor, Antiochos II, but more specific co-operation is not attested.

It is more likely, as we have seen, that Eumenes took the opportunity afforded by his own accession, that is, the change of rule he represented at Pergamon, to press more strongly than Philetairos had done a claim to an independent *dynasteia*. This

[44] See, in general, Will, *Hist. pol.* i. 208–11.

[45] Beloch, *Gr. Gesch.* iv.[2] 1. 593, n. 4; Cardinali, *RP* 13–14; Crampa, *Labraunda,* iii. 1. 113–20; Magie, *Roman Rule,* ii. 733, n. 16, rightly points out the lack of conclusive evidence.

[46] It is most likely, and significant, that Eumenes I was responsible for the first official contact of the dynasty with Delos. The first vase for a Philetaireia festival was dedicated in 262 (Ziebarth, *Hermes,* lii (1917), 427, n. 4; *IG* xi. 2. 224A, 4), and Eumenes' statue (*IG* xi. 4. 1107, = Durrbach, *Choix,* 33) is the earliest known of an Attalid on the island; the base celebrating a victory of Philetairos was almost certainly inscribed during the reign of Attalos I, as I suggest below, 31 n. 8. The development of these contacts, which naturally had a considerable prestige value, was probably first and foremost an expression of Eumenes' independent *dynasteia,* and though doubtless carried through with Egypt's approval, does not imply that Eumenes was that country's vassal.

For the view that the battle at Sardis was decisive to the outbreak of the Syrian War, see, besides Beloch (cited in n. 45), W. W. Tarn, *Antigonos Gonatas* (Oxford, 1913), 314. The accession to the Seleukid throne of the young Antiochos II was perhaps a stronger reason for Ptolemy's advance; cf. Will, *Hist. pol.* i. 208.

attitude is probably reflected also in a Pergamene inscription recording a settlement between Eumenes and groups of mercenaries
settled at Philetaireia and Attaleia, who had recently been in revolt.[47] Attaleia was situated in Lydia, north-east of Thyateira and
some 35 kilometres east of Pergamon;[48] the position of Philetaireia
has not been exactly located, but its designation in the document in
question as being ὑπὸ τὴν Ἴδην places it somewhat north of the
Adramyttene Gulf, in the south-east of the Troad.[49] In this treaty,

[47] *IvP* 13, with addenda, *IvP* i. p. xix, ii. p. 507, = *OGIS* 266; *StV* iii. 481, with
bibliography, p. 149.
[48] G. Radet, *BCH* xi (1887), 168; Cardinali, *RP* 14, n. 6; L. Robert, *Rev. Arch.*
1934, 90–2; *Villes*, 101–2.
[49] The name Philetaireia is to be found in two other Pergamene inscriptions. One,
a dedication, refers to a Eumeneion (*IvP* 240, with addenda, *IvP* ii. p. 509, = *OGIS*
336): Διογένης Ἐπικλέους, | κατασταθεὶς πρὸς τῆι ἐπιμελείαι καὶ | φυλακῆι τῶν ἐν
Φιλεταιρείαι τειχῶν καὶ πυλῶν | καὶ τῶν περὶ τὸ Εὐμένειον ἱερῶν, τῶι δήμωι. This
Philetaireia has been identified with the one ὑπὸ τὴν Ἴδην mentioned in the treaty
with Eumenes, with the conclusion that Eumenes was recognized as κτίστης there
(cf. Cardinali, *RP* 14, n. 8; Meyer, *Die Grenzen,* 99). The second inscription is a
decree honouring the gymnasiarch Diodoros Pasparos, passed in the period of the
Mithridatic wars (*AM* xxxii (1907), 243, no. 4; *IGR* iv. 292; Robert, *Ét. anat.* 45–50;
on the chronology, C. P. Jones, *Chiron,* iv (1974), 191 ff.); this included the
provision (lines 40–3): ἀνεῖναι δὲ | αὐτοῦ καὶ τέμενος ἐν Φιλεταιρείαι, ὀνομάσαν-
τες Διοδώ<δω>ρειον, ἐν ὧι κατασκευασθ[ῆναι] | ναὸν λί[θου] λευκοῦ, εἰς ὃν
ἀνατεθῆναι τὸ ἄγαλμα· ἐν ἧ δ᾽ ἂν ἡμέραι γίνηται ἡ καθιέρ[ωσις] | αὐτοῦ
σ[ταλὴν]αι πομπὴν ἐκ τοῦ πρυτανείου εἰς τὸ τέμενος αὐτοῦ κτλ. The provision for
the procession presupposes that the *temenos,* and therefore the place called
Philetaireia, where it was to be dedicated, were in Pergamon itself or nearby. As the
first editor of the inscription observed, this Philetaireia can hardly have been the
one designated ὑπὸ τὴν Ἴδην, since the latter was a good two days from Pergamon
(H. Hepding, *AM* xxxii (1907), 254–5; cf. L. Robert, *REA* xxxvi (1934), 524; *AvP* ix.
89–90). The procedure laid down in the decree for Diodoros makes it clear that the
Philetaireia concerned was close to Pergamon, although the conclusion that it was a
part of the city, designating the old city of Philetairos as distinct from the city built
by Eumenes II (cf. *AvP* ix. 90), is unlikely, since the use of a dynastic name in this
form of a part of a city is extremely rare, though not entirely unparalleled (cf. the
quarter named *Hadrianos* added to the city of Alexandria by Hadrian: P. M. Fraser,
JEA xxxvii (1951), 105; *Ptolemaic Alexandria,* (Oxford, 1972), 35). It seems more
likely that this Philetaireia was situated in the immediate vicinity of Pergamon.
From this probability we may draw two conclusions: (1) that the Philetaireia of the
treaty with the mercenaries was called ὑπὸ τὴν Ἴδην to distinguish it from the one
closer to Pergamon (and possibly others of the name); (2) that the Eumeneion
attested is to be located in the latter place. Thus the conclusion that Eumenes I was
recognized as κτίστης of Philetaireia ὑπὸ τὴν Ἴδην cannot be maintained, and there
is no reason, on this evidence, to assign the completion of the building at
Philetaireia and Attaleia to the rule of Eumenes I rather than to that of Philetairos.

reference is made to a grant of immunity dated by a Seleukid year (lines 10–11): ἡ ἀτέλεια . . . ἡ ἐν τῶι τετάρτωι καὶ τεσσαρα|κοστῶι ἔτει, i.e. 269/8.[50] Such an exact designation by a Seleukid year, even as a matter of convenience, is hardly accountable after the break with the Seleukids at Sardis. This indication is confirmed by Eumenes' coinage, on which the head of Seleukos is replaced by that of Philetairos, and the legend *ΦΙΛΕΤΑΙΡΟΥ*, a change which points to the recognition of a new era, most probably as a result of the issue at Sardis.[51] If, as is most likely, the construction of Philetaireia and Attaleia was completed before the battle at Sardis, namely before 261 at the latest, their inauguration must be accounted the work of Philetairos, not of Eumenes. Whether, in this case, the work was begun with Seleukid approval, and whether it was completed already under Philetairos, cannot be determined. In any event, arguments put forward for a later date for the revolt of the mercenaries, including the late 250s, are not convincing.[52] It should be mentioned that the positions at Philetaireia and Attaleia

[50] That this was the Seleukid era was rightly argued by Dittenberger, ad loc.

[51] F. Imhoof-Blumer, *Die Münzen*. The attempt of H. Gäbler, *Erythrai* (Berlin, 1892), 51–3, to date the beginning of this coinage to the reign of Attalos I, though followed among others by U. Wilcken, *RE*, s.v. Attalos (9), 2159, was refuted by A. J. B. Wace, *JHS* xxv (1905), 99–100, and by H. von Fritze, *Die Münzen von Pergamon*; cf. U. Westermark, *Das Bildnis*, 12–13.

[52] For a later date see Meyer, *Die Grenzen*, 97–9. It is argued, firstly, that since a copy of the treaty was to be set up in the temple of Apollo in Gryneion, this city must have been in Eumenes' possession. This conclusion is unacceptable, however, in view of the fact that the treaty of συμπολιτεία between Smyrna and Magnesia ad Sipylum, from 243 or 242 (*StV* iii. 492; cf. above, n. 14), was also to be set up in Gryneion (line 85), as rightly noted by Schmitt (*StV* iii, p. 149). Furthermore, copies of Eumenes' treaty were also to be erected on Delos and in the temple of Asklepios at Mytilene, neither of which belonged to him. It is surely clear that the three places designated were sanctuaries of international status, which would give the treaties erected there additional force. The second argument for a later date is that the treaty, which attests Eumenes' possession of territory extending to Philetaireia and Attaleia, must be dated later than Eumenes' acquisition of Myrina, which lay between them and Pergamon, and Myrina, as we have seen, remained a Seleukid city under Antiochos II. This argument ignores the more likely possibility, already argued (cf. n. 43), that Eumenes' claim to direct authority within the area enclosed by the military settlements at Philetaireia and Attaleia, was not immediately and wholly realized. In view of the Seleukids' opposition to Eumenes' independent authority, as expressed at Sardis, and later, it is not surprising that some cities remained under Seleukid authority, despite Eumenes' claim, until a later date. This obviously does not mean that Eumenes' acquisition of direct authority in the area as a whole, as reflected in the treaty with the mercenaries, should be dated later.

cannot necessarily be regarded as definite frontier fortifications, since the location of Attaleia, at least, did not lend itself to this function.[53] The treaty with the mercenaries does, however, add a further indication of the status of Eumenes' *dynasteia*; it shows that he had large groups of mercenaries in his own pay, and that he personally, not the Seleukids, administered the territory in which they were settled.

The geographical limits of the independent rule established by Eumenes can only be approximately established.[54] The literary evidence, that of Polybios and Strabo, refers to the kingdom of Pergamon before the Peace of Apameia as being confined to a small area in Mysia around Pergamon. Polybios, in his admiration of the achievement of Eumenes II, makes what is clearly a simple contrast between the size of the kingdom after Apameia, and that immediately before, that is, during the final years of the reign of Attalos I and the early years of his successor's (xxxii. 8. 3): ὅς γε πρῶτον μὲν παραλαβὼν παρὰ τοῦ πατρὸς τὴν βασιλείαν συνεσταλμένην τελέως εἰς ὀλίγα καὶ λιτὰ πολισμάτια ταῖς μεγίσταις τῶν καθ᾽ αὑτὸν δυναστειῶν ἐφάμιλλον ἐποίησε τὴν ἰδίαν ἀρχήν. The same distinction is valid at xxiii. 11. 7: παραλαβόντες οὗτοι (Eumenes II and Attalos II) μικρὰν ἀρχήν. This evidence therefore cannot be applied to the situation prior to the reign of Attalos I. The distinction made by Strabo, however, in referring to the Roman settlement, seems to be of a wider application (xiii. 4. 2, 624): πρότερον δ᾽ἦν τὰ περὶ Πέργαμον οὐ πολλὰ χωρία μέχρι τῆς θαλάττης τῆς κατὰ τὸν Ἐλαΐτην κόλπον καὶ τὸν Ἀδραμυττηνόν. This designation is more arguably relevant also to the rule of Eumenes I and Attalos I. In the case of Eumenes, confirmation of the validity of this inference can be adduced. A boundary inscription (ὅροι Περγαμηνῶν) from Ketschi-Agyl, 2 kilometres southeast of Cape Hydra at the southern extremity of the Elaitic Gulf, must be dated, according to the highly characteristic letter-forms, to the middle of the third century BC, and it is therefore attributable to the reign of Eumenes I.[55] The military settlements at Philetaireia

---

[53] L. Robert, *Rev. Arch.* 1934, 90–2.
[54] Cf. Meyer, *Die Grenzen*, 97–102, with the reservations expressed above, nn. 43 and 52.
[55] D. Baltazzi, *BCH* v (1881), 283; more fully published in *AvP* I. 1. 95–6.

and Attaleia were also within Eumenes' teritory, although, as has been said, they probably did not mark its boundaries. It is unlikely, however, that Eumenes' territory extended eastward much further than Attaleia, since Thyateira and Nakrasa remained Seleukid until a later date.[56] To the south, the area of Aigai and Temnos is not specifically attested as being under Attalid control until the reign of Attalos I, although it is just possible that Attalos acquired it from Eumenes. In general, however, Strabo's description of the size of the kingdom before the Peace of Apameia can be said to apply to the rule of Eumenes I.

It is probable, therefore, as Strabo indicates, that the Elaitic Gulf, and with it the port of Elaia itself, belonged to the Pergamene sphere of influence from an early date. During the reign of Antiochos I, however, Elaia seems to have been either independent or at least not Attalid, as is shown by the evidence of a land dispute involving the city;[57] it must therefore have been acquired for the first time by Eumenes I, and we may reasonably conclude that he did so at about the same time as his acquisition of nearby Pitane, and in the same circumstances, that is, as part of the positive policy undertaken early in his reign.

We will see in the next chapter that a Pergamene fleet is attested for the first time during the First Macedonian War, but we have no direct evidence as to its origins.[58] A question we would very much like to answer, but at present cannot, is the extent to which this fleet was already developed under Eumenes I. There can be little doubt that with the acquisition of Elaia Eumenes will have taken the opportunity thus provided of strengthening by sea the contacts with Kyzikos and the Black Sea area which had been formed by his predecessor. It is highly likely, then, that the fleet was built up from this date, and was developed over the years to the point where, at the end of the third century, it played a role in Aegean warfare and is first noticed by our literary sources. The importance of Eumenes' acquisition of Elaia can hardly be overstressed as an important factor in the development of the Attalid Kingdom. It remained the chief port of the Attalids at least until Ephesos was given to them in 188.

[56] See below, 43–4, 106.
[57] *OGIS* 335, = *IG* xii Suppl. 142, 144. Cf. Magie, *Roman Rule*, ii. 734, n. 18.
[58] See below, 68–9.

3

THE REIGN OF ATTALOS I

Eumenes I died in 241, and was succeeded by his cousin (once removed) and adopted son, Attalos I.[1] During Attalos' reign we see a development of Pergamene authority in three important respects: Attalos' assumption of the royal title; the emergence of the military and diplomatic power of the king; and a corresponding attempt to expand the area of Attalid influence. We see overall the foundation of more concentrated administrative institutions, which remained the guiding principles of Attalid rule even after the transformation of the kingdom in 188. From the literary sources, and of these especially Polybios,[2] Attalos I emerges as the most able of the Attalids in nearly every respect: militarily he was the most energetic, and he was clearly responsible for the foundation of the military power of Pergamon, both on land and sea, a power which remained a factor of importance to the Attalids in addition to the support which they later hoped, not always with success, to receive from Rome; in the field of diplomacy he had not perhaps the sharp cunning and subtle duplicity to be displayed later by his son, Eumenes II, but his greatest achievement must be reckoned to be his service to the alliance with Rome, and the great advance of the international renown enjoyed by Pergamon as a result of this alliance. That Attalos failed ultimately to establish a lasting hold on the greatly increased kingdom that seemed within his grasp is a measure partly of his own evidently limited intentions, and partly of the ability of his rivals to power in Asia Minor, especially the Seleukid Antiochos III. In contrast with the achievement of his successor, one important point needs finally to be made: that whereas Eumenes acquired an empire determined by and at the disposal of the Roman Senate, Attalos' achievement was entirely

[1] On the date, see above, 10–11. On the adoption, *AM* xxxv (1910), 463–5, no. 45: Εὐμένης Φιλεταίρου | Ἄτταλον τὸν υἱόν. See Appendix i.
[2] See especially xviii. 41.

his own, and in his dealings with Rome he consistently maintained the right to an independent policy.

The reign of Attalos I is best discussed in two parts: firstly the years of almost continuous warfare in Asia Minor, ending with the agreement with Antiochos III; and secondly the final years of the reign when Attalos was the ally of Rome.

(i) Attalos and Asia Minor, 241–216

In assessing the first part of the reign of Attalos I, we are faced with a number of difficulties. The most basic of these is the fact that our knowledge of the details, in terms of topography and chronology, of the military campaigns of the years 241–216, on which Attalos' extended authority was ultimately based, is for the most part, with a significant exception (the campaign of 218, discussed below) extremely sketchy, consisting of facts without the means fully to evaluate their significance. This is true of the events of the 230s and 220s, whose chronology is obscure in the extreme, while for the years 218–202 we suffer an almost total lack of evidence relating to Attalos' position in Asia Minor, in particular in relation to the Seleukid position. Secondly, the evidence that we do have is almost exclusively concerned with the military facts, and the insight that we are afforded into the nature of Attalos' attempts at consolidation, in terms of administrative institutions, is correspondingly limited. The relevant epigraphical evidence, consisting mainly of the inscriptions to the victory monuments set up by Attalos in the sanctuary of Athena in Pergamon, similarly dwells on the military aspect of the situation, recording victories, or what Attalos regarded as victories,[3] and no more. This is not however

[3] One of the small bases dating from the restoration of the precinct of Athena under Eumenes II commemorates a victory in the naval battle off Chios fought in 201 (*IvP* 52, as restored by Holleaux, *Études*, ii. 43–9, = *OGIS* 283): [Βασιλεὺς] Ἄτ[ταλος | Διὶ] κα[ὶ ᾿Αθηνᾶι] Νικ[ηφόρωι | ἀ]πὸ τ[ῆς πρὸς Φίλιππον] | καὶ Μακε[δόνας περὶ Χίον] | ναυμ[αχίας]. (On the date of the inscription, see Kähler, *Gr. Fries*, 187, n. 43.) Polybios' account of the battle, however, shows that Attalos' part in it was hardly distinguished (xvi. 2–8, especially 6, Attalos' escape to Erythrai). We therefore have to reckon with a certain propaganda element in at least some of the monuments erected to commemorate victories claimed by Attalos, a consideration of importance, as we will see, in assessing the role played by the Galatians as Attalos' opponents. The Eumenid restoration of the precinct of Athena is more fully discussed in ch. 4 (iii).

the place to enter into a discussion, which must necessarily be lengthy, of the relationship between the literary and epigraphical evidence for the involved and much disputed chronology of the 230s and 220s: this is done in Appendix ii; here I state only the conclusions reached, in order to proceed directly to an evaluation of their significance.

The successive opponents of Attalos I in the years 241–216 were the Galatians, Antiochos Hierax (in whose army Galatians appeared as allies or, more probably, as mercenaries),[4] the *strategoi* of Seleukos III Soter, and Achaios. Naturally the motives of these enemies in opposing Attalos were various. To the Galatians Attalos stood in the way of their obtaining plunder from the rich lands in the neighbourhood of Pergamon; he had, furthermore, refused to pay the tribute periodically paid to the Galatians by the dynasts of Asia Minor to secure freedom from attack (see below), and he had perhaps encouraged the Greek cities to do the same.[5] The

---

[4] It is not always clear from the evidence whether the Galatians were fighting as allies or as mercenaries of the kings, but their appearance alongside different enemies of Attalos suggests the latter. Launey's argument (*Recherches*, i. 505–6; cf. Cardinali, *RP* 32) that since Attalos names the Galatians before Antiochos Hierax in his victory monuments, they were his principal opponents, and not simply the mercenaries of Hierax, is not convincing; this precedence was probably due as much to the propaganda value to Attalos of emphasizing this aspect of his victories (on which his claim to the royal title was based) as to the relative strength and importance of his opponents, and this consideration applies equally to the monument set up after the death of Hierax by the soldiers who had served under Epigenes (*IvP* 29, = *OGIS* 280; cf. Kähler, *Gr. Fries*, 185, n. 18, and below, Appendix ii).

[5] A decree of Erythrai honouring its board of *strategoi*, probably passed in the early 270s, before the Galatian victory of Antiochos I, shows that the cities as well as the dynasts paid tribute directly to the Galatians (*Syll.*³ 410, = H. Engelmann and R. Merkelbach, *Die Inschr. von Erythrai u. Klazomenai (Inschr. griech. Städte aus Kleinasien*, I, 1972), no. 24. 10–15): πο[λλῶν δὲ φό]|6ων καὶ κινδύνων περι-στάντων καὶ δαπ[άνης οὔσης πρὸς] | εἰρήνην οὐκ ὀλίγης ἐν ἅπασιν διετ[ήρησαν τὴν πό]|λιν καὶ τὴν χώραν ἀκέραιον, ἐπιμεληθέν[τες μὲν τῆς τῶν χρη]|μάτων συναγωγῆς τε καὶ ἀποστ[ολῆς τοῖς περὶ Λεον]|νόριον βαρβάροις ἃ συνετάξατο ἡ π[όλις] κτλ. This payment seems to have been made on a direct basis, as distinct from the Γαλατικά attested in the context of a remission by a Seleukid king, most probably Antiochos I (cf. Habicht, *Gottmenschentum*, 96–9; M. Wörrle, *Chiron*, v (1975), 70; W. Orth, *Königlicher Machtanspruch*, 76 ff.) in a letter to Erythrai (Welles, *RC* 15 (dated to Antiochos II by Welles) = *Inschr. von Erythrai* etc., no. 31), 26–8: καὶ ἀφορο|[λογ]ήτους εἶναι συγχωροῦμεν τῶν τε ἄλλων ἁπάντων καὶ | [τῶν εἰς] τὰ Γαλατικὰ συναγομένων. It is in any event quite clear that a city's financial obligations in this respect could be extremely severe.

Seleukid kings, Seleukos II, Seleukos III, and for a time also Antiochos III, were naturally opposed to Attalos' increasing his *dynasteia* in Asia Minor at their expense, as were Antiochos Hierax and Achaios, nominally as officials in the service of the Seleukids, but each acting eventually in his own interest with a view to establishing a kingdom in Asia Minor independent of Pergamon and of the Seleukid king he originally served. As far as Attalos was concerned, however, all these opponents shared an interest in limiting his authority, and we will see that this part of his reign was entirely committed to defending this authority. His victories over his opponents led, in the case of the Galatians to his assumption of the royal title, and in the case of the Seleukids (including Antiochos Hierax and Achaios) to a temporary military predominance in parts of Asia Minor, especially in Hellespontine Phrygia, Lydia, and Caria. The most important point of discussion in this connection, to be taken up in this chapter, is the extent to which, and manner in which, Attalos was able to exploit this military predominance in terms of the possible extension of his authority in the areas concerned.[6]

A distinction must first be made between the independent action of the Galatians in their plundering activities in western Asia Minor, which threatened the Greek cities over which Attalos claimed authority, or to whom he offered protection, and the part they played in opposition to Attalos as mercenaries in the service of Antiochos Hierax.[7] We know from Polybios, through Livy (xxxviii. 16.14), that Attalos refused to pay the Galatians the usual

[6] Important contributions to an understanding of the chronology of the 230s and 220s are those of Beloch, *Hist. Zeitschr.* lx (1888), 499–512; E. Bickermann, *Berytus,* viii (1944), 76–8. For a good discussion from the Pergamene point of view, see Kähler, *Gr. Fries,* 181, n. 11; cf. more recently, J. Crampa, *Labraunda,* iii. 1. 123–31. Of great importance is the evidence of friendship between Antiochos Hierax and Seleukos Kallinikos in the spring of 236, when the two brothers made a joint dedication of land to the city of Babylon (see Bickermann, loc. cit.); thus Beloch seems to me to have been correct in dating the outbreak of the war and the battle at Ankyra not earlier than 236 (cf. also his *Gr. Gesch.* iv.[2] 2. 543).

[7] Cf. A. Ferrabino, *Atti Accad. Torino,* xlviii (1912–13), 233–44; Magie, *Roman Rule,* ii. 734, n. 20. The view of Beloch (*Gr. Gesch.* iv.[2] 2. 546) and Cardinali (*RP* 23–34) that the great Galatian victory was simply a part of Attalos' war with the Galatians and Hierax, does not not seem to me to fit with the evidence, as I explain below, 33.

tribute, and that he was the first of the dynasts to do so;[8] we know from Polybios directly, as well as from later sources, that he defeated the Galatians in a great battle in Mysia, and that as a result of his victory he took the royal title.[9] These two events, the refusal to pay tribute and the battle in Mysia, must clearly be associated with one another, and the two together must further be associated with the independent marauding activities of the Galatians, and not with their role as mercenaries of Hierax, since, in this latter role, payment of tribute to secure freedom of attack would not come into question. Thus Attalos' Galatian victory is not to be regarded as simply a part of his war with Hierax, a view against which the literary tradition is also to my mind decisive (see below). This conclusion is confirmed by Attalos' dedication to Athena for a victory won over the Tolistoagian Galatians at the sources of the river Kaikos. The victory was commemorated together with Attalos' later victories in the series of dedications which make up the so-called 'long *bathron*' (*IvP* 21–8; *OGIS* 273–9), and also in an entirely separate monument, unique among the victory monuments of Attalos I and surely designed for erection in a prominent position in the precinct of Athena in Pergamon, inscribed (*IvP* 20, = *OGIS* 269) [Βασιλεὺς Ἄτταλος, νικήσας μά]χηι Τολιστ[οαγίους Γαλάτα]ς π[ερὶ πηγὰς] Καΐκ[ου ποταμοῦ, χα]ρι[στ]ή[ριον Ἀθ]η[νᾶι]. This victory was the most lavishly celebrated of the successes of Attalos I, and was evidently regarded by him as the most important; it is for this reason the one most probably to be identified with the victory 'in Mysia' (see n. 9) which led to Attalos'

[8] *Primus Asiam incolentium abnuit Attalus, pater regis Eumenis.* An epigram inscribed on a base at Delos (*IG* xi. 4. 1105, = Durrbach, *Choix*, 31) celebrates a victory won by a Philetairos over Galatians. Since the letters are clearly of the late third century BC (see Durrbach, ad loc.), we may discount the son of Attalos I as the victor, and are left with Philetairos the Founder. Since the inscription was almost certainly made, on this criterion, during the reign of Attalos I, it is very likely, in my view, that the base was erected on Delos by Attalos at the time of his similar resistance to the Galatians. Philetairos, despite his victory, seems, like Antiochos I, to have continued the payment of tribute, a policy which is in accordance with the *ad hoc* nature of the tribute as argued in the text.

[9] Polyb. xviii. 41. 7–8; Strabo xiii. 4. 2, 624. Pausanias i. 25. 2, referring to monuments set up by Attalos on the Athenian Acropolis, refers to one commemorating a battle 'in Mysia': καὶ Γαλάτων τὴν ἐν Μυσίᾳ φθορὰν ἀνέθηκεν Ἄτταλος ὅσον τε δύο πηχῶν ἕκαστον. See further, Appendix ii.

assumption of the royal title (Polyb. xviii. 41.7): νικήσας γὰρ μάχῃ Γαλάτας... ταύτην ἀρχὴν ἐποιήσατο καὶ τότε πρῶτον αὐτὸν ἔδειξε βασιλέα. [10] The date of this victory is clearly of great importance to the chronology of Attalos' titulature, but it cannot be precisely determined. It has been thought that Attalos' refusal to pay the Galatians their usual tribute is best understood as a reversal of policy to be associated with his accession,[11] but this argument misunderstands the nature of the tribute in question. It is unlikely that it was paid by the kings and dynasts on a regular, or annual, basis; it is more likely that the sums involved were offered by them as bribes as the need arose, 'protection money' as we would call it, when the danger from the Galatians appeared to be particularly oppressive, and could not otherwise be averted.[12] The obvious attraction of this expedient was that it avoided the effort and probably even greater expense involved in carrying out military resistance, and it is not surprising that the Galatians came eventually to expect it as a matter of course. In refusing to pay the tribute Attalos was open to attack, and was patently prepared to meet this attack by means of direct military action. This decision may plausibly be associated with a development of the Pergamene army at Attalos' disposal.[13] Eumenes I seems to have relied largely on the employment of mercenaries, as we have seen in the case of Philetaireia and Attaleia; it was probably more economical for him

[10] On these monuments see Kähler, Gr. Fries, 182, who also shows, from Livy xxxviii. 16. 11, that the movements of the Tolistoagians down the west coast of Asia Minor make them the most likely of the groups of Galatians to have made contact with Attalos and thus to have demanded tribute from him.

[11] See, from example, E. Thraemer, Pergamos (Leipzig, 1888), 258. Wilcken, RE, s.v. Attalos (9), 2159–60, rightly discounted this argument, but retained an early date for Attalos' assumption of the royal title on the basis of Polybios' statement (xviii. 41. 8) βασιλεύσας τετταράκοντα καὶ τέτταρα (i.e. 'ruled as king' from 241 to 197). It is clear, however, that Polybios' terminology in such a summary context cannot be pressed, as noted by Beloch, Gr. Gesch. iv.² 2. 546: 'er konnte sich auch ohne arge Pedanterie gar nicht anders ausdrücken'; cf. Kähler, Gr. Fries, 181, n. 11. Wilcken also supposed that the head of Philetairos replaced that of Seleukos on Pergamene tetradrachms as a result of Attalos' assumption of the royal title, but this coinage must be accounted an innovation of his predecessor Eumenes (see above, 24).

[12] Cf. F. Stähelin, Gesch. der kleinasiatischen Galater (ed. 2, Leipzig, 1907), and below, ch. 5.

[13] See, in general, M. Launey, Recherches, i. 438–41.

therefore to pay the occasional tribute. A more developed Pergamene army is attested for the first time during the First Macedonian War by the inscriptions from Delphi recording the honours which the Phocian town of Lilaia bestowed on the members of its Pergamene garrison;[14] especially noteworthy is the appearance for the first time of Pergamene citizens and Μυσοί.[15] We will see later that influence in Mysia formed an important part of the authority conceived of by Attalos for his kingdom. The development of this army probably extended over a number of years, as did the building of a fleet, which also appears for the first time during the First Macedonian War (see below, 68–9), but its origins may well be located in the 230s and 220s, years during which Attalos faced almost continuous hostilities from his neighbours.

We see in any event that Attalos' attitude to the Galatians is not necessarily to be regarded as a reversal of policy implemented at his accession, and on this criterion the time of the Galatians' attack cannot be precisely located. It seems most likely, however, for a number of reasons, that it took place before the Galatians joined forces with Antiochos Hierax. In the first place, the literary tradition does not connect Attalos' victory in any way with the war against Hierax.[16] Secondly, the victory at the sources of the Kaikos was won over the Tolistoagian Galatians alone, whereas in the battle fought at the Aphrodision Attalos faced the Tektosagan Galatians as well as the Tolistoagians and Antiochos Hierax. Thus the Tektosagans most probably joined the struggle at a later date.[17] Also to be considered is the fact that the victory at the Aphrodision was evidently a decisive one (see further, below), and a major

---

[14] *F. Delphes,* iii. 4. 132–5.

[15] *F. Delphes,* iii. 4. 132, 2: Μηνόδωρος Νέωνος Μυσὸς καὶ οἱ ὑφ᾽ αὑτὸν Μυ[σο]ί. The 25 names listed in the third column of this decree have no ethnics and may reasonably be identified as Μυσοί (Launey, *Recherches,* i. 439).

[16] Beloch (*Gr. Gesch.* iv.² 2. 544) has said the opposite: 'dass der berühmte Sieg des Attalos über die Galater aufs engste mit seinen Kämpfen gegen Antiochos zusammenhängt, war schon aus unserer literarischen Überlieferung klar . . . So heisst es bei Justin von Attalos (er nennt ihn rex Bithyniae Eumenes) victorem Antiochum Gallosque adgreditur.' This reasoning is absurd in assuming that the battle mentioned by Justin is the only one to be taken into account in this context: see further, Appendix ii.

[17] On the movements of the Tolistoagians see M. Launey, *REA* xlvi (1944), 217–36; Kähler, *Gr. Fries,* 182.

Galatian attack in the immediately following years is hardly credible. In the chronology argued here the battle at the Aphrodision is dated to the late 230s, and we can accordingly most plausibly date the battle at the sources of the Kaikos to the early 230s, probably, but not necessarily, before the beginning of the war between Antiochos Hierax and Seleukos II. Within this decade a preference for an earlier rather than a later date is suggested by the decisiveness of Attalos' victory, of which there can be no doubt; a longer rather than a shorter interval is to be expected before the reappearance of the Tolistoagian Galatians as Attalos' opponents in the battle at the Aphrodision.[18] These considerations suggest a date for Attalos' Gallic victory within the period 238–235, and it is probable that he bore the royal title for all but the initial years of his rule at Pergamon.[19]

The battle fought at the Aphrodision, which must denote the Pergamene Aphrodision outside the city,[20] in which Attalos defeated the Tolistoagian and Tektosagan Galatians and Antiochos Hierax, is almost cetainly the one mentioned by Trogus, *Prologue* xxvii, in the words *Galli Pergamo victi ab Attalo*, since Trogus' description corresponds more closely with this than with any other battle attested for these years. It is hardly identifiable with the battle fought at the sources of the Kaikos, which was in no way located 'at Pergamon'. The context of the battle in Trogus' narrative is the aftermath of the battle at Ankyra, in which Antiochos Hierax defeated his brother Seleukos II.[21] The battle at Ankyra should most probably be dated to the year 235 (although others have dated it earlier: see Appendix ii), and the battle at the Aphrodision to the last years of the decade, that is, shortly before

---

[18] An interval of some years between Attalos' Galatian victory at the sources of the Kaikos and the reappearance of the Galatians as mercenaries of Hierax was regarded by Kähler (*Gr. Fries,* 83) as a 'schwer vorstellbare Situation', but we would expect a period of inactivity on the part of the Tolistoagians if Attalos' victory was as resounding as our sources would have us believe.

[19] For the epigraphical evidence relating to Attalos' titulature, see Appendix ii; it does not enable a closer dating than that already argued.

[20] The designation τὸ Ἀφροδίσιον in a royal dedication at Pergamon must refer to the precinct outside the city; cf. Beloch, *Gr. Gesch.* iv.[2] 2. 546.

[21] *Seleuci bellum in Syria adversus Ptolomaeum Tryphonem: item in Asia adversus fratrem suum Antiochum Hieracem, quo bello Ancurae victus est a Gallis: utque Galli Pergamo victi ab Attalo Zielan Bithunum occiderint.*

the battles in Lydia, Caria, and Hellespontine Phrygia, of which the first two (*IvP* 27 and 28, from the *bathron*) are mentioned by Eusebios and dated respectively to 229/8 and 228/7.[22] In 227, according to the chronology transmitted by Eusebios, Hierax fled to Thrace, there to meet his death, and to this year and in this context should most probably be dated the battle in Hellespontine Phrygia which Attalos claimed as a victory (*IvP* 22).[23]

In 226/5 Seleukos II was succeeded by his son Seleukos III Soter, [24] who undertook without success to recover the seriously weakened Seleukid position in western Asia Minor. Among the dedications which make up the large *bathron* is one for a victory over 'Lysias and the *strategoi* of Seleukos' (*IvP* 25+26, = *OGIS* 277): ἀπὸ τῆς παρ[ὰ — πρ]ὸς Λ[υ]σίαν | καὶ τοὺς Σελ[εύκου στρατ]ηγο[ὺ]ς μάχης. Another victory over a Seleukid army is celebrated in the series of smaller bases whose inscription is datable to the time of the Eumenid restoration of the precinct of Athena (on which see Appendix ii), and which we should restore (*IvP* 36): [Βασιλεὺς Ἄτταλος | Διὶ καὶ Ἀθηνᾶι] | ἀ[πὸ τῆς—] | πρὸς Ἐ[πιγένην? τὸν] | Σελεύκου σ[τρατηγὸν μάχης].[25] This battle is too often overlooked, and is of particular importance in pointing to a probably continuous Seleukid military undertaking against Attalos during the short reign of Seleukos III. Attalos' opponent Lysias is almost certainly the Λυσίας Φιλομήλου Μακεδών honoured by a Delphian proxeny decree dated to 242 BC.[26] This alliance of the Seleukid king with a dynast of Asia Minor

[22] Eusebios i. 253 Sch. The chronological tradition derives from Porphyrius, Eusebios' source for the chronology of the Hellenistic monarchies. On the tradition, see E. Schwartz, *RE*, s.v. Eusebios, 1378–80 (= *Griech. Geschichtschreiber*, 507–10); R. Helm, *Eranos*, xxii (1924), 1–40.

[23] Polyb. v. 74. 4: μεταλλάξαντος τὸν βίον ἐπὶ Θράκης; Eusebios i. 253 Sch. Eusebios' chronology places Hierax's flight to Thrace immediately after the battle with Attalos in Caria, omitting the abortive attack on Seleukos in Mesopotamia which must come between these two events; that is, Hierax fled from Seleukos, not from Attalos; cf. M. Launey, *Recherches*, i. 505, n. 3, and, on the death of Hierax, Walbank, *Comm.* i. 600.

[24] Beloch, *Gr. Gesch.* iv.² 1. 686, 2. 196.

[25] For the restoration Ἐ[πιγένην], which is extremely likely, see Cardinali, *RP* 44, n. 1 (a Seleukid Epigenes, rival of Hermeias, is known from Polyb. v. 41. 4; cf. Schmitt, *Untersuchungen*, 151–3). The restoration given in the text is more probable than that usually written, following unnecessarily the dedication for the battle with Lysias: πρὸς Ἐ[πιγένην καὶ τοὺς ἄλλους] | Σελεύκου σ[τρατηγοὺς μάχης].

[26] *SGDI* 2736; cf. above, 20 n. 39.

against the King of Pergamon further indicates the intensity of the campaign, but whether this was a voluntary undertaking on Lysias' part or a requirement arising from a subordinate position cannot be determined. This evidence affords no more than a dim and fleeting glimpse of the fortunes of a small dynasty whose origins were similar to those of the Attalids, but which, unlike the Attalids, did not achieve the status of a kingdom.

These two battles fought against Seleukid armies should probably be dated to the years 226–223, that is before Seleukos' advance in person, recorded by Polybios (iv. 48. 7-8), which led to his death, most probably in 223 (see below, n. 27): Σέλευκος γὰρ ὁ νέος ὡς θᾶττον παρέλαβε τὴν βασιλείαν, πυνθανόμενος Ἄτταλον πᾶσαν ἤδη τὴν ἐπὶ τάδε τοῦ Ταύρου δυναστείαν ὑφ᾽ αὑτὸν πεποιῆσθαι, παρωρμήθη βοηθεῖν τοῖς σφετέροις πράγμασιν. ὑπερβαλὼν δὲ μεγάλῃ δυνάμει τὸν Ταῦρον, καὶ δολοφονηθεὶς ὑπὸ τ᾽ Ἀπατουρίου τοῦ Γαλάτου καὶ Νικάνορος, μετήλλαξε τὸν βίον.

Although Seleukos failed entirely to check Attalos' military predominance in western Asia Minor, his opposition was maintained, with more positive results, by his brother, Antiochos III, who succeeded him in the autumn of 223.[27] Antiochos' cousin, or uncle, Achaios,[28] who had already held the position of στρατηγός under Seleukos Kallinikos,[29] was now appointed ἐπὶ τάδε τοῦ Ταύρου, that is to the overall command of Seleukid Asia Minor, a post usurped previously by Antiochos Hierax.[30] It is difficult to assess the implications for Attalos of Achaios' success, although it is clear that for a time Achaios was master of the whole of Attalos' kingdom except the capital (Polyb. iv. 48. 11): τὸν μὲν Ἄτταλον εἰς αὐτὸ τὸ Πέργαμον συνέκλεισε, τῶν δὲ λοιπῶν πάντων ἦν ἐγκρατής. It is likely, however, that Achaios' military predominance was ephemeral and without lasting consequences, and it has left no

[27] On the chronology of Seleukos' death and the accession of Antiochos III, see Schmitt, *Untersuchungen*, 2–3.
[28] For the relationship between Achaios and Antiochos, see Beloch, *Gr. Gesch.* iv.² 2. 204–6; P. Meloni, *Rendiconti dell'Accad. naz. dei Lincei*, viii (1949), 543; Schmitt, *Untersuchungen*, 30–1.
[29] Polyainos iv. 17 (campaign against Hierax): στρατηγοὶ Σελεύκου Ἀχαιὸς καὶ Ἀνδρόμαχος μετὰ πολλῆς δυνάμεως ἐδίωκον. Cf. Beloch, *Gr. Gesch.* iv.² 2. 205.
[30] On this office see Bengtson, *Strat.* ii. 90–115; Schmitt, *Untersuchungen*, 158–60.

trace in contemporary documents. We can more positively conclude that by the year 220 Attalos and Achaios had come to an
understanding. In this year Achaios was proclaimed king in
Laodikeia,[31] and by this act he took for himself most of those parts
of Asia Minor over which the Seleukid king still claimed authority.
Such an act of open rebellion is hardly credible if Achaios remained formally at war with Attalos, no matter how successful he
had previously been. Furthermore, when war broke out between
Rhodes and Byzantion in this same year, 220, Byzantion appealed
to both Attalos and Achaios for assistance.[32] Polybios, who records the event, makes it clear that Attalos was in no position,
being still confined to Pergamon, to take an active part in the war,
but it is hard to imagine that Byzantion would have made such an
appeal to both Attalos and Achaios if the two were still in a state of
open warfare with one another. Thus we may conclude that by 220
some kind of agreement had been reached; whatever the exact
terms, it is clear from Polybios' narrative that for the time being
Achaios maintained his military advantage.

This initial advantage, however, was not maintained. In 218,
while Achaios was occupied with the siege of Selge in Pisidia,[33]
Attalos undertook a military expedition which was clearly aimed at
re-establishing his authority as it was then constituted. Of particular interest is the fact that Achaios' sudden departure left Attalos
free to leave his capital with a large army; we see, that is, that
Achaios had done little to consolidate his position, and Attalos
quickly regained his 'lost' territory. A full account of the expedition is given by Polybios (v. 77–8), and this account remains the
basis for an assessment of the nature and extent of Attalos' rule in
these years.

This series of events ends with the agreement reached in 216
between Attalos and Antiochos III, which probably determined to
a large extent the final outcome in terms of Attalos' position in the

---

[31] Cf. Schmitt, *Untersuchungen*, 164–5.

[32] Polyb. iv. 48. 1–3. It is to be noted that Attalos expressed his support, but could
not implement it (48. 2): ὁ μὲν οὖν Ἄτταλος ἦν πρόθυμος, εἶχε δὲ βραχεῖαν τότε
ῥοπὴν ὡς ἂν ὑπ' Ἀχαιοῦ συνεληλαμένος εἰς τὴν πατρῴαν ἀρχήν.

[33] Polyb. v. 77. 2: κατὰ δὲ τὸν καιρὸν καθ' ὃν Ἀχαιὸς ἐποιεῖτο τὴν ἐπὶ τοὺς
Σελγεῖς στρατείαν.

following years, and was perhaps confirmed by a more formal
treaty a few years later. First, however, we must review the
development of Attalos' position prior to this agreement.

It is not surprising that during these years of almost continuous
military and political instability in the west of Asia Minor we see
very little trace in any of our sources of an attempt on Attalos' part
to consolidate his successes in terms of an expansion of direct
royal authority; it seems rather to have been a case of his maintaining a hold on the little that he initially gained. Before 230 his
military activity was entirely defensive, in the sense that his victories over the Tolistoagian Galatians at the sources of the Kaikos,
and over the combined Galatians and Hierax at the Aphrodision,
clearly arose from action taken in defence of the kingdom he had
inherited at his accession.[34] Thus there was little opportunity
during the 230s for Attalos to increase the area of his direct authority. During the years from 230 to 223 his military activity was
extended further afield, in areas over which he and his predecessors had not previously exercised any kind of authority, namely in
Lydia, Caria, and Hellespontine Phrygia, and for a time Attalos
was militarily predominant in all of them, although — a point which
needs to be stressed — not in all of them at one time; they were,
that is, simply successive theatres of warfare.[35] Polybios says that
in 223 Seleukos III crossed the Tauros to attack Attalos,
πυνθανόμενος Ἄτταλον πᾶσαν ἤδη τὴν ἐπὶ τάδε τοῦ Ταύρου
δυναστείαν ὑφ᾽ αὑτὸν πεποιῆσθαι (see above, 36). This statement, however, represents the attitude of Seleukos (as interpreted
by Polybios!), and not that of Attalos; it is chronologically inexact[36] and certainly exaggerated with respect to the extent to
which Attalos was able to translate his military supremacy into a

[34] The defensive nature of these battles is shown by their respective positions: the
'sources of the Kaikos' were, as Kähler has indicated (*Gr. Fries,* 182), a natural
point of entry for the Galatians into Attalos' kingdom; and at the Aphrodision
Attalos was fighting under the walls of his capital.

[35] For the view, which I regard as incorrect, that Attalos claimed a cumulative
hegemony in western Asia Minor, see, e.g., Crampa, *Labraunda,* iii. 1. 124, who
also sees Attalos' position as a motive for Doson's Carian expedition (following
McShane, *Foreign Policy,* 97–100); this is extremely unlikely.

[36] Polybios compresses the chronology by saying that Seleukos crossed the
Tauros ὡς θᾶττον παρέλαβε τὴν βασιλείαν, whereas he did so in 223, three years
after his accession (see above, 36).

political one. During the years in question, the political vacuum created in western Asia Minor by the defeat of Antiochos Hierax was not left to Attalos alone to fill. In Caria, the intervention of Antigonos Doson in 227, which we may now fortunately regard as a fact, effectively precluded Attalos' continued military predominance, and it is significant that the correspondence from Labraunda, which provides a very full picture of foreign rule in Caria, makes no allusion to any period of Attalid administration.[37] In other areas Attalos continued to face Seleukid military opposition, and at least two major battles with Seleukid armies are, as we have seen, recorded among the inscriptions from the large *bathron* and elsewhere. The lack of positive evidence must preclude certainty, but it is extremely unlikely that Attalos found any opportunity during the 220s to establish a political hegemony in the areas in which he was militarily successful.

This negative aspect of Attalos' ambition is complemented, on the other hand, by his development of relations with Greek cities closer to Pergamon, where the evidence shows a distinct advance from the strictly limited position held by Eumenes I.[38] Herein, to my mind, and not in the field of military expansion, lies the achievement of Attalos I. The most important evidence is, as already noted, Polybios' account of the military expedition carried out by Attalos in 218, to which we now turn. Polybios' narrative (v.

[37] Crampa, *Labraunda*, iii. 1. 124. We also owe to Crampa (*Opusc. Athen.* viii (1968), 171–8) the elimination from the body of evidence relating to this question of a document (Welles, *RC* 29) once thought to have been of the Pergamene chancery and to relate to a supposed period of Attalid rule in Caria following the defeat there of Antiochos Hierax. Its connection with the Attalids has never been a convincing proposition (cf. the doubts already expressed by Bengtson, *Strat.* ii. 100, n. 4), and it can no longer be adduced in support of the conclusion, for which there is no other evidence, that Attalos treated Caria for a time as a Pergamene province.

[38] The best treatments of Attalos' relations with the Greek cities are still those of P. Ghione, *Mem. Accad. Torino*, lv (1905), 67–149, and G. Cardinali, *RP* 81–102; for further discussion see Magie, *Roman Rule*, ii. 939, n. 36. The subject has been taken up more recently by R. B. McShane, *Foreign Policy*, 58–91, who sees the development of Attalos' relations with the cities as amounting to the foundation of a league modelled consciously on that of Doson's mainland league of states and cities. This view seems to me in itself to go far beyond the scope of the evidence; it is presented by McShane by means of comparative arguments that are at best jargonistic and superficial, at worst absurd (e.g. the argument from Polyb. v. 77. 5–6 that Attalos held league meetings!!), and inevitably leads to a distorted view of Attalos' activity and intentions in these years.

77–8) is well detailed in terms of topography, and Attalos' movements can be retraced with some precision.[39] The aim of the expedition was clearly to recover authority over cities and communities in Aeolis and Mysia, that is, close to Pergamon, which had previously fallen to Achaios;[40] thus Attalos went first to the Aeolian cities (v. 77. 2): Ἄτταλος ἔχων τοὺς Αἰγοσάγας Γαλάτας ἐπεπορεύετο τὰς κατὰ τὴν Αἰολίδα πόλεις καὶ τὰς συνεχεῖς ταύταις, ὅσαι πρότερον Ἀχαιῷ προσεκεχωρήκεισαν διὰ τὸν φόβον. After receiving envoys from certain Ionian cities, he turned northward; crossing the Λύκος ποταμός by Thyateira he visited the κατοικίαι τῶν Μυσῶν, the inhabitants of Mysia,[41] received the surrender of Karseai and Didyma Teiche (fortified positions in Mysia left by Achaios in charge of a στρατηγός, Themistokles), crossed the Ἀπίας πεδίον (to be identified most probably with the valley of Balikesir) and Mount Pelekas (part of the Temnos range), and reached the river Makestos (v. 77. 3-9).[42] At this point Attalos' Galatian mercenaries, wearied by the long march, took the opportunity afforded by the omen of an eclipse of the moon to refuse to go any further, and they were settled by Attalos on suitable land by the Hellespont (v. 78. 1–5).[43] After friendly dealings with (χρηματίσας φιλανθρώπως) three cities in the Troad which had remained loyal to him, Lampsakos, Alexandria Troas, and Ilion, Attalos returned μετὰ τῆς δυνάμεως to Pergamon (v. 78. 6).[44]

[39] Holleaux's study in *Études*, ii. 17–42 (which first appeared in 1897) established the basis of our understanding of this campaign; for further topographical discussion (relative to Mysia), cf. L. Robert, *Ét. anat.* 185–98. See also Schmitt, *Untersuchungen*, 262–4.

[40] The attempt of G. Radet, *Revue des Universités du Midi*, 1896, 1–18, to show that Attalos' campaign involved a pursuit of Achaios as far as Pisidia, was refuted in detail by Holleaux, art. cit. (previous note), and was later renounced by the author in the same journal (1897, p. 523).

[41] Pliny, *Nat. Hist.* v. 115: *intus et Thyatira adluitur Lyco.* On the κατοικίαι τῶν Μυσῶν see Robert, *Ét. anat.* 191–4.

[42] The river is called *Megistos* by Polybios (v. 77. 9, περὶ τὸν Μέγιστον ποταμόν), but its identification with the *Makestos* (Pliny, *Nat. Hist.* v. 142) or, more accurately, *Μέκεστος* (Strabo xii. 8. 11, 576) is assured: Cf. W. Ruge, *RE*, s.v. Makestos, 773; Holleaux, *Études*, ii. 38; L. Robert, *Ét. anat.* 187.

[43] On the significance of this settlement see ch. 5. The eclipse (1 Sept. 218) provides one of the very few chronological certainties of the reign of Attalos I prior to his alliance with Rome.

[44] It is important to note from these words, μετὰ τῆς δυνάμεως, that the Galatians evidently constituted only a part, and probably a less significant part, of the forces which accompanied Attalos in 218; see further below, ch. 5.

The most important information supplied by Polybios' account concerns the extent of Attalos' ambition in 218, which corresponds with the conclusions we have drawn on the basis of his activity in the 230s and 220s. Military activity was confined to Aeolis and the Mysian communities; dealings with the Greek cities south of Aigai and Temnos and in the Troad were, on the contrary, conducted on a diplomatic level. This fact is of considerable importance in that the absence of Achaios in Pisidia left Attalos with a free hand in areas further afield, and the limited nature of his activity may therefore be regarded as representative of his intentions. Attalos was clearly as little concerned in 218 with securing a political hegemony in Lydia, Caria, and Hellespontine Phrygia as he seems to have been in earlier years.

It is clear, then, that Attalos treated the Greek cities further from Pergamon rather differently from those in Aeolis and Mysia. In these two areas, as we see from Polybios' narrative, Attalos imposed his authority by force of arms. In Aeolis he aimed at recovering those cities ὅσαι πρότερον Ἀχαιῷ προσεκεχωρήκεισαν διὰ τὸν φόβον. ὧν αἱ μὲν πλείους ἐθελοντὴν αὐτῷ προσέθεντο καὶ μετὰ χάριτος, ὀλίγαι δέ τινες τῆς βίας προσεδεήθησαν. ἦσαν δ' αἱ τότε μεταθέμεναι πρὸς αὐτὸν πρῶτον μὲν Κύμη καὶ Μύρινα καὶ Φώκαια· μετὰ δὲ ταύτας Αἰγαιεῖς καὶ Τεμνῖται προσεχώρησαν, καταπλαγέντες τὴν ἔφοδον. That is, the three cities Kyme, Myrina, [45] and Phokaia returned to Attalos of their own accord, while Aigai and Temnos submitted only to a show of force, τῆς βίας προσεδεήθησαν. The expressions used by Polybios of the attitudes taken by these Aeolian cities, μεταθέμεναι πρὸς αὐτὸν, προσεχώρησαν, καταπλαγέντες τὴν ἔφοδον, suggest that Attalos claimed a considerable degree of control over them, at the very least to the extent of demanding their loyalty to him. We may compare this relationship with that pertaining to Eumenes I and Pitane, where, as we have seen in the previous chapter, the city's

---

[45] The text reads Κύμη καὶ Σμύρνα καὶ Φώκαια, but Wilcken's emendation to Μύρινα (*RE*, s.v. Attalos (9), 2162) is followed here, as is usually done (cf. Holleaux, *Études*, ii. 19, n. 2) to reconcile this sentence with the later reference to Smyrna at v. 77. 6. There is no serious alternative to Myrina, and the three cities, Kyme, Myrina, and Phokaia, are known to have had close relations in the third century, including a common coinage (cf. McDonald, *JHS* xxvii (1907), 159; Walbank, *Comm.* i. 603).

affairs were in some measure subject to the dynast's supervision. We should evidently envisage, that is, an area of territory close to Pergamon in which the Greek cities lost a large measure of their independence to the dynasts. The nature of Attalos' authority over these cities cannot easily be defined, because we lack further evidence of a positive kind. A clearer indication of status may be seen however in the case of Phokaia. During the Antiochic War this city was betrayed to Antiochos and received a Seleukid garrison;[46] then in 188, by the terms of the Roman settlement of Asia, it received back its 'ancestral constitution and the territory which it had before' (i.e. before the war).[47] Thus Phokaia, one of the Aeolian cities which returned willingly to Attalos' allegiance in 218, evidently retained its constitution and the right to the civic ownership of land in the years 218 to 195, during the years of Attalid rule. This does not necessarily mean, however, that Attalos exercised no constitutional control over the city. In Pergamon, and (as we will see) in other cities at a later date, the Attalids preserved the constitutional forms of the independent city, the πάτριον πολίτευμα, and controlled the administration by claiming for themselves the right to appoint certain officials within the administration, above all the στρατηγοί.[48] At Pergamon this measure is seen to be in force already during the rule of Eumenes I,[49] but the procedure is not certainly attested for cities of the Attalid Kingdom before the Peace of Apameia, when the status of the Attalids' authority in Asia Minor was radically altered. It will be argued later that the office of ἐπιστάτης, comparable with that attested for the other Hellenistic kingdoms in the context of the administration of the Greek cities, was introduced to the Pergamene Kingdom by Attalos I, probably when he acquired Aigina in 209.[50] Aigina was however a unique case; it was the personal possession of the king, and at the time of its acquisition it constituted his only territory outside Asia Minor. Attalos' rule in Aigina

---

[46] Livy xxxvii. 9. 1–4; 11. 5; cf. Appian, *Syr.* 25: ὑπήκοος Ἀντιόχου.

[47] Polyb. xxi. 46. 7: ἀπέδωκαν δὲ καὶ Φωκαιεῦσι τὸ πάτριον πολίτευμα καὶ τὴν χώραν, ἣν καὶ πρότερον εἶχον.

[48] See below, ch. 4 (ii).

[49] *IvP* 18, = *OGIS* 267, lines 21–2 (appointment of the στρατηγοί at Pergamon by Eumenes I). This kind of royal appointment is discussed below in ch. 7.

[50] See below, 74–5.

may not necessarily be taken as a reflection of his rule in cities
closer to Pergamon and acquired at an earlier date. In the case of
Phokaia, moreover, the institution of an ἐπιστάτης is not compatible with the fact that the city evidently retained its ancestral
constitution after 218.

It is probable then that Attalos demanded the loyalty of the
Greek cities and communities in Aeolis and Mysia, and supported
this demand by force of arms in 218, but that he did not interfere,
beyond this requirement, in their internal administration. This
conclusion will be seen to correspond with the nature of Attalos'
activity in the first twenty years of his reign, which was defensive
and not expansive; in maintaining his authority in Aeolis and
Mysia against the interference of his successive enemies, and of
these especially Achaios, who for a short time most effectively
deprived him of his authority, it was support for his military
undertakings that Attalos most required from the cities and communities concerned. Further evidence in support of this indication
may be cited for Thyateira. This city is not mentioned in Polybios'
account of the campaign of 218, perhaps because it had not allied
itself with Achaios, but in crossing the Λύκος ποταμός Attalos
passed through its territory,[51] and he probably took the opportunity of confirming its loyalty; it is unlikely, at least, that he
ignored it altogether. That Thyateira lost a measure of its independence after 218 is shown by a dedicatory inscription of Roman
imperial date emanating from this city, and set up by οἱ ἀπὸ
βασιλέων 'Αττάλου καὶ Εὐμένους κατοικοῦντες Μερνούφυτα
'Ηρακλησασταί.[52] A *cistophoros* of Thyateira, formerly dated to
year 2 of the reign of Eumenes II (BA EY B), indicated on that
chronology that Thyateira was Attalid in 196/5, and it was argued
that the *katoikoi* of the dedication were originally settled in the
territory of Thyateira, as the joint names suggest, at the end of
Attalos' reign and the beginning of Eumenes', that is, in 197.[53]
Now that this *cistophoros,* together with others of the same series
(dated BA EY B and Δ), has been convincingly redated to a later
period,[54] there is no evidence that Thyateira remained under At-

[51] See above, 40.
[52] Keil and von Premerstein, *Bericht über eine Reise in Lydien,* 27, no. 51.
[53] Robert, *Villes,* 39–40.
[54] E. S. G. Robinson, *Num. Chron.* xiv (1954), 1–7; L. Robert, *Villes,* 252–60.

talid control continuously from 218 to the outbreak of the Antiochic War, and the literary evidence suggests otherwise. In 201,
when Philip V of Macedon invaded Pergamene territory, Thyateira
seems still to have been under Attalos' control,[55] but it is probable
that this control was lost to Antiochos III in 198, when he in turn
invaded Attalos' kingdom; there is positive evidence in the narrative of Livy to the effect that Eumenes II no longer controlled the
city in 190 and had probably not done so for some time (xxxvii. 8.
7): *is* (sc. Eumenes) *cum magnam praedam agi posse dixisset ex
hostium agro, qui circa Thyatiram esset, hortando perpulit
Livium, ut quinque millia militum secum mitteret. missi ingentem
praedam intra paucos dies averterunt.*[56] In the light of this interpretation of the evidence, we must conclude that the settlement
was originally established by Attalos I before 198, and probably
before Philip's invasion of 201, when Attalos became involved for
the second time in an Aegean war, and that it was refounded by
Eumenes II after 188. The status of Thyateira is therefore certainly
relevant to Attalos' position after 218, and shows that in addition to
expecting the loyalty of the Greek cities he regarded himself as
entitled to establish colonies in their territory.

Further evidence of the implications for the cities and communities of Aeolis and Mysia of their enforced loyalty to Attalos
can be inferred only indirectly from our sources. In particular, we
have no direct evidence as to whether they were required to pay
tribute, but the fact that the Ionian city of Teos, which was bound
to Attalos by συνθῆκαι, had to pay a large amount of tribute, as we
will see, renders it extremely likely that the same obligation was
demanded at least in Aeolis, where Attalos' control was, as we
have seen, much tighter. It was naturally an important incentive to

[55] Polyb. xvi. 1. 7: Philip, after destroying the Pergamene Nikephorion, ὥρμησε
τὰς μὲν ἀρχὰς ἐπὶ Θυατείρων. It has rightly been inferred from this passage that
Thyateira was at this time in Attalos' possession; cf. Holleaux, *Études*, iv. 247–55;
Robert, *Villes*, 38. It should be noted that Philip did not necessarily attack
Thyateira, or even reach it; the words ἐπὶ Θυατείρων indicate the direction of his
march (Holleaux, *Études*, iv. 249, n. 1).

[56] Cf. Livy xxxvii. 37, attesting further Antiochos' occupation of the city before
the battle at Magnesia: *regia castra circa Thyatiram erant.* Schmitt (*Untersuchungen*, 273, n. 3) has pointed to the unlikelihood of Eumenes' taking part in a
raid on a recent possession; it is therefore more reasonable to regard Thyateira as a
loss of 198, eight years earlier.

a Hellenistic monarch in ensuring the loyalty of the Greek cities that he gained thereby more substantial support in his military undertakings. It seems most likely, then, that Attalos envisaged a supply of money and men in the cities whose loyalty he enforced. In Mysia, the situation was rather different. *Μυσοί*, as has already been mentioned, constituted a part of the Pergamene garrison which occupied the city of Lilaia during the First Macedonian War, a fact which indicates that the communities of Mysia supplied men rather than money;[57] this is an understandable procedure in the case of a country which was made up almost entirely of village communities (κατοικίαι τῶν Μυσῶν).[58]

We should take account, finally, of a letter written by Attalos in 205 to Magnesia on the Maeander in reply to that city's request for recognition of its newly inaugurated festival for Artemis Leukophryene.[59] In agreeing to the request Attalos speaks not only for himself, but also for 'the cities under me' (12–13: ἠξίουν δὲ καὶ τὰς ὑπ' ἐμὲ πόλε[ις] | ἀποδέξασθαι ὁμοίως; 19–20: καὶ αἱ πόλεις δὲ αἱ [πειθόμε]|ναι ἐμοὶ ποιήσουσιν ὁμοίως). The cities concerned can only be those of Aeolis, and the terminology used by Attalos shows that they remained firmly under his control, in a manner and to a degree comparable with the control exercised by Eumenes I over Pitane. In sum, the evidence for the years 218 to 201 suggests the following conclusions as to the nature of Attalos' authority in Aeolis and Mysia: it is clear that he claimed the right to their loyalty (this right extending to substantial support in time of war) and, furthermore, to their subordination to his will in matters of foreign policy, as well as the right to use their land for the settlement of military colonists; it is probable, on the other hand, that he did not appoint resident officials in these cities or interfere in their constitutional procedure. They were, in other words, administratively independent, but in terms of external policy they were subject to the directions of the King of Pergamon.

Turning to the cities further from Pergamon, to the south in Ionia and to the north in Hellespontine Phrygia, we see, as already

[57] See above, 33.
[58] On the Mysian communities, see L. Robert, *Ét. anat.* 194; Launey, *Recherches,* i. 436–7.
[59] *IvM* 22, = *OGIS* 282; Welles, *RC* 34.

noted, a different relationship between king and city. The evidence for these areas is fuller, although in some respects equally confusing. In particular, the συνθῆκαι mentioned by Polybios do not tell us very much about the obligations they incurred, beyond the fact that they were entered into voluntarily by the cities concerned: ἧκον δὲ καὶ παρὰ Τηίων καὶ Κολοφωνίων πρέσβεις ἐγχειρίζοντες σφᾶς αὐτοὺς καὶ τὰς πόλεις. προσδεξάμενος δὲ καὶ τούτους ἐπὶ ταῖς συνθήκαις αἷς καὶ τὸ πρότερον, καὶ λαβὼν ὁμήρους, ἐχρημάτισε τοῖς παρὰ τῶν Σμυρναίων πρεσβευταῖς φιλανθρώπως διὰ τὸ μάλιστα τούτους τετηρηκέναι τὴν πρὸς αὐτὸν πίστιν (v. 77. 5–6). The use of the word ἐγχειρίζειν, 'to entrust', is of significance in that Polybios used it on several occasions to denote a relationship between king and city, or between one city and another, in which the weaker voluntarily seeks the protection of the stronger, and three examples are especially noteworthy as the phraseology is identical with that pertaining to Teos.[60] Kalynda, seeking independence from Kaunos in 163, turned to Rhodes (xxxi. 5. 3): ἀγωνιῶντες δὲ τὸ μέλλον πρεσβεύειν μὲν ... (lac.) ἐγχειρίζοντες σφᾶς αὐτοὺς καὶ τὴν πόλιν.[61] In 219, during the war of the allies, the city of Phialeia, threatened by an Aitolian attack (iv. 79. 8), διαπρεσβευσάμενοι πρὸς τὸν Φίλιππον ἐνεχείρισαν σφᾶς αὐτοὺς καὶ τὴν πόλιν.[62] The expression is used, finally, of a city's seeking the protection of Rome (xviii. 49.1): ἐάν, τὸ δὴ λεγόμενον, τρέχωσι τὴν ἐσχάτην, ἐπὶ τοὺς Ῥωμαίους καταφεύξονται καὶ τούτοις ἐγχειριοῦσι σφᾶς αὐτοὺς καὶ τὴν πόλιν. These parallels serve to clarify the position taken by Teos in 218, as Polybios describes it. As in the other cases cited, the idea implied is not one of conquest or subjection, but of protection sought by the city against a danger,

---

[60] For other uses of ἐγχειρίζειν by Polybios, see A. Mauersberger, *Polybios-Lexikon* (Berlin 1956–), s.v. (65 examples). The word is also used in public documents of the 'entrusting' of civic offices to a person, e.g. in *IG* ii.² 1028, 72: παραλαβὼν τὴν ἐ[γ]χειρισθεῖσαν ἑαυτ[ῶι πί]στιν ὑπὸ τοῦ δήμου; cf. *IG* ix. 2. 1103, 13–14; Holleaux, *Études*, ii. 186. In itself it in no way implies surrender or loss of independence.

[61] On this event see Magie, *Roman Rule*, i. 110; ii. 957, n. 71; 1391 n. 59. Rhodes subsequently occupied the city and its possession was confirmed by the Senate (xxxi. 5. 5: συνέβη δὲ καὶ τὴν σύγκλητον αὐτοῖς βεβαιῶσαι τὴν τῶν Καλυνδέων κτῆσιν). This does not, however, affect our interpretation of the original intention as expressed in the word ἐγχειρίζειν.

[62] Cf. F. W. Walbank, *Philip V of Macedon* (Cambridge, 1940), 46.

the danger in this case clearly being the return of Achaios. A single
term will not adequately define this relationship, but the nearest to
hand is 'protectorate' rather than 'overlordship'; words such as
'subjection', and 'dependence', which are more usually applied in
this context,[63] are inappropriate to the position of the cities which
sought Attalos' protection.

This interpretation of Polybios' evidence is of considerable importance in clarifying the status of Teos in the last decade of the
third century. In the middle of this decade, most probably in 204,
following the example of a number of cities of western Asia Minor,
Teos instituted a festival to honour its god, Dionysos, and dis-
patched the usual envoys throughout the Greek world to request
the ἀσυλία of its territory.[64] Among extant replies to this request
are those of the Aitolians, the Amphiktyons, Delphi, and a large
number of Cretan communities.[65] The decrees of Delphi and of the
Amphiktyons are datable to one of the years 204/3–203/2; that of
the Aitolians more precisely to the Panaitolika of February–March
203.[66] The replies of some of the Cretan communities, which
should also be dated to one of these years,[67] refer to assistance
afforded to the envoys of Teos by representatives of Philip V and

[63] Cf. Cardinali, *RP* 101 (Teos listed as 'Attalid' as distinct from 'free'); Meyer,
Die Grenzen, 105. See also below, n. 76.

[64] See P. Herrmann, *Anadolu,* ix (1965), 29–159 (cited in the following notes by
the author's name alone).

[65] Two copies have been found of the Aitolian and Delphian decrees. AITOLIANS:
(a) copy from Teos: *SGDI* 1411, = *Syll.*[3] 563, *IG* ix.[2] 1. 192; (b) from Delphi: *F.
Delphes,* iii. 2. 134a. DELPHI: (a) from Teos: Ad. Wilhelm, *GGA* clx (1898), 218, =
SGDI 2675; (b) from Delphi: *Syll.*[3] 565, = *F. Delphes,* iii. 2. 134c. AMPHIKTYONS:
Syll.[3] 564, = *F. Delphes,* iii. 2. 134b. Letter of the ATHAMANIAN KINGS, Theodoros
and Amynandros: Wilhelm, *GGA* clx (1898), 217, = Welles, *RC* 35. CRETAN COM-
MUNITIES: *SGDI* 5165–80, = *Inscr. Creticae,* I, p. 4, no. 1 (Apollonia); p. 25, no. 52
(Arkades); p. 30, no. 1 (Biannos); p. 62, no. 8 (Knossos); p. 101, no. 1 (Istron);
p. 111, no. 2 (Lato); p. 292, no. 1 (Rhaukos); II, p. 2, no. 1 (Allaria); p. 63, no. 17
(Axos); p. 118, no. 2 (Kydonia); p. 161, no. 21 (Eleutherna); p. 243, no. 3 (Polyrrhenia); p. 291, no. 1 (Sybritos); III, p. 31, no. 2 (Hierapytna).

[66] The chronological basis of these decrees, including the fact that the replies of
the Greek communities should be dated to the years 205–203, was established by
Ad. Wilhelm, *GGA* clx (1898), 216–20. Cf. G. Klaffenbach, *IG* ix.[2] 1., p. 51 (on no.
95); Herrmann, 94.

[67] Cf. G. Colin, *F. Delphes,* iii. 2, p.136; Holleaux, *Études,* iv. 178–203; W. Ruge,
RE, s.v. Teos, 547–50. The dating of the Cretan decrees to 193, the year of the reply
of the Roman praetor (see below, n. 73), though followed in spite of Wilhelm by
Blass (on *SGDI* 5165–80) and Cardinali (*Riv. di fil.* xxxv (1907), 13) is unsupportable.

Antiochos III, and it is clear from these circumstances that Teos
was acting in the matter without reference to its relationship with
the King of Pergamon. On the contrary, it has long been recognized that the intervention of Philip was due to his status as
προστάτης of the Cretan communities, while the part played by
Antiochos showed a direct relationship between Teos and the
Seleukid king.[68] An inscription discovered more recently at Teos
(Sivrihissar) has confirmed and clarified this position.[69] This inscription records a decree of Teos honouring Antiochos III and his
queen, Laodike, as well as part of a letter written by the king to the
city acknowledging the honours paid to him. The decree refers in
detail to Antiochos' part in the negotiations, and to his own recent
recognition of the ἀσυλία of the city, and was therefore probably
passed in 203.[70] Of particular interest is the fact, now attested for
the first time, that Antiochos appeared in person in the city,
strengthening the impression of a firm relationship between the
two (I. 17–18): παρελθὼν εἰς τὴν ἐκκλησίαν αὐτὸς | ἀνῆκε τὴ[ν]
πόλιν καὶ τὴγ χώραν ἡμῶν ἱερὰν καὶ ἄσυλον κτλ. Antiochos'
presence at Teos may be dated to 204, when he is known to have
been in Asia Minor following the return from his eastern campaigns,[71] a date which fits well with a declaration of ἀσυλία in the
Greek mainland in the following spring.

It is clear from this evidence that by 204 Teos no longer depended on its former relationship with Attalos I of Pergamon. As
long as Teos is regarded as an Attalid subject, or as part of the
Attalid Kingdom, in the years from 218 to 204, this sequence of
events presents a major difficulty in that Attalos must, in these
circumstances, have suffered the 'loss' of Teos as a kind of *fait
accompli,*[72] in spite of the good relations which, as we will see, are

[68] Magie, *Roman Rule,* ii. 942–3, n. 39; *Buckler Studies,* 168, n. 3; Ruge, *RE* s.v.
Teos, 550; Walbank, *Philip V,* 121, n. 3. The view of Holleaux (art. cit. n. 67), that
Philip was at the time master of Teos, having captured the city in 201, was extreme
and failed to explain the position taken by Antiochos; it also led to chronological
difficulties.

[69] Herrmann, art. cit. (n. 64).

[70] See Herrmann's commentary, 93–7.

[71] Polyb. xv. 25. 13, in an account of events in Egypt following the death of
Philopator, says that Agathokles Πέλοπα μὲν ἐξέπεμψε τὸν Πέλοπος εἰς τὴν Ἀσίαν
πρὸς Ἀντίοχον τὸν βασιλέα. On the date of this event, see Wilhelm, *Wien. Anz.* lvii
(1920), 57; Schmitt, *Untersuchungen,* 233, n. 2; Herrmann, 96.

[72] So Herrmann, 106–18, esp. 112: 'es sieht eher danach aus, dass Attalos in
diesem Falle ein fait accompli in Kauf nehmen musste' etc.

evident between Attalos and Antiochos for at least a part of the time before the outbreak of the Second Macedonian War. What is more, the action of the Roman Senate in 193, in adding its name to the list of states which recognized the inviolability of Teos, thereby endorsing the part played by Antiochos, would be difficult to understand if Antiochos had acquired the city forcibly from Rome's friend and ally.[73] This legalistic view of Teos' status does not, however, adequately account for its relationship with Attalos, and later with Antiochos; in fact such a view never corresponds with the largely indefinite relations between a Hellenistic monarch and a Greek city.[74] Polybios says that Teos placed itself under Attalos' influence by looking to him for protection; this is not to say that the city was thenceforth a subject city or a part of Attalos' kingdom. It is more likely that Attalos simply retained his status of defender, or protector, of Teos, Kolophon, and the other Ionian cities, up to 205, the year of the Peace of Phoinike which ended the First Macedonian War. Attalos had played little part in this war, having had to return to defend his kingdom in 208 when it was invaded by Prusias I of Bithynia. Of the war with Prusias we know little more than the fact, but it is probable that it was ended in 205 at the same time as the Peace of Phoinike, bringing a short period of tranquillity to western Asia Minor before the invasion of Philip in 201.[75] It is not surprising that Teos, in this short period of peace, no

[73] A letter of M. Valerius Messalla, the praetor of 193 (*Syll.*[3] 601), confirmed the status of Teos as ἱερὰν καθῶς καὶ νῦν ἐστιν καὶ ἄσυλον καὶ ἀφορολόγητον ἀπὸ τοῦ δήμου τῶν Ῥωμαίων. For the circumstances, which included again the mediation of envoys of Antiochos, see Holleaux, *Études*, iv. 200–203, who explained the late date of Teos' request to Rome in terms of his belief that the city remained under the control of Philip, Rome's enemy, until 196, when Antiochos gained control and could act as mediator. Now that we know that Antiochos' influence at Teos is to be dated much earlier than previously supposed, this explanation cannot stand; cf. Herrmann 141–2. In the present state of our evidence the question must remain open.

[74] Cf. the remarks of A. H. M. Jones, *The Greek City from Alexander to Justinian* (Oxford, 1940), 95.

[75] On the war between Prusias and Attalos see Habicht, *RE*, s.v. Prusias (1), 1092–3; *Hermes*, lxxxiv (1956), 94. Habicht rightly envisages a separate treaty concluded between them at about the time of the Peace of Phoinike. I see no good reason, however, to discount the authenticity of their appearance among the *adscripti* to the Peace of Phoinike (Livy xxix. 12.14), since their hostilities had had a bearing on the Macedonian War. Most suspect among the names of the *adscripti* are Athens and Ilion, but all the others can be defended. For the greatly varied modern opinion on this question, ranging from complete acceptance (e.g. J. P. V. D. Balsdon, *JRS* xliv (1954), 32–5) to total rejection (Habicht, *RE*, s.v. Prusias (1), 1093), see the bibliography to *StV* iii. 543 (Peace of Phoinike).

longer sought Attalos' protection, and the fact that its συνθῆκαι with Attalos were renewed in 218 indicates that the relationship was largely of an *ad hoc* nature, that is, it was related to the state of military activity in western Asia Minor. In passing under the more direct influence of Antiochos III on his return from the East in 204, Teos did not cease to be an Attalid city (which it had never been) and henceforth become a Seleukid city,[76] terms which so far from defining status avoid the problems involved; rather, in a time of comparative peace, it felt free to look to a new protector. This, then, is the nature of the change in Teos' status; the reasons for it are more clearly apparent from the decree honouring Antiochos, to which we now return.

The decree attests clearly for the first time the nature and extent of the obligations which in general we would expect Teos to have incurred in looking to Attalos for protection. It has long been thought, although mostly for the wrong reasons, that Teos paid some form of tribute to Attalos in 218,[77] and this conclusion has been established as a fact by the decree, where we find specific references to such payments:

I. 10–20 (Antiochos) παραγενόμενος ἐπὶ τοὺς καθ' ἡμᾶς τόπους ἀπο-
κατέστησε τὰ πράγματα εἰς συμφέρουσαν κατάστασιν καὶ ἐ-
πιδημήσας ἐν τῇ πόλει ἡμῶν καὶ θεωρῶν ἐξησθενηκότας
ἡμᾶς κα[ὶ] ἐν τοῖς κοινοῖς καὶ ἐν τοῖς ἰδίοις διά τε τοὺς συνεχεῖς
πολέμου[ς] καὶ τὸ μέγεθος ὧν ἐφέρομεν συντάξεων καὶ βουλόμενος
τά τε πρὸς τὸν θεὸν εὐσεβῶς διακεῖσθαι ὧι καθιέρωσεν ἡμῶν τὴν πόλιν
καὶ τὴν χώραν (καὶ) θέλων χαρίζεσθαι τῶι τε δήμωι καὶ τῶι κοινῶι τῶν
περὶ τὸν Διόνυσον τεχνιτῶν παρελθὼν εἰς τὴν ἐκκλησίαν αὐτὸς
ἀνῆκε τὴ[ν] πόλιν καὶ τὴν χώραν ἡμῶν ἱερὰν καὶ ἄσυλον καὶ ἀφορολόγητον κ[αὶ] τῶν ἄλλων ὧν ἐφέρομεν συντάξεων βασιλεῖ Ἀττάλωι ὑπεδέξατο ἀπολυθήσασθαι ἡμᾶς δι' αὐτοῦ κτλ.

I.32–4 (Teian envoys had been sent to Antiochos, and he) ἐνεφάνισε
τούτοις
[ὅτι πα]ραλέλυκε τὴμ πόλιν εἰς ἀεὶ καθότι ἐπηγίλατο ὧν συνετάξα-
[μεν φ]όρων βασιλεῖ Ἀττάλωι.

The terminology here is imprecise; we read first ὧν ἐφέρομεν συντάξεων (19), and later ὧν συνετάξαμεν φόρων (33–4), although

[76] So Ruge, *RE*, s.v. Teos, 547–50; cf. Herrmann 108: 'tatsächlich ist Teos in den Jahren 205/3 seleukidisch gewesen bzw., wie wir jetzt sagen können, geworden.'
[77] e.g. by Ghione, art. cit. (n. 38), 94; Cardinali, *RP* 93–4; Meyer, *Die Grenzen*, 105, who lists Teos with 'tributpflichtige Städte' as distinct from 'freie verbündete'.

it is to be noted that in the second context the decree records the reply of Antiochos. A distinction between the terms φόρος and σύνταξις is clearly evident in the fourth century, including Alexander's administration of the Greek cities of Asia Minor, but it cannot be taken for granted that the distinction was maintained at the end of the third century.[78] In the Attalid Kingdom as it was constituted after the Peace of Apameia, we meet a variety of terms to denote the payment of money by a city to a king: φόρος, τέλεσμα, πρόσοδοι, but the exact differences in their connotations remain obscure.[79] We cannot even be certain that the term φόρος always denotes a regular, i.e. annual tribute, although this seems to be the usage in a document dating from the reign of Attalos II and concerning a city under Pergamene control.[80] Overall the evidence seems to show that, as distinct from the term φόρος, which acquired the role of a general designation (as is apparent, for example, in the concept of ἀφορολογησία), the terms σύνταξις, τέλεσμα, and so on, were used imprecisely and even indiscriminately. It is therefore not necessarily valid to argue from the text under discussion that Teos paid Attalos I specifically categorized φόρος and σύνταξις, since this too would presuppose that the terms are used precisely, whereas they clearly are not. Further-

[78] For a statement of the case for maintaining a strong distinction between the terms σύνταξις and φόρος, see H. Francotte, *Les Finances des cités grecques* (Paris, 1909), 77–86; on the Attalids, 81, where the position is summed up as follows: 'substituer le phoros à la syntaxis, c'est substituer un régime de contrainte sans réserves à un régime de liberté.' This conclusion is in my view too rigid for the nature of relations between city and suzerain in the Hellenistic period, which I have touched on in the text. On the other hand, A. Heuss, *Stadt und Herrscher*, 106–111, argued too dogmatically against the distinction at this date. There seems, for example, to be a distinction in the letter of Alexander to Priene, *OGIS* 1, 9–15: τὸ δὲ - - καὶ Μυρσ[- - - καὶ - - - - | κ]αὶ π[ᾶσαν τὴν πέριξ] χώρα[ν | γ]ινώσκω ἐμὴν εἶναι, τοὺς δὲ κα|τοικοῦντας ἐν ταῖς κώμαις ταύ|ταις φέρειν τοὺς φόρους. τῆς | δὲ συντάξεως ἀφίημι τὴμ Πριη|νέωμ πόλιν, κτλ. Herrmann's point in this connection (see below), that reference is in one case to a city, and in the other to villages, seems to me to strengthen rather than weaken the case for a distinction. Naturally one cannot assume that the distinction was maintained absolutely over a hundred years later, but it seems likely that chanceries were aware of some difference in concept between the two terms. For further discussion of this question, cf. Magie, *Roman Rule*, ii. 829, n.14; Herrmann, 101–5.

[79] See below, ch. 4 (ii).

[80] Amlada: Swoboda, Keil, and Knoll, *Denkmäler aus Lykaonien*, no. 74 II; Appendix iv, no. 23; this document is discussed below, 102.

more, the fact that Antiochos declared Teos ἱερὰ καὶ ἄσυλος καὶ
ἀφορολόγητος does not mean that the city had formerly paid
regular φόρος in addition to σύνταξις, since the formula was an
abstract one, used to denote the future status of a city's inviolability.[81] It is more likely that Teos had previously been required to
pay occasional contributions to Attalos, which were sometimes
called συντάξεις and at other times, more generally, φόροι, than
that these payments were regular and specific. It is not until a later
date in the development of the Pergamene Kingdom that we find
the payment of regulated tribute to the sovereign.

Further evidence of these obligations is to be found in the terms,
as reported by Polybios, of the Roman settlement of Asia Minor in
188 BC. Here we read among the requirements laid down for the
Greek cities (xxi. 46. 2): ὅσαι (sc. τῶν αὐτονόμων πόλεων) δ'
Ἀττάλῳ σύνταξιν ἐτέλουν, ταύταις ἐπέταξαν τὸν αὐτὸν Εὐμένει
διδόναι φόρον.[82] This is translatable in two ways: either, 'they (the
Roman commissioners) required those cities which had paid σύνταξις to Attalos to pay the same (amount of) tribute to Eumenes',
or, 'they required those cities which had paid σύνταξις to Attalos
to pay the same as φόρος to Eumenes'. Of these two alternatives,
the first seems to me in itself the more likely; this involves regard-
ing σύνταξις and φόρος as being interchangeable, in the sense that
φόρος could denote any kind of tribute payment, which, as we
have seen, seems to be the case in the third and second centuries
BC. This preference with respect to Polybios' meaning is supported
by his terminology in describing, at an earlier point in the narra-

---

[81] It is the conclusion of Herrmann, 101–5, that in addition to a regular φόρος,
Teos paid Attalos συντάξεις, but this assumes that the declaration of ἀφορολογησία (I. 18) means that Teos had necessarily paid a regular φόρος up to that point, an
assumption which is not justified by the confused terminology used in the decree. A
declaration of ἀφορολογησία meant only that the city would not be required in the
future to pay tribute, regardless of previous requirements. The term is included in
the letter of Messalla (*Syll.*[3] 601; see above n. 73), 19–21: κρίνομεν εἶναι τὴν πόλιν
καὶ τὴν χώ|ραν ἱερὰν καθὼς καὶ νῦν ἐστιν καὶ ἄσυλον καὶ ἀφορο|λόγητον ἀπὸ τοῦ
δήμου τοῦ Ῥωμαίων, and in the letter of the Athamanian kings (see n. 65), 7–8:
σ[υ]γχωροῦμεν εἶναι καὶ τὴν | πόλιν ὑμῶν καὶ τὴγ χώραν ἱερὰν καὶ ἄσυλον καὶ
ἀφορολόγητον. None of these had a personal interest in payment of φόρος; the
declaration was simply part of the usual form of recognition (cf. Herrmann, 140–1),
and was not meant to refer to the ending of taxation at that moment in force.
[82] Cf. Livy xxxviii. 39. 8: *quae partium Antiochi fuerant aut stipendiariae Attali
regis, eas omnes vectigal pendere Eumeni iusserunt.*

tive, the general provisions envisaged by the Senate for the settlement of Asia Minor (xxi. 24. 8): τῶν (δὲ) πόλεων τῶν Ἑλληνίδων
ὅσαι μὲν Ἀττάλῳ φόρον ὑπετέλουν, ταύτας τὸν αὐτὸν Εὐμένει
τελεῖν, ὅσαι δ' Ἀντιόχῳ, μόνον ταύταις ἀφεῖσθαι τὸν φόρον. The
construction of this sentence around the antithesis ὅσαι μὲν Ἀττάλῳ — ὅσαι δ' Ἀντιόχῳ, requires that the term φόρος be
used of former payments both to Attalos and to Antiochos, and this
usage therefore confirms the general connotation of the term
φόρος. In the case of Teos, then, the city certainly paid Attalos
σύνταξις and φόρος, but it is most probable that the two terms
refer to the same thing, and the fact that these payments were
evidently severe constitutes the most likely motive for the city's
turning to Antiochos in 204.

Another inscription requires mention in the context of tribute
payment, although its relevance is doubtful.[83] This document is a
decree of Teos recording its decision to buy land for the Ionian
Guild of Dionysian τεχνῖται, whose seat was then at Teos (5–9):
ἀγοράσαι δὲ αὐτοῖς καὶ κ[τῆ|μα] ἔγγεον ἐν τῆι πόλει ἢ τῆι χώραι
ἀπὸ δρα(χμῶν)𐅅X | [καὶ] προσαγορεύεσθαι τὸ ἀγορασθὲν κτῆμα
ἱερὸν ὃ ἀν[έθη|κε] ὁ δῆμος τῶι κοινῶι τῶν περὶ τὸν Διόνυσον
τ[ε|χ]νιτῶν, ὃν ἀτελὲς ὢν ἡ πόλις ἐπιβάλλει τελῶν. Of the six
thousand drachmai required for the purchase of the land, three
thousand were to be provided ἐγ βασιλικοῦ, that is, from royal
funds (15–18): τὸ δὲ ὑπ[ο|λι]πὲς δρα(χμὰς) XXX δότωσαν οἱ
εἰσιόντες ταμίαι ἐκ τ[ῶν | πρ]ώτων δοθησομένων αὐτοῖς ἐγ
βασιλικοῦ εἰς τ[ὴν | τῆ]ς πόλεως διοίκησιν. These two procedures,
the payment of τέλη ('duties'), and the receipt of money from royal
funds, have hitherto suggested a relationship with an Attalid rather
than a Seleukid king,[84] although this criterion alone does not
decide the matter; all we can say is that these practices are better
attested for the Attalids. A more substantial argument is the fact

[83] R. Demangel and A. Laumonier, *BCH* xlvi (1922), 312–19, no. 2 (*SEG* ii. 580).
Cf. L. Robert, *Ét. anat.* 39–44 (supplements 2–5; commentary 16–23). The text is
reproduced in A. W. Pickard-Cambridge, *The Dramatic Festivals of Athens* (ed. 2,
rev. Gould and Lewis, Oxford, 1968), 314, no. 9.
[84] Cf. Holleaux, *Études*, ii. 95–6 (chronology: 96, n. 2); Ruge, *RE*, s.v. Teos, 562
(dates the inscription before 225); E. Bickermann, *Hermes*, lxvii (1932), 68; W.
Hahland, *ÖJh* xxxviii (1950), 92–4; Herrmann, 102, n. 105.

that the Attalids are known to have taken a great interest in the
welfare and prosperity of the τεχνῖται when Teos became a tributary city in 188.[85] The Ionian Guild is attested for the first time by an
Aitolian decree of 235, and it is unlikely that it was founded much
before this date;[86] in this case the only alternative royal funds are
those of the Seleukid Antiochos III, who can reasonably be
excluded on the ground of his recognition of the city as
ἀφορολόγητος in 204;[87] nor is it likely that the city had paid taxes
to Antiochos at an earlier date, since the decree honouring him
complains so bitterly of the demands made by Attalos. For these
reasons a connection with the Attalids is a sounder proposition.
The document has commonly been dated to the reign of Attalos I,
but a date after the Peace of Apameia seems far more likely.[88] The
criterion of the letter forms is not by itself decisive, since they are
compatible with a date in any of the three periods, 228–223,
218–201, and that immediately following the Roman settlement.[89]
On historical grounds the first of these periods appears to be the
least likely, while Holleaux's argument that the decree gives the
impression of relations recently established between the city and
the Guild of τεχνῖται is not convincing;[90] since these relations were
never very stable, it is not necessarily to be concluded that the
buying of land and voting of honours by the city implies the Artists'
recent arrival. Furthermore, the only other evidence for payment

[85] See below, ch. 4 (ii).

[86] *F. Delphes*, iii. 3. 218B, 6–7: ἔδοξε [τοῖς Αἰτωλοῖς ἀπ]ῳδόμεν τοῖς τεχνίταις
τά[ν | τε ἀσφάλεια]ν καὶ τὰν ἀσυλίαν τοῖς ἐπ᾽ Ἰ[ωνίας καὶ Ἑλλησπό]ντου κτλ. On
the origins of the Ionian *koinon*, see G. Klaffenbach, *Symbolae ad historiam
collegiorum Artificum Bacchiorum* (Berlin, 1914), 17–21; Pickard-Cambridge,
Dram. Festivals, 291–4.

[87] Holleaux, *Études*, ii. 96, n. 2.

[88] Cf. Bengtson, *Strat.* ii. 220. For the earlier date: Holleaux, Ruge, Hahland (see
n. 84).

[89] Cf. Holleaux, loc. cit. (n. 87). The letters bear some resemblance to those of the
Korrhagos decree, but this point cannot be pressed. In this case I do not think that
the letters can determine a dating one way or the other.

[90] Holleaux, loc. cit.; cf. Hahland, *ÖJh* xxxviii (1950), 92. Equally flimsy seems
to me an argument introduced by Herrmann (102, n. 105) that subventions from the
royal treasury are not likely to have been made at a time recent to the passing of the
decree for Antiochos, which attests heavy συντάξεις; this is to assume an understanding of royal financial policy that we simply do not have, and it is worth pointing
out that the city which honoured Korrhagos received royal subventions although it
had previously been paying substantial πρόσοδοι to the king.

from the royal treasury concerns the city which passed the decree honouring Korrhagos, στρατηγός of Eumenes II in Hellespontine Phrygia, after the Roman settlement had put Pergamene authority over Greek cities on a much surer footing (9–12):[91] (Korrhagos) ἠξίωσεν τὸν βασιλέα ἀποδοθῆναι . . . τὸ εἰς τὰ ἱερὰ καὶ πόλεως διοίκησιν ἀργύριον κτλ. This parallel, and the implication, mentioned above, of the change in Teos' status in 188, when the Attalids first took a serious interest in the welfare of the τεχνῖται, strongly suggest that the inscription in question, and the financial procedure attested by it, should be dated not to the reign of Attalos I, but to that of Eumenes II, and more exactly, to the years immediately following the Roman settlement, namely to the same time as the decree honouring Korrhagos. Its relevance to the period of Attalos' relations with Teos in 218 should therefore in all probability be discounted.

At this point we may usefully summarize the conclusions reached from this evidence as to the implications of Teos' relations with Attalos. In 218 the city entrusted itself to him on the basis of συνθῆκαι which had been arranged at an earlier date. From this date, and possibly earlier, the city was required to pay a vaguely defined form of tribute, sometimes of a considerable amount. The position of Teos can thus be said to lie somewhere between freedom and dependence; an exact definition is unattainable and was probably not meant to be attainable. It seems certain, however, that Teos enjoyed a greater measure of freedom by virtue of its συνθῆκαι than did the communities of Aeolis and Mysia, whose status was closer to full subjection to Attalos. When hostilities in Asia Minor involving Attalos came to a temporary halt in 205, probably at the time of the Peace of Phoinike which ended the Aegean War, Teos felt free to turn to Antiochos III, who had recently returned from the East and now supported the cause of Teos in its request for the general recognition of its ἀσυλία. This recognition was duly accorded in 204/3 by the Greek communities, and in 193 by the Roman Senate. Teos' relations with Attalos had been based entirely on military considerations, and it is not surprising that after long years of war it should turn to a different protector in a peaceful cause.

[91] Holleaux, *Études*, ii. 73–125. See below, ch. 4 (i).

This evidence leaves a clear impression that Teos became eventually dissatisfied with the terms of its relationship with Attalos. In the case of the neighbouring city of Kolophon, the evidence usually cited for its relations with the Pergamene King must now be redated, partly on the basis of the conclusions reached above. In the closing years of the third century, Old Kolophon, the city visited by Attalos I, established a settlement at Notion (Colophon Nova);⁹² although independent of the old city, the new settlement was attached to it by συμπολιτεία,⁹³ and its inhabitants were called, according to a decree of Magnesia on the Maeander, Κολοφώνιοι ἀπὸ θαλάσσης.⁹⁴ A decree of the new city records the decision to institute a festival of the νέοι and ἐφῆβοι to celebrate the γενέθλιος ἡμέρα of Athenaios, the youngest of the sons of Attalos I.⁹⁵ Holleaux has shown further that other members of the Attalid royal family were honoured with Athenaios in having their εἰκόνες erected by the city in the sanctuary of Apollo Klarios.⁹⁶ Holleaux argued, from the absence of any specific reference to Eumenes II, that the decree was passed before his accession in 197, and therefore necessarily shortly before 197, since Athenaios cannot have been born earlier than 220.⁹⁷ More recently, a later date has been urged on the basis of the letter forms of the inscription,⁹⁸ to which an important historical consideration must now be

⁹² Cf. Cardinali, *RP* 94, n. 4; Holleaux, *Études*, ii. 53.
⁹³ L. Robert, *Rev. Phil.* x (1936), 158, n. 6, 165–6; *Villes*, 62.
⁹⁴ *IvM* 53, 75–9: Κολοφώνιο[ι οἱ τὴν] | ἀρχαίαν πόλ[ιν οἰ]κ]οῦντες distinguished from Κολοφώνιοι ἀ[πὸ] | θαλάσσης.
⁹⁵ Th. Macridy, *ÖJh* viii (1905), 161–3, no. 1, as interpreted by Holleaux, *Études*, ii. 51–60 (and simultaneously, but in less detail, by A. Brueckner, *ÖJh* ix (1906), Beibl. 58–9); Appendix iv, no. 20.
⁹⁶ Holleaux, *Études*, ii. 58.
⁹⁷ Ibid. 59; on the birth of Athenaios see also Meischke, *Symbolae*, 26.
⁹⁸ Habicht, *IvP* iii., p. 28, n. 5. Much depends on the restoration of lines 2–5; Holleaux restored: [σταθῆναι δὲ] τὴν εἰκόνα | [ἐν τῶι ἐπιτηδειοτάτωι τόπωι (?) τοῦ ἱεροῦ πλησίον | [τῶν εἰκόνων τῶν ἀδελφῶν Ἀθηναί]ου καὶ τῆς μητρὸς | [αὐτῶν βασιλίσσης Ἀπολλωνίδο]ς. Cf. A. Brueckner, *ÖJh* ix (1906), Beibl. 58–9: πλησίον | [τοῦ πατρὸς θεοῦ βασιλέως Ἀττάλ]ου καὶ τῆς μητρὸς | [θεᾶς βασιλίσσης? Ἀπολλωνίδο]ς. Neither restoration is completely satisfactory, but the construction imposed by Brueckner (στῆσαι δὲ τὴν εἰκόνα - - - πλησίον τοῦ πατρὸς κτλ.) is particularly unfortunate. It is difficult to see in these circumstances how Attalos' name can have been included at this point (cf. Holleaux, *Études*, ii. 58, n. 3): it is not then so surprising that Eumenes' name is also lacking, and it should be noted that the omission of a royal name in a civic decree is often misleading and rarely decisive, a point which will be discussed further in Appendix iii (203, n.14).

added: that after 205 Attalos' influence in Ionia was weakened by the end of the military undertakings on which the συνθῆκαι with Teos and Kolophon, and other cities, were based. The honours voted to Athenaios cannot be dated before 205, when he will have been too young, and a date between the years 205 and 197 seems extremely unlikely. Although the period from 197 to 188, that is, during the first ten years of Eumenes' reign, remain a possibility, a date after the Roman settlement is by far the most convincing, since we have other evidence of cities instituting similar cults to honour the Attalids at this time.[99] It needs to be added that such a cult does not necessarily imply a subject status on the part of the city concerned (Colophon Nova was declared free of tribute in 188),[100] since the practice is known to have been followed by independent cities, for example Kos and Miletos.[101] This important point will be taken up in a later chapter; at this point the redating of this decree leaves us with no additional evidence to clarify the status of Kolophon in the years 218 to 201.

It remains to consider Attalos' dealings with the cities in Helles-pontine Phrygia. The status of these cities is even more clearly one of friendship rather than of allegiance. It appears from Polybios' narrative that Attalos visited them because his settlement of the Galatians by the Hellespont brought him into the area, rather by chance than by design (v. 78. 6): Ἄτταλος μὲν οὖν, ἀποκαταστήσας τοὺς Αἰγοσάγας εἰς τὸν Ἑλλήσποντον καὶ χρηματίσας φιλανθρώπως Λαμψακηνοῖς, Ἀλεξανδρεῦσιν, Ἰλιεῦσι, διὰ τὸ τετηρηκέναι τούτους τὴν πρὸς αὐτὸν πίστιν, ἀνεχώρησε μετὰ τῆς δυνάμεως εἰς Πέργαμον. On the other hand, the words τετηρηκέναι τὴν πρὸς αὐτὸν πίστιν suggest the existence of a previous relationship during the war with Achaios, one perhaps based on συνθῆκαι, as is the case with the Ionian cities. This does not necessarily mean, however, that their terms were the same as those of the Ionian cities; it is extremely unlikely, for example, that they paid Attalos tribute, since they were free cities after 188.[102] Nor did the Hellespontine cities 'entrust' themselves to Attalos in

---

[99] See below, ch. 6.
[100] Polyb. xxi. 46. 4; see below, ch. 4 (ii).
[101] See below, 155. Kolophon was regarded as a subject city by Cardinali, *RP* 86, and, on the basis of the cult, by Holleaux, *Études*, ii. 60.
[102] On the status of these cities after 188, see Schmitt, *Untersuchungen*, 284.

the manner of Teos and Kolophon. On the contrary, Polybios' narrative shows that Attalos' dealings were on the basis of a free alliance, spontaneous support rather than contrived co-operation. Thus Attalos' relationship with Lampsakos, Ilion, and Alexandria Troas may be compared with that pertaining to Kyzikos; in the case of Ilion, evidence cited in the next chapter reveals a further parallel in the form of the kind of Attalid benefactions already known for Kyzikos in the case of Philetairos. They were all important free cities whose friendship was especially valuable to Attalos because, like Kyzikos, they facilitated the important Pergamene trade with the Black Sea area.[103] They sympathized with Attalos, but owed him no allegiance.

*

The conclusion of the preceding discussion has been that Attalos' main contribution to the growth of his kingdom in the years 241 to 218 lay in his development of firmer diplomatic contact with Greek cities further from Pergamon, enabling him to find stronger and more substantial support in his wars against successive local opponents. In examining the extent to which Attalos subsequently maintained the position he gained in 218 two important events have to be taken into account: the counter-attack made by Achaios in the years 218 to 216, and the agreement reached in 216 between Attalos and Antiochos to co-operate in eliminating Achaios. Of neither event do we possess significant details. The first is recorded by Polybios as follows (v. 77. 1):[104] Ἀχαιὸς δὲ ποιησάμενος ὑφ' ἑαυτὸν τὴν Μιλυάδα καὶ τὰ πλεῖστα μέρη τῆς Παμφυλίας ἀνέζευξε, καὶ παραγενόμενος εἰς Σάρδεις ἐπολέμει μὲν Ἀττάλῳ συνεχῶς, ἀνετείνετο δὲ Προυσίᾳ, πᾶσι δ' ἦν φοβερὸς καὶ βαρὺς τοῖς ἐπὶ τάδε τοῦ Ταύρου κατοικοῦσι. Although the extent of Achaios' success in these years is unknown, it is probable that Attalos found himself again in difficulties, for such circumstances best explain his willingness to come to terms with Antiochos in the late spring of 216 (v. 107. 4):[105] Ἀντίοχος δὲ

---

[103] On this aspect of the Attalids' economic policy cf. M. I. Rostovtzeff, *Ramsay Studies*, 365–6.

[104] Schmitt, *Untersuchungen*, 263.

[105] On the κοινοπραγία see Schmitt, *Untersuchungen*, 264–7; on the date, 264, n. 1.

μεγάλῃ παρασκευῇ χρησάμενος ἐν τῷ χειμῶνι, μετὰ ταῦτα τῆς θερείας ἐπιγενομένης ὑπερέβαλε τὸν Ταῦρον, καὶ συνθέμενος πρὸς Ἄτταλον τὸν βασιλέα κοινοπραγίαν ἐνίστατο τὸν πρὸς Ἀχαιὸν πόλεμον. This agreement (κοινοπραγία) was one of military co-operation designed to achieve a specific purpose, and not a formal treaty,[106] but there is further evidence that the good relations between Attalos and Antiochos were maintained after the capture and death of Achaios in 213 had put an end to the immediate ground of co-operation between the two kings. A treaty between them is recorded, this time with the title συνθῆκαι, in the literary evidence relating to the Roman negotiations with Antiochos after his defeat at Magnesia in 189:

Appian, *Syr.* xxxviii: Scipio addresses an embassy from Antiochos and alludes to the compensation that would be required of him: ἀποδοῦναι (sc. Antiochos) ... Εὐμένει ὅσα λοιπὰ τῆς πρὸς Ἄτταλον τὸν Εὐμένους πατέρα συνθήκης ἔχει.

Polybios xxi. 17. 6 expresses the same negotiations as follows: ἀποδοῦναι δὲ καὶ Εὐμένει τετρακόσια τάλαντα (τὰ) προσοφειλόμενα καὶ τὸν ἐλλείποντα σῖτον κατὰ τὰς πρὸς τὸν πατέρα συνθήκας.

It is extremely unlikely that the agreement reached in 216 constituted the kind of formal treaty attested by these passages, although we need not necessarily conclude that the συνθῆκαι had been concluded only shortly before the year 189 in which reference is made to them.[107] If, as seems correct, we regard the συνθῆκαι as a treaty of later date and closer definition than the κοινοπραγία, the most likely date for its conclusion is immediately or shortly after the death of Achaios, namely in 213 or 212. In the years 212 to 205/4 Antiochos was in the east of his kingdom, and on his return in 204 his activity in western Asia Minor was hardly conducive to friendly relations with the King of Pergamon. It is also possible that in the years before the outbreak of the Second Macedonian

---

[106] Schmitt, *Untersuchungen,* 264, n. 1.

[107] I find unconvincing Schmitt's argument (*Untersuchungen,* 265), 'doch ist kaum anzunehmen, dass der Seleukide noch nach fast drei Jahrzehnten die vergleichsweise niedrige Summe schuldig geblieben wäre.' On the contrary, payments of such obligations in instalments, over a period of time, is a well-attested procedure at this time; the treaty which ended the war between Attalos II and Prusias II, for example, was drawn up on this basis, Prusias being obliged to pay Attalos 500 talents over a period of twenty years (Polyb. xxxiii. 13. 6: πεντακόσια δὲ τάλαντα κατενεγκεῖν ἐν ἔτεσιν εἴκοσι).

War, Attalos was largely responsible for propagating the belief in, and danger of, an alliance between Antiochos and Philip V of Macedon. This would have been an unconvincing attitude to adopt if he himself had also concluded a formal alliance with Antiochos within the last few years. Since relations between the two kings were strongest in the years 216 to 212, it is to this period, shortly after the informal κοινοπραγία had lapsed with the defeat of Achaios, that the συνθῆκαι most naturally belong.[108]

The terms of the κοινοπραγία and the συνθῆκαι are unknown, but it has usually been concluded that Attalos gained from his co-operation with Antiochos, at least to the extent that he was able to recover the position he had achieved in 218.[109] As far as it goes this view is probably correct, since Antiochos cannot have hoped to gain Attalos' co-operation in 216 without making some form of concession; on the other hand Achaios was at the time of the

[108] Antiochos and Philip: *StV* iii. 547. It seems most likely that the 'pact' between Antiochos and Philip V was an informal agreement to co-operate, or even simply an understanding not to interfere with one another's interests. Such an agreement could very easily have been understood later to have amounted to a partition of the Egyptian Empire, and it is highly probable that Attalos and the Rhodians used the rumour (which is all it can have been) in order to convince the Senate of the existence of a danger (cf. Appian, *Maked.* 4. 2: καὶ τήνδε τὴν δόξαν, ἐκταράσσουσαν ἅπαντας 'Ρόδιοι μὲν 'Ρωμαίοις ἐμήνυσαν; cf. D. Magie, *JRS* xxix (1939), 32–44; *Roman Rule*, ii. 750, n. 42); whether the Senate took the threat seriously is another matter (see below, n. 151). Magie has perhaps gone too far in denying the existence of any kind of agreement (although he was quite right in stressing the importance of the rumour of its existence, which is what really matters), but Schmitt's attempted defence of the tradition (*Untersuchungen*, 237–61) does not establish the authenticity of a formal treaty, whose existence is most unlikely. See also E. Badian, *Gnomon*, xxxviii (1966), 715–16.

Two dedications from Pergamon should be mentioned in the context of relations between Attalos and Antiochos. One (*IvP* 189, = *OGIS* 236) is a statue base of Zeuxis, στρατηγός and ἐπὶ τῶν πραγμάτων of Antiochos III (cf. Ad. Wilhelm, *Wien. Stud.* 1907, 11–13; L. Robert, *Nouvelles Inscr. de Sardis*, I. 9–14); the base is inscribed Ζεῦξιν Κυνάγου | ὁ δῆμος. The other (*IvP* 182, = *OGIS* 240) is a base of the king himself: Βασιλέ[α μέγαν 'Αντίοχ]ον | [β]ασιλέως Σ[ελεύκου Καλλι]νίκου | [Πρω]τᾶς Μεν[ίππου νομ]οφύλαξ. The official nature of these dedications implies at least that Antiochos was at the time *persona grata* in Pergamon, and since the statue of Antiochos, where the restoration of the title μέγας seems assured, cannot be dated before 205 (Holleaux, *Études* iii. 159–63), it appears that we must envisage a short period of good relations between Attalos and Antiochos after Antiochos' return from the East in 204. That these good relations lasted for more than a few months is, however, most unlikely.

[109] See the references given by Schmitt, *Untersuchungen*, 266, n. 2.

conclusion of the agreement at least as much a threat to Attalos as he was to Antiochos, perhaps more so, and it is arguable that Attalos stood to gain more from the κοινοπραγία in immediate terms than Antiochos. It is therefore unlikely that Attalos was able to achieve more than a return to the status quo of 218.

More important, however, is the consideration that this is the first recorded treaty between Attalid and Seleukid kings; it therefore marks a decisive point in the development of relations between the two dynasties. Previously, as we have seen, the Seleukids were always concerned with limiting the Attalid *dynasteia*, and it is unlikely that they even acknowledged its independent status. Now, however, the formal constitutional commitment to συνθῆκαι implies a direct recognition by Antiochos of this independent status, and of Attalos as an equal king.[110] We may therefore reckon as the most important concession that Antiochos made to Attalos the first Seleukid recognition of the Attalid Kingdom as a separate and sovereign *dynasteia*.

Further specific conclusions remain tentative. In 218 the Hellespontine cities of Lampsakos, Alexandria Troas, and Ilion affirmed the loyalty to Attalos which they had shown during the war with Achaios. In view of this attitude taken by the leading cities of the area, it is unlikely that Antiochos was able to reassert Seleukid influence in the Troad before the two invasions of Asia Minor in 198 and 197. Pergamene influence in the Troad may therefore be accounted a specific gain of the wars ending with the agreement of 216 and the συνθῆκαι.[111]

The subject status after 216 of the Aeolian cities close to Pergamon is confirmed in the case of Thyateira by the inscription at-

[110] Agreements between kings in the Hellenistic period were obviously not always called συνθῆκαι; much clearly depended on the circumstances of the agreement. Thus an agreement to end hostilities was often called, as we would expect, διαλύσεις (e.g. *StV* iii. 428 (Peace of 311), 448 (ephemeral peace between Demetrios Poliorketes and Kassandros in 302)). Of the terms used, however, συνθῆκαι is constitutionally the most formal, and necessarily involves a mutual recognition of status.

[111] Schmitt (*Untersuchungen*, 165) points to the possibility that the cities of the Troad had eventually fallen to Achaios, and that Polybios v. 78. 6 merely says that they remained loyal to Attalos, i.e. they resisted as long as they could. This view cannot be discounted, but it seems to me not to be what Polybios means, in the context of the section as a whole.

testing Attalos' settling of κατοίκοι in its territory, and in general terms, as we have seen, by the reference in Attalos' reply to Magnesia on the Maeander to αἱ ὑπ' ἐμὲ πόλεις, etc.[112] The fact that reference was made in the Roman settlement to taxes paid to Attalos further suggests that the situation apparent in 218 was also in force in the following years. In these respects then, Attalos seems to have recovered the position he held in 218. On the other hand, Pedroli's extreme view that after 216 Attalos 'possedesse dell' Asia Minore i territori al nord di una linea ideale che dal mare ed immediatamente a messogiorno di Colofone si estende fino all' alta valle del Sangario, e di qui fino all' Ellesponto; e però all' incirca tutta l'antica satrapia di Frigia all' Ellesponto',[113] is neither based on specific evidence nor related to the realities of Attalos' position in earlier years, in which such aggrandizement of the kingdom does not come into question, and it was rightly discounted by Cardinali. Cardinali's own view, however,[114] which was endorsed by Ernst Meyer,[115] by M. Holleaux,[116] and by L. Robert,[117] that Attalos retained in 216 all his conquests of two years earlier, needs modification in accordance with the differing status of the subject communities in Aeolis and Mysia, and the allied cities in Ionia and Hellespontine Phrygia, where status varied from city to city. Attalos most probably recovered the authority he had exercised in 218, but the extent of direct authority, which was confined to Aeolis and Mysia, remained unchanged.

The situation in Mysia, however, was certainly less stable after 216. As already noted, the nature of the country permitted only a tentative and partial kind of authority, and no treaty could by itself guarantee Attalos' position there. In the years following Attalos' expedition of 218 its position is unclear, but the fact that Μυσοί appear in Attalos' army during the First Macedonian War shows that his control was at least partially maintained in the years following the agreement with Antiochos. In all probability, how-

[112] See above, 45.
[113] U. Pedroli, *Il Regno di Pergamo* (Turin, 1896), 30–1. Cf. Cardinali, *RP* 81–3.
[114] *RP* 86.
[115] *Die Grenzen,* 103–4.
[116] *Études,* ii. 60.
[117] *Villes,* 40, n. 3.

ever, the status of Mysia remained vague, in the sense that no single ruler exercised authority over the whole country; it has been shown, for instance, that although Attalos continued to recruit soldiers from the country he was by no means the only ruler at the end of the third century to do so.[118] Mysia may therefore be seen rather as a natural recruiting ground for Hellenistic armies than as a country of sustained political importance.

This conclusion concerning the status of Mysia may serve to clarify a vexed problem arising from a reference to Mysia in the terms of the Roman settlement of Asia Minor in 188 BC. According to Polybios (xxi. 46.10) the territories awarded to Eumenes II included Μυσούς, οὖς πρότερον αὐτὸς παρεσκευάσατο; according to Livy (xxxviii. 39.15), *Mysiam, quam Prusia rex ademerat*. It has been generally recognized that Polybios' text as we have it is corrupt, and that Livy transmits the correct original.[119] The identification of Mysia, however, remains problematical. It is unlikely to have been the whole of the area adjoining Pergamon, that is, Mysia proper, since the area is more closely defined: *quam Prusia rex ademerat*. It is also most unlikely that Prusias ever penetrated so close to Pergamon. On the other hand, the idea that Attalos gained an even temporary control over an entire area further from Pergamon, such as Mysia Olympene and the later Phrygia Epiktetos, both of which have been suggested in this context, seems to be ruled out by the literary evidence, which unanimously stresses the smallness of the Attalid Kingdom before 188.[120] Furthermore, Polybios' reference to Μυσοί suggests a part and not the whole of a country. In these circumstances we should think rather of territory on the borders of Mysia, and most probably that between Mysia and Phrygia Epiktetos, whose boundaries

---

[118] On the recruitment of Mysians in the Hellenistic armies, cf. Launey, *Recherches*, i. 436–9.

[119] Cf. Cardinali, *RP* 82, n. 2; Meyer, *Die Grenzen*, 150, n. 2; Magie, *Roman Rule*, ii. 758, n. 56; Habicht, *Hermes*, lxxxiv (1956), 91. Mommsen, *Römische Forschungen*, ii. 538, alone attempted to emend the text of Livy (*Prusia* to *pridem*).

[120] Mysia Olympene: Cardinali, *RP* 82, n. 2. Phrygia Epiktetos: Meyer, *Die Grenzen*, 115; Magie, *Roman Rule*, ii. 759 (with reservations); Habicht, art. cit. (n. 119), 92; Schmitt, *Untersuchungen*, 266, 276–8. On the evidence for the size of the kingdom before 188, see above, 25.

were never clearly defined in antiquity.[121] We know, in particular, that certain communities in this border area were sometimes assigned to Mysia,[122] and we may reckon that Attalos' control in Mysia spilled for a time into the area known later as Phrygia Epiktetos, but this does not mean that the country as a whole may be accounted a part of his kingdom.[123] We are dealing, in other words, with the border territory between the kingdoms of Pergamon and Bithynia, and, given the unstable situation in Mysia, it is not surprising that this territory remained disputed until the time of the Roman settlement. Prusias is known to have been actively hostile to Attalos on at least two occasions, in 208 and in the years preceding the Antiochic War.[124] On the first occasion Prusias invaded Attalos' kingdom, an action which must have brought him into the intervening territory in Mysia;[125] as we have seen, it is by no means certain that Attalos was able to maintain the hegemony in this area as a whole to which he aspired in 218. It is admittedly plausible that the loss to Prusias at this date of a part of Mysia will have been rectified by the peace which we may date to 205,[126] but it is hardly likely that this was the only occasion on which Prusias invaded Mysia. As a border land between the two kingdoms the country was naturally liable to frequent attempts on the part of each king to maintain a stronger and more widespread influence there than his rival. For this same reason it would constitute territory which required settlement in 188, whatever the situation at that moment. It is not necessarily to be concluded that at the time of the Roman settlement the territory concerned was still in Prusias' possession; only that it had been disputed, and remained in dispute. It is probable that Prusias took the opportunity afforded

---

[121] Cf. Habicht, art. cit., 92, with particular reference to Strabo xii. 4. 4, 564: χωρὶς τὰ Μυσῶν καὶ Φρυγῶν ὁρίσματα· διορίσαι δὲ χαλεπόν.

[122] Strabo xii. 8. 12, 576: τῆς δ' ἐπικτήτου Φρυγίας Ἀζανοί τέ εἰσι καὶ Νακολία καὶ Κοτιάειον καὶ Μιδάειον καὶ Δορύλαιον πόλεις καὶ Κάδοι· τοὺς δὲ Κάδους ἔνιοι τῆς Μυσίας φασίν. Cf. *OGIS* 446 (Kadoi): ὁ δῆμος ὁ Μυσῶν Ἀββαειτῶν. This evidence shows only that the boundaries were unclear; the areas as a whole were usually carefully distinguished, e.g. in Strabo xii. 4.1, 563.

[123] Attalid rule at Aizanoi is attested by an inscription of Hadrianic date: see below, 97 n. 84.

[124] Cf. Habicht, *RE*, s.v. Prusias (1), 1092–3; 1097–8.

[125] Livy xxviii. 7. 10.

[126] See above, n. 75.

by Antiochos' invasion of Attalos' kingdom in 198 to strengthen his position in the disputed area, but that his position was maintained there for the following ten years is doubtful.[127]

These considerations lead to the conclusion that the Mysians concerned lay on the border of Mysia proper and were later included in Phrygia Epiktetos; that owing to the nature of the country neither Attalos nor Prusias was able to maintain a more than ephemeral hold there, although both made the attempt on various occasions; and that the disputed area was settled in Eumenes' favour in 188. In this respect, then, Attalid influence in Mysia under Attalos I may be compared with that pertaining at a later date in Galatia, to the extent that similar conditions rendered impossible a settled and lasting control over the whole country.[128]

(ii) Attalos and the Aegean, 215–197

We have seen Attalos, during the first twenty-five years of his reign, in the role not of an ambitious would-be empire builder, but of a cautious and defensive ruler, concerned with strengthening his kingdom rather than with expanding it, and indeed for most of the time preoccupied with defending its very existence from the threats presented by successive enemies. To strengthen his military position Attalos formed closer relations with Greek cities in Ionia and the Troad, but we have seen that in terms of direct rule the situation hardly changed from the time of his predecessor. Finally, in the years preceding Antiochos' departure for the eastern campaigns, the Seleukid and Attalid kings came to an agreement, eventually constituted under the formal title συνθῆκαι, which at the very least confirmed Attalos' sovereignty in Aeolis and Mysia. Attalos' achievement in the years preceding his alliance with Rome can be summarized as the consolidation of authority within the kingdom left to him by Eumenes I, and the foundation of stronger diplomatic relations outside it. One could

---

[127] Schmitt, *Untersuchungen*, 276–8, argued that Prusias invaded the area concerned in 198, necessarily before Eumenes' accession (cf. Polyb. xxxii. 8. 3); as I do not believe that either Attalos or Prusias exercised such a definite control in this area as to constitute incorporation in their respective kingdoms, I do not think that this point can be pressed.

[128] On Galatia, see further below, ch. 5.

not do better than recall the words of M. Holleaux, written with reference to Attalos' campaign of 218, but applicable to the reign as a whole: 'circonspect et avisé, calculant juste ses intérêts, limitant ses entreprises à ses moyens d'action, et se hâtant d'accomplir, sitôt que s'en offre l'occasion, des besognes immédiatement utiles.'[129]

A few years after the agreement with the Seleukid king, Attalos took part in the so-called First Macedonian War as Rome's ally against Philip V of Macedon. The nature of Attalos' involvement, and above all the motives for his enmity to Macedon in the light of his cautious policy of earlier years, must form an important part of our discussion. Scholars have suggested various reasons for Attalos' alliance with Rome. The most extreme view has been expressed, surprisingly, by the same scholar whose more apposite words have been quoted above; written twenty-four years later, this view sees Attalos, in the second half of his reign, attempting to found an empire in the Aegean after his failure to increase his kingdom in Asia Minor; to 'escape to the west', even to re-form the old kingdom of Lysimachos.[130] In such a scheme, Philip would appear as Attalos' natural enemy, and in Holleaux's brilliant picture of Roman relations with the East, Attalos appears as the ready ally of Rome, concerned to persuade the Senate of the usefulness of its intervention, but equally anxious to secure such powerful support for the grandiose intentions he now allegedly entertained for the expansion of his kingdom. This view, needless to say, presents a picture of Attalos' intentions very different from the one argued in the preceding pages, and we would have to suppose a dramatic change of policy; it is, however, untenable and must be refuted.

Other views see Philip as the natural enemy of Attalos in the

[129] *Études*, ii. 42.

[130] *Rome, la Grèce et les monarchies hellénistiques au IIIe siècle av. J.-C.* (Paris, 1921), 204–5, especially 205: 'dominer l'Aigée, y prendre la place quittée par l'Egypte, y prévenir la Macédoine et lui enlever ce qu'elle y tient déjà, occuper les Cyclades et même l'Eubée, pénétrer au Sud jusqu'au coeur des mers grecques, pousser au Nord jusqu'aux îles et aux rivages de Thrace, puis s'étendre, s'il se peut, vers la Chersonèse, se saisir des détroits, et, chevauchant sur l'Europe et l'Asie, restaurer l'éphémère empire de Lysimaque.' In this list of imputed intentions, only the words 'y prévenir la Macédoine' seem to me to be realistic.

latter's opposition to the Seleukids and to Prusias I of Bithynia, Philip's ally;[131] and Attalos as the natural enemy of Philip in his defence of his kingdom in Asia Minor.[132] Neither of these two points of view is realistic; the first overlooks the important fact that Attalos and Antiochos were formal allies during the years preceding the outbreak of the Macedonian War, as well as the consideration that Prusias' intervention on Philip's behalf took place some years after the outbreak of the war, and cannot therefore have been a factor determining Attalos' policy before it; the second argument is equally untenable in view of the fact that Philip was at this date not a direct threat to Attalos' position in Asia Minor, even as suzerain of Caria, where Attalos did not have lasting interests at this date; this threat was, once again, a later development in Aegean politics.[133]

More important, however, is the consideration that all these approaches to the problem presuppose a total commitment on Attalos' part from the very beginning of the war with Philip. A closer examination of the facts shows that this assumption is not justified; on the contrary, it will be seen that Attalos had little enthusiasm for the war and took part only when persuaded to do so by his allies and only to such an extent as would satisfy them.

We must consider, firstly, the circumstances in which Attalos became Rome's ally, and the implications of this alliance. Although these circumstances are not entirely clear, it is certain at least that the initiative lay not with Attalos, but with his prospective allies, and of these with Aitolia more than Rome. In interpreting the literary tradition, represented in full at this point only by Livy, we have to be careful in distinguishing the evidence derived from Polybios from that which can be ascribed to one or another of the Roman annalists, and in assessing their respective values. Livy's account of the Roman treaty with Aitolia, which we should probably date to the year 212, although compressed and evidently

[131] G. De Sanctis, *Storia dei Romani* (Turin, 1907–64), iii. 2. 416.
[132] U. Wilcken, *RE*, s.v. Attalos (9), 2163.
[133] Prusias: see Holleaux, *Rome, la Grèce*, 206, n. 1. Philip and Caria: Crampa, *Labraunda*, iii. 1. 127–31.

selective, was almost certainly derived from Polybios;[134] the terms
show that Attalos' co-operation was envisaged but not presup-
posed (Livy xxvi. 24. 8–9): *igitur conscriptae condiciones, quibus
in amicitiam societatemque populi Romani venirent* (sc.
Aetoli),
(9) *additumque ut, si placeret vellentque, eodem iure amicitiae
Elei Lacedaemoniique et Attalus et Pleuratus et Scerdilaedus
essent, Asiae Attalus, hi Thracum et Illyriorum reges.* As is well
known, Rome avoided total involvement in the war even after this
treaty with Aitolia, and it is probable that Attalos' participation
was suggested in the hope that the availability of the Attalid fleet
would complement the power of Aitolia by land, and thereby
further reduce Rome's direct obligations. The fleet appears for the
first time, and then only briefly (see below) during this war, at
which point it was evidently a force of some strength, but we have
no direct evidence as to the circumstances of its construction. The
fact that a fleet is not attested by Polybios in the campaign of 218
hardly provides a *terminus post quem* for its construction, as has
been thought,[135] since Attalos' strictly military activity in that year
was confined to areas of Aeolis and Mysia in which naval activity is
hardly to be expected; in other areas his dealings were political,
and in one case (the Troad), not originally envisaged. So the
argument that Attalos began the construction of a fleet some time
after 218 as a part of his plan to turn to the west, does not have any
firm basis in the evidence. It is more probable that the fleet was
built up gradually over a number of years, and in particular after
the acquisition of the important harbour position of Elaia, probably in the reign of Eumenes I, as a means of improved communi-
cations and especially of closer contact with the Greek mainland,
which was always an important factor in Attalid foreign policy.
There is no evidence to show that the fleet was developed in
pursuit of an expansive or aggressive policy.

[134] The most thorough analysis of the literary tradition is that of K.-E. Petzold,
Die Eröffnung des zweiten römisch-makedonischen Krieges (Berlin, 1940), but it
suffers from a dogmatic attitude taken towards the value of the various elements of
the tradition. For the treaty with Aitolia, see Schmitt's commentary, *StV* iii. 536.
On the date, see especially G. Klaffenbach, *Der römisch-ätolische Bündnisvertrag
vom Jahre 212 v. Chr. (SB Berlin*, 1954); G. A. Lehmann, *Untersuchungen z.
historischen Glaubwürdigkeit des Polybios* (Münster, 1967), 10–134.
[135] As argued, for example, by Holleaux, *Rome, la Grèce*, 205–6, n. 2.

Although the availability of the fleet was an attraction to his allies, we see clearly that Attalos' own part in the war was from the beginning of a vague and undefined nature, and it is unlikely that a formal alliance with Rome was concluded before the time of the Peace of Phoinike which ended the war; it is more probable that Attalos' position remained one of informal *amicitia*.[136] This conclusion is indicated in particular by Polybios' reference in a later context (200 BC) to Attalos' activity as based on a κοινοπραγία (xvi. 25. 4): θεωρῶν (Attalos) δ' αὐτοὺς (the Roman commissioners) καὶ τῆς προγεγενημένης κοινοπραγίας μνημονεύοντας ... περιχαρὴς ἦν. This term was used, as we have seen, of Attalos' co-operation with Antiochos in the war with Achaios, and denotes a commitment to military assistance for the time being rather than the conclusion of a formal treaty. Such military assistance seems to have been the nature of Attalos' involvement, to which we now turn.

Attalos' short and casual involvement hardly supports the notion of a scheme on his part of expansion in the Aegean. The invitation to Attalos to take part in the war was probably made in 212. So far from seizing this golden opportunity of an 'escape to the West', Attalos did not appear in Aegean waters until the year 209, and then only when the Aitolians, still left to bear the brunt of the fighting and evidently desperate to secure Attalos' active participation, offered him the honorary title of League ἡγεμών together with the prestigious island of Aigina, recently acquired by them, at the nominal price of thirty talents, as a base for the Pergamene fleet.[137] The following year Attalos returned to his capital on receipt of news of Prusias' invasion of his kingdom, a diversion probably engineered by Philip, and he took no further active part in the war. Apart from Aigina, which constitutes a special case, Attalos achieved no territorial gains as a result of his participation.

This activity, viewed objectively, suggests informal co-operation rather than a formal alliance, and corresponds with the conclusion reached above as to Attalos' initial relationship with Rome. It also corresponds with our view of Attalos' policy with regard to his kingdom; we see him still, that is, cautious and

[136] K.-E. Petzold, *Die Eröffnung*, 14–18.
[137] Polyb. xxii. 8. 10; cf. *BSA* lxvi (1971), 1–2.

reserved, hesitant to commit himself to ambitious schemes, and
more concerned with the preservation of his small kingdom, and
the authority it represented, than with its aggrandizement. We
have seen that the initiative in securing Attalos' albeit ephemeral
co-operation lay in a large measure with the Aitolians. This fact is
of importance in that it was with Aitolia that Attalos' relations
were, at that time, in the context of the Roman alliance, the
strongest. It is well known that, at a date before 219, Attalos had
financed the building of the fortifications of the Aitolian stronghold
of Elaos;[138] less frequently noticed is the equally significant appearance of the ethnic Ἀτταλεύς in Aitolian manumissions from
the end of the third century, pointing to the existence in Aitolia at
that date of a city named Ἀτταλεία whose foundation, or, more
probably, refoundation, may be dated to the time of the First
Macedonian War, or earlier.[139] We are bound, then, to reckon with
a closer Pergamene relationship with Aitolia than that suggested
by the single fortification of Elaos. This impression is strengthened
by evidence relating to Attalos' activity at Delphi, then under
Aitolian control. Attalos' predecessors had established cordial
relations with Delphi, but their generosity was probably limited to
direct financial support. This policy was taken a step further by
Attalos, as elsewhere, by the more direct expedient of adding to
the buildings of the sacred precinct. This took the form of a terrace
built to the north-east of the Temple of Apollo and including a small
stoa; the scale of the building was compact, and the most interesting feature of the construction is the choice of its site, as close as
possible to the temple and thereby in an area so constricted that to
allow room for the new terrace a breach had to be made in the
sacred *peribolos* wall, for the first time since the reconstruction of
the area in the sixth century.[140] The size and position of the
building indicate a cult purpose — the stoa was not simply a shelter
from the rain — as does the dedication of the whole complex to

[138] Polyb. iv. 65. 6–7: Ἀττάλου τὴν περὶ αὐτὸ κατασκευὴν ἀναδεξαμένου τοῖς
Αἰτωλοῖς.

[139] Cf. Klaffenbach on *IG* ix.² 1. 95 (204/3; cf. 107): '*nimirum hoc oppidum
Ἀτταλεία denominatum est a rege Attalo I de Aetolis bene merito.*' On the origins
of Attalos' relations with Aitolia (which are very obscure) see also McShane,
Foreign Policy, 101, n. 29.

[140] For a description of the site see G. Roux, *BCH* lxxvi (1952), 141–96.

Apollo: [Βα]σιλε[ὺς ῎Ατταλ]ος ['Απ]όλ[λ]ων[ι]. An Amphiktyonic decree dated most probably to 223/2 BC[141] records regulations for the use of the portico, and leaves the impression that abuses of the precinct had arisen since its construction (lines 7–11): ἐν τὰν παστά[δα τὰν ἀνατεθεῖσαν τῶι θεῶι] | ὑπὸ τοῦ βασιλέ[ω]ς 'Ατ-τάλου μηθενὶ εἶμ[εν ἐξουσίαν πλὴν βασιλέως] | ἀναθεῖναι μηθέν, μηδὲ σκανοῦν μηδὲ π[ῦρ ἀνάπτειν ἐντὸς ἢ ἐκτὸς] | τὰς παστάδος κτλ. It is likely then, from this evidence, that the construction of the terrace should be dated to the earlier years of Attalos' reign, most probably the 230s, although there is no reason to associate the construction with any of Attalos' military successes, as has been done.[142]

It is to be noted, finally, that it was Attalos' policy, in Delphi and elsewhere, not simply to finance building operations of this kind, as his predecessors seem to have done, but to provide skilled workers to carry out the actual operation; we hear at Delphi in 197 of one Dameas, ὁ παρὰ τοῦ βασιλέως 'Αττάλου ὁ ἐπὶ τῶν ἔργων τῶν βασιλικῶν.[143] The implementing of this more ambitious policy at Delphi may be accounted one of the factors leading to Attalos' friendly relations with Aitolia.

It can hardly be coincidence, then, that it was the Aitolians with whom Attalos had the strongest relations at the time of the out-break of the First Macedonian War; they whose treaty with Rome envisaged Attalos' co-operation; and they at whose call Attalos finally appeared with a fleet in the Aegean in support of the Roman alliance. In this connection lie the origin and motive of Attalos' at first reluctant appearance in the alliance formed against Philip, and any notion of personal ambition on Attalos' part at this time must be discounted.

It is probable that Attalos, together with Prusias I of Bithynia, was entered as one of the *adscripti* to the Peace of Phoinike which ended the First Macedonian War in 205.[144] It is at any rate certain that Attalos' position in relation to the Roman alliance remained

---

[141] *Syll.*³ 523 (Pomtow). Cf. Wilhelm, *ÖJh* viii (1905), 12–13; R. Flacelière, *Les Aitoliens à Delphes* (Paris, 1937), 407, no. 38b.

[142] e.g. by McShane, *Foreign Policy*, 101: 'Attalus I built a portico at Delphi to celebrate his Gallic victories.'

[143] *SGDI* 2001; Appendix iv, no. 4; cf. Daux, *Delphes*, 499.

[144] On the authenticity of the *adscripti*, see above, n. 75.

informal. In the years from 205 to 200, however, the situation in the Aegean changed dramatically with the emergence of Philip of Macedon as a threat to the islands and to Attalos' position in western Asia Minor. The piratical expedition of Dikaiarchos, the worshipper of Lawlessness and Impiety, which we should prob-ably date to the year after the Peace of Phoinike,[145] must have been the first clear indication of the reality of this new threat. Attalos and Rhodes stood to suffer most: Attalos from Philip's now clear designs on the cities of the Hellespont,[146] and Rhodes from his support of the Cretan pirates. With their commerce and prosperity equally threatened, it is not surprising to find Attalos and Rhodes co-operating in the following years, as the threat merged into reality, in resisting Philip's advance. So far from being an un-natural alliance, as has usually been assumed, it was the inevitable reaction to a common danger. Of particular importance is their common policy, now well attested by epigraphical evidence,[147] of challenging Philip's position in Crete (a position of great impor-tance to his ambitions in the Aegean) by concluding alliances with groups of Cretan cities, thereby controlling the supply of Cretan mercenaries.

It seems most likely, however, from the limited evidence, that of these two powers Rhodes was the more belligerent at the time of the outbreak of the Second Macedonian War, owing largely to the vigorous policy of her admiral Theophiliskos. Polybios states explicitly that Theophiliskos was the driving force behind the alliance, being mainly responsible for securing Attalos' participa-tion in the naval battle off Chios, in which the combined Attalid and Rhodian fleets proved to be a good match for Philip, although

---

[145] Polyb. xviii. 54. 8; Diodoros xxviii. 1. Holleaux, *Études*, iv. 124–45, establi-shed the date of the expedition as either 205 or 204; of these the later year seems by far the more likely.

[146] Polybios designates as Dikaiarchos' objectives in 204, τὰς Κυκλάδας νήσους καὶ τὰς ἐφ᾽ Ἑλλησπόντου πόλεις (54. 8). This policy of aggression against the Hellespontine cities, which was carried further in 202, and which directly threat-ened both Attalos' interests there and his contacts with the Black Sea area, must have been a decisive factor in determining Attalos' more positive policy as devel-oped after 202.

[147] For Attalid treaties with Cretan communities see P. Ducrey and H. van Effenterre, *Kret. Chron.* xxi (1969), 277–300; P. Ducrey, *BCH* xciv (1970), 637–59; Appendix iv, no. 3; for the Rhodian treaties, *StV* iii. 551 (Hierapytna), 552 (Olus). Note that Hierapytna was the common ally of Rhodes and Attalos.

both sides claimed the victory.[148] In these events we see again Attalos' reluctance to become involved in an Aegean war, shown also by the fact that he had not taken part in the earlier engagement between the Rhodian and Macedonian fleets at Lade.[149] The death of Theophiliskos at Chios doubtless also goes a long way to explain the marked hiatus in the activity of Rhodes and Attalos prior to their appeal to Rome. This appeal took place in 200, after Philip's escape from his enemies' siege in Bargylia; for its motive we need surely look no further than the consideration that Attalos and Rhodes had after three major attempts (Lade, Chios, Bargylia) failed to contain Philip, and to keep him from plundering Attalos' own territory,[150] and the probable feeling after the death of Theophiliskos that the alliance was by itself not powerful enough. For the first time we see Attalos taking an energetic initiative in Aegean affairs, indeed the main advocate — or so it seems — of the renewal of the war with Macedon. This policy, so far from being a reversal of his earlier policy, should be seen as a logical development of it; no longer able to defend his kingdom by his own resources, he sought the help of the power which seemed most able to support him.[151]

[148] For the narrative of the battle, Polyb. xvi. 2–8; Philip's claim to victory is at 8. 2. For Attalos' victory dedication, see above, n. 3. The initiative of Theophiliskos, 9. 4: ἠνάγκασε δὲ τὸν Ἄτταλον μὴ μέλλειν κτλ.

[149] Polyb. xvi. 10. 1: τὸν δ' Ἄτταλον μηδέπω συμμεμιχέναι. Although Holleaux put forward positive arguments for dating the battle off Chios before that of Lade (*Études*, iv. 218–22), I regard as more convincing the chronology proposed by De Sanctis, *Stor. Rom.* iv. 1. 10, n. 27, in which the battle of Lade is followed by Philip's invasion of Pergamon and the battle off Chios, in that order. Cf. Walbank, *Philip V*, 307–8.

[150] Polyb. xvi. 1, discussed by Holleaux, *Études*, iv. 247–55 (with the chronological reservation expressed in the previous note; cf. Walbank, *Philip V*, 308).

[151] I cannot discuss fully here the political and diplomatic circumstances of Roman intervention in the Second Macedonian War; nor the various attitudes at Rome at the time. As I have said (above, n. 108), the existence of a formal treaty between Antiochos and Philip seems extremely unlikely, but an informal working agreement cannot be ruled out. What mattered was the reporting of the rumour at Rome, although it is not likely that such a report played a decisive part in determining Roman policy in 200; no one in Rome can have believed in the possibility of a direct threat from the East (see H. Bengtson, *Die Welt als Geschichte*, v (1939), 176–7, = *Kleine Schriften zur alten Geschichte* (Munich, 1974), 251–2). More important considerations to the Senate at this time surely were that Philip was supporting lawlessness in the eastern Aegean, and that Roman intervention to restore order there had become feasible with the ending of the war with Carthage (on this second point, see Niese ii. 590; Petzold 24–5).

This appraisal of Attalos' policy in relation to the Roman alliance leads to the conclusion that the main motive continued to be the defence, and not the extension, of his kingdom. In fact, Attalos achieved two territorial gains as a result of the alliance with Rome, namely the islands of Aigina and Andros.[152] Aigina remained an island of some considerable prestige in the Hellenistic period, and must have appeared to Attalos as an asset of value, particularly as its possession provided him with a base close to the Greek mainland, with whose cities it remained his concern to promote friendly relations, but its acquisition was not due to any substantial initiative on Attalos' part. Andros was acquired in 199, during the Second Macedonian War, but the circumstances, beyond the fact that Attalos had taken part in its capture from Philip, are unclear. We have only Livy's statement, *ea ab Romanis regi Attalo concessa* (xxxi. 45. 7); we cannot be sure that it had the same status, in the sense of being a possession of the king, as Aigina.

We see, then, that Attalos never envisaged the Roman alliance as a means of territorial expansion. Such ideas of Attalos as an empire-builder are the fantasies of modern historians. With our sights thus narrowed we are able to assess more fairly Attalos' own achievement. He did not create a new kingdom; rather he devoted his resources to strengthening the existing kingdom — modest as it was in size — and to establishing a diplomatic standing in the Greek world which it never lost.

We may however reasonably attribute to Attalos, in the context of his rule over Aigina, the application of an institution which was later extended to other cities of the enlarged kingdom. Aigina and Andros are of particular importance in assessing the development of institutions of Attalid rule in that they were subject possessions whose acquisition can be dated firmly to the reign of Attalos I, and whose institutions can therefore be assigned with a high degree of probability to him. In particular, the presence of an ἐπιστάτης at Aigina, attested by a decree of the city dating from the reign of Attalos II, indicates that this was an Attalid institution before the

---

[152] Attalid interests in Euboia, including Attalos' temporary possession of Oreos (Livy xxxi. 46. 16; cf. *IvP* 50, = *OGIS* 288) were shortlived; in 196 Flamininus prevented the Roman commissioners from finally ceding Eretria and Karystos, and even Oreos, to Eumenes II (Polyb. xviii. 47. 10–11; Holleaux, *Études*, v. 40, n. 1).

extension of the kingdom in 188.[153] It is more likely that the ἐπιστάτης had existed in Aigina from the time of its acquisition, than that the office was introduced suddenly in 188, since the status of Aigina was not changed in that year. It is unlikely, however, as has already been pointed out (above, 42), that the office was introduced by Attalos into any of the cities of Asia Minor, whose status was much less closely defined; but we can be reasonably sure that Attalid rule in Aigina provided a precedent for similar institutions that were implemented throughout the kingdom after 188. It will be shown in a later chapter that the development of royal cults of the Attalids also owes its origins in some measure to Attalos' rule in Aigina and Andros.

Of equal importance in this connection is the indication that a garrison was imposed in Aigina after Attalos acquired it in 209. That this was the case is shown by a dedication of the garrison members, which is datable to the reign of Attalos I:[154] Διὶ καὶ ᾿Αθῆναι |ὑπὲρ βασιλέως | ᾿Αττάλου |Σατυρῖνος, Καλλίμαχος |καὶ οἱ ὑπ' αὐτοὺς ἡγεμόνες |καὶ στρατιῶται. As I have attempted to show elsewhere, this body was not an army in the field during the First Macedonian War, as no Pergamene army was engaged in Aigina at this time; it was therefore a garrison put in later.[155] In fact the presence of a garrison is attested by Livy during the Second Macedonian War,[156] but we have no evidence as to its permanence. It seems likely, however, that the status of Aigina as a naval base rendered the island liable to almost continuous military occupation by Attalos. Although this policy may be seen as an important precedent for Attalid practice elsewhere at a later date, for example on the frontier with Galatia,[157] it seems to have been the exception rather than the rule. The Attalid garrison in a Greek city remained, as we will see, a rarity.

[153] *IG* iv. 1, = *OGIS* 329. See *BSA* lxvi (1971), 4.
[154] *EA* 1913, 90–92; *ISE* i. 36.
[155] *BSA* lxvi (1971), 1–6.
[156] xxxi. 25. 1 (200): *quia praesidium Attali ab Aegina Romanique ab Piraeo intraverant urbem.*
[157] See below, ch. 5.

4

THE ATTALID KINGDOM AFTER
THE TREATY OF APAMEIA

The Attalids were the great opportunists of the Hellenistic world, and none more so than Eumenes II, who succeeded his father Attalos towards the end of 197.[1] His reign marked the height of Pergamene power and splendour, as characterized by the extensive rebuilding of the citadel of Pergamon,[2] and it has left us in the Great Altar and its sculptures one of the finest monuments of antiquity.[3] Eumenes was rewarded for his loyalty to Rome in the war with Antiochos III of Syria with an extended kingdom which far surpassed the previous Attalid Kingdom in terms of size and extent of authority, although it was, as we shall see, based on it. The new kingdom made proportionately greater demands on the Attalid system of administration, and at the same time the incorporation of Teos, the seat of the Ionian Guild of Dionysian *technitai*, allowed Eumenes and his successors new scope in the development of royal cults. These aspects of Attalid rule will demand most of our attention in this and the following chapters.

The events of the reign of Eumenes II are well documented by the narratives of Polybios and Livy, and a fairly dependable chronological framework can be established. Eumenes extended his father's policy of forming friendships with the states of the Greek mainland by concluding an alliance with the Achaian League which Polybios calls (in 185) 'the ancestral alliance'.[4] The

[1] On the date, see above, 10 n. 6.

[2] Strabo xiii. 4. 2, 624; the chronology and details of the building programme under Eumenes II are discussed by A. Schober, *ÖJh* xxxii (1940), 151 ff., and more fully by Kähler, *Gr. Fries,* 136 ff.

[3] See, in addition to *AvP* III, Kähler, *Gr. Fries,* part I. The best readily available photographs of the friezes known to me are those in E. Schmidt, *The Great Altar of Pergamon* (London, 1965), but the text is not of the same standard. Carl Humann's drawings of the figures of the friezes are beautifully reproduced in *Der Pergamon Altar* (Dortmund, 1960).

[4] Polyb. xxii. 7. 8.

Attalid fleet again served the purpose of the alliance, assuming an active role in two expeditions directed against Nabis of Sparta in 195 and 192,[5] and the alliance is further attested in action during the war with Antiochos by a dedication of the League made after the battle of Magnesia in honour of Eumenes' brother, the future Attalos II.[6] It is clear that Eumenes, like his father, enjoyed close and lasting relations with the states of central and southern Greece,[7] and these relations are also illustrated by an important but not often cited passage of Polybios, which refers to widespread honours paid to Eumenes in the Peloponnese.[8] By means of large donations at Delphi, Attalos I and Eumenes II also strengthened their friendship with the Aitolians, their allies in the Macedonian wars, and this friendship is reflected in the many honours paid to the Attalids at Delphi, more than to any other dynasty.[9] These relations were all inspired by the now established Attalid policy of winning friends by acts of generosity, a policy noted among others by Livy (xlii. 5.3): *cum Eumenis beneficiis numeribusque omnes Graeciae civitates et plerique principum obligati essent.* The lavish use of their wealth remained as much a corner-stone of the Attalids' foreign policy after 188 as it had been before.

In 216 Antiochos III seems to have recognized Attalos I as an equal king and his kingdom as a sovereign state, and he is the first of the Seleukids for whom such action is attested. We know nothing further of the relations between the two kings until 198, when Antiochos, after returning from successful operations elsewhere in his kingdom, turned his attention again to Asia Minor and took the opportunity of attacking the kingdom of Attalos at a

[5] Livy xxxiv. 29. 4; *IvP* 60–63, = *Syll.*[3] 595, 605.

[6] *IvP* 64, = *Syll.*[3] 606.

[7] The evidence of Attalos I's interest in central Greece and the Peloponnese consists of chance references, e.g. Polyb. iv. 65. 6, where we learn that Attalos had financed the building of the walls of the Aitolian stronghold of Elaos. He was honoured by the Sikyonians after redeeming sacred land of Apollo for them; later he received an annual sacrifice there (Polyb. xviii. 16; see below, 147). For Eumenes see also Appendix iv, no. 19 (Thebes).

[8] xxvii. 18; in 170/69, when the whole of Greece was concerned with the imminent war with Perseus, the Achaians considered revoking all their honours, but a more moderate proposal, supported by Polybios himself, was adopted (xxvii. 7. 8–14). The affair characterizes dramatically the Attalids' high regard in the Peloponnese and their concern to maintain it.

[9] Daux, *Delphes,* 502–11.

time when the latter was particularly unable to defend it.[10] Antiochos' behaviour is difficult to understand, for no sooner was Attalos dead than he offered a marriage-alliance to Eumenes, whose refusal Eumenes claimed to his credit in his speech to the Roman Senate in 189.[11] The importance of Antiochos' actions lay in the consequence that the Roman alliance replaced the need for at least nominal co-operation with the Seleukids as a major requirement of Attalid foreign policy. This freedom from Seleukid influence is reflected in a number of institutions of Attalid rule after the Treaty of Apameia had confirmed the position: in the regional administration, which departed from the Seleukid satrapal system; in the titles and functions of officials; and in the new royal coinage, the *cistophoros,* first minted on a general basis after the Treaty of Apameia (see part ii below). In terms of practical politics this situation formed for a time a far more decisive and substantial support to Attalid independence. After the Roman settlement of 188 BC the King of Pergamon could deal with the Seleukid problem from a position of strength, and the results are startling.

In Asia Minor the new kingdom awarded to Eumenes II created its own problems, and Eumenes was faced for the rest of his reign with the enmity of Bithynia and Pontos, as well as the danger presented by the apparent readiness of the Galatians to ally themselves with any enemy of Pergamon, as they had done in the previous reign. One of the most important aspects of the external policy of the Attalids in the years after Apameia was therefore the need to keep control over Galatia, which they did not annex formally as a province although perhaps they could have done (see chapter 5), and Cappadocia, which they achieved by a dynastic marriage (see Appendix iii) and, when necessary, by direct interference.

[10] Livy xxxii. 8. 9–10. The authenticity of this invasion in 198, as distinct from the one in the following year, is convincingly defended by E. Badian, *Cl. Phil.* liv (1959), 82–3 (= *Studies in Roman History* (Oxford, 1964), 114) and by Schmitt, *Untersuchungen,* 269 ff.

[11] Polyb. xxi. 20. 8–9; Appian, *Syr.* 5. The most convincing date for this offer is 195, after the marriage of Antiochos' children Antiochos and Laodike at Seleukeia in 196/5 (Schmitt, *Untersuchungen,* 13–14), and the meeting of Antiochos and Hannibal at Ephesos in the autumn of 195 (Holleaux, *Études,* v. 180–3), where it occurs in Appian's narrative; see also below, Appendix iii, n.7.

The immediate causes of the war which Eumenes fought with Prusias I of Bithynia are unknown, and we have no continuous narrative of its course, the literary evidence being confined to occasional references.[12] A decree of Telmessos, dated to 184 and therefore during Attalid rule, honours Eumenes for a great victory over 'Prusias, Ortiagon, and the Galatians and their allies', and acclaims Eumenes as *Soter,* saviour.[13] The content of the decree suggests the context of a war in progress, and establishes a chronology whereby the peace is to be dated a little after 184/3. Eumenes' victory provided a suitable occasion for the first celebration of the reorganized Pergamene Nikephoria, which we must date to 181; it probably also earned Eumenes the title *Soter,* first attested by the decree of Telmessos just mentioned, and referring more probably to this war than to the earlier, Antiochic, war.[14]

No sooner was peace concluded with Prusias than Eumenes faced another enemy, Pharnakes of Pontos. This new war was under way in 183/2, when envoys of Eumenes and of Pharnakes appeared in Rome and the Senate agreed to send out *legati.* The most substantial piece of evidence on the course and nature of this war is Polybios' account of the treaty concluding it in 180/79.[15] The principal action evidently took place in Galatia and Cappadocia, and this fact illustrates the rivalry of the kingdoms of Asia Minor for control of these important areas. In the settlement Pharnakes was required to evacuate the Galatians' territory and to revoke συνθῆκαι previously concluded with them; Attalid interests in both Galatia and Cappadocia were firmly reasserted.

As a result of the enormous increase of their kingdom in 188 the Attalids were for the rest of their history far more concerned with Asian affairs, and far less than before with the events of the Aegean. It was a sign of the times when in 175/4 Eumenes II placed on the Seleukid throne the new king, Antiochos IV Epiphanes, whose elevation is described by Appian (*Syr.* 45), and equally

[12] For an account of this war see Niese iii. 70 ff.; Habicht, *Hermes,* lxxxiv (1956), 93 ff.; *RE,* s.v. Prusias (1), 1086–1107.

[13] Appendix iv, no. 7; see also no. 8 (Panion, Thrace).

[14] On the chronology, see Habicht, *Hermes,* lxxxiv (1956), 99; on the title, L. Robert, *Rev. Phil.* lx (1934), 284–5; *Ét. anat.* 73, n. 1.

[15] xxiii. 9. 3; the treaty is at xxv. 2; cf. xxiv. 14.

remarkable that Eumenes and his brothers, and the deceased Attalos Soter, should be lavishly honoured in an Athenian decree relating to these events.[16] Furthermore, we know from a fragment of Diodoros (xxxi. 32a) that when Epiphanes died in 164/3, Eumenes went so far as to crown at Pergamon a rival to the successor Demetrios, and this pretender was later brought to the throne by Attalos II, after the defeat and death of Demetrios (Strabo xiii. 4. 2, 624). Such interference in Seleukid history was a by-product of Roman intervention. It is not surprising that Eumenes was only vaguely interested in the Roman war with Perseus, although the extent of his commitment is unclear; on the other hand, Rome could not deal as finally with the King of Pergamon as she chose to do with Rhodes.[17]

The Galatians remained a major problem in Asia Minor, for the Greek cities as well as the monarchies. Attalid troops had taken part in the campaign of Manlius in 189 (Polyb. xxi. 33–40; Livy xxxviii. 12–38), and its successful outcome had been, according to Polybios (xxi. 40. 2) a cause of greater joy to the inhabitants of Asia Minor than the prospect of freedom from Antiochos. Those inclined to dub Eumenes a lackey of Rome and a traitor to Hellenism[18] are reminded that he now assumed responsibility for Galatia despite evident Roman disapproval,[19] and secured a victory comparable in its outcome to that of Manlius, and certainly as beneficial to the safety of the Greek cities. (The details of this war will be discussed in chapter 5.) Polybios is explicit that Eumenes' popularity among the Greek cities increased as he took a more independent line (xxxi. 6. 6): καθ' ὅσον ἐδόκουν οἱ Ῥωμαῖοι

---

[16] *IvP* 160, = *OGIS* 248; Holleaux, *Études,* ii. 127–47.

[17] H. H. Schmitt, *Rom und Rhodos* (*Münchener Beiträge zur Papyrusforschung und antiken Rechtsgeschichte,* 40, 1957), 157 ff.

[18] There is no evidence to support the generalization that Eumenes 'was everywhere disliked as being Rome's jackal, the traitor to Hellenism' (W. W. Tarn, *Hellenistic Civilisation* (ed. 3, London, 1952), 29). It is precisely evidence of this kind that we most lack for Eumenes' reign; what there is is confined mainly to scraps of Rhodian propaganda, which naturally depict Eumenes in an unfavourable light.

[19] Note the events surrounding Attalos' visit to Rome in 168/7 (Polyb. xxx. 1–3; Livy xlv. 19). The Senate's suspicions were directed at Eumenes personally because of his behaviour during the war with Perseus. Rome's contribution to a solution of the Galatian problem in these years was precisely nil.

βαρύτερον τῷ Εὐμένει προσφέρεσθαι, κατὰ τοσοῦτο συνέβαινε τοὺς Ἕλληνας προσοικειοῦσθαι, φύσει τῶν ἀνθρώπων ἀεὶ τῷ θλιβομένῳ τὴν εὔνοιαν προσνεμόντων. We are surely entitled to believe then that Eumenes died in the favour of many of the Greek cities of Asia Minor.[20]

Eumenes was already ill during the war with Pharnakes, when his brother Attalos assumed much of the burden of the war, and by 168/7 his death was expected.[21] According to the chronological indications afforded by Strabo, he died in 160/59, and documentary evidence from Delphi allows a closer dating: Eumenes was certainly alive until the late autumn of 159, and furthermore his brother Attalos had been co-regent during the last months of his life.[22]

The personality of Attalos II is markedly different from that of Eumenes, for although he is in many ways the most likable of the Attalids, he clearly did not have the forcefulness and diplomatic ability which his father and his brother had shown in turn. It had been, for example, the recovery of Eumenes that had put an end to the war with Pharnakes. Strabo informs us that Eumenes left the kingdom to Attalos as *epitropos* of the younger Attalos (the future Attalos III), Eumenes' son by Stratonike (xiii. 4. 2, 624; see Appendix i). The fact that Attalos called himself king and ruled until his own death, which occurred certainly well after the majority of his nephew,[23] probably reveals the intention of protecting the succession in much the same way as Antigonos Doson had done for Philip V of Macedon.[24]

Under Attalos II, Attalid foreign policy continued, although on a

[20] Note especially the decree of the Ionian *koinon* passed in Eumenes' honour in the winter of 167/6, immediately after he was refused entry into Italy by the Roman Senate; it is quoted extensively in Eumenes' reply to the *koinon* (*OGIS* ii. 763, = Appendix iv, no. 13; cf. Holleaux, *Études*, ii. ch. xi, esp. 169–71, and below, part ii). Eumenes was particularly commended for bringing peace (lines 11–13).

[21] Polyb. xxiv. 5. 2; xxx. 2. 5.

[22] See above, 10 n. 7.

[23] On the chronology, see below, Appendix i.

[24] Antigonos Doson was first *epitropos* and later *basileus:* see the study of Dow and Edson, *Harv. Stud.* xlviii (1937), esp. 163 ff. The distinction between guardianship and usurpation is examined by A. Aymard, *Études d'histoire ancienne* (Paris, 1967), 230 ff. The careful attention Attalos II paid to the guardianship of his nephew is now further demonstrated by a royal letter about the man who was appointed his mentor (Appendix iv, no. 24).

less independent basis, to be concerned almost exclusively with Asian affairs. According to Polybios (xxxii. 12) Attalos' first act on succeeding to the throne was the restoration of his personal friend Ariarathes (V) to the throne of Cappadocia, and Polybios rightly notes that this was an example of Attalos' general policy.[25] It is probable, then, that Attalos was anxious to make sure of his friends before dealing with his enemies.[26] These enemies were for the most part, as in the previous reign, Galatia and Bithynia. Royal correspondence with the friendly priest Attis at Pessinous makes it clear that Attalid control over Galatia, barely established under Eumenes II, was lost under Attalos II.[27] Attalid hostility to Bithynia reached a final climax. We have a good if brief narrative of Attalos' war with Prusias II in the *Mithridateios* of Appian (3–7), supplemented by substantial fragments of Polybios' history (xxxii–xxxiii). Both these accounts are written in Attalos' favour, and the only documentary evidence, a dedication of Attalos himself, naturally confirms the implications of the literary sources, that Prusias was completely in the wrong.[28]

Of Prusias' initial treachery there can be little doubt; according to Appian the Senate ordered Prusias to make peace with Attalos on the frontier, taking with him only a thousand men, instead of which he advanced with his entire army and destroyed the Pergamene Nikephorion.[29] On the other hand, Attalos resorted to the now standard Attalid practice of dealing with potential and real enemies by removing them from their thrones and installing friends in their places; by the time Attalos was dead, this policy had been successfully applied to Syria and Cappadocia, as well as Bithynia.[30]

[25] xxxiii. 12. For Attalos' early friendship with Ariarathes at Athens, see *Syll.*[3] 666, a joint dedication to their teacher Carneades.

[26] Note Appian's comment (*Syr.* 45) on the motives of Eumenes and Attalos in supporting Antiochos IV: ἑταιριζόμενοι τὸν ἄνδρα.

[27] See below, ch. 5.

[28] *IvP* 225, = *OGIS* 327.

[29] *Mithr.* 3; Polyb. xxxii. 15. According to both accounts, Prusias' destruction of the Nikephorion constituted his second attack on Attalos. According to Polybios, Prusias went on to loot the rich country around Thyateira, as Philip V of Macedon had done in 201 (xvi. 1. 6–7; Holleaux, *Études*, iv. 248–51; L. Robert, *Ét. anat.* 112–13; Magie, *Roman Rule*, ii. 1197, n. 42).

[30] Appian, *Mithr.* 4–7; for Syria, see Hopp, *Untersuchungen*, 79–85.

Attalid forces assisted Rome in the final subjugation of Macedon in 149,[31] and in the sack of Corinth three years later,[32] and with the latter event the narrative of Polybios (or what is left of it) comes to a close. For the rest of the reign of Attalos II, and for that of his successor, we are left, apart from the comparatively meagre epigraphical evidence, with literary references that are either fragmentary or incidental, or both. For most events we badly miss context and detail, and the loss of a good contemporary source is irreparable. Little more than the fact is known of Attalos II's probably important campaign against the Thracian king Diegylis, son-in-law of Attalos' former enemy, Prusias II of Bithynia (Appian, *Mithr.* 6), which is dated by a dedication to the year 145,[33] and the end of Attalos' reign is shrouded in darkness.

The preoccupation of Eumenes II and Attalos II with Asian affairs is further exemplified by their activity on the southern shore of Asia Minor, where the cities of Selge and Amlada in Pisidia evidently tried to resist Attalid influence after the Galatian troubles of the 160s. Both Eumenes and Attalos undertook military campaigns in the area, but the short literary notices recording them do not say much about the background and circumstances of these events.[34] Also of great importance is Attalos' foundation of Attaleia in Pamphylia,[35] which, together with his building activity in the harbour at Ephesos (see part ii below), indicates his concern to promote trade in the kingdom. Attaleia faced Cyprus, the eastern Mediterranean, and the realm of the Ptolemies, and the choice of this position confirms the tendency of the Attalids after the Treaty of Apameia to turn away from co-operation and economic intercourse with the Seleukids.

The anecdotal nature of the literary evidence for the reign of the

---

[31] Strabo xiii. 4. 2, 624; cf. Niese iii. 334.

[32] Pliny, *Nat. Hist.* xxxv. 24; cf. Niese iii. 352.

[33] *OGIS* 330; Hopp, *Untersuchungen*, 96–8.

[34] For Selge we have the notice of Trogus, *Prol.* xxxiv; Strabo xii. 7. 3, 571 says that the Selgians διεμάχοντο πρὸς τοὺς βασιλέας ἀεί (by οἱ βασιλεῖς Strabo often means the Attalids). Cf. Hopp, *Untersuchungen*, 70. The situation of Amlada is discussed more fully below, 102.

[35] Strabo xiv. 4. 1, 667. Attaleia was founded more probably in the early years of Attalos' reign, when he was campaigning in Pisidia, than in 189 in connection with Manlius Vulso's campaign in the area; Hopp, *Untersuchungen*, 102–4 considers both dates possible.

last of the Attalids, Attalos III Philometor, has already been discussed; it tells us more about the man than about the events of his
reign.[36] He figures hardly at all in the final fragments of Polybios'
history,[37] and we are left with a mainly hostile tradition about him
that has excessively coloured modern opinion. The epigraphical
material shows that Attalos III continued to defend Attalid interests in military terms,[38] and that he was responsible for a significant and highly individual development of the royal cults of the
kingdom (see chapter 6).

His decision to bequeath the kingdom to Rome [39] must be seen in
the context of his own personality and rule, and not in terms of a
postulated dependence on Rome beginning in the previous reign or
even earlier, for Attalos' predecessors were well able to defend
their kingdom even when the Senate refused or declined to support
them. Attalos' bequest is the first instance of the will of a Hellenistic monarch in favour of Rome being put into effect. There was a
theoretical precedent, known from an inscription from Cyrene, in
the decision in 155 of Ptolemy Physkon (the future Euergetes II,
then King of Cyrene) to leave his kingdom to Rome as a last resort,
should he die with no one of his choice to succeed him; it is even
possible that Attalos knew of Physkon's decision from his contacts
in Rome, although Physkon's will was not implemented and was
probably not made public until a later date.[40] Attalos' action later

[36] See above, ch. 1.

[37] The testimonia are given in Appendix i below.

[38] *IvP* 246, = *OGIS* 332 honours Attalos on his return from a successful military
expedition, perhaps in Thrace; cf. Hopp, *Untersuchungen*, 111, n. 25.

[39] Still important is Cardinali's study 'Le morte di Attalo III e la rivolta di
Aristonico', in *Saggi . . . offerti a G. Beloch* (1910), 269–320; for an excellent
modern discussion see Hopp, *Untersuchungen*, 121–47.

[40] *SEG* ix. 7, = *Ann. ép.* 1932, 80. According to this text a copy of the will was to
be sent to Rome. Wilcken, *SB Berlin*, 1932, 317–36, argued that the will was not
published until 96 BC, when Rome finally acquired Cyrene, but the Senate may have
known the terms in 155, and the information could therefore have reached Attalos.
An earlier origin of this practice may be seen in the decision of Nikomedes I of
Bithynia (died *c*.255: Beloch, *Gr. Gesch.* iv.² 2, p. 213) to secure the succession for
the children of his second marriage by naming specific guardians outside his own
kingdom, namely Herakleia, Kios, Byzantion, and the Kings of Macedonia and
Egypt (Memnon 22, = *FGrHist* 434, F14). In the event, despite these precautions,
Ziaelas, half-brother of the designated heirs, succeeded in gaining the throne (see
Magie, *Roman Rule*, ii. 1195, n. 35).

constituted a precedent for Nikomedes IV of Bithynia.[41]

The transition to Roman rule was hindered by the resistance of Aristonikos. Now that Aristonikos can be seen as a dynastic aspirant to a *paternum regnum,* as his coinage, which calls him King Eumenes, indicates, we are spared further speculation about social upheaval in the Attalid Kingdom and especially at Pergamon.[42] Aristonikos failed to win support from the Greek cities of the kingdom, probably because they had already been promised their freedom in Attalos' will,[43] and he resorted to the mobilization of slaves as a desperate strategic measure. He failed not as a social revolutionary, but as the last claimant to the throne of the Attalids.

(i) The New Provinces

We have now traced the history of the Attalid Kingdom to the point where under Attalos I it became an independent and sovereign kingdom able to maintain alliances and exert influences beyond its own frontiers as Attalos and his predecessors chose to place them. The origins of this expansive policy lay in a need to defend the kingdom against the Galatians[44] and other enemies; they did not arise from and did not lead to thoughts of empire or even of expanding the area of direct royal authority. Attalos' treaties with the important Greek cities, reviewed above,[45] served the interests of both parties, city and king, and enabled Attalos to collect συντάξεις for the support of his professionalized armies. There is no evidence whatever within the area of direct authority which Attalos inherited from Eumenes I of a regional administration or of a system of direct government over the Greek cities concerned; the coincidence of certain institutions with those of the Pergamene constitution, as indicated by the prescripts of extant decrees, is not in itself necessarily indicative of a centralized policy, since the city of Pergamon did not have an untypical constitution, but one which other cities might be expected to share in ordinary circumstances.

[41] Magie, *Roman Rule,* ii. 1200, n. 49.
[42] E. S. G. Robinson, *Num. Chron.* xiv (1954), 1–7; Hopp, *Untersuchungen,* 145–7.
[43] Hopp, *Untersuchungen,* 143–4.
[44] See also below, ch. 5.
[45] See above, 39–58.

We shall see later that the Attalids were able to exploit the constitutional arrangements in some cities to their own advantage, but
there is no evidence that they manipulated or prescribed the forms
of the constitutions themselves.[46] Attalos' administration was
noticeably geared to the military requirements of his reign, and
apart from their commitment to support him in this area of royal
activity we have no indication in the available evidence that the
cities in the immediate territory of Pergamon were not allowed to
lead a full and independent civic life.

Whatever the exact nature and extent of royal rule during the
reign of Attalos I, it is clear at least that at the end of his reign the
kingdom was hardly any bigger than it had been at the beginning.
Polybios ascribes to Philip V of Macedon the following commen-
dation of Eumenes II and Attalos II:[47] παραλαβόντες οὗτοι μικρὰν
ἀρχὴν καὶ τὴν τυχοῦσαν ηὐξήκασι ταύτην, ὥστε μηδεμιᾶς εἶναι
καταδεεστέραν. The most recent losses were those of 198 when, as
the evidence suggests, Antiochos III seized large areas of Attalid
territory, enabling him to march through this territory again in the
spring of 196 without any apparent opposition from Eumenes.[48]
During the war in which Eumenes fought against Antiochos on the
side of Rome, many Attalid cities close to Pergamon, including
Phokaia and Thyateira,[49] remained in Seleukid possession, and the
Attalid Kingdom for a while almost ceased to exist, but at the end
of this war Eumenes was rewarded for his loyalty to Rome with a
kingdom which in terms of size and security of tenure was something the Attalids had not known before. In this chapter we shall
examine the implications of this new situation in terms of the royal
administration and the precedents on which it drew.

In 188 BC the Roman settlement of Asia Minor imposed new
obligations on the King of Pergamon by altering totally the constitutional basis on which the kingdom was founded. Eumenes II
had not merely foreseen but had welcomed these obligations in his
speech delivered to the Roman Senate in 189, the year after the

---

[46] See further below, 104–9.

[47] xxiii. 11. 7. See also xxxii. 8. 3: (Eumenes) παραλαβὼν παρὰ τοῦ πατρὸς τὴν
βασιλείαν συνεσταλμένην τελέως εἰς ὀλίγα καὶ λιτὰ πολισμάτια.

[48] Schmitt, *Untersuchungen*, 271–3, and especially 273.

[49] See above, 42, 43–4.

defeat of Antiochos III at Magnesia:[50] οὐδενί φαμεν δικαιότερον
εἶναι παραχωρεῖν ὑμᾶς τῶν ἐκ τοῦ πολέμου γεγονότων ἄθλων
ἤπερ ἡμῖν. It was not simply a matter of an increase of territory that
was at issue, because the terms by which the increase was made
represent something quite different from previous Attalid experience. We shall see in particular that the basis of Attalos' expansion
of royal influence beyond his formal frontiers was swept aside
together with these frontiers by the terms imposed by Rome.[51]
Polybios' account of the settlement as it related to Eumenes
specifies both areas and individual cities that were assigned to him
as gifts. These included, in Europe, Chersonesos, Lysimacheia
and 'the adjoining strongholds and *chora* which Antiochos had
ruled', and in Asia, 'Hellespontine Phrygia, Greater Phrygia, the
Mysians whom Prusias had previously taken, Lycaonia, Milyas,
Lydia, and the cities of Tralles, Ephesos, and Telmessos'.[52] This
provision suggests that the administration of the areas concerned
was left in Eumenes' hands, and we look for confirmation and
clarification of this situation to a number of contemporary documents relating to two of the areas specified in the Roman settlement, namely Chersonesos and Hellespontine Phrygia. In addition
we now have evidence for a third region, centred on Ephesos. In all
cases the attested names and institutions .show a departure in
terminology from the Seleukid satrapal system, but it will be seen
that the new institutions do not indicate, as is often maintained, the
influence of any other single administrative system.

An inscription of Roman date from Sestos honouring a benefactor refers to Straton ὁ στρατηγὸς τῆς Χερρονήσου καὶ τῶν κατὰ
τὴν Θράικην τόπων, evidently a royal appointee of earlier date. A
dedication from a village near ancient Thyateira mentions the area
in the same words in connection with a campaign of Attalos II
undertaken there in 145; it refers to 'the . . . soldiers who crossed
in year 15 to the *topoi* in Chersonese and Thrace'. It will be evident

---

[50] Polyb. xxi. 19–21, especially 21. 9.

[51] See below, 98 ff.

[52] xxi. 46. 9–11 (the corresponding passage of Livy is xxxviii. 39. 7–40. 1). For a
geographical analysis of these awarded territories see Magie, *Roman Rule,* ii.
758–64, n. 56; Walbank, *Comm.* iii. 163–75. The status as gifts is at 46.10: ταύτας
μὲν οὖν ἔδωκαν Εὐμένει τὰς δωρεάς. The phrase translated here as 'the Mysians
whom Prusias had previously taken' is discussed above, 63–5.

that the name of the area as defined in these inscriptions corresponds closely with the designation given in the Roman settlement of 188, namely 'Chersonesos and Lysimacheia and the adjoining strongholds and *chora*'. To this evidence we may now add a recently published inscription from Ephesos which attests one Demetrios son of Apollonios, 'keeper of the seal' and στρατηγὸς ἐπί τε Ἐφέσου καὶ τῶν κατ' Ἔφεσον τόπων καὶ Καΰστρου πεδίου καὶ τὸ Κιλβιανόν (sic).[53]

The most substantial evidence for the Attalids' institutions of provincial administration is an inscription relating to Hellespontine Phrygia.[54] The stone was found at Bursa (ancient Prusa) and records a decree honouring a man named Korrhagos son of Aristomachos, but it has been firmly established that the honouring city was not Prusa itself.[55] Holleaux's exhaustive study of the letter-forms established termini of *c.* 225 and 150 BC; this means that the decree must refer either to Seleukid or to Attalid rule, since during these years the territories of Hellespontine Phrygia came under no other authority.[56] There is no specific reference in the decree to either kingdom, and the only royal designation is the anonymous ὁ βασιλεύς.

Ἔδοξεν τῆι βουλῆι καὶ τῶι δήμωι· Μενέμαχος
Ἀρχελάου εἶπεν· ἐπεὶ Κόρραγος Ἀριστομάχου
Μακεδών, τεταγμένος στρατηγὸς τῶν κα-
θ' Ἑλλήσποντον τόπων, διατελεῖ τὴμ πᾶσαν
5   σπουδὴν καὶ εὔνοιαν προσφιρόμενος εἰς τὸ συν-

[53] Thrace: *OGIS* 339, = J. Krauss, *Inschr. von Sestos und der Thrakischen Chersones* (*Inschr. griech. Städte aus Kleinasien*, XIX, 1980), no. 1 (with full commentary); *OGIS* 330. Compare the title of the third-century Ptolemaic official Hippomedon, στρατ[ηγὸς ἐφ' Ἑλλησπόντου καὶ τῶν ἐπὶ Θράικης τόπων (IG XII. 8. 156, = *Syll.*³ 502; Bengtson, *Strat.* iii. 178). Ephesos: Appendix iv, no. 25.

[54] Homolle, *CRAI* 1921, 269 ff. (editio princeps), superseded by Holleaux, *BCH* xlviii (1924), 1–57 (*Études,* ii. 73–125), the most thorough analysis and necessarily the starting point of any discussion of the text. On the date, which is discussed below, and other additional points, see the important remarks of G. De Sanctis, *Riv. di fil.* iii (1925), 68–78. The text appeared as *SEG* ii. 663 (cf. iv. 716). See the useful discussion in Bengtson, *Strat.* ii. 211–26.

[55] Holleaux, *Études,* ii. 114–15; De Sanctis, *Riv. di fil.* liii (1925), 70–1. Holleaux argued persuasively in favour of Apollonia on the Rhyndakos, not far from ancient Prusa where the stone was found. Magie's arguments for Abydos (*Roman Rule,* ii. 1011–13) are not acceptable in themselves since Abydos was probably not Attalid at the argued date (see below, n. 140).

[56] Holleaux, *Études,* ii. 75–81, 85–6.

αὔξεσθαι τὸν δῆμον, καὶ κοινῆι καὶ ἰδίαι τοῖς ἐν-
τυγχάνουσιν τῶν πολιτῶν εὔχρηστον αὐτὸν
παρασκευάζει, ὑπό τε τὴν παράληψιν τῆς πόλεως
ἠξίωσεν τὸν βασιλέα ἀποδοθῆναι τούς τε νό-
10 μους καὶ τὴν πάτριον πολιτείαν καὶ τὰ ἱερὰ τεμέ-
νη καὶ τὸ εἰς τὰ ἱερὰ καὶ πόλεως διοίκησιν ἀργύριον καὶ
τὸ τοῖς νέοις ἔλαιον καὶ τὰ ἄλλα ἅπερ ἐξ ἀρχῆς ὑπῆρ-
χεν τῶι δήμωι, ἐνδεῶς τε ἀπαλλασσόν-
των τῶν πολιτῶν διὰ τὸν πόλεμον παρά
15 τε αὐτοῦ ἐχαρίσατο εἰς τὰς δημοτε-
λεῖς θυσίας βοῦς καὶ ἱερεῖα, καὶ τῶι βασιλε[ῖ]
μνηθεὶς ἐξεπορίσατο σῖτον εἰς σπέρμα
καὶ διατροφήν, καὶ τὰς ἰδίας ἑκάστωι τῶν
πολιτῶν κτήσεις συνέσπευσεν διαμεῖν[αι]
20 τοῖς τε μὴ ἔχουσιν δοθῆναι ἐκ τοῦ βασιλικοῦ,
καὶ ἀτελείας ἐπικεχωρημένης πασῶν
τῶν προσόδων ὑπὸ τοῦ βασιλέως ἐτῶν
τριῶν ἔσπευσεν καὶ ἄλλα δύο ἔτη ἐπιδοθῆ-
ναι, βουλόμενος εἰς εὐδαιμονίαν καὶ ἐπίδο-
25 σιν καταστῆσαι τοὺς πολίτας, ἀκόλουθα πράσσων τῆι
τοῦ βασιλέως προαιρέσει · ἵνα δὲ καὶ ὁ δῆμος φαί-
νητα(ι) ἀποδιδοὺς χάριτας ἀξίας τοῖς αὐτὸν
εὐεργετοῦσιν, δεδόχθαι τῶι δήμωι · [ἐπαινέσαι τε]
Κόρραγον τὸν στρατηγὸν κα[ὶ στεφανῶσαι αὐτὸν]
30 χρυσῶι στεφ[άνωι κτλ.]

'A decree of the *boule* and the people, on the motion of Menemachos son of Archelaos. Considering that Korrhagos the Macedonian, son of Aristomachos, after being appointed *strategos* of the regions around the Hellespont, constantly shows every enthusiasm and good will for the advancement of the people and publicly and individually puts himself at the service of the citizens; that after the acquisition of the city he asked the king to restore the city's laws and ancestral constitution and its sacred precincts, as well as providing funds for the sacred and civil administration and oil for the use of the *neoi* and everything else formerly available to the people; that when the citizens were in severe hardship as a result of the war he provided at his own expense oxen and other animals for the public sacrifices, and having notified the king he provided corn for sowing and for sustenance, urged that each individual should keep his own possessions and that those with nothing should be provided for out of royal funds, and also urged that immunity from all taxes granted by the king for three years should be extended for another two years, wishing to endow the citizens with prosperity and generosity in accordance with the king's policy. So that the people may be seen to show suitable gratitude to its benefactors, the people have decided as follows: to commend Korrhagos the *strategos*, to crown him with a gold crown, [etc.].'

The decisive argument in favour of associating the decree

with Attalid rule arises from the name given to the region: οἱ καθ᾽ Ἑλλήσποντον τόποι. Under Seleukid rule the area was called, more typically, ἡ ἐφ᾽ Ἑλλησπόντου σατραπεία, and the corresponding official was called στρατηγὸς ἐφ᾽ Ἑλλησπόντου.[57] When Attalos I defeated Antiochos Hierax in Hellespontine Phrygia, he named the area similarly in his dedication to Athena,[58] Φρυγία ἡ ἐφ᾽ Ἑλλησπόντου, and the province retained this Seleukid name in the Roman settlement as recorded by Polybios.[59] Since the year 188 BC is thus established as the *terminus post quem* of the designation found in the decree from Bursa, this decree cannot be associated either with Seleukid rule or with a supposed period of Attalid rule under Attalos I (already discounted in the previous chapter for other reasons),[60] and so Attalid rule after the Roman settlement alone remains in question.

This view receives support from literary evidence, which also enables us to date the decree more exactly. According to Livy, a man named *Corragus macedo* took part with Eumenes' brother Athenaios in the Galatian campaign of Cn. Manlius Vulso in 189,[61] and again, as *Eumenis praefectus,* in an invasion of the Thracian kingdom of Kotys in 171.[62] The implication is that Corragus, whom we may reasonably identify with the Korrhagos of the Bursa decree, was appointed *praefectus* (i.e. *strategos*) between the years 189 and 171, clearly suggesting a connection with the foundation of the new Attalid province of Hellespontine Phrygia in 188 BC. The expression ὑπό τε τὴν παράληψιν τῆς πόλεως, 'after the acquisition of the city', is the regular one used in such circumstances to denote the assumption of authority by a new power. It does not refer to Korrhagos' appointment, since then we would expect the addition παρὰ τοῦ βασιλέως, 'by the king'; it refers

---

[57] Ibid. 85; see *OGIS* 221. III (Welles, *RC* 11, 3–4); Bengtson, *Strat.* ii. 12–13.

[58] *OGIS* 274. Dittenberger restored ἐφ᾽ Ἑλλ[η]σ|[πόντωι], but *OGIS* 221 and Polyb. xxii. 46, where Ἑλλησπόντου is found, provide closer parallels of administrative usage than the other literary references he gives (note 5 to *OGIS* 274). The genitive is tacitly preferred by Holleaux, *Études,* ii. 85, n. 4 (cf. 84, n. 2).

[59] xxi. 46. 10.

[60] See above, 57–8.

[61] xxxviii. 13. 3.

[62] xlii. 67. 4.

rather to a complete change of authority.[63] In this case the cause of the change can only have been the terms of the Roman settlement, and the war referred to in the decree in connection with the city's hardships is the Antiochic War, in which Antiochos III invaded Asia Minor and no doubt brought the city concerned under his control, as he did with Phokaia.[64]

We may conclude, then, that the areas assigned to Eumenes in the Roman settlement were, in the cases for which we have evidence, renamed and placed under the authority of royal *strategoi*. We turn now to consider another phenomenon attested by the texts so far cited, the designation *topoi*. The term is a familiar one in other Hellenistic kingdoms, especially in the Seleukid Kingdom

[63] See De Sanctis, loc. cit. (n. 54) 71 ff.; Rostovtzeff, *SEHHW* iii. 1472, n. 44. Holleaux, *Études*, ii. 118 ff., observed that the expression παραλαβὼν τὰ πράγματα and its variants refer to acquisition of authority rather than to military conquest, but did not make the distinction between transfer of command within one authority and the transfer of that authority itself. In cases where an existing authority passes to a new official or to a succeeding king, the predecessor or the person by whom the authority is delegated is named; for the Ptolemies see *OGIS* 55 (a decree of Telmessos), 7–9: Πτολεμαῖος ὁ Λυσιμά|[χο]υ, παραλαβὼν τὴν πόλιν παρὰ βασιλέ|[ως Πτ]ολεμαίου τοῦ Πτολεμαίου κτλ., and *Syll*.[3] 463 (a decree of Itanos), = *I. Cret*. iii. p. 83, no. 7: Βασιλεὺς Πτολεμαῖος | παραλαβὼν τὰν τῶν Ἰτανίων πόλιν καὶ πολίτας | παρὰ τοῦ πατρὸς βασιλέως Πτολεμαίου, καὶ τῶν | προγόνων, κτλ. *OGIS* 90 (the Rosetta Stone) refers to the date of Ptolemy Epiphanes' accession (line 47) as the year ἐν ἧι παρέλαβεν τὴν βασιλείαν παρ(ὰ) τοῦ πατρός. For the Attalids see Polybios' reference to the succession of Eumenes II at xxxii. 8. 3, quoted above, n. 47.

Another instance of the simpler formula used of Korrhagos' appointment in the decree from Bursa is provided by Polyb. xxvii. 13 (an excerpt of unknown context) with reference to Ptolemy Makron, *strategos* of Cyprus under Ptolemy VI: παραλαβὼν τὴν νῆσον ἔτι νηπίου τοῦ βασιλέως ὄντος. See Bengtson, *Strat*. ii. 216, n. 4; Walbank, *Comm*. iii. 311. We have already met another relevant example in the acquisition of Pitane by Eumenes I as attested by *OGIS* 335, line 141 (see above, 19, 21): Εὐμένης παραλαβὼν τὰ πράγ[ματα] κτλ. The inscriptions from Labraunda supply a further example comparable to the position of Korrhagos in Olympichos' acquisition of authority over Mylasa (*Labraunda*, iii. 1., no. 8, line 13): παραλαβόντες γὰρ τὴν [ὑμετέραν πόλιν] κτλ. (on the liberation of Mylasa by Seleukos II see Crampa, op. cit., ch. 3).

[64] See above, 42 and n. 46 there; Cf. Rostovtzeff, *SEHHW* ii. 635. On the date of the decree from Bursa see De Sanctis, loc. cit. (n. 54); Bengtson, *Strat*. ii. 213–17. Holleaux associated the decree with later events, but eventually subscribed to De Sanctis' date (*BCH* liv (1930), 248, n. 2; cf. *Études*, ii. 116, n. 2). It should be noted that 188 is the date of the παράληψις τῆς πόλεως, and not necessarily that of the decree, which can be dated to any of the years immediately following this event.

and in Egypt, but its range of meanings and applications is wide.[65] For the Attalid Kingdom it has to be determined whether it has any consistent signification relative to the regional administration as a whole, such as that of a collection of small areas or communities as distinct from cities, as in the Seleukid Kingdom and in Egypt. It is found with an apparently similar connotation in lists of *epheboi* from Pergamon, in the heading 'from the places' (ἀπὸ τόπων) which introduces groups of names each consisting of the personal name followed by the patronymic and the formula τῶν ἀπό or ἐκ, 'of those from' a named place. A full designation of this type would read, for example: 'Apollonides, son of Athenaios, of those from Daskylion.'[66]

An interesting feature of these formulae is that they stand in place of the more usual ethnic. Those who are designated foreigners (ξένοι) in other lists are named with the conventional adjectival ethnic, so that those ἀπὸ τόπων must be regarded as belonging to a different category.[67] Nor are the designations in the lists of those ἀπὸ τόπων those of places attached by *sympoliteia* to another city, since we know that such places were designated by a

---

[65] See Rostovtzeff, *SEHHW* i. 561–2, iii. 1450, n. 327. On Seleukid usage see also Bickermann, *Institutions des Séleucides* (Paris, 1938), 198, 302; Bengtson, *Strat.* ii. 10–12, 211. Rostovtzeff's and Bengtson's view of the term *topoi* as exact usage in the Attalid as well as the Seleukid kingdoms is disputed here.

[66] The heading ἀπὸ τόπων is preserved only in one list, that published in *AM* xxxv (1910), 434, no. 19: ἀπὸ τόπων | Ἀρτέμων Ἀσκληπιάδου τῶν ἀπὸ - - - | Ἀσκλάπων Μελανίππου τῶν ἐξ - - - | Μηνογένης Ἀσκληπιάδου τῶν ἐκ - - -. Regrettably in this instance the right-hand edge of the stone is not preserved. There are other lists of *epheboi* in which the names are compiled in the same way, and the heading ἀπὸ τόπων may be restored to them; *AM* xxxv (1910), 426, no. 12, col. ii includes the following complete names:

> Μ[ητρ]όδωρος Ἀσκλάπωνος τῶν ἐξ Ἄββου κώμη[ς]
> Ἀνδρικὸς Ἀσκληπιάδου τῶν ἐξ Ἀπιασίωνος ἀγροῦ
> Ἀπολλωνίδης Ἀθηναίου τῶν ἐγ Δασκυλίου
> Ἀπολλώνιος Μητροδώρου τῶν ἀπὸ Μασδύη[ς]
> Ἀπολλωνίδης Διονυσοφάνου τῶν ἐκ Τίμνων
> Ἀσκληπιάδης Μηνοφάντου τῶν ἀπὸ Μασδύη[ς]

Other such lists are *AM* xxxii (1907), 440 ff., nos. 309–14, 322, 324, 326–7, 329, 331?; *AM* xxxv (1910), 422 ff., no. 11, col. i, lines 1–9.

[67] For a list of ξένοι see *AM* xxxv (1910), 422, no. 11. The heading also occurs in a fragment of another list, *AM* xxxii (1907), 435, no. 297.

formula including the name of the city concerned.[68] The *topoi* referred to in the ephebic lists formed a separate category representing communities that were outside civic life, for example τῶν ἐξ Ἄββου κώμης.

For a number of reasons, however, it seems unlikely that the *topoi* mentioned in the ephebic lists have anything directly to do with the terms used in the Attalid names for Chersonese and Hellespontine Phrygia. In the first place, the lists are certainly confined in scope of reference to ephebes from the immediate area of the city of Pergamon that can be related to the direct authority exercised by Eumenes I. Furthermore, among the provisions of the Pergamene decree passed after the death of Attalos III,[69] people called Μασδυηνοί are included among the soldiers who were to receive the citizenship of Pergamon, and their home may be identified with the name Μασδύη or Μαζύη, which appears frequently in the ephebic lists in the formula of those ἀπὸ τόπων.[70] Clearly then, the Μασδυηνοί constituted a military settlement in the immediate area of the city, and they did not have Pergamene citizenship in the royal period. They were in fact, as I have argued generally, outside civic life in administrative and constitutional terms.

A further argument may be added. If the *topoi* of the ephebic lists are to be related to the regional *topoi*, we must expect a closer definition in the former than the simple ἀπὸ τόπων, such as ἀπὸ τῶν τόπων τῶν ἐν Χερρονήσωι, or whatever the case may be. The fact that the designation is simply ἀπὸ τόπων reinforces the conclusion that it refers to a single area, which in the circumstances

[68] Thus in the list cited in the previous note a man named Epikrates son of Diodoros is designated Στρατονικεὺς τῶν ἀπὸ Ἰνδειπεδίου. This designation has nothing to do with the formula of those ἀπὸ τόπων, who have no ethnic at all in the lists. Stratonikeia is so qualified to distinguish it from other cities of the same name, as L. Robert has shown (*Villes*, 43–82), and so Epikrates appears in the list of ξένοι with what is an ordinary designation of origin, as is clear from the form of the other names in his list (e.g. Ἀρτέμων Τηλέφου Τιαρηνός).

[69] *OGIS* 338, = *IGR* iv. 269.

[70] Not with the Paphlagonian town of Mastya, as the similarity of names once wrongly suggested; see Magie, *Roman Rule*, ii. 1036, n. 8.

must be that of the city of Pergamon.[71] The places so designated included military settlements of the kind specified above, and these are probably comparable to the *katoikoi* attested for Ptolemaic Egypt[72] and the 'Macedonian foundations' mentioned by Strabo,[73] but in general terms we may envisage village communities outside city life such as that at Abboukome mentioned in the lists.

It may now be asked whether this conclusion helps us to understand the nature of the designation *topoi* in the Attalid regional administration. The first thing one notices is that in this context the application is inconsistent and less exact, referring in the Korrhagos decree to a whole region and in the dedication following Attalos II's Thracian campaign to certain parts of a region.[74] Indeed in the second document it is most unlikely that the term *topoi* implies any constitutional significance whatever, being rather a generic designation meaning 'places', since Attalos' campaign took him, according to the literary evidence, to parts of Thrace, including the territory of King Diegylis, that were beyond the frontiers of his kingdom.[75] In the decree from Sestos, however, the term *topoi* seems to have more exact connotations, being within the Attalid Kingdom and probably denoting known rather than unknown areas.[76]

This varying use of the term is consistent neither with Ptolemaic practice (the most likely parallel) nor with usage at the Attalid capital as argued from the evidence of the ephebic lists. When the term is used so inconsistently, we are bound to question the validity of the claim that in the Attalid provinces the *topoi* as attested in the texts cited were an extension of the local Pergamene usage. It seems unlikely, in the circumstances, that the word *topoi* as applied to the provinces had any precise or consistent constitu-

[71] The implications of this conclusion for the civil administration will be noticed below in chapter 7.

[72] Bengtson, *Strat.* iii. 73–5.

[73] See L. Robert, *Ét. anat.* 193, n. 2.

[74] Korrhagos is called simply (lines 3–4) στρατηγὸς τῶν καθ' Ἑλλήσποντον τόπων. Attalos' dedication (*OGIS* 330) refers to οἱ κατὰ Χερρόνησον καὶ Θρᾴκην τόποι.

[75] For a review of the evidence see Hopp, *Untersuchungen*, 96–8.

[76] See above, 87.

tional significance, and it is more likely that it was a convenient generic formula for describing different regional phenomena not precisely expressible in other terms. It cannot be compared with the Seleukid *toparchiai* in Syria, for which a specific official is attested.[77] In the Attalid Kingdom the only office associated with the *topoi* for which we have evidence is that of the *strategos* of the whole province.

In 188 BC Eumenes II received a number of formerly Seleukid military settlements, *katoikiai* in another special sense of the word.[78] Although evidence of the Attalid administration of these communities is in general terms extremely thin, a good example is to be found in the settlement of the territory of Telmessos, which passed into Eumenes' hands along with that city. A stone now in the museum at Izmir preserves a letter written by Eumenes II to his official Artemidoros, whose title is unfortunately not given. He was responsible for the *katoikoi* of the village of the Kardakes in the territory of Telmessos, who had petitioned him on the grounds of a number of severe hardships, in particular the inability to pay a σύνταξις, here a poll-tax of four Rhodian drachmas and one obol per head. In his letter Eumenes promises considerable assistance to the community, including the sending of an architect to advise on the reconstruction of dilapidated fortifications and — most important — a reduction of the poll-tax to one Rhodian drachma and one obol. We see Eumenes here as in the Korrhagos decree concerned to safeguard the welfare of the community which had appealed to him, and to ensure its prosperity by means of positive measures which are probably typical of Attalid policy as applied to the inherited Seleukid *katoikiai*.[79]

It is unlikely that these communities have any exact correlation with the *topoi* of the Attalid provinces discussed above; for one thing we have seen that the term is used without any evident

---

[77] *OGIS* 752; Bengtson, *Strat.* ii. 22–3.

[78] On the Seleukid κατοικίαι see Rostovtzeff, *SEHHW* i. 499–501; Bengtson, *Strat.* ii. 68–9, both of whom contest the view of Bickermann, *Inst. Sél.* 72 ff. (cf. L. Robert, *Ét. anat.* 191–3) that the colonies were not military in character. See now G. M. Cohen, *The Seleucid Colonies (Historia* Einzelschr. 30, 1978).

[79] The text was mentioned by L. Robert, *Ét. anat.* 375, n. 1, and was published by M. Segre in *Cl. Rhodos* ix (1938), 190 ff. An improved text will be found in Maier, *Mauerbauinschriften*, i. 76 (= *SEG* xix. 867).

consistency, and for another the former Seleukid *katoikiai* or military settlements were of a nature very different from the Mysian *katoikiai,* villages not specifically military in character, which we have found reason to relate to the local Pergamene *topoi* mentioned in the ephebic lists. For this reason and others we must not regard the organization of the enlarged kingdom created in 188 BC as an extension of the organization of the Mysian communities formerly administered by the dynasts and kings at Pergamon. On the contrary, it is probable that the Attalids maintained without change the Seleukid system of administering the military *katoikiai* by means of *strategoi*; such at least is the implication of a dedication made by the members of a colony near Lydian Apollonis in 154/3:[80]

Βα[σ]ιλεύ[οντο]ς ’Αττάλου | ἔτους ζ΄ [μ]ην[ὸ]ς Ξανδίκο[υ]‖ ο[ἱ ἐκ .]εσπούρων Μακεδό|νες ὑπὲρ τοῦ Δερ|κ[υλί]δου τοῦ αὐτῶν στρα|τ[ηγο]ῦ ἀρετῆς ἕνεκεν κα[ὶ] | εὐδ[όξ]ου [ἀνδ]ρ[α]γαθίας ἧς | ἔχ[ω]ν διατε[λ]εῖ εἴς τε | [τὸν βασιλ]έ[α καὶ] ἑ[α]υτού[ς].

It seems probable that the Attalids were anxious to promote the prosperity of these newly acquired communities by easing their financial burdens and by maintaining existing administrative institutions, thereby disturbing as little as possible the relations of the colonists with their suzerain. In this respect the Attalids evidently did not depart from the methods used by the Seleukids. The same seems to be true, according to the limited evidence, of the Attalid administration of the temples of the kingdom, whose rich lands rendered them an important source of revenue, as they had been under the Seleukids.[81] The little that we know of the Attalids' treatment of temple lands indicates that they subscribed to the methods used in other Hellenistic kingdoms. Their maintenance of control over the administration, and in particular the financial administration, of the temples is shown by the royal appointment of a *neokoros* to the temple of Artemis at Sardis,[82] and a tax-exemption is attested by an inscription from

[80] *AM* xxiv (1899), 230, no. 68; fuller text *ap.* Keil and von Premerstein, *Reise,* 47, no. 95. Cf. Bengtson, *Strat.* ii. 207.

[81] For the continuity of temple administration see Jones, *Greek City,* 42 ff.; Rostovtzeff, *SEHHW* ii. 648–9 (with the reservation expressed below, n. 84).

[82] Appendix iv, no. 5, lines 7–11: ὁ βασιλεὺς . . . κατέστησεν νεωκόρον τῆς θεοῦ.

Soma in the upper Kaikos valley recording a letter written by Attalos II during Eumenes' reign to the *katoikoi* of Apollo Tarsenos.[83] Most important, the Attalids maintained the policy known for other Hellenistic monarchies of assigning land to temples in the kingdom, as I believe is shown by an inscription of Hadrianic date from Aizanoi in Phrygia.[84]

It may be useful at this point to summarize what has been said. We have evidently to assign the institutions and procedures of Attalid rule after 188 BC to various precedents. It seems likely, from the disappearance in Attalid records of the designation *satrapeia*, previously applied by the Seleukids in Asia Minor, that the Seleukid satrapal system was replaced by a different and less closely defined system. Within this framework, however, a number of detailed administrative institutions were retained from the Seleukid organization, particularly in areas such as the military settlements whose tradition of allegiance to the Seleukids could not be ignored, and the temple-lands which had always preserved a semblance of independence, where it will have been in the Attalids' interest to render the change of suzerainty as inconsequential as possible. Finally, it needs to be emphasized that the Attalid administration after 188 BC was not simply an extension of the administration applied hitherto in the small area of direct authority about Pergamon, and there is no evidence for supposing that it was based on or even greatly influenced by Ptolemaic practice. There is no significance in the designation *topoi* since this was in Attalid usage a vague and inconsistent term applied to provinces and to areas beyond them, and it does not seem to have had for the

[83] Welles, *RC* 47. Boehringer's attempt (*AvP* ix. 92) to ascribe the authorship of this letter to Attalos I before his assumption of the royal title has been convincingly refuted by Kähler, *Gr. Fries* 182. On tax-exemption in the Hellenistic period see Holleaux, *Études*, ii. 112–13.

[84] The inscription (*Bull. Mus. Imp. Rom.* lxvi (1938), 44–8, = E. M. Smallwood, *Doc. Ill. Principates of Nerva, Trajan and Hadrian*, 165, no. 454) refers to *fines Iovi c[rea?]tori et civitati Aezanitarum datos [a]b Attalo et Prusia regibus.* The kings are most probably Attalos I and Prusias I: see T.R.S. Broughton in *Studies .. in honor of A.C. Johnson*, 236–50; Habicht, *Hermes*, lxxxiv (1956), 93 ff. Compare the Seleukid donation of land attested by *OGIS* 262.

This evidence cannot justify the view of Rostovtzeff, *SEHHW* ii. 648, that the king could seize temple land or income, or his statement, 'at Aezani in Phrygia the kings, both Seleucid and Attalid, exercised the right of partial confiscation.' See the important remarks of Jones, *Greek City*, 309–10, n. 58; Broughton, loc. cit.

Attalids the specific connotations which it had for the Ptolemies and the Seleukids. The positive conclusion to be drawn is that the Attalids' methods of rule as implemented after 188 BC drew on a wide range of Hellenistic institutions and were determined, as with the Attalids generally, by expedience and opportunism, not being based exclusively or even predominantly on any one system of administration.

(ii) The Greek Cities

According to the literary evidence, the status of each Greek city in 188 depended, at least as far as the payment of tribute was concerned, on its record during the war with Antiochos, and this principle can usually be seen to have applied in individual cases.[85] Miletos co-operated with a Roman fleet operating in the area of the city in 190; in 188 its sovereignty was respected to the extent that its sacred lands, evacuated during the war, were restored in full, and later Miletos concluded a private treaty with Herakleia.[86] Thus in theory Miletos, pro-Roman during the war, was left independent afterwards. Ephesos, on the other hand, surrendered only after the defeat of Antiochos at Magnesia, and was one of the 'gifts' granted to Eumenes II by the Roman settlement.[87] Tralles surrendered at the same time and suffered the same fate.[88] For Telmessos, another 'gift' city, the evidence is less clear, but Seleukid sympathies are suggested by its coinage and its use of the Seleukid era at a later date, and it seems likely that it too assisted Antiochos in the war with Rome.[89]

There is evidence moreover that subject cities of the old kingdom of Eumenes I and Attalos I became independent if they had earned the right. Aigai is a case in point: this city's record during

[85] Polyb. xxi. 46. 2–3; Livy xxxviii. 39. 7–8; xxxvii. 53. 28. See the valuable study of Bickermann, *REG* i (1937), 217–39; Schmitt, *Untersuchungen,* 278–85; Walbank, *Comm.* iii ad loc; Préaux, *Monde hell.* i. 161–3.

[86] Livy xxxvii. 16. 2; 17. 3; Polyb. xxi. 46. 5. The treaty with Herakleia: *Syll.*³ 633. Miletos and Herakleia evidently passed under Rhodian influence for a time; the treaty they concluded established the principle that neither should do anything ὑπεναντίον τῆι πρὸς Ῥοδίους συμμαχίαι (line 35). This συμμαχία is not otherwise attested (see Fraser and Bean, *Rhodian Peraea,* 109).

[87] Ephesos' surrender: Livy xxxvii. 45. 1.

[88] Ephesos and Tralles as gift cities: Polyb. xxi. 46. 10.

[89] See Magie, *Roman Rule,* ii. 762.

the war is unknown, but its name appears, not as part of the Attalid Kingdom, but as a fully sovereign city and entitled to compensation from Prusias, in the συνθῆκαι concluded between Attalos II and Prusias II of Bithynia in 154, together with Methymna, Herakleia, and Kyme, cities certainly independent at the time.[90] Other cities, subject to the King of Pergamon and known to have been attacked by Prusias, such as Elaia, Thyateira, and Temnos, do not appear separately in the treaty; so we may infer that Aigai, once an Attalid subject, had its independence restored in 188, presumably on the basis of its behaviour during the war with Antiochos.[91]

This principle was evidently subject to exceptions. Magnesia on the Maeander surrendered to Rome at the same time as Ephesos and Tralles, but unlike these two it was privileged by the Scipios and remained an independent city outside Attalid jurisdiction, evidently maintaining on its own account friendly relations with Teos, a tributary city after 188, as we shall see.[92] This case is not likely, however, to have been an exception in principle, because the treatment afforded to Magnesia depended on the personal authority of the Scipios and not on senatorial policy generally.

The treaty also stipulated, as we saw in the previous chapter, that cities which had paid σύνταξις to Attalos I should henceforward pay φόρος to Eumenes. It is clear then that the Roman settlement was more careful in its treatment of the Greek cities than in its apparently wholesale allocation of entire provinces. Although the Chersonese was assigned to Eumenes and became part of an Attalid province, some of its cities remained indepen-

[90] Polyb. xxxiii. 13. 8. Methymna later entered into private diplomatic relations with Rome (*Syll.*[3] 693). Kyme was freed of tribute obligations in 188 (Polyb. xxi. 46. 4). We have good evidence for the autonomy of Herakleia after 188: *Syll.*[3] 618 records a letter of Cn. Manlius Vulso (on the identification see n. 1 in *Sylloge* ad loc.) to the city in 188 confirming its autonomy. As we have seen (n. 86 above), the city concluded a treaty with Miletos which attests its membership of a Rhodian συμμαχία.

[91] For the evidence of Aigai's coinage, see below, 111.

[92] Tacitus, *Ann.* iii. 62: *proximi hos Magnetes L. Scipionis et L. Sullae constitutis nitebantur: quorum ille Antiocho hic Mithridate pulsis fidem atque virtutem Magnetum decoravere, uti Dianae Leucophrynae perfugiam inviolabile foret.* The sovereignty of Magnesia is reflected in documents relating to the city's dispute with Priene, in which Mylasa was the arbitrator (*IvM* 93, = *Syll.*[3] 679). Relations with Teos: *IvM* 97.

dent and were listed as αὐτονομούμενοι in the peace concluded
between Eumenes II and Pharnakes of Pontos in 179.[93]
Lysimacheia, however, was specifically given to Eumenes in 188,
along with the Chersonese and τὰ προσοροῦντα τούτοις ἐρύματα
καὶ χώραν, and Diodoros refers to the city as being subject to
Attalos II.[94]

We have now seen that four cities were assigned to Eumenes as
gifts in 188: Ephesos, Tralles, Telmessos, and Lysimacheia. To
these we should perhaps add Magnesia ad Sipylum, which is
similarly designated by Livy.[95] It should be admitted immediately
that if we did not have this specific evidence about the gift cities we
would not easily discern from other sources any major difference
in status from other cities which passed in varying degrees of
subjection under Attalid control, and it is unlikely that the designation as 'gifts' which Polybios records had any precise constitutional implications. There is no literary record of oppression as
there is in the case of the Rhodian treatment of the Lycian cities,
also categorized as gifts in 188;[96] even Rhodian propaganda directed against Eumenes did not touch on this subject.

It is unlikely, then, that the Senate intended any particular status
by the title 'gifts', and it would be unprofitable to look for one in the
epigraphical evidence. We now know that after 188 BC Ephesos
was the centre of an administrative region and the seat of a regional
strategos. A gymnasial dedication attests Eumenes' interest in the
gymnasium, a policy applied by the Attalids to Greek cities of
whatever status, notably Miletos.[97] Eumenes was a benefactor at
Ephesos and at Miletos, and we shall consider later the possibility
that, despite or perhaps because of their different status, these two

[93] Polyb. xxv. 2. 13.
[94] Polyb. xxi. 46. 9; Diod. xxxiii. 14. 2.
[95] Livy xxxvii. 56. 3: *et nominatim Magnesiam ad Sipylum.*
[96] The ambiguity of Rome's definition of the status of Lycia and the subsequent
dispute with Rhodes on this question of course obscure the issue (see Fraser and
Bean, *Rhodian Peraea,* 111 ff.), but I am concerned here with Polybios' terminology as applied to the original ruling (xxii. 5. 4): τοῖς δὲ Ῥοδίοις χαριζόμενοι
προσένειμαν ἐν δωρεᾷ τοὺς Λυκίους.
[97] Appendix iv, no. 25; J. Keil, *Wien. Anz.* xxii (1951), 331–6, no. 1, = *SEG* xvii.
510: [Ἑρμεῖ] Ἡρακλεῖ καὶ βασιλεῖ Εὐμένει. For the restoration [Ἑρμεῖ] see J. and
L. Robert, *Bull.* lxvi (1953), 169, no. 178. See in general Préaux, *Monde hell.* i.
265–6.

cities competed for royal favour. It is enough here to confirm that there is no evidence that Ephesos was treated specially in internal constitutional terms after 188 BC.

Telmessos is the first city known to have called Eumenes *Soter*; this was done in a decree of 184 BC passed in gratitude for Eumenes' defence of Asia Minor against Prusias, the Galatians, and other enemies.[98] Clearly, however, this kind of spontaneous honouring of the saviour king is a feature of Greek civic life irrespective of constitutional status, and therefore has no special significance in the case of Telmessos.[99]

We pass to Tralles. There is evidence, lacking for the other cities, that Tralles was a royal residence of the Attalids: both Vitruvius and Pliny refer to a royal palace in the city.[100] A decree of Tralles honouring a judge from Phokaia refers to μουσικοὶ ἀγῶνες celebrated at Tralles in honour of Eumenes II, but such activity again is not necessarily to be associated with subject status.[101]

In the case of Lysimacheia evidence is lacking, but that already adduced is enough to demonstrate that an enquiry which sets out merely to determine which cities were 'subject' and which 'free' after 188 BC will be misleading in the way that defining status for the cities under Attalos I was seen to be misleading.[102] There is also the difficulty that the literary accounts of the Roman settlement, and very probably the Roman settlement itself, did not set out to explore the connotations of a city's status. The accounts in Polybios' and Livy's narratives are (at times on their own admission) selective, and dwell in particular on the issue of tribute.[103] In

[98] Appendix iv, no. 7.

[99] See below, ch. 6.

[100] Vitruvius ii. 8. 9: *Trallibus domus regibus Attalicis facta*; Pliny, *Nat. Hist.* xxxv. 49: *domum Trallibus regiam Attali*.

[101] See below, ch. 6, and Appendix iv, no. 6, lines 10–11. Other cities, apart from those discussed in this and the previous chapter, known to have been subject at some time to the Attalids are Priapos (Strabo xiii. 1. 14, 588), Skepsis (Strabo xiii. 1. 54, 609), Nakrasa (if *OGIS* 268 emanates from there: see Robert, *Villes*, 36, n. 6), and Phrygian Apameia, where an ephebic cult of Eumenes II and Attalos II is attested (*MAMA* vi. 173; J. and L. Robert, *Bull.* 1939, no. 400); the evidence of Apameia's coinage is discussed later in this chapter.

[102] See above, ch. 3 (i).

[103] See e.g. Livy xxxviii. 39. 7: *civitatium autem cognitis causis decem legati aliam aliarum fecerunt condicionem*. On tribute as a mark of subjection see Jones, *Greek City*, 102–12; Préaux, *Monde hell.* ii. 438.

considering all the evidence, literary, epigraphical, and numismatic, our analysis must seek to determine how status affected civic life and prosperity, how it restricted independence and freedom, and how it was regarded by the Attalids, in whose hands it was placed by the will of the Roman Senate.

A high degree of subjection to the Attalids entailed by tributary status after 188 has been alleged on the premiss that the kings could, and did, demand additional payments when they required them, apart from the regular φόρος, but on closer analysis this premiss dissolves into nothing.[104] The Pisidian city of Amlada was required to pay a τέλεσμα as well as φόρος during the major Galatian war of Eumenes II in the 160s, according to a letter of his brother Attalos to the city on the subject.[105] The status of Amlada in relation to the Attalids is quite unclear, but this letter seems to deal with conditions imposed by the circumstances of war (such as the taking of hostages) rather than with an episode in the context of continuous Attalid rule.[106]

[104] See Rostovtzeff, *SEHHW* iii. 1475, n. 55.

[105] Appendix iv, no. 23. On *telesma*, see Welles, *RC*, p. 369.

[106] Information on the status of Amlada is derived from a group of documents dealing with wartime conditions (Swoboda, Keil, and Kroll, *Denkmäler aus Lykaonien,* nos. 74–5; Appendix iv, nos. 22–3); see now in general Hopp, *Untersuchungen,* 70–4, and on the chronology, 71, n. 80. The documents are: I. The end of a letter whose authorship is unclear; II. A letter (*OGIS* 751; Welles, *RC* 54) headed Ἄτταλος Ἀμλαδέων τῆι πόλει καὶ τοῖς γεραιοῖς; III. A badly preserved letter, headed [βασιλεὺς Ἄτταλος Ἀμλαδέων τ]ῆι πόλει καὶ τ[οῖς γεραιοῖς]. Of these three letters, only the last can be dated firmly to a specific reign, from a reference in it to Eumenes' son Attalos, the future Attalos III (lines 4–5). The writer of this letter is therefore Attalos II; letter II, the most important, was written by Attalos before his accession, and the events referred to in the letter, including the remission of Amlada's payments to the king, may be associated with the war of this king involving the Pisidian city of Selge, attested by the *Prologue* to Trogus xxxiv: *ut mortuo rege Asiae Eumene suffectus Attalus bellum cum Selegensibus habuit et cum rege Prusia.* The recent death of Eumenes II, and the proximity of the war with Prusias, which broke out about 154, place the war with Selge in the 150s, not long after the accession of Attalos II. It is therefore clear that Amlada was heavily taxed during this war, but it cannot be assumed that these circumstances applied in peacetime conditions (*contra* Hopp, 70). The fact that, according to letter II, Amlada paid yearly tribute, establishes the city's subject status at that time, but this status may have arisen from the city's behaviour in the war as well as from any other definite cause; there is, furthermore, no specific evidence that the Attalids received Amlada in 188 BC. Whatever the case, it is clear that the conditions attested for Amlada, a frontier-city necessarily involved in the continual bouts of warfare undertaken by the Attalid kings in the area (cf. Meyer, *Die Grenzen,* 154; Welles, *RC* 54 ad loc.), cannot be regarded as typical of the Attalids' treatment of other tributary cities, whose circumstances were different.

An inscription from Sardis to be dated to the early second century BC records remissions of tribute and other concessions allowed to a city of whose name only the initial T has been preserved on the stone;[107] it includes the provision (lines 16–19):
[ἀ]πὸ δὲ τοῦ ὀγδόου ἔτους διδόναι τρε[ῖς ἀναφορὰς] | [ἐκ] πασῶν τῶν γινομένων προσόδων πα[ρ᾿ ἕκαστον] | ἐνιαυτὸν ἀργυ[ρ]ίου μνᾶς εἴκοσι καὶ ἄλλ[ως μὴ ἐν]|οχλεῖσθαι εἶν[αι] δὲ αὐτοὺς ἀ[φ]ρουρήτ[ους] κτλ. . . . The tone and language of this document are somewhat reminiscent of the Attalid chancery, but no proof whatever is attainable in the present state of the text. The city concerned may have been Temnos, as the editors of the inscription suggested, and the circumstances the same as those of the decree for Korrhagos, namely the aftermath of the Antiochic War, but many such contexts may be adduced with no less plausibility. In short, none of the evidence usually cited indicates Attalid policy with regard to taxation in general terms and in normal circumstances.

The city for which we have the clearest evidence as regards status as a tribute-paying city after 188 BC is Teos. We know that Teos paid a considerable σύνταξις to Attalos I, as we saw in the previous chapter, and according to the terms of the Roman settlement it should have paid φόρος thereafter.[108] A letter written by Eumenes II to the Ionian Guild of Dionysian *technitai,* whose seat was then at Teos, tells us a good deal about the relationship between the king and the city.[109] Fragmentary though the letter is, it is very probable that Teos, like the Guild, could be bound by royal *prostagmata* and that by this means a settlement could be imposed on the city concerning its dispute with the Dionysian

---

[107] *Sardis* vii. 1, no. 2.

[108] Before the discovery of the decree honouring Antiochos III and Laodike (see above, ch. 3, n. 64), there was no specific evidence that Teos was a tributary Attalid city after 188. Its subject status was inferred by Cardinali (*RP* 94) from (i) the city's allegiance to Antiochos during the war with Rome (cf. Livy xxxvii. 27–8), and (ii) the direct treatment afforded to Teos by Eumenes II in its dispute with the Dionysian *technitai* (see below). The fact that Teos interceded at Rome for its daughter-city Abdera in 167 (*Syll.*³ 656) is regarded by Magie, *Roman Rule,* ii. 959, and Walbank, *Comm.* iii. 167–8, as evidence that Teos was then independent, but this approach is too dogmatic; it is quite feasible that a Greek city could send an embassy to Rome while being tributary to a king, especially in the special circumstances relating to the question of Abdera.

[109] *IvP* 163, = Welles, *RC* 53.

technitai.[110] The same machinery is known to have been used in the context of Attalid rule in Aigina, a possession of the King of Pergamon,[111] and a decision of Attalos III concerning the important priesthood of Dionysos Kathegemon at Pergamon was also communicated as a *prostagma*, as recorded in Attalos' letter to Kyzikos on the subject, dated 135 BC.[112] The word was used, as is well known, of royal decisions, and sometimes of the decisions of subordinate officials, in other Hellenistic kingdoms.[113] It is clear from the constitutional terms employed in the surviving correspondence that Eumenes was more than just an arbitrator in the dispute between the city and the Guild of *technitai*, because the embassy of the Guild, to which reference is made, envisaged a settlement imposed by the king if it proved to be necessary:[114] εἰ δὲ μὴ διδό|ναι οὕτως ἐμαυτὸν ὅπως εἰς ὁ[μόνοια]ν ἀποκατα|στήσας, βεβαι[ῶς ὑμῖν εἰς τὸν λοιπ]ὸγ χρόνον | [τὰ ε]ἰ̣ς εἰ[ρηνὴν καὶ εὐνο-μίαν συντείνοντα - - - -]. The expressions used of royal decisions, all introduced by either κρίνω or ὑπολαμβάνω, determine the extent of royal authority implied in the settlement.[115]

According to a decree of Teos honouring a citizen of Magnesia on the Maeander, the *strategoi* of Teos had a constitutional function similar to their counterparts at Pergamon; the prescript reads[116] τιμ]ούχων καὶ στρατηγῶν γνώμη. We have already noticed a similar procedure at Pitane and Phokaia, and to these instances we may add from the Attalid Kingdom the cities of

[110] Fränkel restored *IvP* 163. C, 7–8 κ[ατὰ τὰ δόγμα]|τα τῶμ βασιλέων, but Holleaux's restoration (*Études*, iii. 205) κ[ατὰ τὰ προστάγμα]|τα was adopted by Welles, and is followed here.

[111] *OGIS* 329, 14–15.

[112] *IvP* 248, = *OGIS* 331. III, 41–3, = Welles, *RC* 66, 16–18.

[113] See the valuable analysis of Holleaux, *Études*, iii. 205–11. For the Ptolemies see also M. - Th. Lenger, *Corpus des ordonnances des Ptolémées* (Brussels, 1964), and in general, Préaux, *Monde hell.* i. 272–3, ii. 599–601.

[114] Welles, *RC* 53 I.A, lines 6–9.

[115] See, in the text, II. C, line 15; III. B, line 8, C, line 9; IV. C, line 12. Compare the case of Hierocaesarea and Thyateira, whose dispute was settled *regis* [*con*]-*stitutionibus* (Keil-von Premerstein, *Zweite Reise*, 13, no. 18). A letter written to Priene concerning a settlement between that city and Miletos (*IvPr* 27, = Welles, *RC* 46) is, I believe, a document of Roman rule and not the letter of an Attalid, and in any event the text is too fragmentary to allow conclusions concerning constitutional prodecure.

[116] *IvM* 97, 30–47.

Phrygian Hierapolis, Sardis, Tralles, Magnesia ad Sipylum, and an
unnamed city replying to a communication of Magnesia on the
Maeander.[117] This constitutional machinery is less frequently attested outside the Attalid Kingdom;[118] more significantly, it forms
a part of the constitution of the city of Pergamon from the beginning of the Attalid dynasty, as Pergamene decrees from the early
third century onwards attest.[119] We are therefore led to ask
whether this state of affairs entitles us to believe that the kings of
Pergamon determined or interfered in any way with the constitutions of tributary and subject cities. The frequent occurrence of the
constitutional machinery whereby the *strategoi* introduced matters for consideration to the popular assembly, notably at Teos
which we know was a tributary city after 188, is the sole indication
that it reflects Attalid policy in general terms. The only other
evidence that can be adduced relates to a single city. A decree from
Bakir (ancient Nakrasa), but not necessarily of that precise prove-
nance, dated βασιλεύοντος Ἀττάλου, πρώτου | ἔτους, and there-
fore issued by a city of the Attalid Kingdom, honours a certain
Ἀπολλώνιος Μελεά|γρου ἐπιστάτης.[120] The term ἐπιστάτης is
well attested in the Hellenistic period as a governing magistrate in a
subject city,[121] and in the Attalid Kingdom it was used of Kleon's
office at Aigina;[122] in the present case there can be no doubt that

---

[117] Hierapolis: *OGIS* 308; Sardis: Appendix iv, no. 5, lines 1–2; Tralles: *BSA* xxix
(1927–8), 68–71; Magnesia: *AM* xxiv (1899), 411; the unnamed city: *IvM* 87, =
OGIS 319.

[118] Notably at Priene under Lysimachos (*OGIS* 11), and at Smyrna under
Seleukos II (*OGIS* 229).

[119] See below, 165 n. 23.

[120] *OGIS* 268; cf. Robert, *Villes*, 36, n. 6. The decree is dated by Robert, followed
by Bengtson, *Strat.* ii. 248, to the reign of Attalos II or III, on the premiss (as yet not
argued in full) that the *basileia* mentioned in line 6 honoured Zeus Basileios and not
the kingship of Attalos I, as Wilcken, *RE*, s.v. Attalos (9), 2159, and Meyer, *Die
Grenzen*, 98, thought. The issue in my view remains open: Attalos I did not fall short
of divine honours elsewhere (see ch. 6), and we find a parallel to the royal *basileia* in
the Βασίλεια at Alexandria (P. M. Fraser, *Ptol. Alexandria*, ii. 382, n. 341).

[121] See Holleaux, *Études*, iii. 217–19, and his list, 253–4, supplemented by
Robert, *Hellenica*, vii, p. 22; Bengtson, *Strat. passim*. On the Seleukid *epistates*
see also Welles, *RC*, p. 187, n. 3, 188, n. 4, and on the Ptolemaic *epistates*, Préaux,
Monde hell. ii. 419–20. One example of the office is known from Bithynia: L.
Robert, *Ét. anat.* 228–35; cf. Bengtson, *Strat.* ii. 245; Rostovtzeff, *SEHHW* iii.
1481, n. 75. For the Rhodian *epistatai* of the Peraea, see Holleaux, *Études*, i.
409–17; Fraser and Bean, *Rhodian Peraea*, 86–94.

[122] *OGIS* 329, 34–5, with Dittenberger's n. 19.

Apollonios was *epistates* of the city which passed the decree in his honour. If, as seems likely, the stone came from a city near Nakrasa, such as Akrasos or Stratonikeia, the city concerned was situated in the area of direct authority established by Eumenes I and exploited by his successor, and we know that the area around Thyateira, including Nakrasa and the upper Kaikos valley, was in Attalid hands some years before the Roman settlement, in fact already during the reign of Attalos I.[123] Aigina also was an acquisition of Attalos I, and it is therefore very likely that the office of *epistates* was introduced into subject cities by this king rather than Eumenes II.

The decree also refers to another office previously held by Apollonios: καὶ πρότε|ρον δὲ στρατηγὸς τῆς πόλεως κατασταθείς. This constitutes the only indication of the method of appointment of the civic *strategoi* in the Attalid Kingdom outside the capital; as such it is tantalizingly vague, but two parallels can be cited in determining the significance of the verb κατασταθείς used of the appointment. The same word is used of Eumenes I's appointment of the Pergamene *strategoi*,[124] and in a Megarian decree of the appointment of Hikesios of Ephesos at Aigina by Eumenes II.[125] It seems likely, then, that Apollonios' office was a royal appointment, although this is not specifically stated, as was his later office of *epistates*.[126]

In the light of this evidence we have reasonable grounds for believing that the King of Pergamon appointed *epistatai* and *strategoi* in the subject cities; that, in other words, he interfered in and perhaps restricted the constitutional functions of these cities. This does not necessarily mean however that the constitutions as a whole were similarly determined, since the king could have made use of existing institutions, as he did perhaps at Pergamon itself, but it is possible that he favoured the type of constitution found at Pergamon and encouraged cities within his kingdom to adopt it. At this point then, we may usefully consider the exact nature of the

---

[123] Robert, *Villes*, 31–40.

[124] *OGIS* 267. II, 1–2: οἱ κατασταθέντες ὑπ' Εὐμένους στρατηγοί.

[125] *Syll.*[3] 642: ὁ κατασταθεὶς ἐπ' Αἰγίνας ὑπ[ὸ τοῦ βασ]ιλέως Εὐμένους. See my remarks in *BSA* lxvi (1971), 3–4.

[126] See Bengtson, *Strat.* ii. 248–9.

office of *strategos* in Greek cities that were subject to Attalid authority.

In Attalid usage the term *strategos* connotes one of two civil offices: either a regional governor, such as Korrhagos and Demetrios, or a member of a collegiate board, as at Pergamon and the other cities already mentioned. It is never clearly attested in a military sense. The copious body of inscriptions which provide information concerning the organization of the Attalid army attests no military office higher than that of ἡγεμών, whether referring to a garrison or to an army in the field. In the decrees from Delphi honouring the members of a garrison put into the town of Lilaia by Attalos I, their ranks are designated as οἱ στρατιῶται καὶ ἡγεμόνες,[127] and the same formula is used with reference to the armies at Philetaireia and Attaleia under Eumenes I,[128] and with reference to an Attalid force at Aigina in the time of Attalos I.[129] All this is in striking contrast to Seleukid and Ptolemaic titulatures, in which the military *strategos* is separately designated.[130]

We may conclude then that in the Attalid Kingdom the office of *strategos* was civil (in two senses) and not military.[131] It may be thought significant that Livy's Corragus, *praefectus Eumenis,* whom we have identified with the *strategos* Korrhagos, fought with Manlius against the Galatians in 189, but even he was subordinate in the command of the Attalid contingent to a member of the royal family, Athenaios,[132] and the fact that Corragus (Korrhagos)

[127] *F. Delphes,* iii. 4. 132–5; part of 133 is now conveniently reproduced in Moretti, *ISE* ii, no. 81; note there the typical formulas οἱ στρατιῶται καὶ ἀγεμόνες οἱ μετὰ Θρασ[υμάχου] and τόν τε Θρασύμαχον καὶ το[ὺ]ς μετὰ αὐτοῦ στρατιώτας καὶ ἡγεμόνες.
[128] *IvP* 13, = *OGIS* 266, 19–20: Παράμονος καὶ οἱ ἡγεμόνες καὶ οἱ ὑφ᾽ αὐτοὺς στρατιῶται.
[129] *Eph. Arch.* 1913, 90–2, = Moretti, *ISE* i, no. 36. I have reproduced and discussed the text of this small round red-painted altar in *BSA* lxvi (1971), 4–5 (photograph, pl. 2). See also *IvP* 29, = *OGIS* 280.
[130] See *OGIS* 217, = Welles, *RC* 39 (cf. Wilhelm, *Wien. Anz.* lvii (1920), 40–2).
[131] The application of the term *strategia* to the mercenary body in Philetaireia in the document recording the settlement with Eumenes I (ch. 2, n. 47) does not in my view necessarily mean that their commander, Paramonos, was called *strategos,* as Bengtson, *Strat.* ii. 198 ff., argues. The significance of the titulature of Philopoimen, στρατηγὸς καὶ ἐπὶ τῆς σφραγῖδος under Attalos II (see below, 132) is unclear (Bengtson, loc. cit.).
[132] Livy xlii. 67. 4.

was a regional *strategos* does not have a direct bearing on his military office in the field. In fact this instance is typical of Attalid practice: the largely mercenary armies were invariably commanded, at least in the more important campaigns for which we have evidence, by the king or a near relative of the king, and in the case of Eumenes II, very often by one of his brothers.

This analysis determines the nature of the office held by Apollonios, as attested by the decree from Bakir, στρατηγὸς τῆς πόλεως. The possibility that he was a military governor in charge of a garrison can be discounted. Since he is called *strategos* 'of the city', the collegiate civic magistracy common in cities of the Attalid Kingdom alone remains in question. We have found reason to believe that he was appointed to this office by the king, a practice likely to be repeated in other cities of the kingdom, for which evidence is lacking. On the other hand we have found no cogent evidence to suggest that the office itself, let alone the constitution as a whole, was of the king's design or imposition; since the office was, as we have seen, a civic one and a typical Greek one at that, it seems reasonable to think that the king made use of an existing institution in order to establish a personal control over the constitutional features of the cities concerned, as he did at Pergamon.[133]

The widespread appointment of royal officials in cities is attested by an excerpt from Diodoros' history which refers to the hostile attitude of Attalos III to officials of his father's reign:[134] τῶν δὲ ἄλλων φίλων τῶν ἐπ᾽ ἐξουσίᾳ στρατιωτῶν ἢ πόλεων τεταγμένων οὓς μὲν ἐδολοφόνησεν, οὓς δὲ συλλαβὼν πανοικίους ἀνεῖλε. The construction of the sentence suggests a general description of officials rather than the designation of a specific office, ὁ ἐπὶ πόλεως, since in fact Diodoros' expression is οἱ ἐπ᾽ ἐξουσίᾳ . . . πόλεων, and a comparison with the office called ὁ ἐπὶ πόλεως at Pergamon can carry little weight.[135] It seems more plausible to regard Diodoros' description as embracing the titles *strategos* and *epistates* attested by the epigraphical evidence we have been considering.

We may conclude, then, that tributary cities of the Attalid Kingdom enjoyed freedom in the matter of constitutional form, but that it was a freedom limited by the king's appointment of *strategoi* and *epistatai*. The evidence of the king's power to issue *prostagmata* in the case of Teos further indicates the status of a tributary city, since the king could certainly treat one such city on the same terms as another. These limitations apart, all our evidence suggests that the tributary cities continued to lead an independent civic life, and no evidence of the imposition of garrisons or military governors in normal circumstances has come down to us.

We have seen that the main burden imposed on these cities was the obligation to pay tribute, and it is in these terms that they are designated in the accounts we have of the Roman settlement of 188 BC. It was doubtless this obligation more than any other that determined a city's relationship to the king at Pergamon. With this consideration we may associate in part the Attalids' concern to influence probouleutic functions by virtue of their personal appointment of *strategoi*, because one important aspect of these functions was the administration of finances, at Pergamon and elsewhere.[136] A further line of enquiry in this regard may be found in the cities' coinage, which has undergone a thorough re-examination in recent years.[137]

It has now been established that cities independent of the Attalids after 188 began or continued to issue gold coins or tetra-

---

[136] See below, 167–8.
[137] The groundwork on these coins was done by F. Imhoof-Blumer, *Die Münzen,* 28–35, and H. von Fritze, *Die Münzen von Pergamon*; these studies established a stylistic sequence for the coins. Important among recent works are: E. S. G. Robinson, *Num. Chron.* xiv (1954), 1–7; U. Westermark, *Das Bildnis,* who argued that the old dynastic coinage bearing the head of Philetairos ended in 190; D. Kienast, *Jahrb. für Numismatik und Geldgesch.* xi (1961), 159 ff., with bibliography, 163–86; Robert, *Villes,* 252 ff.; H. Seyrig, *Rev. Num.* v (1963), 19 ff. For a summary of discussion on this question see now F. S. Kleiner and S. P. Noe, *The Early Cistophoric Coinage* (American Numismatic Society, *Numismatic Studies,* xiv, 1977); A. Giovannini, *Rome et la circulation monetaire en Grèce au IIe siècle av. Jésus-Christ (Schweiz. Beitr. zur Altertumswiss.* 15, 1978).

drachms in their own right,[138] whereas no independent coinage is attested for cities known to have been tributary to the Attalids. Many of these tributary cities issued a new coin, the *cistophoros,* which was minted initially at Pergamon, Ephesos, and Tralles, on a different standard from that of the Attic tetradrachm, and which, as we shall see, was most probably introduced as the exclusive coinage of the kingdom in 188 BC. This cistophoric coinage was limited to cities known to have been tributary to the Attalids after 188 BC, and recent numismatic research has indicated its status as a royal coinage minted at Attalid cities, the chief mint being at Pergamon, which provided also for the issues of Synnada, Sardis, and Apameia.[139]

The consistent pattern of the coinages of the Greek cities of Asia Minor after the Roman settlement is clear from the following table, which lists the issues of twenty-seven cities whose status in known from literary or epigraphical evidence:

City	Status	Coinage
Alabanda	independent	independent
Alexandria Troas	independent	independent
Colophon Nova	independent	independent
Ephesos	gift city	cistophoric
Herakleia by Latmos	independent	independent
Ilion	independent	independent
Kibyra	independent	independent
Kos	independent	independent
Kyme	independent	independent
Kyzikos	independent	independent
Lampsakos	independent	independent
Magnesia on the Maeander	independent	independent
Magnesia ad Sipylum	gift city (Livy)	no independent coinage

[138] Seyrig, 19; see also the table below. Some of these cities are of special interest in view of their previous relations with Pergamon, notably Kyzikos, Lampsakos, Ilion, the Kolophonians of Notion, Alexandria Troas, and Smyrna (see ch. 3 above). Note that Kyme and the Kolophonians of Notion were specifically freed of the obligation to pay tribute in 188 (Polyb. xxi. 46. 4). For relations between Ilion and the Attalids, see Welles, *RC* 62 (as interpreted by Robert, *BCH* liv (1930), 348–51; *Op. Minora Selecta* i. 167–70), a royal letter written probably by Attalos II; it refers to a purchase of land by the king from the temple of Athena at Ilion, and to previous benefactions of oxen and drivers (compare the sending of artists to Delphi by Attalos II (*Syll.*³ 682; Daux, *Delphes,* 509) and of an architect to the *katoikoi* in the territory of Telmessos by Eumenes II (above, 95).

[139] Seyrig, 21–2. As Seyrig shows, the single *cistophoros* of Smyrna is of a later date, and was clearly a special issue.

Miletos	independent	independent
Myndos	independent	independent
Mytilene	independent	independent
Priapos	tributary	no independent coinage
Rhodes	independent	independent
Sardis	tributary	cistophoric
Skepsis	tributary	no independent coinage
Smyrna	independent	independent
Telmessos	gift city	no independent coinage
Temnos	tributary	no independent coinage
Tenedos	independent	independent
Teos	tributary	no independent coinage
Thyateira	tributary	cistophoric
Tralles	gift city	cistophoric

It seems from this evidence that a city's coinage after 188 was directly related to its status as fixed by the Roman settlement of that year: independent cities were free to issue their own coinage, whereas cities made tributary to the Attalids lost this right. If this is so, then cities which continued after 188 to issue their own coins were evidently not Attalid subjects; the independent status of Aigai, argued above on other grounds, would thus be confirmed, as would that of Parion, Abydos, Myrina, Lebe'dos, and Phaselis.[140]

[140] Seyrig, 20. The case of Abydos is particularly interesting, in that Abydos has been thought to be an Attalid subject from 188, and even, by Magie (see below), as possibly the city which issued the decree honouring Korrhagos discussed above in part i. The status of Abydos is however unclear; in 196 it was declared free (Polyb. xviii. 44. 4; Holleaux, *Études*, iv. 317–18, n. 4; Schmitt, *Untersuchungen*, 284), but Antiochos' garrison still held the city in 190 (Livy xxxvii. 9. 11–12; xxxiii. 38.4). We do not know how the city was treated by Rome in 188, but Magie's view (*Roman Rule*, ii. 1012–13) that 'for its surrender to Antiochus it would naturally have been awarded to Eumenes' is untenable, in view of explicit evidence, in the case of Phokaia (Polyb. xxi. 46. 7; see above, 42 n. 46), that a city betrayed to Antiochos, and then held by a garrison and not by loyalty, was not treated in 188 as if it had joined the cause voluntarily. Abydos' independent coinage probably dates from shortly after the third Macedonian war (Seyrig, 20, n. 2), and may have begun with a commemorative issue; thus a short period of Attalid rule after 188 is not precluded on this criterion, and is perhaps supported by an inscription from Ilion mentioning a certain Chaireas, ὁ τεταγμένος ἐπ' Ἀβύδου; it would be difficult to assign this clearly royal appointment to anyone but an Attalid king (cf. Bengtson, *Strat.* ii. 242). All we can say with certainty is that Abydos was independent from about 170; if it was subject to Eumenes between 188 and that date, the reason for such a status is not clear.

The oldest coins of the cistophoric coinage, judged on stylistic grounds, are issues of Pergamon, Ephesos, Tralles, Sardis, and Apameia; although at one time dated, as individual issues of each city, to the end of the third century BC and even earlier,[141] it is clear from the history of these cities, from the dominance of the Pergamene mint in the coinage, and above all from the fact that the coins were issued by all of them, and minted in the three major Attalid cities, in the same period, that is, as a common coinage, that the origins of the coinage must be dated to the years after 188 BC, when the cities concerned were assigned to Eumenes II by the terms of the Roman settlement of Asia Minor. It is only in this period of the second century that the necessary common political circumstances can be adduced for all the cities in explanation of such a coinage.[142]

In the case of Pergamon it is probable that the coinage was issued before 188 BC, in addition to the dynastic coinage bearing the head of Philetairos, which, it now seems, continued to be minted after 188 BC. Livy mentions *cistophori* among the booty of three Roman triumphs of the Antiochic War in 190 and 189, and these references cannot be dismissed as anachronistic designations of a number of different coinages, as is usually done.[143] Livy's evidence does not necessarily emanate from badly informed annalistic sources, since the exact details he gives suggest archival material of the kind gathered for the Augustan publication of the *fasti triumphales*; and the objection that Glabrio, who triumphed in 190, could not have had *cistophoroi* in his booty because neither of his defeated opponents, the Aitolians and

[141] Kleiner and Noe, 10–18.

[142] Seyrig, 22 ff.; Giovannini 15. *Cistophoroi* from Thyateira, Apollonis, and Stratonikeia, bearing the letters *BA EY* followed by *B* or *Δ*, have been shown by Robinson (cited above, n. 137) to be issues of Aristonikos, who called himself Eumenes III; cf. L. Robert, *Villes*², 252 ff. Kleiner and Noe date the introduction of the common coinage to about 166 BC, after Eumenes' successful Galatian war of the early 160s. They argue, on the basis of a coin hoard from Mektepini in Phrygia (N. Olçay and H. Seyrig, *Le Trésor de Mektepini en Phrygie*, Paris, 1965) that the dynastic coinage bearing the head of Philetairos continued after 188 BC, and postulate a short overlap with the new cistophoric coinage, but a longer one is possible; moreover the historical circumstances they adduce as contextual evidence are not especially convincing. For the dominance of the Pergamene mint in the coinage, see Kleiner and Noe, 120–4.

[143] xxxvii. 46. 2 (M'. Acilius Glabrio in 190); xxxvii. 58. 4 (L. Aemilius Regillus in 189); xxxvii. 59.1 (L. Cornelius Scipio Asiaticus in 189). Cf. Seyrig, 24, n. 1; Kleiner and Noe, 18, n. 58. For the chronology of the late dynastic coinage, see Kleiner and Noe, 14–16.

Antiochos III, ever circulated the coin, cannot stand, because Antiochos at least could easily have acquired quantities of the coins when his son Seleukos raided Attalid territory and besieged Pergamon in 190.[144] I regard it as probable, then, that *cistophoroi* were minted at Pergamon before, although not long before, 188 BC, as well as tetradrachms bearing the portrait of Philetairos, and that the cistophoric coinage was imposed on tributary cities in or shortly after 188 as the sole currency of Eumenes' newly acquired kingdom, with Pergamon as the chief mint and others at Ephesos and Tralles. This fact attests clearly Eumenes' intention of rendering his subjects financially dependent on their suzerain, and is consistent with the Attalids' persistent concern to control the finances of their kingdom personally, another consequence of which we saw earlier in their direct appointment of civic *strategoi*.

The fact that the cistophoric coinage was not circulated outside the kingdom throws light on Eumenes' economic policy in more general terms.[145] So far from co-operating economically with the Seleukids after 188, as Rostovtzeff thought,[146] Eumenes was evi-

[144] Seyrig, 24, n. 1; Seleukos' invasion of 190: Livy xxxvii. 18; Appian, *Syr.* 26. The invasions of 198 and 197 also come into consideration: see above, 77–8.

[145] On this question, see Seyrig, 25–6; Kleiner and Noe, 124–5.

[146] *Anat. Stud. Buckler* 277 ff.; *SEHHW* ii. 654 ff. Rostovtzeff argued, from the abundance of autonomous tetradrachms from western Asia Minor found in Syrian hoards of the second century BC, that Eumenes II inherited a surplus of metal in 188, and therefore co-operated with the Greek cities and with the Seleukids by supplying them with this metal. This view has been decisively criticized by Seyrig, 26–8; in fact, circulation of these tetradrachms in the Seleukid Kingdom is as notable before 188 as after, and remained always a free circulation, as distinct from the royal Seleukid currency. Furthermore, the policy of financial monopoly, introduced into his kingdom in the form of the *cistophoros* in 188 BC, testifies against the notion of an 'entente cordiale' with the Seleukids after that date.

O. Mørkholm, *Antiochus IV of Syria* (Copenhagen, 1966), 51–63, believes in a political and economic co-operation between the Attalids and the Seleukids when Antiochos IV came to the throne. Apart from the circumstances of Antiochos' elevation, which seem to me to amount to little more than a typical example of Attalid opportunism, there is little evidence to support this view, and still less to support that of a 'triple alliance of Pergamon, Cappadocia, and Syria' after 175 (Mørkholm, 55). The fact that Antiochos shared the same contacts in the Greek world as Eumenes proves nothing, since many of them, especially Delphi and Delos, received the attention of most powerful states and kingdoms at this time. Again, Antiochos' policy of friendship with Miletos, a city according to Mørkholm 'within the Pergamene sphere of influence', simply reflects another aspect of that city's determination to advance its own position by courting the favour of any benefactor willing to assist it (on this policy see further below); it says nothing for the relations between the benefactors. Finally, as Mørkholm admits (57–8), Antiochos was willing to help rivals of Pergamon as well as friends; Rhodes is a case in point (Livy xli. 20. 7; *Syll.*[3] 644–5).

dently concerned to establish a rival economy, whose coinage was on a standard different from that of the Attic tetradrachm circulated in the Seleukid Kingdom, and whose status therefore suggests circumstances other than co-operation in trade with the Seleukids. Although he was no doubt aware of the example of this policy shown by the Ptolemies, it is hardly valid in the present state of the evidence to regard Eumenes' implementing of a currency monopoly as a sign of direct Ptolemaic influence; rather it suggests that same policy, argued above, whereby the Attalids after 188 adopted institutions of different origins as they suited the circumstances of the new kingdom. We have seen that the Attalids were always concerned to control personally the institutions of financial administration in the various parts of their kingdom: the Greek cities, the *katoikiai,* the temples, and, as Cardinali has shown, the capital, where this policy was probably implemented early in the dynasty's history.[147] This policy did not, however, reach the proportions of the highly centralized economic and fiscal system developed by the Ptolemies, of which the currency monopoly was only one aspect; it would be wrong, therefore, to suppose that Eumenes was directly influenced to any great extent by Ptolemaic practice in making provision for the financial administration of his kingdom after the Treaty of Apameia.

The status of a 'free' or non-tributary city in relation to the Attalid Kingdom is more difficult to determine. The difficulties can best be considered by comparing the fortunes of the two cities for which the evidence is most informative: the gift city of Ephesos and the free city of Miletos. In the case of Miletos the material to hand allows us to draw a very distinct picture of the relations between the city and the king. Perhaps the most significant conclusion to be drawn from it is that at Miletos Eumenes II was almost certainly called a god in his lifetime.

The entire body of evidence with which we are concerned dates from the reign of Eumenes II; some of it has been familiar for a long time, while some is more recent.[148] As we have seen, Miletos was

---

[147] G. Cardinali, *Mem. Accad. Bologna,* x (1915–16), 181–93; see below, ch. 7. The responsibility for finances of the provincial *strategos* is shown by a *cistophoros* bearing the letters *ΚΟΡ(ΡΑΓΟΣ) ΑΡ(ΙΣΤΟΜΑΧΟΥ)*; Seyrig, 29–31.

[148] The texts are given in Appendix iv, nos. 13–17.

given its freedom in 188 as a reward for co-operation in the Antiochic War. The status of the city before the war is unclear; there is certainly no evidence that it was a Ptolemaic city at the end of the third century and in all probability it was completely independent.[149] There is no ground in the Roman settlement, as recorded by Polybios, on which Miletos could have been expected to pay tribute to Eumenes, and its independence was in all ways assured. The city's territory almost certainly included that of Myus, a small town whose sacred lands were a constant cause of dispute with its more powerful neighbours. This was undoubtedly so at the end of the third century, when Miletos billeted some Cretan mercenaries in the territory of Myus.[150] As a result of the expedition of Philip V in Asia Minor in 201, Miletos temporarily lost its independence, and Myus was given by the invader to Magnesia on the Maeander,[151] but the former situation was restored when Miletos concluded a separate treaty with Magnesia in 196, which set the boundary between the two cities at the River Hybandos.[152] The territory of Myus was presumably included in the sacred lands which were specifically restored to Miletos in 188.

The most important of the documents we are to consider is a long letter of Eumenes II addressed to the Ionian *koinon* (Appendix iv, no. 13), which quotes extensively (lines 5–37) the Ionian decree passed in his honour to which his own letter is a reply. It is the key to the chronological problems involved in attempting to form a secure sequence of documents, and thereby a sequence of events. Holleaux's thorough analysis of the contents of the letter and its historical content[153] established that the winter of 167/6, when Eumenes is likely to have been at Delos (lines 1–5) and his Galatian war was still in progress, is the date which best suits all the implications of the letter, and this date has rightly been accepted since. The decree, as passed on to us by Eumenes' letter, attests honours voted to him both by the *koinon* and by Miletos alone. The honours of the *koinon* are conventional: the donation of a gold

---

[149] Holleaux, *Études,* iii. 135–6; Rehm, *Das Delphinion in Milet* (*Milet* i. 3, Berlin, 1914), 267, 323.

[150] *Milet* i. 3. 33E; Magie, *Roman Rule,* ii. 883, n. 81.

[151] Polyb. xvi. 24. 9; Holleaux, *Études,* iv. 230 ff.

[152] *Syll.*[3] 588, line 30.

[153] Holleaux, *Études,* ii. 153–78.

crown, the erection of a gilded statue anywhere in the territory of the *koinon*, honours to be announced at the festivals of the *koinon*, Eumenes to be met and congratulated by representatives of the *koinon*. The more significant part is contained in Eumenes' reply: he offers to provide an income for the celebration of his ἡμέρα ἐπώνυμος at the festival of the Panionion,[154] and to pay for the statue, which he chooses to be put up (lines 59–60) [ἐν τῶι ἐψη]|φισμένωι ἡμῖν ὑπὸ Μιλησ[ίων τε]μένε[ι].

One of the Ionian envoys who met Eumenes at Delos (line 3) was Eirenias son of Eirenias, a prominent citizen of Miletos about whom a good deal is now known. He is also mentioned in the surviving portion of the city's decree in honour of Eumenes (Appendix iv, no. 14), in the capacity of envoy of the city to the king; Eumenes in reply (lines 16–18) γράματα (*sic*) ἀπέσταλκεν — δι' ὧν τά τε ὑπὸ Εἰρ[η]|νίου ἐμφανισθέντα αὐτῶι ἐχθέμενος κτλ. Holleaux's identification of the date of this mission on behalf of the city with that of the mission on behalf of the *koinon* is the weakest part of an otherwise dependable chronological framework, although it has been accepted, for example, by Welles.[155] This identity of occasions, based solely on the fact that on each occasion the Milesian envoy was Eirenias, is certainly suspect. There is no other reason to date the decree of Miletos to the year 167/6, and a later date is also arguable.

We pass to the third document, a decree of the Milesian *boule* which honours Eumenes' brothers Attalos and Athenaios in addition to the king himself (Appendix iv, no. 15).[156] The principal honours of course go to Eumenes, and include the celebration of his γενέθλιος ἡμέρα. As Holleaux argued, this celebration implies that the *temenos*, still referred to as 'voted' (ἐψηφισμένον) in Eumenes' letter (lines 59–60), had been completed, and we may therefore conclude that the decree of the *boule* is the later of the

---

[154] This celebration is not proposed in the extant part of the decree, and may have been Eumenes' own idea.

[155] Holleaux, *Études*, ii. 174–5; Welles, *RC*, p. 214: 'it appears . . . that Irenias, the Milesian member of the League embassy, had carried a special message to the king.' This identification is not accepted however by Daux, *BCH* lix (1935), 227.

[156] The omission from these honours of Philetairos, the youngest of the sons of Attalos I, may be explained by an early death. The last record of him relates to the year 171 (Livy xlii. 55. 7); cf. Hoffmann, *RE* s.v. Philetairos (3), 2162; Hopp, *Untersuchungen*, 31–2.

two documents. Although there is no indication that Eumenes is dead,[157] his brother and eventual successor, Attalos II, is called in this decree βασιλεὺς Ἄτταλος (lines 39–40). We have already seen that Delphian decrees dated in the year of Amphistratos (160/59) establish the fact that Attalos II was given the royal title before the death of Eumenes II late in 159.[158] An Athenian decree in honour of an unknown *oikeios* of Eumenes II, passed earlier in the same year, 160/59,[159] cannot therefore refer in its last surviving line to Eumenes' death, but must refer to the act of establishing the co-regency. When I examined the stone, now in the Epigraphical Museum in Athens (inv. 7526), I obtained a number of new readings, notably these in the important final line: - - - - *KAINYN-EYMENO . . THNAPX* - - - -. Following Daux's suggestions, we may restore this line as follows: καὶ νῦν Εὐμένο[υς] τὴν ἀρχ[ὴν παραδόντος (or ἐπιτρέψαντος) τῶι ἀδελφῶι Ἀττάλωι].

The importance of this text lies in the fact that it provides a *terminus post quem,* or even *ad quem,* for Attalos' assumption of the royal title, whereas Delphian chronology presents us with a *fait accompli.* For our present purpose, it proves that the decree of the *boule* of Miletos cannot be much earlier than 160/59. It may be later, because the possibility remains that Eumenes was already dead and Attalos had succeeded him;[160] if so it will not be much

[157] On this point, and others concerning the chronology under discussion, see G. Daux, *BCH* lix (1935), 226–9.

[158] See above, 10 n. 7.

[159] *IG* ii.² 953; Appendix iv, no. 18; W. B. Dinsmoor, *The Athenian Archon List in the Light of Recent Discoveries* (New York, 1939), 190, with references.

[160] This possibility depends on the interpretation drawn from the words (ὅπως) ἡ εἰς τὸμ βασιλέα μνήμη διαφυλά[σσητ]αι (lines 37–8), which do not necessarily mean that Eumenes was no longer alive. An Athenian decree in honour of Pharnakes I of Pontos and his recently acquired queen, Nysa, passed in the archonship of Tychandros, that is in the same year as *IG* ii.² 953 discussed above, 160/59, included the provision ἀναγγέλλειν δὲ τῶι βασιλεῖ τὸν κ[εχ]ειροτονημένον, ὅτι ὁ δῆμο[ς π]ειράσεται . . . πάντα τὰ πρὸς δόξαν καὶ μνήμην [αὐτῶι ἀνήκο]ντα συγκατασκευάσαι κτλ. (*Inscr. Délos,* 1497 bis, lines 50 ff.). Pharnakes was most certainly alive at the time; see also Mørkholm, *Antiochus IV,* 54.

In his letter to the Ionian *koinon,* Eumenes makes the offer already referred to in the words (lines 54–6) προσόδους ὑμῖν τὰς ἱκανὰς ἀνα[[θήσ]ω ἀφ' ὧν ἕξετε τὴν καθήκουσαν ἡμῖν [ἀνατιθ]έναι μνήμην. The expression can then refer to a living king. If Eumenes had died between the time the *temenos* at Miletos was voted and the time of the passing of the decree of the *boule* of Miletos, we would expect a more explicit reference to his death in the later document, and I am more inclined to believe that Eumenes was still alive when the *temenos* had been completed and the statue had been erected.

later.[161] The most important implication of this chronology so far as the present argument is concerned is that the building of the *temenos* voted to Eumenes II in the decree quoted in the king's letter, and the erection of the statue therein as requested by the king in the same letter, were almost certainly achieved during his lifetime.[162]

The last two documents with which we are concerned have been published more recently than the others; one was found in 1960, the other known, but not published, before. One is a decree of Miletos honouring its prominent citizen Eirenias (Appendix iv, no. 16), and it establishes as a fact what had previously been conjectured, that Eumenes of Pergamon provided the capital for the gymnasium at Miletos, this being in the case of the Attalids a well-attested practice.[163] Previously it had been known only that the same Eirenias had been appointed overseer in the construction of the gymnasium.[164] It may have been at this juncture that Eumenes sent a letter to the city, and that the city passed the decree in his honour of which the text is our no. 14. Or it may have been later still.

The last decree to be considered here (Appendix iv, no. 17) is the final link in justifying the assertion expressed above, that Miletos called Eumenes a god in his lifetime. Found rebuilt into a wall in 1903, it was referred to by Ruge,[165] but remained unavailable until published by P. Herrmann along with the new decree concerning Eirenias.[166] For the precise chronological relationship of this to the other Milesian documents, the reader is referred to the commentary attached to that publication. For our purpose the important point is that the text is certainly a Milesian decree ratified by

[161] This point depends on Rehm's revised dating of 'the second god after Menekrates' (lines 27–8); see Holleaux, *Études,* ii. 177–8. Although this chronological point is not by any means precise to the year, it justifies the statement I have made in the text.

[162] See the previous two notes. Holleaux's point (*Études,* ii. 173), 'il n'est pas croyable que la mise en état du τέμενος consacré par les Milésiens ait exigé de bien longs délais', should also be taken into account.

[163] L. Robert, *Ét. anat.* 85, n.3. Ephesos: *SEG* xvii. 510.

[164] Th. Wiegand, *Siebenter vorläufiger Bericht über die von den Königlichen Museen in Milet und Didyma unternommenen Ausgrabungen* (*Abh. Berlin,* Anhang, 1911), 29.

[165] *RE,* s.v. Myus, 1436.

[166] *Ist. Mitt.* xv (1965), 71–117.

the people of Myus, at the time in *sympoliteia* with Miletos;[167] it is to be dated before the erection of the statue of Eumenes II in his *temenos* at Miletos, since the decree was to be inscribed on its base (lines 7–8): ἀναγραφῇ δὲ καὶ τόδε τὸ ψήφισμα εἴς τε τὸ βῆ[μα ἐφ᾽ οὗ]| σταθήσεται ἡ τοῦ βασιλέως εἰκών. According to the chronology argued above, this places the decree, with near certainty, in Eumenes' lifetime, and the proposition is confirmed by the evidence of the decree itself. Throughout, there is reference to one king, ὁ βασιλεύς, who must of course be Eumenes; in particular, the king whose *eikon* was to be set up in Miletos (line 8) must be the same as the king, in no way distinguished, to whom envoys of the city were to be sent (lines 10 ff.). If Eumenes were no longer alive, and Attalos had succeeded him, we would expect a distinction to be made between the dead king and the living, for example in line 12: παρακαλεῖν τὸν βασιλέα Ἄτταλον. The decree includes a provision for the sale of a priesthood of Eumenes (lines 4–5): ὅπως ἱερωσύνη πραθ[ῇ ἡ βασιλέως] Εὐμένους θεοῦ.[168] Thus, according to our chronology, which is confirmed at every point, the priesthood and the divine title were associated with Eumenes during his lifetime.

There was nothing new in the city of Miletos calling a royal benefactor a god; it had done this for Antiochos II after the murder of Timarchos, as Appian informs us:[169] δεύτερος δὲ Ἀντίοχος . . . θεὸς ἐπώνυμον ὑπὸ Μιλησίων γίγνεται πρῶτον. The worship of Antiochos and that of Eumenes constitute the type of cult instituted spontaneously by a grateful but not necessarily subject city, as distinct from the dynastic cult established as a result of royal wish.[170] Its place in the context of Attalid royal cults as a whole will be examined in a later chapter, but at this point the political implications of Miletos' extravagant attitude to honouring Eumenes, an attitude not paralleled to our knowledge elsewhere in the Attalid Kingdom, require some consideration.

At both Ephesos and Miletos, one the possession of Eumenes according to the terms of the Roman settlement, the other a free

---

[167] Herrmann, 90 ff.

[168] I see no objection to the restoration of βασιλέως at the end of line 4. The absence of the royal title would call for some explanation.

[169] *Syr.* 65. See W. Orth, *Königlicher Machtanspruch*, 153–6.

[170] Habicht, *Gottmenschentum*, 160 ff.

non-tributary city by the same terms, the institution of the gymnasium became, by his will, the responsibility of the king. At Ephesos he received a normal gymnasial dedication associating him with Hermes and Herakles, as was usual;[171] at Miletos the honours were extended to amount to a regular cult of the living king. Thus Miletos, and not Eumenes' own city of Ephesos, may be regarded as a centre of his cult, in addition to the capital Pergamon and Teos. This condition would be more readily attributable to a subject city.

It is arguable, however, that of these two cities, Ephesos was in a better position after the Roman settlement had placed the city in Eumenes' hands. Whereas Miletos depended on royal favour for any benefits she might receive, Ephesos, as a part of the kingdom and probably its largest port, was automatically destined to prosperity, and it doubtless emerged from the Roman settlement as a city enjoying advanced royal patronage. In fact we know that Ephesos ranked high in the Attalids' regard, and we have specific evidence of building activity, always a sure sign of prosperity, under Attalos II.[172] The city was the centre of an Attalid administrative region; at least two Ephesians, Hikesios and Megon, reached high rank in the royal administration, and a third, whose name is not known in full, was chosen to be the mentor of the young Attalos III.[173]

Miletos, on the other hand, was in a different position, having rather to fend for itself for its economic prosperity. There are indications that its harbour was beginning to silt up, and that its trade by sea was in decline,[174] whereas Ephesos still enjoyed the

[171] Cf. *OGIS* 230 (Hermes, Herakles, and Antiochos Megas at Soli); *AM* xxviii (1903), 358 ff. (Ptolemy, Hermes, and Herakles at Samos).

[172] Strabo xiv. 1. 24, 641, mentions Attalos II's project of building a mole at the mouth of the harbour with the idea of deepening the entrance to accommodate larger ships; although unsuccessful, it is an indication of the growing volume of trade passing through the harbour. Strabo says of the city in his own day, αὔξεται καθ' ἑκάστην ἡμέραν, ἐμπόριον οὖσα μέγιστον τῶν κατὰ τὴν Ἀσίαν τὴν ἐντὸς τοῦ Ταύρου. Ephesos also enjoyed a fuller trade by land with the East. Strabo traces, on the evidence of Artemidoros, the important route from Ephesos which reached as far as the Euphrates (xiv. 2. 29, 663).

[173] For Hikesios and Megon, see below, 133–5. The mentor of Attalos III: Appendix iv, no. 24.

[174] Strabo xvi. 635.

advantage afforded by Lysimachos early in the third century BC of a new and better site for its harbour.[175] It was doubtless for this reason that the Milesians worked so hard to attract the king's attention and seized every opportunity to honour him. No wonder they were so grateful to Eirenias, who had the king's ear.[176] As a centre of Eumenes' worship the city would attain two important aspirations: the guaranteed goodwill of the king whose cult was celebrated, and the commercial prosperity that any important cult brought to a Greek city.[177] It is clear that in both these respects Ephesos held an advantage by virtue of its status, and if Miletos was to remain competitive it had to adopt a positive policy to gain and keep the king's favour. This evidently is what it did, and with great success.

Evidently, then, the terms 'free' and 'subject' do not adequately define the status of cities which enjoyed contacts with the Attalid Kingdom. The evidence we have discussed does not allow us to draw sharp distinctions between a free and a tributary or subject city, apart from the issue of tribute obligation. The information it does convey concerns the king's readiness to be as well-disposed to the latter as to the former, and shows that a city in the possession of the king in all probability led as independent a civic life as a free city, such as Miletos. It also enjoyed the advantage of royal patronage, a privilege which the free city sought by other means.

(iii) Festivals of Athena

So far in this chapter we have been considering the implications of the Roman settlement in mainly political terms, and we may now usefully turn to examine another facet: the process by which the cult and festivals of Athena, the most important of Pergamon's gods, were enhanced and transformed as a means of religious propaganda in line with the new standing of the King of Pergamon in the Greek world. We shall also see in a later chapter how cults of Dionysos were used to advance the status of the royal cult.

[175] Ibid. xiv. 1. 21; cf. Magie, *Roman Rule*, ii. 921, n.13.

[176] See the city's decree in his honour (Appendix iv, no. 16). These close relations between Miletos and the Attalids were maintained in the reign of Attalos II, when statues of the king and his brother Athenaios were erected in Miletos (*OGIS* 320–1).

[177] Habicht, *Gottmenschentum*, 165 ff.

Athena was a goddess with many aspects, and was well suited to the role of a city's presiding deity: she was a protector, a bringer of victory, a patron of learning and art, and she had associations with the oldest cities of the Greek mainland and Asia Minor. All these attributes were exploited by the Attalids, as they were by others in the Hellenistic period. A temple of Athena was built at Pergamon probably at the beginning of the third century BC, when Philetairos still acknowledged the suzerainty of Lysimachos, and it was sufficiently important by the time of Eumenes I to be the depository of the Pergamene copy of his treaty with the mercenaries at Philetaireia and Attaleia.[178] A festival called Panathenaia is attested at about the same time by the decree of Pergamon honouring the city's *strategoi,* but nothing further is known of it.[179]

In the reign of Attalos I the evidence for the cult of Athena becomes more copious and more significant, corresponding to Attalos' series of military victories and his proclaimed kingship. An enlargement of the temple and precinct of Athena in the city predating the great Eumenid restoration is probably to be considered the work of Attalos I early in his reign, as a means of accommodating the massive monuments he dedicated to Athena.[180] The figure of Athena on the dynastic coinage undergoes some change in Attalos' reign, greater emphasis being laid on the spear she is holding and less on the shield, developments which may plausibly be related to Attalos' military activity, in particular his victory over the Galatians at the river Kaikos.[181]

One of the few pieces of literary evidence for the cults of Athena at Pergamon records the occurrence of ἀγῶνες for Athena in 220. Polybios writes (iv. 49. 3), with reference to the outbreak of commercial war between Rhodes and Byzantion in this year, that Prusias I of Bithynia could be expected to take the side of the Rhodians: ἠρέθιζε δ' αὐτὸν καὶ τὸ δοκεῖν Βυζαντίους πρὸς μὲν Ἄτταλον εἰς τοὺς τῆς Ἀθηνᾶς ἀγῶνας τοὺς συνθύσοντας ἐξαπεσ-

[178] *OGIS* 266, = *StV* iii. 481 (discussed above, 22–5). Ohlemutz, *Kulte,* 16–23, dates the foundation of the temple to the first decade of the third century BC. On the temple of Athena as a state archive, see ibid. 23, 55–7.

[179] *IvP* 18, = *OGIS* 267 (discussed below, ch. 7).

[180] *AvP* ii. 55–6; Ohlemutz, *Kulte,* 28–9; Kähler, *Gr. Fries,* 135; the monuments are listed and considered in Appendix ii.

[181] *MvP* II. 7, 9, 12, 15; III. 4; Ohlemutz, *Kulte,* 34–5.

ταλκέναι, πρὸς αὐτὸν δ᾿ εἰς τὰ Σωτήρια μηδένα πεπομφέναι. This evidence has been interpreted to suggest that Attalos' festival was a recent foundation in 220,[182] but the emphasis of novelty lies surely on Prusias' Soteria (about which nothing further is known), and the passage cannot in my view be expected to afford precise chronological clues about Attalos' festival. All we can say is that in 220 Attalos was celebrating important games for Athena, whose description by Polybios suggests something other than the older Panathenaia, and which may plausibly be associated, like the other more definite cult phenomena, with Attalos' victories and assumption of the royal title.

At some time towards the end of Attalos' reign, or more probably at the beginning of the reign of Eumenes II, Athena was given the cult name *Nikephoros*, 'bestower of victory'. With this phenomenon we have also to associate two other names which are known chiefly from epigraphical sources, the festival of the Nikephoria, and the site outside the city called Nikephorion. It is possible that this titulature was not all introduced at the same time; that is to say, that Athena was called *Nikephoros* before the idea of a Nikephorion or of Nikephoria was conceived, but this is most unlikely, and the evidence is best understood as reflecting a single concept, as is usually done. Of the three names, only that of the Nikephorion occurs in literary sources, in Polybios, Strabo, and Appian, in all cases fortunately in securely dated contexts. First Polybios: his narrative of the year 201, when Philip V of Macedon was raiding Attalid territory, refers *inter alia* to Philip's destruction of the Nikephorion (xvi. 1. 6): ἐπεὶ δὲ τὸ Νικηφόριον ἐλυμήνατο, τὸ μὲν ἄλσος ἐκτεμών, τὸν δὲ περίβολον διαρρίψας, τούς τε ναοὺς ἐκ θεμελίων ἀνέσκαψε, πολλοὺς καὶ πολυτελεῖς ὑπάρχοντας, κτλ. After his defeat in 197, Philip was required to put the damage right, and he agreed to do so (xviii. 2. 2), but we do not know whether he kept his promise. Strabo attributes a renovation of the site to Eumenes II, as we shall see, but this does not necessarily mean that Philip had not kept his word, since the Eumenid restoration took place in the 180s, by which time Pergamon had suffered another invasion, that of Seleukos in 190 (Livy

---

[182] For example by Ohlemutz, *Kulte*, 34.

xxxvii. 18; Appian, *Syr.* 26). Appian also refers to a later destruction of the site, that by Prusias II of Bithynia in 155 (*Mithr.* 3; cf. Polyb. xxxii. 27).

Now this evidence needs careful consideration, because at first sight Polybios seems to suggest that the Pergamene Nikephorion was in existence already in the reign of Attalos I, and this is frequently taken to be the case, leading necessarily to the conclusion that Attalos was also responsible for designating Athena as *Nikephoros* and for the foundation of the Nikephoria, which are on this view to be identified with the ἀγῶνες for Athena recorded for 220.[183] But Polybios, in saying that Philip destroyed the Nikephorion in 201, may well be referring to the name current in his own day,[184] and it is to be noted that Polybios speaks of 'many temples' on the site, which suggests an extended application of the name beyond that of the original cult centre. The place may not formerly have had a name, and Philip's promise to restore the site related, of course, to the renovation which eventually became the famous Nikephorion.

The evidence of Attalos' monuments throws further doubt on the accepted view, because all the extant dedications are made to Athena without the cult epithet *Nikephoros,* with the exception of a small group which we may now consider. This group (*IvP* 51–6, 58) comprises a number of not very substantial fragments of small round bases commemorating individual victories; in two cases they are dedicated to Athena Nikephoros, one celebrating the victory over the Tolistoagians, the other the victory over Philip V at Chios in 202.[185] Another piece (*IvP* 55 A) has the first three letters of the name *Nikephoros,* but the royal name has not been preserved. This meagre evidence for the cult name is in striking contrast to the series of large monuments, none of which calls Athena *Nikephoros.* We cannot simply assume that all the dedica-

---

[183] Holleaux, *Études,* ii. 61–2; Ohlemutz, *Kulte,* 33–4; Klaffenbach, *MDAI* iii (1950), 99 ff. The site of the Nikephorion has not been identified; for a discussion of the probabilities, see Ohlemutz, *Kulte,* 36–7.

[184] Kähler, *Gr. Fries,* 187, n. 43.

[185] *IvP* 51, = Kähler, *Gr. Fries,* 190, n. 56; *IvP* 52, = *OGIS* 283: see below, 196 n. 5. Segre, in his important study cited below, n. 192, thought that the Nikephoria were founded by Attalos after the battle off Chios, but this is not a good context even regardless of other considerations (see above, 28 n. 3).

tions to Athena Nikephoros were placed in the Nikephorion outside the city rather than in the city temple from which the known
monuments come,[186] because Attalos, as we have seen, envisaged
the precinct in the city as the context of his grandest monuments,
and it would be difficult to imagine the even grander monuments to
be expected of a postulated new Nikephorion. Furthermore,
Eumenes placed his dedications to Athena Nikephoros in the
city's temple even after the known rebuilding of the Nikephorion
outside the city.

There remains the question of the two small bases which are
certainly dedications in the name of King Attalos to Athena
Nikephoros. Although usually dated to the last years of Attalos'
reign, the less regular letter-forms are markedly different from the
material associated with the 230s and 220s, and also from Attalos'
dedication of booty from Aigina in 210 (*IvP* 47, = *OGIS* 281), and
are closer to the inscriptions from the 190s and later. Kähler has
plausibly suggested that these bases are to be dated to the Eumenid
rebuilding of the precinct of Athena in the city, when, as he shows,
old blocks and bases were reused in addition to new material
brought in.[187] Athena's cult name *Nikephoros* is at this date to be
regarded as Eumenes' addition, and in support of this chronology
is the appearance of what must be Eumenes' name in one of the
fragments of the group under consideration (*IvP* 56 B).

On this chronological view, the first appearance of Athena
Nikephoros in the Pergamene inscriptions is the dedication of
Eumenes II commemorating his victory in alliance with the

[186] As does Ohlemutz, *Kulte,* 34.
[187] *Gr. Fries,* 135–6, with n. 46. An examination of the stones in the Pergamon
Museum in Berlin undertaken by the author in 1969 confirmed this chronology. The
rather crude letters of the small bases under discussion differ markedly from the
more precise work of Attalos' larger monuments, and are directly comparable with
some of Eumenes' own dedications, especially *IvP* 63 (see Kähler, *Gr. Fries,* 190,
n. 56). Eumenes' reconstruction of the precinct of Athena involved the use of old
material for new inscriptions and the reinscription of a number of bases dating from
Attalos' reign. The first dated example of this use of old material is the base
celebrating victory in the second war against Nabis of Sparta and the ensuing
campaign against Antiochos III in Greece (*IvP* 62, = *Syll.*[3] 605 A), and since its
erection must be dated after 189, the beginning of the project culminating in an
enlarged precinct dedicated to Athena Nikephoros most plausibly belongs to this
period, along with the rebuilding of the Nikephorion outside the city, which pre-
ceded the first celebration of the panhellenic festival.

126   *Attalid Kingdom after the Treaty of Apameia*

Achaian League over Nabis of Sparta in 195.[188] This local affair
cannot however be the reason for the designation *Nikephoros* and
the cult activity associated with it; we must go back a few more
years to the Attalid victory in the alliance with Rome over Philip V
of Macedon in 197, on which account Polybios, doubtless reflecting Greek sentiment generally, praised Attalos I (xviii. 41. 9) as
ἀγωνιζόμενος ὑπὲρ τῆς τῶν Ἑλλήνων ἐλευθερίας.

It may be regarded as an understandable tribute on Eumenes'
part that shortly after his accession in 197 he instituted the cult of
Athena Nikephoros and the festival of the Nikephoria to celebrate
this victory for freedom won by his father. We know that Eumenes
was concerned to advance the status of Athena at Pergamon in
other ways, by propagating a spurious legendary origin of the cult,
for instance.[189] The first coinage bearing the legend *AΘHNAΣ
NIKHΦOPOY* should also be dated to his reign,[190] and we may
reasonably postulate that festivals called Nikephoria were celebrated in the 190s.

A further opportunity to promote the cult of Athena came with
the victory over Antiochos III in 189 and the Roman settlement of
the following year. During the years immediately following the
settlement Eumenes implemented that grand design of rebuilding
and extending Pergamon which occupied the rest of his reign and
required new circuit walls to encompass the much enlarged city.
Athena received much of the attention; a magnificent two-
storeyed temple, whose *propylon* bore a dedication to Athena
Nikephoros, the adjoining library housing Eumenes' precious
collection of books, and a new statue of Athena Parthenos modelled on the Athenian original betokened her continued importance.[191] Of equal importance to all this activity, and arising in part
out of it, was the reinstitution of the Nikephoria as a 'crowned'
panhellenic festival, first celebrated on this basis in 181, and attested by a series of documents concerning the recognition of the

[188] *IvP* 60, = *Syll.*[3] 595 A; cf. Kähler, *Gr. Fries*, 187, n. 43.
[189] *IvP* 156; cf. Ohlemutz, *Kulte*, 16.
[190] *MvP* I. 19, 20; Ohlemutz, *Kulte*, 39.
[191] Strabo xiii. 4. 2, 624, quoted below; see also the studies cited above, n. 2. For
the temple of Athena Nikephoros, see *IvP* 149; E. Rohde, *Griech. und röm. Kunst
in den staatlichen Museen zu Berlin* (1968), 49 and pl. 36.

new festival and the ἀσυλία of the Nikephorion, to which we must now turn.

The documents are decrees of the Aitolians and the Delphic Amphiktyons recording acceptance of Eumenes' invitation to the festival, which consisted according to this evidence of 'crowned' games, the musical part ἰσοπύθιος and the athletic and equine parts ἰσολύμπιος (the Amphiktyonic decree is dated to 182/1 and provides the chronological key to these events); a letter of Eumenes to a Carian city, most probably Iasos; and a letter to Kos, of which a second substantial fragment providing important new information was published by Segre in 1948.[192] A great deal of difficulty has been removed, and argument eliminated, from our understanding of these texts now that it has been convincingly shown that the reorganized celebrations attested by them took place regularly every five years, and at no time every three years, as was formerly taken for granted on the basis of a decree of Pergamon honouring Metris, the priestess of the ninth Nikephoria: the trieteric festival mentioned there is not the Nikephoria, but the Dionysia.[193] This conclusion confirms Segre's restoration of line 16 of Eumenes' letter to Kos, already supported by comparison with the texts dealing with the foundation of the Leukophryena at Magnesia on the Maeander, and all the ingenious proposals for explaining or avoiding the alleged inconsistency may be dispensed with.[194] Eumenes' invitation is, as Segre recognized, to a penteteric festival (Appendix iv, no. 12, lines 15–17): διεγν[ωκότες δὲ συντελεῖν αὐτῆι πα|ν]ήγυρίν τε διὰ πεν[ταετηρίδος καὶ μουσι-|κο]ὺς καὶ γυμνικοὺς [καὶ ἱππικοὺς ἀγῶνας].

In this letter Eumenes takes a personal credit for the establish-

---

[192] Aitolian decree: *Syll.*³ 629, = Daux, *Delphes*, 299–301, = *F. Delphes*, iii. 3. 240. Amphiktyonic decree: *Syll.*³ 630, = Daux, *Delphes*, 293–5, = *F. Delphes*, iii. 3. 261; cf. Daux, *BCH* lxxviii (1954), 370–1. Eumenes' letters: to a Carian city, probably Iasos: Welles, *RC* 49; cf. Segre (cited below); to Kos: Welles, *RC* 50; (with new fragment found in 1938) M. Segre *ap.* Robert, *Hellenica*, v (1948), 102–28; see Appendix iv, nos. 9–12. On the chronology, see L. Robert, *BCH* liv (1930), 332–8; G. Klaffenbach, *MDAI* iii (1950), 99–106.

[193] C. P. Jones, *Chiron*, iv (1974), 183–9.

[194] Segre envisaged two phases in the reorganization, but Klaffenbach showed conclusively that all the documents under consideration refer to the same procedure of 182/1. Klaffenbach's restoration in line 16, διὰ πεν[θ' ἡμέρων], taken to mean 'lasting for five days' is not possible: see J. and L. Robert, *Bull.* 1952, no. 127.

ment of the cult, the designation *Nikephoros* (lines 5–7, with Segre's restoration: [Νικηφόρον] | τε προσηγορεύκαμεν, [καλλίστην νομίζον]|τες εἶναι καὶ οἰκειοτάτη[ν τὴν προσω]|νυμίαν ταύτην), and two previous celebrations (lines 9–10: δὶς γὰρ ἤδη παρακληθέ[ντες ὑφ' ἡμῶν τάς τε] | πανηγύρεις ἃς τότ[ε κατηγγείλαμεν ἀποδέξασθε] | φιλοφρόνως). Even allowing for royal exaggeration, this evidence seems to confirm the conclusion we have already reached, that the festival of the Nikephoria so-called was an institution of Eumenes II in the first years of his reign, and not of his predecessor Attalos I. We saw reason earlier to associate the cult epithet *Nikephoros* with the victory over Philip V of Macedon in 197, and we may reasonably date the two 'earlier' celebrations of Nikephoria referred to in Eumenes' letter to the 190s, before the outbreak of war with Antiochos III intervened. A date in the years after the Antiochic War is not convincing, because Eumenes was then occupied with the restoration of the Pergamene Nikephorion, which Strabo describes in the context of the building programme datable to the 180s (xiii. 4. 2, 624): κατεσκεύασε δ' οὗτος τὴν πόλιν καὶ τὸ Νικηφόριον ἄλσει κατεφύτευσε καὶ ἀναθήματα καὶ βιβλιοθήκας καὶ τὴν ἐπὶ τοσόνδε κατοικίαν τοῦ Περγάμου τὴν νῦν οὖσαν ἐκεῖνος προσεφιλοκάλησε. The completion of the Nikephorion, and Eumenes' defeat of the Galatians and Prusias I of Bithynia celebrated in the decree of Telmessos which hailed Eumenes as *Soter* in 184/3, (Appendix iv, no. 7) doubtless provided the occasion for refounding the Nikephoria as στεφανῖται ἀγῶνες, as the decrees of the Aitolians and the Amphiktyons call them, but the inspiration of the new Nikephoria must be located in the defeat of Antiochos and the greatly increased authority attained by Eumenes in the resulting Roman settlement, just as the older Nikephoria had been the result on a more modest scale of the defeat of Philip V of Macedon.

The Nikephoria remained the most important Pergamene festival until after the formation of the Roman province, and the priestesses of Athena Nikephoros held an important position in the city's life, as inscribed bases honouring three of them attest: these are Metris, priestess of the ninth Nikephoria τοῦ στεφανίτου ἀγῶνος, 149 reckoning on a penteteric basis, the year of Attalos II's victory over Prusias II of Bithynia; Biton, priestess of the fourteenth Nikephoria in 129; and Asklepias, priestess of the eighteenth Nikephoria in 113.[195] It was probably a regular practice for the city to honour its priestess in a year in which Nikephoria were held; this is a further indication of the importance of the festival both to Pergamon and to the king, as an outward sign to the Greek world of his authority and influence after the Treaty of Apameia.

(iv) Officials of the Royal Administration

Like other Hellenistic monarchies, the Attalids evolved an administrative bureaucracy that was separate from the civil administration of the capital (to be discussed in chapter 7); most of our information comes as usual from epigraphical sources relating to the positions and activities of high-ranking officials.[196]

Around the king stood a group of close advisers, of whom some, but not all, were his relatives. At their head was the office of ὁ ἐπὶ τῶν πραγμάτων, one holder of which, Menogenes son of Menophantes, has recorded his title in a series of dedicatory inscriptions from Pergamon honouring members of the royal family.[197] The peak of his career is to be dated to the reign of Eumenes II, according to a decree from Nakrasa in which he is the honorand:[198]

[οἱ περὶ Νά]κρασον Μακεδόνες
[Μηνογ]ένην Μηνοφάντου,
[συγγενῆ] βασιλέως Εὐμένου,
[καὶ νο]μοφύλακα, ἀρετῆς ἕνεκεν
[καὶ ἀνδρα]γαθίας καὶ εὐνοίας
[πρός τε τὸ]μ βασιλέα καὶ ἑαυτούς.

This dedication shows that Menogenes was concerned with the

---

[195] Metris: *IvP* 167, = *OGIS* 299; Biton: *IvP* 223, = *OGIS* 322; Asklepias: *IvP* 226, = *OGIS* 324. For the chronology, see Jones 188–9, correcting the 'traditional' trieteric dates given by Ohlemutz, *Kulte*, 49–50, and elsewhere.

[196] There is a valuable synthesis of the evolution of the Hellenistic bureaucracies by Rostovtzeff, *SEHHW* ii. 1079 ff. For the Attalids, see Cardinali, *RP* 205 ff.; G. Corradi, *Studi Hellenistici* (Turin, 1929) 347 ff.; Hopp, *Untersuchungen*, 98–101.

[197] *IvP* 171–6, = *OGIS* 291–6. The title survives in full only in *IvP* 174 (*OGIS* 294), but it can be restored in all the others.

[198] *IvP*, ii. p. 504, no. 176a, = *OGIS* 290, with the revisions of L. Robert, *Villes*, 75–6. Robert's restoration ['Α]κρασον is not followed, however, since the singular form Νάκρασος (or Νάκρασον), which he rejected, is now attested: see P. Herrmann, *SB Wien* clxv. 1 (1969), 7–36; J. and L. Robert, *Bull.* 1970, no. 512.

affairs of an old subject city of the Attalids, and it is possible that the office he held gave him responsibility for the area of direct authority inherited from the rule of Eumenes I, the nature of which was discussed in chapter 2. No regional *strategos* is attested for this area, and it is very likely that, like other parts of the kingdom, it was administered by the officials of the royal administration.

Menogenes was most probably appointed to the office of ὁ ἐπὶ τῶν πραγμάτων in the later part of Eumenes' long reign, since his name appears again together with those of Athenaios and Sosandros, relatives of Attalos II, in a letter written by Attalos to the priest Attis at Pessinous, whose activities will be reviewed in the next chapter (Welles, *RC* 61). This chronology is supported by the evidence of a dedication made by Menogenes to Attalos II (*IvP* 174, = *OGIS* 294), in which Attalos is named without the royal title and was therefore not yet king:

> Ἄτταλον βασιλέω[ς Ἀττάλου]
> Μηνογένης Μηνοφάν[του,]
> ὁ ἐπὶ τῶν πραγμάτων, ἀρ[ετῆς ἕνεκεν]
> καὶ εὐνοίας τῆς εἰς ἑ[αυτόν].

The king drew heavily for members of the royal administration on a close circle of friends and relatives, as is shown by the frequent appearance in both literary and epigraphical records relating to Pergamon of the king's σύντροφοι (companions) and συγγενεῖς (relatives). Their service to the king assumed many forms, and the family about which we know most, that of Sosandros and Athenaios, provides the clearest examples.[199] The evidence is derived mainly from three royal letters concerning their priesthoods of Sabazios and Dionysos Kathegemon, of which the first (Welles, *RC* 65) is addressed by Attalos II to his cousin Athenaios. He calls Sosandros, the son-in-law of Athenaios, his σύντροφος, and says that he had been appointed priest of Dionysos Kathegemon by his brother Eumenes. He was therefore priest at the beginning of Attalos' reign, and according to the same letter he continued to hold the office until ill health prevented him. This chronological point is of importance, because it shows that he was still priest of Dionysos Kathegemon when he served as military

[199] *OGIS* 331, = Welles, *RC* 65–7; cf. Ohlemutz, *Kulte,* 90 ff. See also the dedication *IvP* 221, as interpreted by H. von Prott, *AM* xxvii (1902), 161 ff.

commander of a Pergamene force which defended Elaia against Prusias II of Bithynia in 157/6, an event recorded by Polybios (xxxii. 25.10): (Prusias) οὐδὲν δὲ πράττειν δυνάμενος διὰ τὸ Σώσανδρον τὸν τοῦ βασιλέως σύντροφον εἰσεληλυθότα μετὰ στρατιωτῶν εἴργειν αὐτοῦ τὰς ἐπιβολάς, ἀπῆρεν ἐπὶ Θνατείρων. We also learn from Attalos' letter to Athenaios, and from a letter of Attalos III to Kyzikos, dated to 135 BC, that Sosandros' son-in-law Athenaios was appointed to the important priesthood of Sabazios during Sosandros' lifetime, and that when Sosandros died, Athenaios succeeded him, combining the two priesthoods, of Dionysos Kathegemon and Sabazios, in one person.[200]

It is clear then from this evidence that the king was served in his royal administration by families rather than individuals, the son (or son-in-law) succeeding to the position held by his father even when he held another position already. The priesthood of Sabazios was of course a special matter in that Sabazios was particularly associated with Queen Stratonike, who brought the cult from Cappadocia, and it was natural that the priesthood would be preserved in the family of Sosandros and Athenaios, who were related to the royal family: we cannot therefore reasonably infer a general policy from this instance alone. There is however further evidence pointing to the same conclusion.

First to be considered are two inscriptions attesting σύντροφοι of Attalos II. One, from Pergamon,[201] is a popular dedication for one Apollonides son of Theophilos:

> ὁ δῆμο[ς]
> Ἀπολλωνίδην Θεοφίλ[ου],
> τὸν σύντροφον τοῦ βασιλ[έως,]
> ἀρετῆς ἕνεκεν καὶ εὐνοίας [τῆς]
> 5 πρός τε τὸν βασιλέα καὶ ἑα[υτόν].

The other is a dedication of Attalos II from the Athenian agora in honour of another Theophilos, undoubtedly the brother of the Apollonides attested at Pergamon:[202]

---

[200] See, in addition to the references given in the previous note, my remarks on the cult of Sabazios at Pergamon and its political implications, in *BSA* lxvi (1971), 8–9.

[201] *IvP* 179, = *OGIS* 334.

[202] *Hesperia*, xxiii (1954), 252, no. 33, = *SEG* xiv. 127; cf. *Hesperia*, xxvi (1957), 86; Habicht, *Gnomon*, xxx (1958), 317.

[βασ]ιλεὺς Ἄτταλος βα[σιλέως Ἀττάλου]
καὶ βασιλίσσ[η]ς Ἀ[πολλωνίδος]
[Θ]εόφιλον Θε.........|/εα
[τ]ὸν ἑαυτοῦ σύντροφον ἀρετῆ[ς] ἕνεκ[α]
[τῆ]ς εἰς ἑαυτὸν καὶ τὸν δῆμον τὸν Ἀθηναίων.

We turn now to another relationship. A certain Andronikos is mentioned by Polybios (xxxii. 16) as leader of a Pergamene embassy to Rome during the reign of Attalos II which pleaded the case against Prusias II of Bithynia, and in the *Mithridateios* of Appian (*Mithr.* 4–5) he figures prominently in a subsequent plot to overthrow Prusias. He was evidently an important figure about whom we know all too little, and we may, with Fränkel, identify him as the honorand of a fragmentary decree which deals *inter alia* with the proceedings of an embassy, and calls the honorand a σύντροφος of Attalos II:[203]

[ἐπὶ πρυτάνεως ..] οδώρου· γνώμη σ[τρατηγῶν· ἔγνω δῆμος· ἐπεὶ
........]
[... σύντρο]φος τοῦ βασιλέως ἔν τε τοῖ[ς ἀναγκαιοτάτοις καιροῖς]
[σπουδ]αίας χρείας παρείσχηται τῶι τε βασιλ[εῖ καὶ τῶι δήμωι κτλ.]

A dedication of the same reign from the Samian Heraion honours a man whom we may identify as Andronikos' brother: Philopoimen son of Andronikos, *strategos* and 'keeper of the seal':[204]

> βασιλεὺς Ἄτταλος
> βασιλέως Ἀττάλου
> Φιλοποίμενα Ἀνδρονίκου
> τὸν στρατηγὸν καὶ ἐπὶ τῆς
> 5   σφραγῖδος ἀρετῆς ἕνεκα
> καὶ ἀνδραγαθίας καὶ τῆς
> πρὸς αὐτὸν εὐνοίας
> Ἥραι.

This Philopoimen was commander of the Pergamene forces present at Corinth in 146 (Paus. vii. 16. 1 and 8), and according to an anecdote recorded by Plutarch (*Mor.* 792) was the favourite adviser of Attalos Philadelphos towards the end of his life.

---

[203] *IvP* 224, = *OGIS* 323. The phi of σύντροφος is discernible from a squeeze I made of the stone in Berlin in 1969.

[204] *AM* xliv (1919), 30, no. 16, = *SEG* i. 374, = *IGR* iv. 1712; a photograph will be found *ap.* Tölle, *Die Antike Stadt Samos* (Mainz, 1969), 26. Another holder of the office of ἐπὶ τῆς σφραγῖδος was the *strategos* Demetrios at Ephesos (Appendix iv, no. 25; see above, 88); see on this title Bengtson, *Strat.* ii. 209.

The part played by these σύντροφοι, collectively also called ἀναγκαῖοι, was an active and important one, both in implementing royal policy, as did Menogenes at Nakrasa, and in helping to form it, as we see most clearly in the letter written by Attalos II to Attis already mentioned. Attalos had evidently met Attis at Apameia, and the two had discussed the possibility of military action against a band of Galatians (see below, chapter 5); returning to Pergamon, Attalos consulted the ἀναγκαῖοι: ἐλθόντων ἡμῶν | εἰς Πέργαμον καὶ συναγαγόντος μου οὐ μόνον Ἀθήναιον | καὶ Σώσανδρον καὶ Μηνογένην, ἀλλὰ καὶ ἑτέρους πλείο|νας τῶν ἀναγκαίων κτλ. It was one of these, Chloros, who urged a policy of conciliation with Rome, and the king himself finally subscribed to it, although the decision remained his.[205] No other document of the Attalid chancery illustrates so well the factors which determined royal decisions and the means by which they were reached.

Apart from the office of ὁ ἐπὶ τῶν πραγμάτων and the general designations σύντροφοι and συγγενεῖς we do not know what titles, if any, these close advisers held. There are other terms attested by epigraphical evidence which connote those especially favoured by the king, but these terms are of a generic nature, and conform to the pattern established in other Hellenistic kingdoms, where various grades of φίλοι are attested.[206] It may be convenient to list the evidence relating to the Attalids at this point.

(1) φίλος

IG ii.[2] 945 (Syll.[3] 651), lines 8–9. Decree honouring Diodoros (Eumenes II): Διόδωρος φί[λος] | ὑπάρχων τῶι βασιλεῖ Εὐμένει. This is the only Attalid example of the unqualified title φίλος, and examples of higher grades of φίλοι are likewise rare: one such is Megon of Ephesos, who is mentioned by Eumenes II in letters written to Iasos and Kos concerning the reorganization of the

[205] Attalos uses the word κρίνω of this final decision: ἔκρινον οὖν εἰς μὲν τ[ὴ]ν Ῥώμην ἀεὶ πέμπειν κτλ. Cf. Cardinali, *RP* 205–6, and on the significance of the word κρίνω in connoting a royal decision, Welles, *RC*, p. 83.
[206] On these titles, see G. Corradi, *Studi Hell.* 318 ff.; A. D. Momigliano, *Athenaeum*, xi (1933), 136–41; Holleaux, *Études*, iii. 220 ff. (from *BCH* 1933). On the Seleukid φίλοι see also Bickermann, *Inst. Sél.* 41 ff. It is important to note that the graded status of the φίλοι (four grades according to Momigliano) were evidently common to all the Hellenistic monarchies, and the Attalids were therefore following normal practice.

Pergamene Nikephoria (see above, iii):

Kos: Appendix iv, no. 12:[207] Μέγωνα [᾽Εφέσιον, τῶν φίλων τῶν προ-?] | τιμωμένων παρ᾽ ἡμῖν.

Iasos: Appendix iv, no. 11: Μ]έγωνά τε τῶν φίλων ἐν τιμῆι [τῆι πρωτῆι (or μεγίστηι) παρ᾽ ἡμῖν ὄντα (or ὄντα παρ᾽ ἡμῖν)].

Another is attested by a dedication from Attondae (*MAMA* vi. 68): Σόλων ᾽Αττάλου, φίλος πρῶτος.

These titles are more common in the Seleukid, Pontic, and, above all, the Ptolemaic administrations,[208] and it is perhaps not surprising that they should appear less frequently in our evidence for the more closely centralized Attalid administration.

(2) παρὰ τῶι βασιλεῖ διατρίβων, κτλ.

IG ii.² 947, lines 15–17. Decree honouring Theophilos (?166/5): ἐπειδὴ Θεό[φιλ]ος Περγ[α|μηνὸς εὔνο]υς ὑπάρχων τῶι [δή]μ[ω]ι πρότερόν τε διατρίβων [παρὰ τῶι βασι|λεῖ Εὐμένει] καὶ ἐν τιμε[ῖ ὦν] παρ᾽ αὐτῶι κτλ.

This is surely the man we have already met as σύντροφος of Eumenes II; the present titles may then be considered as honorary rather than constitutionally specific.

Appendix iv, no. 26 (decree of Kyme): ᾽Επίγονος Δαμοκράτευς Ταραντῖνος | διατρίβων παρὰ τῷ βασιλεῖ ᾽Αττάλῳ.

(3) οἰκεῖος

IG ii.² 953, lines 6–7. Decree honouring a man whose name has not survived on the stone (160/59): [οἰκ]εῖος ὢν τοῦ βασιλέως Εὐμένους κτλ.

(4) τῶν προτιμωμένων

IG ii.² 946 (*Syll.*³ 655, with the supplements of Ad. Wilhelm, *Wien. Anz.* 1921, 81), line 8: Μένανδρος Περγαμηνὸς τ[ῶν μάλιστα πισ-τευομένων καὶ τιμωμένων] παρὰ τῶι βασιλεῖ Εὐμένει κτλ.

Although the evidence is not copious, it seems likely from the cases reviewed that these were in the main honorary titles with no particular constitutional or administrative significance; the case of Theophilos bears this out, as do Menogenes and Philopoimen,

---

[207] The restoration is that of Holleaux, *Études*, iii. 222, which is preferable to that of Momigliano, art. cit. 140: [τῶν πρώτων (*sc. φίλων*) καὶ προ]τιμωμένων.

[208] See the studies cited above, n. 206.

because they had specific titles in addition to the apparently honorary ones. We may conclude, then, that a number of the royal advisers did not have official titles designating particular spheres of authority or activity, but were employed in diverse capacities as the king chose.

It is important to point here to the fact that at least three citizens of Ephesos served important roles in the royal administration. One, Megon, has been mentioned above, as a φίλος of the highest category. A second, Hikesios, was ὁ κατασταθεὶς ἐπ' Αἰγίνας (*Syll.*³ 642), and a third, whose name is not known, was appointed by Attalos II to be the mentor of his nephew, the future Attalos III (Appendix iv, no. 24). It is probable then that when Ephesos became Attalid in 188, it provided the royal administration with a number of officials who were able to reach high rank, and it is not surprising that the king drew on the considerable administrative experience of this city. This policy corresponds to the high regard for Ephesos which we have elsewhere attributed to the Attalid kings in other contexts, but the extent to which this policy was applied, and whether it was applied to other cities besides Ephesos, cannot in the present state of the evidence be adequately determined. It is significant in this regard, however, that Ephesos and Tralles, as we saw earlier, played an important part as royal mints after the Treaty of Apameia in addition to the principal mint at Pergamon.

5

THE GALATIANS

An event which was to have the greatest repercussions throughout the subsequent history of Asia Minor was the entry of the Galatians in 278/7,[1] at the very time when Philetairos was consolidating his position at Pergamon. Records of their activity and of their relations with the dynasts at Pergamon are naturally more complete for the reigns of Attalos I and his successors, while for the first thirty years or so of their occupation we rely on the chance evidence of contemporary documents and traditions preserved in the works of local historians and transmitted to us by later writers. It is only by these means that we can examine their methods and aims, as well as the reactions of the Greek cities and other inhabitants of Asia Minor. The only useful reference to the Galatians' activities as a whole is a curious one in Strabo (xii. 5. 1, 566): κατέσχον δὲ τὴν χώραν ταύτην (i.e. Galatia) οἱ Γαλάται πλανηθέντες πολὺν χρόνον καὶ καταδραμόντες τὴν ὑπὸ τοῖς Ἀτταλικοῖς βασιλεῦσι χώραν καὶ τοῖς Βιθυνοῖς, ἕως παρ' ἑκόντων ἔλαβον τὴν νῦν Γαλατίαν καὶ Γαλλογραικίαν λεγομένην.[2] This is the only evidence of a general nature to suggest that the Attalid rulers were concerned with the settlement of Galatians, although clearly it cannot be accepted as it stands. There is specific evidence of this policy in the case of Attalos I, as we shall see, but none refers to settlement of Galatians within Pergamene territory. That Philetairos won a victory over a band of Galatians seems to be shown by a metrical dedication inscribed on a base at Delos; the Philetairos is not specified, but the letter-forms point almost cer-

---

[1] Pausanias x. 23. 14 dates the entry of the Galatians into Asia Minor to the year of the Athenian archon Demokles, 278/7. See, in general, F. Stähelin, *Gesch. der kleinasiatischen Galater*, 7 ff.; M. Launey, *Recherches*, i. 490 ff.; M. Wörrle, 'Antiochos I, Achaios der Ältere und die Galater', in *Chiron*, v (1975), 59–87. On the chronology, see M. Launey, *REA* xlvi (1944), 218, n. 2, and below, n. 6.

[2] References to particular methods used by the Galatians in their raids can be found in Livy xxxviii. 16. 12–13, and in the decree of Priene mentioned in the text (*IvPr* 17, = *OGIS* 765).

tainly to Philetairos the Founder.[3] If authentic, this victory occurred at about the same time as the victory of Antiochos I, attested
by Appian but undated;[4] the two battles may have been connected
with the same subsidiary movement of the Galatians but there is no
reason to believe that the celebration of Philetairos' success was
due to participation in Antiochos' victory rather than to a separate
victory.

In addition to his own direct action against the Galatians
Philetairos is known to have offered substantial assistance to at
least one independent city, Kyzikos.[5] The chronology of
Philetairos' donations is fairly well established; they include
money, supplies, and contributions to the φυλακὴ τῆς χώρας,
notably in 278/7, when a band of Galatians passed close to the
territory of Kyzikos on its route to the interior of Asia Minor.[6] In

[3] *IG* xi. 4. 1105, = Durrbach, *Choix*, 31. This inscription is discussed above and
dated to the reign of Attalos I, 31 n. 8.

[4] *Syr.* 65. Cf. Stähelin, 12–14; the colourful account in Lucian, *Zeuxis* 8–11, is
defended by B. Bar-Kochva, *Proc. Camb. Phil. Soc.* cxcix (1973), 1–8, who dates
the battle to 'shortly after April 272'. Segre's date, 278/7 (*Athenaeum,* viii (1930),
53–6) seems to me to be too early in view of the rest of the chronology; *c.* 272, after
the end of the first Syrian war, is preferable, although a date shortly before the
outbreak of this war, *c.* 276/5, is also possible (so Launey, *REA* xlvi (1944), 234, n. 1;
Magie, *Roman Rule* ii. 731, n. 12). See now M. Wörrle, *Chiron,* v (1975), 65–72.

[5] *OGIS* 748; see above, 15 n. 20.

[6] The inscription records the donations of Philetairos listed according to the years
of the Kyzikene eponymous magistrates, as follows:

Gorgippides	money for ἀγῶνες and φυλακὴ τῆς χώρας.
Bouphantides	ἀτέλεια τῆς λείας.
Phoinix	φυλακὴ τῆς χώρας.
Poseidon	money εἰς ἔλαιον καὶ συναγωγὴν τῶν νέων.
Diomedon	supplies ἐν τῶι πολέμωι τῶι πρὸς τοὺς Γαλάτας γενομένωι.

The first editors dated Diomedon to 278/7 from the reference under his name to a
Galatian war; this chronology however raises a difficulty in dating Gorgippides as
early as 282/1. Dittenberger (*OGIS* ad loc., n. 7) argued an alternative chronology,
associating the reference ἐπὶ Βουφαντίδου, πολεμηθείσης τῆς χώρας with the wars
involving Antiochos I, Nikomedes of Bithynia, and Antigonos Gonatas, thus making Phoinix the magistrate of 278/7, the year of the Galatians' arrival in Asia Minor.
This chronology has been convincingly endorsed by Launey, in *REA* xlvi (1944),
217 ff., where a relief from Kyzikos showing Herakles fighting an opponent (which
Launey showed to be a Galatian), and also dated ἐπὶ Φοίνικος ἱππάρχου (cf. *BCH*
lvi (1932), pl. xxv), was shown to have represented an appeal from the city to the
god when threatened by an attack from the Galatians under Loutarios; these,
according to Livy's account of their entry into Asia Minor (xxxviii. 16), had to pass
near Kyzikos to rejoin the Galatians under Leonnorios. M. Segre adopted a
chronology earlier than this by two years (*Athenaeum,* viii (1930), 488 ff.), and
subsequently one earlier by one year (*Athenaeum,* xii (1934), 437, n. 2).

gratitude, the city instituted a festival named Philetaireia in his honour (see below, chapter 6).

The aims of the Galatians seem from the beginning to have been settlement and security. Their attack on Ilion, according to Strabo a 'kind of village-town' (κωμόπολίς τις ἦν), and according to Demetrios of Skepsis as recorded by Strabo in the same passage (xiii. 1. 27, 594), very much in decline before the Antiochic War, was evidently inspired by their need for a stronghold: Ἡγησιάναξ δὲ τοὺς Γαλάτας περαιωθέντας ἐκ τῆς Εὐρώπης ἀναβῆναι μὲν εἰς τὴν πόλιν δεομένους ἐρύματος, παραχρῆμα δ' ἐκλιπεῖν διὰ τὸ ἀτείχιστον. When defeated by the dynasts of Asia Minor, they were dealt with by the assignation of settlements; after Attalos' great victory they were settled in the part of Greater Phrygia which became Galatia, in all probability by Mithridates II of Pontos, who had received this territory on the occasion of his marriage with Laodike, the sister of Seleukos Kallinikos.[7] It was probably for similar reasons that the Galatians entered the service of kings as mercenaries or as allies:[8] Attalos of Pergamon after their defeat (see below), Antiochos Hierax, the kings of Bithynia and, above all, the kings of Pontos. The Καρικά of Apollonios, according to Stephanos of Byzantion, s.v. Ἄγκυρα, referred to the settlement by Mithridates I (died 266) and Ariobarzanes (266–256) of Galatians in alliance with them against Egypt; this is good evidence that the Galatians attached themselves from the beginning to the kings of Pontos, by whom they were given lands in exchange for military service, rather than to the kings of Bithynia, from one of whom they had received the initial invitation to cross into Asia.[9] We have records of three significant Galatian revolts in these years: the first in Pontos in the reign of Ariobarzanes in which the king himself perished, the second during the war of the Seleukid brothers, and the third during the expedition undertaken by Attalos I of Pergamon in 218 BC. In the last two cases, where we have evidence, the

[7] Strabo xii. 5. 1, 566, quoted above; Pausanias i. 4. 5, 8. 2. Justin xxxviii. 5. 3 (marriage-alliance between Mithridates II and Seleukos Kallinikos, *c*. 245). I follow here the conclusions of Ed. Meyer, *Geschichte des Koenigreichs Pontos* (Leipzig, 1879), 43–51, as offering the best explanation of the Strabo passage. For other views, see Magie, *Roman Rule,* ii. 731, n. 13.

[8] On the status of the Galatians serving in the kings' armies see above, 29 n. 4.

[9] *FGrHist* 740, F14. The death of Mithridates I: Diod. xxiii. See Ed. Meyer, op. cit. (n. 7), 43 ff.

Galatians were dealt with by means of settlement.[10] For this reason it seems likely that during the years when Philetairos and Eumenes I successively ruled at Pergamon, some Galatians, who (as we know) plundered western Asia Minor and were defeated by Philetairos, were settled in the small area of Pergamene territory then established and formed an important part of its consolidation.

For the reign of Attalos I the evidence becomes clearer and more substantial. We have already found reason to relate the activities of the Galatians in the early years of his reign to the individual alliances he concluded with numerous Greek cities and confirmed in 218 (see above, chapter 3), and this point can now be elaborated. There is a body of local evidence concerning Galatian attacks on Greek cities; in addition to the evidence for Ilion, already cited, we have a number of honorary decrees voted by Greek cities in recognition of the bravery of individuals during Galatian attacks. A decree of Priene honours a certain Sotas for bravery and initiative in defending the city against a Galatian attack, and a similar decree of Erythrai honours the entire board of *strategoi* for the part they played in defending their city against an attack from Galatians under Leonnorios. Among Philetairos' donations to Kyzikos, according to the decree of that city already discussed (*OGIS* 748), were quantities of corn contributed ἐν τῶι πολέμωι | τῶι πρὸς τοὺς Γαλάτας γ[ενομένωι] (lines 18–19). A private dedication of a man from Thyateira thanking Apollo for rescuing the man's son ἁλοὺς ὑπὸ τῶν Γαλάτων may also be connected with these activities.[11] In the case of Miletos, as of Ilion, a Galatian raid was recorded (according to Parthenius) by a local historian, Aristodemos of Nysa, and the city's resistance is celebrated in an epigram attributed to Anyte (*AP* vii. 492).[12] Finally, an inscription from Denizli

---

[10] Revolt and settlement under Antiochos Hierax: Justin xxvii. 2; under Attalos I: Polyb. v. 78.1–5.

[11] Priene: *IvPr* 17, = *OGIS* 765. Erythrai: see above, 29 n. 5. Thyateira: Keil-von Premerstein, *Zweite Reise*, no. 19; Magie, *Roman·Rule*, ii. 730–1, n. 11. See in general on this evidence M. Wörrle, *Chiron*, v (1975), 63–4.

[12] Parthenius viii. 1 ff. This evidence may however relate to later events: see Rehm, *Milet*, i. 245; Parthenius' story of a man of Miletos who travelled to Gaul in search of his captured wife implies a Greek awareness of the Gauls and their geography that is not easily attributable to the early third centrury, before the Romans appeared on the scene: see A. D. Momigliano, *Alien Wisdom* (Cambridge, 1975), 57–60; A. S. F. Gow and D. L. Page, *The Greek Anthology, Hellenistic Epigrams,* Anyte xxiii (commentary, ii. 89 ff., 103 f.), = Page, *Epigr. Graeca,* Anyte xxii: the epigram relates the suicide of Milesian women captured by the Galatians.

near Izmir published in 1975 records a decree of the settlements of Neonteichos and Kiddioukome, dated to the month Peritios of the forty-fifth year of the joint rule of Kings Antiochos and Seleukos (=Jan. 267), honouring two officials of the elder Achaios, Banabelos and Lachares, for redeeming prisoners captured by the Galatians in the πόλεμος Γαλατικός.[13]

Evidently then traditions developed on the theme of resistance to the Galatians in the first half of the third century, a resistance in which the Greek cities concerned took considerable pride. With the Greek cities Attalos I of Pergamon was equally a victim of the Galatians; he too chose to defy them by refusing the usual tribute they exacted,[14] and it is in this context that the alliances concluded by Attalos should be placed, although, as we have seen (above, chapter 3), they subsequently served other purposes. We now see more clearly the significance of Attalos' great victory at the river Kaikos and his assumption of the royal title; as successful defender of the Greek cities of western Asia Minor he could justly call himself king.

According to the literary sources the Galatians now moved eastwards and were settled in territory belonging to Mithridates II of Pontos. Some, however, evidently remained in Attalid territory to serve in Attalos' armies, including, according to Polybios (v. 77. 2), the army which accompanied him on his military expedition of 218. We have found reason to believe that this policy was a common one perhaps already exercised by his two predecessors as well as by other rulers in Asia Minor. The implication of Polybios' statement is that these Galatians had been settled in Attalid territory, and we may infer from what we have seen of their intentions that this settlement was a major incentive for enlisting with Attalos, just as the Galatians who served with the kings of Pontos were rewarded with lands in their kingdom.

We may conclude then that the Galatians who swarmed into Asia Minor in 278/7 resorted to two chief means of survival: their periodic demands from dynasts and cities alike for tribute in exchange for freedom from attack, and their enlistment in the service

---

[13] M. Wörrle, *Chiron*, v (1975), 59–87.

[14] Livy xxxviii. 16; on the nature of this tribute, see above, ch. 3. The Galatians evidently demanded tribute from the cities as well as the dynasts, as the decree of Erythrai mentioned above shows. Cf. Magie, *Roman Rule*, ii. 732, n. 15.

of the dynasts, from the invitation of Nikomedes to their partial settlement by Mithridates of Pontos. As far as the Attalids are concerned, however, they no longer served in any significant way as mercenaries after the reign of Attalos I; from that time they appear in our sources rather as their enemies. In fact, relations between the Galatians and Attalos I also are not straightforward; we have seen that he took a band of Galatians with him on his expedition of 218, but his intention may have been as much to find a location for their settlement as to use them as a contribution to his military power, a consideration that is indicated by their attitude when they revolted, and by Attalos' readiness to comply with their demands for settlement.[15]

Attalos' great victory at the river Kaikos should be regarded, according to the evidence of his monuments, as a victory over the Galatians fighting for their own ends, and not as a part of his later war with Antiochos Hierax, with whom Galatians served as mercenaries,[16] but there is no indication in the admittedly scant evidence of a major Galatian war fought in its own right until the hostilities of the 160s which we shall consider very shortly. We have in this connection to recognize two aspects of the Galatians' activities: their raids on Greek cities and on the territories of Bithynia and Pergamon, in which context should be placed Attalos' victory at the river Kaikos; and their co-operation as mercenaries with the enemies of Pergamon, namely Antiochos Hierax, Prusias I of Bithynia, and Pharnakes I of Pontos, which became the principal feature of Galatian hostility to Pergamon in the reigns of Attalos' successors.[17] We have seen that during the war with Pharnakes in particular, Pergamene interests in Galatia were directly threatened, and there is some evidence that in the years following this war Eumenes undertook to consolidate his authority in the area, an essential step as long as the Galatians were prepared to fight alongside his enemies. We may now turn to consider the chronology and significance of this activity.

[15] Polyb. v. 78. Note especially 78. 3: (Attalos) χρείαν μὲν αὐτῶν οὐδεμίαν ὁλοσχερῆ κομιζόμενος. Up to this time the Galatians had shown themselves to be precarious allies, often proving to be as much a liability as an asset to the kings they served; see the cases cited by Launey, *Recherches*, i. 492 ff.

[16] Magie, *Roman Rule*, ii. 734, n. 20; see above, ch. 3, and below, Appendix ii.

[17] Antiochos Hierax: see above, ch. 3. Prusias I: 79. Pharnakes: 79; cf. Polyb. xxv. 2. 4.

142   *The Galatians*

After the defeat of Perseus of Macedon, the Galatians, Perseus' former allies, launched a surprise attack on Eumenes. A Pergamene embassy was sent to Rome in 168, and P. Licinius Crassus, the Roman consul of 171, arrived in Asia in 167 ostensibly to patch up a peace at Smyrna.[18] The initiative failed, however, and Eumenes resorted to direct military intervention in Galatia. We have only fragmentary and incidental references to this intervention in the literary sources: most important of these is a fragment of Diodoros' history (xxxi.14), which lacks context but which informs us that Eumenes πᾶν τὸ Γαλάτων ἔθνος ὑποχείριον ἐποιήσατο.[19] This strongly implies an intention to retain control in Galatia beyond the immediate consequences of military conquest, and accordingly indicates a new feature in Attalid policy with regard to the Galatians.

Further evidence in this regard may be found in Eumenes' correspondence with Attis, the priest of Kybele at Pessinous, one of the principal religious centres of Galatia.[20] According to this correspondence it was through Attis' collaboration that the Attalids maintained a control over the country, or rather the part of it

[18] Polyb. xxix. 22. 4; cf. xxv. 6.3; xxix. 9. 13; Livy xlv. 34. 10. Cf. Niese, iii. 200. For P. Licinius Crassus, see T. R. S. Broughton, *Magistrates of the Roman Republic* (New York, 1951), i. 416 (cos. 171), 435 (envoy in 167).

The Pergamene embassy to Rome in 168 included Eumenes' brother Attalos (Polyb. xxx. 1–3; Livy xlv. 19), and Krates of Mallos, the foremost Stoic in Pergamon and a leading figure in Pergamene scholarship (Suetonius, *de grammaticis* 2: *Crates . . . missus ad senatum ab Attalo rege . . . sub ipsam Ennii mortem* (= 169)). In view of the date, the name of the king must be a mistake for Eumenes II, as R. Pfeiffer has indicated (*History of Classical Scholarship*, 235, n. 2); the suggestion of Hansen, *Attalids*, 121, n. 166, that for *ab Attalo* we should read *cum Attalo*, does not explain *rege*, since Attalos II did not share the royal title this early; Pfeiffer's approach is therefore the correct one. On Krates at Pergamon, see Pfeiffer, 235–46.

It is clear from Polybios' account of Attalos' mission that the Senate's main concern at this time was with limiting Eumenes' power, rather than with solving the Galatian problem; note especially Polyb. xxx. 1. 6: τῶν γὰρ πλείστων Ῥωμαίων ἀπηλλοτριουμένων τῆς τοῦ βασιλέως Εὐμένους εὐνοίας.

[19] A probable victory monument of this war is *IvP* 165 (with an additional fragment published in *AM* xxvii (1902), 90, no. 74). A Delphian decree accepting a festival of Sardis for Athena and King Eumenes refers to Eumenes' war as [τὸν μέγιστον] κίνδυνον (*OGIS* 305, lines 11–12, with Dittenberger's note 12). I have already emphasized the importance of Eumenes' Galatian victory to his standing in the Greek world (above, 80); this importance was first realized by Cardinali, *RP* 103 ff.

[20] *OGIS* 315, = Welles, *RC* 55–61.

centred on Pessinous, and the second of the letters shows that they
personally supported Attis' position at Pessinous in the face of
rivalry from his own family, doubtless as a quid pro quo for his
co-operation (Welles, *RC* 56, lines 3-7): ἐκομισάμην τὴν παρὰ σου
ἐπιστολήν, | ἐν ἧι διεσεσαφήκεις μου περὶ τῶν [τ]ε κα|τὰ τὸν
ἀδελφόν σου Αἰοιόριγα γεγραμ|μένων. ὀρθῶς οὖν καθ᾽ ὑπερ-
βολὴν δι|ίστω κτλ. The position of Attis at Pessinous is in some
ways comparable to that of the priest Korris at Labraunda in the
third century; both seem to have held their positions as of family
right, and both depended largely on the favour of the dynasts.[21]

The letters are mainly concerned with the need for periodic
military activity in Galatia, and there are several references to
Pergamene armies stationed there. The permanence of this situation is further indicated by the complaints of Prusias II of Bithynia
to the Roman Senate in 165/4 that Galatia remained under the
occupation of Pergamene troops, as though the need for them, that
is, the duration of Eumenes' war, was already over.[22] This is not to
say, however, that Galatia was treated as an Attalid province on
the lines of the territories acquired in 188 BC. The evidence points
rather to a series of major campaigns undertaken in the early 160s,
which strengthened Attalid influence in the area but required continued military occupation and secret collaboration with Attis at
Pessinous. It was important, as the Galatians' activities in recent
years had shown, that Attalid influence in Galatia should be maintained, but it is extremely unlikely that the Attalids ever regarded
Galatia as part of their kingdom, or controlled more than certain
parts of the country at any one time.

Under Attalos II this already limited control in Galatia evidently
weakened. The last substantial item in the correspondence with
Attis is a letter in which Attalos refers to the need for military
action, but admits that this course could not be adopted for fear of
Rome's disapproval.[23] There is evidence none the less that Attalos
maintained military activity in the area on a limited scale. According to Trogus (*Prol.* xxxiv), *mortuo rege Asiae Eumene suffectus
Attalus bellum cum Selegensibus habuit et cum rege Prusia.* As we

21 See, on Korris, J. Crampa, *Labraunda,* iii. 1. 75 ff.
22 Polyb. xxx. 20. 2–3; cf. Niese ii. 200 ff.
23 *OGIS* 315 VI, = Welles, *RC* 60.

have seen, this war is to be dated to the 150s, in the first years of Attalos' reign. It was clearly not a major war of the kind fought by Eumenes in the 160s; its main objective was evidently to maintain authority in the area of Galatia adjoining Selge and Amlada, and to secure the allegiance of frontier positions such as these.[24] This evidence supports the implications of Attalos' letter to Attis, that he wished to avoid total commitment in Galatia, and had no intention of attempting to control the entire country.

It is possible, furthermore, that Galatians served as allies or as mercenaries in the pay of Prusias II during the war with Attalos, as can be inferred from the words of Trogus just quoted: *bellum cum Selegensibus. . . et cum rege Prusia*. Although the evidence is too limited to allow certainty on this point, it is clear that Attalos' control over Galatia continued to be piecemeal and tentative; that his wars were of a local nature not designed to support a direct administration in the country as a whole; and that vigorous measures were taken to establish the co-operation of the important strategic positions at Selge and Amlada. This evidence, then, confirms the conclusions reached for Eumenes' reign as to the status of Galatia in relation to the Attalid Kingdom as a whole. Galatia could never be regarded as a single entity, let alone be controlled as such, but it comprised distinct groups of occupation such as that centred on Pessinous. It was with one or another but not with all of these groups that the dynasts of Asia Minor concluded alliances and from one or another that they recruited mercenaries from time to time as the need arose in the third and second centuries BC. Eumenes II and Attalos II of Pergamon did not undertake military intervention in Galatia in order to increase their kingdom but in order to counter the influence of their enemies, who rightly saw the Galatians as a means of containing Attalid power and authority.

[24] See above, 102.

6

ROYAL CULTS

Like their contemporaries in other dynasties, the Attalids received a wide range of secular and religious honours from the cities of Asia Minor and the Greek mainland, and the nature and scale of these honours is a reflection of their authority and renown in the eyes of those who honoured them: again the reign of Attalos I and the creation of the new kingdom in 188 appear to mark the important stages in their development.

Certain distinctions have to be borne in mind in any consideration of Hellenistic royal cults, and these are especially important in the case of the Attalids. The first, and most important, is the difference between worship and deification.[1] From the reign of Attalos I onwards Attalid kings were the objects of wide and varied cult practice, both within and beyond the limits of their kingdom, but it was not until after 188 BC that any of them was called a god in name, and then it was usually done after death, with the single known exception of Miletos, whose circumstances were reviewed in a previous chapter.[2] A second distinction concerns motive. It was one thing for the king to enforce a centralized imperial cult of himself or members of his family, of the kind now well attested for the Seleukids under Antiochos III, and quite another for a city to institute an individual cult on its own initiative and in circumstances arising from its relations with a particular king.[3] We

---

[1] Habicht, *Gottmenschentum,* 206 ff.; see also the remarks of Préaux, *Monde hell.* i. 238 ff.

[2] See above, 114–19.

[3] For the centralized Seleukid cults, see Holleaux, *Études,* iii. 165–81 (from *BCH* 1930); Welles, *RC* 36–7; Wilcken, *SB Berlin,* 1938, 298–321; Robert, *Hellenica,* vii (1949), 1–29 and *CRAI* 1967, 281–94. For the Attalid cults, see in general Cardinali, *RP* 139–72; Daux, *BCH* lix (1935), 210–30; *AvP* ix. 84 ff.; Habicht, *Gottmenschentum,* 124–6; and, for cults associated with Dionysos, H. von Prott, *AM* xxvii (1902), 161–88 (with Robert, *Ét. anat.* 25–6); Ohlemutz, *Kulte,* 90 ff.; P. M. Fraser, *REA* liv (1952), 242 ff.; A. W. Pickard-Cambridge, *Dram. Festivals,* 279 ff. Hansen, *Attalids,* 453 ff. adds nothing of importance to the discussion.

need, finally, to remember that it was not the lot or prerogative only of subject cities to worship or otherwise honour the kings who were their suzerains; free cities could and frequently did honour with equal or greater extravagance those who were their benefactors. As a corollary to this, the presence of a royal cult in a city is not necessarily a mark or indication of its status, as we shall shortly see at Miletos, Kos, and elsewhere.

We may further divide the honours paid to the Attalids broadly into the secular and religious kind (although the distinction is not always a real one), the first consisting mainly of eponymous festivals called Attaleia, Eumeneia, or whatever name was appropriate, and the second of worship and deification as differentiated above. The earliest known eponymous festivals are the Philetaireia and Eumeneia on Delos, which, unlike those to be considered shortly, were initiated and financed by the dynasts themselves and are an indication of their claims to dynastic standing in the Greek world rather than of its recognition.[4]

At Kyzikos we hear of a festival named Philetaireia, which is probably to be associated with the support that Philetairos gave to the city when it was under threat from the Galatians in the 270s; it was the city's method of expressing gratitude to its benefactor and conforms with practices throughout the Hellenistic world in the third and second centuries.[5] Comparable are the Eumeneia at Pergamon itself, which are mentioned in the city's decree honouring its board of *strategoi* and are not to be associated simply with Eumenes' position as dynast: he is called *Euergetes,* and the honours are such that any Greek city might bestow on a benefactor.[6]

Honours of this kind continue in the reign of Attalos I, and their extent and location are predictably more widespread in accordance with the extended range of contacts he established, especially through his alliance with Rome, in the Aegean and on the Greek mainland. In this context we may put the Attaleia associated with the gymnasium at Kos; these were probably instituted on

[4] *IG* xi. 2. 224A, line 4; see further above, 22 n. 46.
[5] *CIG* 3660, line 15; see Robert, *Ét. anat.* 199–201; Habicht, *Gottmenschentum,* 124. See also above, 15 n. 20.
[6] *OGIS* 267, discussed below, 166–8.

behalf of Attalos I and are a further sign of that king's concern to
cultivate allies in the south-west Aegean as a support against the
threat of Philip V of Macedon in the early years of the third
century.[7] The newly attested Attaleia at Aiolian Kyme may also be
connected with the first Attalos, and specifically with the diplomatic activity of 218 in which Kyme played an important part
(see above, chapter 3 (i)), but the city's decree in which they are
mentioned is probably to be dated to the reign of Attalos II, and so
this later bearer of the name may be the honorand of the Attaleia.[8]

Attalos I was the first of his dynasty to receive cult honours in
the full sense. At Sikyon, according to a passage of Polybios which
has survived out of context, he received an annual sacrifice, and a
colossal statue of him was placed beside that of Apollo in the
agora, an act rendering him effectively σύνναος with Apollo.[9] An
inscription in Athens which in my view records a decree of Aigina,
refers to Attalos as being made σύνναος with the island's hero
Aiakos and also mentions the setting aside of *temene* (plural),
although the context and details of the honours are not preserved
on the stone.[10] This text is to be dated to the last years of the third
century, after Attalos had acquired the island in 210, and it is also
to this time that we may date the establishment at Athens of a
priesthood of Attalos and a tribe named after him.[11] These cult
activities constitute a major advance in honours paid to the Attalids, and were later to provide precedents for the honours enjoyed by the last of the dynasty, Attalos III Philometor. They are to
be regarded as a direct result of the great renown won by Attalos in
the Greek world by his defence of Greek freedom both against the
Galatians in Asia Minor, and as Rome's ally against Philip V of
Macedon in Asia Minor and the Aegean.[12]

These cults instituted for Attalos I were none the less occasional

---

[7] *Syll.*[3] 1028, = F. Sokolowski, *Lois sacrées des cités grecques* (Paris, 1969), 165,
A. 8. See now S. M. Sherwin-White, *Ancient Cos* (*Hypomnemata*, li, 1978), 132–3.
[8] G. Petzl and H. W. Pleket, *Chiron*, ix (1979), 73–81; Appendix iv, no. 26.
[9] xviii. 16.
[10] *IG* ii.[2] 885; Appendix iv, no. 2; I discussed this text in *BSA* lxvi (1971), 1–12.
[11] *IG* ii.[2] 5080; the priesthood is probably to be associated with the creation of the
tribe Attalis in 200 BC (Polyb. xvi. 25. 9; Cardinali, *RP* 145–6).
[12] See Polyb. xviii. 41. 9, which refers to Attalos ἀγωνιζόμενος ὑπὲρ τῆς τῶν
Ἑλλήνων ἐλευθερίας.

and *ad hoc*, and despite the great advance in his authority achieved when he took the royal title, there is no evidence of a systematic ruler-cult at Pergamon or elsewhere in the kingdom during his reign.[13] The evidence usually adduced in support of the view that Attalos was deified when he died has little substance and virtually no chronological force. The base *IvP* 59 is dedicated to βασιλέα - - - | θεὸν Σω[τῆρα], and even if Attalos' name is restored here, the date of the inscription may well be much later than his death, as the letter-forms indicate. In another base (*IvP* 171, = *OGIS* 291), usually restored βασιλέα Ἄ[τταλον θεὸν] | καὶ Εὐεργέτην, the supplement called for is surely [Σωτῆρα] | καὶ Εὐεργέτην.[14]

It was not until after 188 that the further step was taken of instituting regular priesthoods of the Attalids and of calling the king θεός; this chronology may be further established by a review of the known instances. The principal cults were established at Pergamon and Teos; when the latter became a tributary city in 188, Eumenes II was quick to exploit its position as seat of the Ionian Guild of Dionysian *technitai*.[15] The full name of this Guild, τὸ κοινὸν τῶν περὶ Διόνυσον τεχνιτῶν τῶν ἐπ' Ἰωνίας καὶ Ἑλλησπόντου, is first attested by an Aitolian decree of about 235, and it corresponds closely to the name of the region which became an Attalid province in 188.[16] The unification of the cults of Dionysos was effected by associating the activity of this Guild with that of the cult body of Dionysos Kathegemon which had been instituted at Pergamon probably by Attalos I; the associated Guilds were called τὸ κοινὸν τῶν περὶ Διόνυσον τεχνικτῶν τῶν ἐπ' Ἰωνίας καὶ

[13] The Basileia attested by *OGIS* 268 are of doubtful relevance here: see above, 105 n. 120 (*contra* Cardinali, *RP* 153, n. 3).

[14] Boehringer, *AvP* ix. 86, regarded the development of the ruler-cult as dating from the reign of Attalos I, but the evidence he cites relates with the exception of Aigina to places outside the kingdom and does not attest a ruler-cult in the form in which it developed later at Pergamon and elsewhere. The altars dedicated to Attalos at Pergamon (*IvP* 43–5) are of a private nature, and their date is uncertain.

[15] See in general Pickard-Cambridge, *Dram. Festivals*, 291–4.

[16] *F. Delphes*, iii. 3. 218B, lines 6–7. It has been thought that this full title dates from 188 and relates to the Attalid acquisition of Hellespontine Phrygia (so von Prott, *AM* xxvii (1902), 161 ff.; Ohlemutz, *Kulte*, 98–9), but the evidence of the Aitolian decree discounts this view. It seems likely, on the contrary, that the Attalids' regional name corresponded to a name already in use by the Guild. See in general above, 53–4, 103–4.

Ἑλλησπόντου, καὶ τῶν περὶ τὸν Καθηγεμόνα Διόνυσον.[17] This amalgamation of the worship of Dionysos at Pergamon and at Teos, which was to outlast the Attalid dynasty,[18] provided a suitable context in which the cults of members of the Attalid royal family could be placed, and is a further attestation of the Attalid policy of associating their own honours with those of a deity or hero, of the kind which we see in practice at Sikyon (Attalos I and Apollo), Aigina (Attalos I and Aiakos), and at Pergamon itself (Eumenes II and the twelve gods, Attalos III and Asklepios).[19]

The creation of the enlarged kingdom in 188 occasioned the institution of a direct form of ruler-cult, again centred chiefly on Pergamon and Teos. This cult arose from a new practice of recognizing members of the royal family as becoming gods when they died. In a decree of Hierapolis honouring Apollonis, the queen of Attalos I, it is said that she μεθέστηκεν εἰς θεούς.[20] The date of this decree cannot be exactly determined, but we may be sure that it was passed after 188 for reasons that will be mentioned shortly. At a later date, the death of Attalos III was expressed in a decree of Pergamon in the words [μεθισ]τάμενος ἐξ ἀν|θρώπων.[21] This practice of deifying a royal person on death plays an important part in Attalid ruler-cults, and we will do well to establish its chronology before exploring its significance.

Although Attalos I is posthumously called θεός, the designation and its associated priesthood are not attested until after 188, and we have no evidence of a cult before this date. The first priest-

---

[17] For the joint name, see Robert, *Ét. anat.* 445–50 (Michel, *Rec.* 1014): *IG* xi. 4. 1136 + 1061, = Durrbach, *Choix*, 75 (Pickard-Cambridge, *Dram. Festivals,* 314, no. 10 (a)). See also G. Klaffenbach, *Symbolae,* 17ff.; Daux, *BCH* lix (1935), 226ff.

[18] It is attested in the same form in a letter of Sulla to Kos confirming privileges of the Ionian Guild (81–79 BC): M. Segre, *Riv. di fil.* lxvi (1938), 253 ff. (Pickard-Cambridge, *Dram. Festivals,* 318, no. 13). This evidence was overlooked by Ohlemutz, *Kulte,* 98: 'nach dem Erlöschen der Pergamenischen Dynastie schwindet aus dem Titel der Hauptverbandes der Techniten in Teos der Zusatz καὶ τῶν περὶ τὸν Καθηγεμόνα Διόνυσον.' Ohlemutz's view, following von Prott, that Dionysos Kathegemon was being worshipped as the ἀρχηγέτης τοῦ γένους of the Attalid dynasty, was based on evidence whose relevance was discounted by Robert, *Ét. anat.* 25–6.

[19] *OGIS* 332 (discussed below); note lines 26–7: [στε]|φανηφορῆσαι πάντα ἕκασ-τον στεφανηφόρον τῶν Δώδεκα θεῶν καὶ βα|σιλέως Εὐμένου.

[20] *OGIS* 308, line 4.

[21] *OGIS* 338, lines 4–5.

hoods we hear of are those of the living Stratonike and the deceased Apollonis at Teos, and of Eumenes II during and after his lifetime at Pergamon and Teos; all these cult phenomena likewise fall in the period after 188, and it is a plausible contention that this year, in view of its importance to the Attalids, marks the beginning of royal cult activity. In the case of Eumenes, von Prott demonstrated many years ago that the cults to which the priesthoods belonged were introduced at Pergamon and Teos by Kraton son of Zotichos, *auletes* and priest of the Ionian Guild of Dionysian *technitai*.[22] The evidence for this event is provided by two decrees of the Guild honouring Kraton: the first is undated,[23] but the second is dated by a priesthood of Eumenes, evidently newly introduced:[24] ἐπὶ ἱερέως Σατύρου, καὶ ἀγωνοθέτου κ[αὶ] | ἱερέως βασιλέως Εὐμένου Νικοτέλου[ς]. Since the first decree refers to the combined Guild of Dionysian *technitai* at Teos and of Dionysos Kathegemon at Pergamon in the form mentioned earlier, it follows that both decrees, and accordingly the introduction of Eumenes' priesthood at Teos, must be dated after 188, when this combination occurred.

At about the same time, or at any rate after 188, when she was betrothed to Eumenes, Stratonike also received a priesthood at Teos, according to an honorary decree of that city.[25] Although neither Eumenes nor Stratonike was called a god, the deceased Attalos I and his queen Apollonis were so called, and Apollonis furthermore was to be worshipped as σύνναος with Aphrodite (lines 4–5): τῶν δὲ θυσιῶν ἐπιμεληθῆναι τὸν ἱερέα τ[ῆς | Ἀφρο]δίτης καὶ θεᾶς Ἀπολλωνίδος Εὐσεβοῦς. At Hierapolis, as we have seen, it was said of Apollonis that she μεθέστηκεν εἰς θεούς, and the chronology of this terminology may also be dated fairly securely within a range of a few years. In the decree of Hierapolis Apollonis is called γυνὴ μὲν θεοῦ βασιλέως Ἀττάλου, μήτη[ρ] | δὲ βασιλέως Εὐμένου Σωτῆρος, and since Eumenes' epithet *Soter*

[22] *AM* xxvii (1902), 161–88 (see above, n. 3).

[23] Durrbach, *Choix*, 75; improved text *ap.* Daux, *BCH* lix (1935), 210 ff.

[24] Michel, *Rec.* 1016 A (O. Lüders, *Die Dionysischen Kunstler* (Berlin, 1873), 179–80).

[25] Robert, *Ét. anat.* 9–20. On the betrothal of Stratonike, see Appendix iii.

was bestowed in the 180s during his war with Prusias I of Bithynia
and the Galatians,[26] Apollonis' death is placed in the years after
about 184. In fact it was probably later still, since Polybios states
that she long outlived her husband, who died in 197.[27]

Towards the end of his life Kraton moved from Teos to Perga-

[26] See above, 79 and n. 13. Eumenes is also called *theos* and *Soter* in a dedication from Pergamon of an altar by the members of a Dionysiac cult (*AM* xxvii
(1902), 94, no. 86): βασιλεῖ Εὐμένει θε[ῶι] | Σωτῆρι καὶ Εὐεργέ[τηι] | οἱ βάκχοι τοῦ
εὐαστοῦ θ[εοῦ]. This honour has generally been regarded as posthumous
(Boehringer, *AvP* ix. 90; Ohlemutz, *Kulte*, 93; Hansen, *Attalids*, 465), although this
is difficult to establish on historical grounds without producing a circular argument.
The letters of the inscription, however, clearly indicate a date in the second half of
the second century, and therefore after Eumenes' death: all have well-developed
apices, and omicron and (dotted) theta are large, occupying the whole depth of the
line, suggesting a date not much later than 150 (cf. Paepcke, *de Pergamenorum
litteratura*, 16, on theta; Holleaux, *Études*, ii. 78). Sigma is a well-developed form
with parallel arms, and in general the letters suggest a date more advanced than that
of the Korrhagos decree (the 180s: see above, 106–10), where many of the letters
appear in more transitional forms (cf. Holleaux, *Études*, ii. 76–81), and of Eumenes'
dedications, inscribed during the 180s (especially *IvP* 62 and 64; cf. Kähler, *Gr.
Fries*, 187, n. 43). A date after Eumenes' death in 159 is probable on these criteria.

[27] Attalos II died in 138 an old man, according to Strabo xiii. 4. 2, 624. Since he
had ruled for twenty-one years after the death of his brother, we may estimate his
age at over eighty when he died, and according to a reference in Lucian (*Macrob.*
12) he died at the age of eighty-two. He was therefore born in about 220. Attalos was
the second son of Attalos I and Apollonis, and Apollonis can therefore hardly have
been born later than 238 (cf. Fränkel, *IvP* i, p. 88). On the other hand, since Attalos I
died in 197 in old age (Strabo, loc. cit.), and Apollonis long outlived him, she must
have been young at the time of her marriage to Attalos; we can accordingly place
her birth with some hope of accuracy in the years 240–238. In 188 she would then
have been about fifty, and Polybios, in a short encomium on Apollonis (xxii. 20. 3)
says that she long outlived her husband (καίτοι χρόνον οὐκ ὀλίγον ὑπερβιώσασα
τἀνδρός), implying that she died in old age; this passage includes a reference to a
visit made by Apollonis with her sons Eumenes and Attalos to Kyzikos, and
concludes, ταῦτα δ᾽ ἐτελέσθη ἐν Κυζίκῳ μετὰ τὴν διάλυσιν τὴν πρὸς Προυσίαν τὸν
βασιλέα, but it is clear that the reference to Apollonis formed a digression prompted
by an account of events relating to Kyzikos now lost, and it is to these events, and
not to Apollonis' visit, that the chronological point refers (see Habicht, *Hermes*,
lxxxiv (1956), 98).

Apollonis is mentioned in the Athenian decree (*IvP* 160, = *OGIS* 248; Holleaux,
Études, ii. 126–47) passed in 175/4 after the accession of Antiochos IV and honouring Eumenes II and his brothers, but we need not assume (*contra* Hopp, *Untersuchungen*, 33) that Apollonis was necessarily alive at the time, since she is named
alongside the certainly deceased Attalos I (lines 43–5): ἐπαινέσαι δὲ καὶ τοὺς γον-
εῖς | αὐτῶν, τόν τε βασιλέα Ἄτταλον καὶ τὴμ βασίλισσαν | Ἀπολλωνίδα.

mon,[28] and he founded there a Guild attested under the name
Attalistai but probably founded in the lifetime of Eumenes II and
originally called *Eumenistai*; this Guild is referred to as his creation in a letter written to it by Kraton after Eumenes' death and
dated to 153/2 (*OGIS* 325). Only the prescript survives:

[βασιλε]ύοντος 'Αττάλου Φιλαδέλφου, ἔτους ἑβδόμ[ου],
[μηνὸς Δ]ύστρου, ἐπὶ δὲ ἱερέως τῶν τεχνιτῶν Κρατίν[ου],
[καὶ ἀγων]οθέτου καὶ ἱερέως θεοῦ Εὐμένου 'Αρισταίου, Κράτω[ν Ζω-]
[τίχο]ν τοῖς 'Ατταλισταῖς τοῖς ὑφ' ἑαυτοῦ συνηγμέ[νοις - - - -].

The absence here of a priesthood of the living king, Attalos II,
suggests that this was a lifetime office and not, like that of the
deceased king, an eponymous one. It does not necessarily mean
that the *Attalistai* were concerned only with the cult of the dead
king, if von Prott is correct in arguing that the organization was
founded under Eumenes II and originally called *Eumenistai*;[29]
there is furthermore no evidence here of a priesthood of the deceased Attalos I. We may reasonably suppose that the Guild was
established in order to honour Eumenes in his lifetime, and the
honours correspond to those awarded to Eumenes and Stratonike
at Teos.

It may be useful at this point to summarize what has been said so
far. The institution of royal priesthoods and the practice of posthumous deification and worship of the Attalids took place in or
shortly after 188, as a further result of the increase in the king's
power and authority in that year. The centres of these cults were at
Pergamon and Teos, although decrees of other places, such as
Hierapolis, attest a more extensive participation. Pergamon and
Teos were united in the worship of Dionysos, and in both cities a
priesthood of the living Eumenes was established. At Teos, and
perhaps at Pergamon, Eumenes' queen, Stratonike, also received
a priesthood, together with the deceased Apollonis, who was to be
σύνναος with Aphrodite.

[28] In an honorary decree of the Isthmian Guild (Michel, *Rec.* 1016 C), Kraton is
called Περγαμηνός, the only recorded instance. There is no means of dating this
decree precisely, but it belongs logically to Kraton's later activity, and we know
from a decree of the *Attalistai* passed after his death that he died at Pergamon
(*OGIS* 326, lines 15–16: μεταλλάσσων τὸν βίον ἐν Πε|ργάμωι; cf. Daux, *BCH* lix
(1935), 219).

[29] *AM* xxvii (1902), 174, n. 2; Ohlemutz, *Kulte,* 101, n. 30.

Two related problems need to be considered in connection with these cults. In the decree of the *Attalistai* already mentioned there is a reference to an Attaleion (*OGIS* 326, lines 20–1): τὸ δὲ ᾽Ατ-τάλειον τὸ πρὸς τῶι θεάτρωι, ὁ καὶ ζῶν καθιερώκει. There is no indication, however, as to whether this Attaleion was in Pergamon or in Teos. The fact that the decree comes from Teos perhaps suggests the latter,[30] but a further reference to the house of the *Attalistai,* which is said to have been 'near the palace', points rather to Pergamon, although the two buildings may not have been in the same city, and there is no particular reason why there should not have been a royal palace at Teos as well as at Pergamon, as there was at Tralles. We have already noted that Kraton spent the later part of his life at Pergamon, and founded the *Attalistai* (or *Eumenistai*) in this period. It is more likely, then, that both the *Attalistai* and the Attaleion were located in the capital, and were associated features of Kraton's work.[31]

There is, secondly, the question of where the cult was located in Pergamon. A group of buildings situated to the north of the Altar *peribolos* has been given the name *'temenos* of the ruler-cult' by the excavators: it is argued that since the site was occupied by houses into the Hellenistic period, the cult later practised there must have been introduced by the Attalids, but all known cults of gods introduced by them were located outside the city.[32] It is probable that the area was rebuilt and augmented in the time of Eumenes II,[33] and this activity may be associated with the institution of the centralized cult in 188, but the circumstantial nature of the evidence precludes certainty. It is also possible that this complex of buildings included the Attaleion as well as the Eumeneion mentioned in the probably post-Attalid dedication (*OGIS* 336) discussed in a previous chapter, but it is more likely that this Eumeneion was situated outside Pergamon.[34]

After 188 priesthoods of deceased kings were a regular feature of royal cult practice in the Attalid Kingdom; since they are mentioned in a Pergamene decree passed after the formation of the

[30] So Dittenberger ad loc., n. 13; Kern, *RE,* s.v. Attaleion, 2156.
[31] Cardinali, *RP* 151, n. 1; Ohlemutz, *Kulte,* 100-1, with references; 101, n. 29.
[32] *AvP* ix. 85 ff.
[33] Kähler, *Gr. Fries,* 153, n. 22.
[34] See above, 23 n. 49.

Roman province, they must have outlasted the Attalid dynasty itself.[35] Such royal cults are also attested at the Pergamene gymnasium under Attalos III. A decree of Pergamon passed in his reign probably in honour of a gymnasiarch seems to associate Attalos with the Founder Philetairos, and possibly with Eumenes II, as recipients of an annual sacrifice on 'the altar dedicated by the *neoi*':[36]

[πα]‖ραστήσας θυσίας ὡς καλλίστας τῶι τε Φιλεταίρωι καὶ Ἀττάλωι τῶι Φιλομήτορι βασιλεῖ καὶ τῶι το[υτοῦ πατρὶ θεῶι Εὐμένει ἐν τῶι βωμῶι τῶι καθιδρυμέ]‖νω[ι] ὑπὸ τῶν νέων ἐπιτελέσαι τὰ καθήκοντα συντετελέσθαι ἐν τῶι ἐπάνω μηνὶ τῆι [ὀγδόηι - - -].

There is also reference to the dedication of cult statues, ἀγάλματα, and specifically one of Philetairos; in Schröder's restoration we read (lines 19–20): το[ῦ δὲ θεοῦ βασιλέως Εὐμένου καὶ τοῦ θεοῦ Ἀττάλου καὶ τοῦ Φιλεταί]‖ρου τοῦ Εὐεργέτου καὶ τοῦ Ἀττάλου τοῦ Φιλομήτορος βασιλέως ἀγά[λματα ἀνατιθέναι]. Although retained with reservations by Dittenberger, this supplement is clearly unsatisfactory; in particular, the reference to θεὸς Ἄτταλος (without royal title) is unlikely in the context of the honours as a whole, so far as we can determine them. The name of Philetairos seems assured, despite the otherwise unattested epithet *Euergetes,* because it occurs elsewhere in the text,[37] and the following is therefore a more consistent supplement: το[ῦ δὲ θεοῦ βασιλέως Εὐμένου τοῦ Σωτῆρος καὶ τοῦ Φιλεταί]‖ρου τοῦ Εὐεργέτου καὶ τοῦ Ἀττάλου τοῦ Φιλομήτορος βασιλέως ἀγά[λματα ἀνατίθεναι]. The gymnasial cult of the king was an important feature of the Attalid ruler-cult after 188. We find it also at Phrygian Apameia, where a decree (probably of the 160s) honours the gymnasiarch Kephisodoros: γυμνασιαρχήσας... καὶ τιμηθεὶς ὑπὸ τῶν νέων ἀνέθηκεν ἀγάλματ[α βασιλέως Εὐμένους καὶ] Ἀττάλου τοῦ ἀδελφοῦ βασιλέως;[38] at Ephesos, as we have seen elsewhere;[39] on Andros, where another decree honouring a gymnasiarch refers to the dedication of ἀγάλματα of the king in

[35] *AM* xxxiii (1908), 375, no. 1.

[36] Schröder, *AM* xxix (1904), 152 ff., = *OGIS* 764, lines 38 ff.

[37] At line 39 quoted above, and at line 36: ἐν τῆι ἐξέδραι ἐν ἧι τὸ τοῦ Φιλεταίρο[υ ἄγαλμα καθιδρύται].

[38] *MAMA* vi. 173, with the revisions of J. and L. Robert, *Bull.* 1939, no. 400.

[39] See above, 100 and n. 97.

Parian marble and the performance of sacrifices on the king's
γενέθλιος ἡμέρα;[40] and at Pergamon, whose gymnasiarch Agias
was honoured, probably in the final years of the reign of Attalos
III, by a civic decree which refers to the celebration of the kings'
ἐπωνύμοι ἡμέραι.[41] The king also enjoyed gymnasial cults in cities
outside, or probably outside, the Attalid Kingdom, usually in
association with the celebration of the king's γενέθλιος ἡμέρα, and
the phenomenon as a whole shows that the existence of such a cult
does not necessarily indicate the status in relation to the Attalids of
the city concerned. It is unlikely, for instance, that Colophon Nova
was ever a subject of the Attalids, yet there Athenaios, the brother
of Eumenes II, was honoured by the νεοί and ἐφήβοι with the
celebration of his γενέθλιος ἡμέρα, as provided by a decree which
is probably to be dated to the middle of the second century; it is
also likely that other members of the royal family had already been
honoured in having their εἰκόνες set up by the city in the sanctuary
of Apollo Klarios.[42] On Kos, the γενέθλιος ἡμέρα of Eumenes II
was celebrated on the 6th Artemision each year, and his priesthood
is also attested there: these phenomena are further signs of an
Attalid influence at Kos which began to be felt in the second
century when Ptolemaic power was waning.[43] Also noteworthy in
the context of gymnasial honours is a priesthood of Attalos II or III
at Sestos, which is brought to our notice by a decree of Roman
date.[44] We examined the case of Miletos in detail in chapter 4;
there, Eumenes was voted in his lifetime a *temenos*, celebration of
his γενέθλιος ἡμέρα, and divine status, and the link with the
gymnasium is especially significant in that Eumenes provided
funds to finance its building, in line with Attalid policy elsewhere.[45]

[40] Appendix iv, no. 21; see also Robert, *Hellenica,* xi–xii (1960), 116–25.

[41] *AM* xxxiii (1908), 379–81, no. 2, line 22.

[42] Appendix iv, no. 20; see also Appendix iii, 205.

[43] *Syll.*³ 1028, etc. (see above, n. 7). For the priesthood, see G. Patriarcha, *Bull. Mus. Imp. Rom.* iii (1932), 28, no. 25; Habicht, *Gottmenschentum,* 125–6 (with further unpublished evidence mentioned, 125, n. 3); Sherwin-White, *Ancient Cos,* 132–3.

[44] *OGIS* 339, lines 26–7. A closer identification of the king is not possible: see Hopp, *Untersuchungen,* 115, n. 50.

[45] Robert, *Ét. anat.* 85, n. 3; see above, 118.

Among the priesthoods used in the dating formula of the Pergamene decree of Roman date mentioned earlier is that of the *theoi
philadelphoi*: καὶ ἱερέως θεῶν φιλαδέλφω[ν - - -]. Jacobsthal, the
original editor of the text, conjectured that the *theoi philadelphoi*
were Philetairos and Athenaios,[46] the younger brothers of
Eumenes II and Attalos II, but this identification seems unlikely
since neither of them became king or shared the diadem, and it is
most improbable that they received epithets of the kind invariably
associated with kingship. Since Eumenes II and Attalos II are both
known to have been called *Philadelphos*, the former admittedly
only once and in strange circumstances, it is a stronger possibility
that they are to be identified as the *theoi philadelphoi*, and this
identification is strengthened by the appearance of a priesthood of
Attalos Philadelphos preceding the one under consideration in the
prescript of the decree.[47] The title and priesthood must have been
bestowed on the royal brothers on or after the death of Attalos II
by his successor, Attalos III, who accordingly may be judged to
have considerably advanced the status and scope of the cults of his
deceased predecessors first envisaged after the Roman settlement
in 188.

Despite this advancement of the royal cult, however, Attalos III
seems not to have taken the further step of allowing himself to be
called a god in his lifetime. One of the most important documents
of his reign is an inscription found at Elaia and recording a civic
decree of (most probably) Pergamon;[48] in the decree the city
celebrates the return of Attalos to his capital after a victorious
military expedition by awarding him a gold crown, setting up his

[46] See above, n. 35.

[47] The testimonia for Attalos' title are given by Cardinali, *RP* 171; to these should
be added *AM* xxxii (1907), 427, no. 272; *AM* xxxiii (1908), 375, no. 1; *BCH* lii (1928),
440, n. 8. On Eumenes' title *Philadelphos*, which occurs once (*OGIS* 302) see
below, Appendix i, n. 23. Whatever the true explanation, the title is undeniably
attested for Eumenes, and its single occurrence is paralleled by that of Attalos II's
title *Soter* (*BCH* lii (1928), 440 n. 8).

[48] *OGIS* 332, on which see A. D. Nock, *Harv. Stud.* xli (1930), 1–62, esp. 22–5 (=
Essays on Religion and the Ancient World, i. 218–22); Wilhelm, *Neue Beiträge*
V (*SB Wien*, ccxiv, 4, 1932), 38–9 (= *Akademieschriften*, i. 280–1); Hopp, *Unter-
suchungen*, 111–13. On the origin of the decree see also Robert, *Ét. anat.* 17, n. 1;
Ohlemutz, *Kulte*, 89 (against the view held here); J. and L. Robert, *Bull.* 1968, no.
441.

cult statue, ἄγαλμα, in the temple of Asklepios Soter, ἵνα ἦ[ι] σύνναος τῶι θεῶι, and the erection of an equestrian statue, εἰκών, next to the altar of Zeus Soter in the agora, with the further provision (lines 11 ff.) of a daily sacrifice 'to (*or* for) the king': ἑκάστης τε ἡμέρας ὁ στε|φανηφόρος καὶ ὁ ἱερεὺς τοῦ βασιλέως καὶ [ἀ]γωνοθέτης ἐπιθυέτωσαν λιβανωτὸν | ἐπὶ τοῦ βωμοῦ τ[οῦ] Διὸς τοῦ Σωτῆρος τῶι βασιλεῖ. As Nock has pointed out, the dative τῶι βασιλεῖ 'is at least ambiguous' and could mean 'to the king' rather than 'for the king', the second sense usually being expressed in the form ὑπὲρ τοῦ βασιλέως;[49] similarly the Attaleia established at Delphi in 160/59 'for' Attalos II, are explained in the words [καθ]ὼς διατέτακ[ται] | ὑπὲρ τὸν βασιλέα Ἄτταλον.[50] It seems probable, then, that Attalos III was to be the *recipient* of the daily sacrifice in the agora. Provision is also made in the decree for an elaborate procession on the eighth of the month, the day on which Attalos 'came to Pergamon', to take place every year from the prytaneion to 'the *temenos* of Asklepios and the king' (comparable therefore to the *temene* voted to Attalos I on Aigina); and further offerings and festivities are devised for the occasions on which 'he visits the city' (line 26, ὅταν δὲ παραγίνηται εἰς τὴν πόλιν ἡμῶν). These honours at Pergamon clearly approach the concept of deification in the king's lifetime as closely as possible short of actually calling him a god, and they may be regarded in the present state of the evidence as the furthest point reached in the elaboration of royal cult-practice in the Attalid Kingdom. Outside the kingdom it seems to have been surpassed only by the exceptional case of Miletos.

Festivals instituted in the name of an Attalid king, or associating the king with a god, continued after 188 to be celebrated in the Greek world both within and beyond the scope of Attalid authority; we know of μουσικοὶ ἀγῶνες βασιλεῖ Εὐμένει Σωτῆρι at Tralles,[51] Ἀττάλεια καὶ Εὐμένεια καὶ Νικηφόρια at Aigina,[52] and

[49] Nock, *Essays,* i. 220.

[50] *Syll.*[3] 672, = Daux, *Delphes,* p. 686 C, = Pouilloux, *Choix d'inscriptions grecques* (Paris, 1960), 58, no. 13.

[51] Appendix iv, no. 6.

[52] *OGIS* 329, lines 40–1.

'Aθαναῖα καὶ Εὐμένεια celebrated at Sardis after Eumenes' Galatian victory.[53] Comparable honours are also recorded for cities
that were, unlike those just mentioned, independent, notably
Eumeneia and Attaleia at Delphi and at Athens,[54] where the motive for the foundation was either gratitude for some benefaction
(invariably financial, as at Delphi), or a wish to participate in the
honours voted generally to the king after some important event,
such as Eumenes' Galatian war. They do not have any great
significance in terms of the royal cult, since they were instituted in
the king's name (ὑπὲρ τοῦ βασιλέως) rather than 'for' or 'to' him.

[53] *F. Delphes* iii. 3. 241.
[54] See the texts cited above, 10 n. 7.

7

THE CITY OF PERGAMON

The city of Pergamon holds a unique position among the capitals of the Hellenistic monarchies. Like all of them, it was the residence of the dynast and the administrative centre of the kingdom. It also functioned as an independent Greek city, at least in constitutional terms. But, unlike any of them, it existed as a royal residence before the evolution of the kingdom, even taking into account the ephemeral and insubstantial expansion under Attalos I. Put simply, whereas Pella, Antioch, and Alexandria were the chief cities of kingdoms already in existence, the Attalid Kingdom was built around Pergamon and after its acquisition, as a feature additional to the existing civic community, whose separate political and constitutional identity was maintained. In this regard, then, the distinction between royal and civil institutions becomes especially meaningful, and the relationship between city and sovereign assumes a dual aspect, as the character of the city changes, in that we have to envisage a relationship between dynast and city developing into one between a king and his capital.

Our first concern is with the position of the dynasts — that is, Philetairos, Eumenes I, and, for a few years of his reign, Attalos I — in relation to the city of Pergamon. From this will arise the question of the extent to which and manner in which (so far as they can be determined) this relationship changed with the assumption of the royal title by Attalos I in the early 230s.

A question we cannot fully answer in the present state of our evidence is the degree of change introduced to the constitution of Pergamon by the first two dynasts. In the first place we have very few indications in our sources relating to the constitution before the arrival of the dynasts,[1] a deficiency which obviously makes it

[1] For the pre-Attalid city see Cardinali, *RP* 1–4, to whose account there is little to add by way of fact. See also the references given by Magie, *Roman Rule,* ii. 725, n.2. The constitutional aspects of the following survey owe much to the work of Cardinali, *RP* 244–302, as well as to that of Swoboda, *Rh. Mus.* xlvi (1891), 497–510, and of G. Corradi, *Studi Ellenistici,* 347 ff. For the evolution of the Hellenistic bureaucracies in general, see also the valuable synthesis of Rostovtzeff, *SEHHW* ii. 1078–81.

difficult to locate and assess changes made by them. There is also the problem, discussed already in another context, of their status *vis à vis* the Seleukids, and the measure of their freedom to interfere in and determine civic policy. We have concluded that Philetairos owed much, in his relations with Greek cities, to his Seleukid patronage,[2] and it seems very likely, with this consideration in mind, that Philetairos effected little change in the civic order of Pergamon, which remained nominally a Seleukid city. We can in fact hardly expect significant developments to the advantage of the dynast before the battle at Sardis in 262, which elevated him, as we have found reason to believe, to a much higher level of self-determination. It is, significantly, to Eumenes I that we must ascribe the first major constitutional development in the city under the Attalids. As has already been noted, Eumenes certainly played a part in the development of the dynast's authority, in and around Pergamon, considerably more significant than is customarily accredited to him, and with more evidence datable to his reign it is highly probable that this picture would emerge even more clearly.

There is clear evidence at least that Eumenes manipulated the existing democratic form of political institutions in Pergamon to his own advantage; this procedure was to become, as we have seen, the basis of the Attalids' relations with dependent Greek cities. It was always their policy to take advantage of existing institutions, rather than create new ones, and for the creation of this idea Eumenes must take most of the credit. It is clear from the Pergamene record of the treaty of *isopoliteia* with Temnos, already discussed in a previous chapter,[3] that the legislative process at Pergamon in the fourth century was normally directed through the usual channels of *probouleuma* and discussion in the *ekklesia*.[4] Although the treaty with Temnos may date from the early years of Philetairos' rule, it cannot be later, and this shows that the *boule* and *ekklesia* existed and were of political importance before the

---

[2] See above, 16–19.
[3] *IvP* 5; *OGIS* 265, = *StV* iii. 555. See above, 16–17.
[4] [ἔγνω βο]υλὴ καὶ δῆμος· γνώμη στρατηγῶν. See Swoboda, art. cit. (n. 1), 497.

arrival of Philetairos.[5] The same may be said of the *strategoi*, who proposed the motion concerning the treaty with Temnos; although we have no certain evidence to the effect, it seems most likely that this was the normal procedure carried over from the pre-Attalid city. It is not likely that Philetairos can have been responsible for an innovation of such fundamental importance; nor credible that, if this were the case, he would not have been remembered in the city's history in more explicit terms than the formal designation *neos ktistes*, which we encounter by chance at a much later date.[6]

It seems clear, then, that the three principal organs of legislative procedure under the dynasts, *boule, ekklesia,* and *strategoi,* were simply a continuation of an existing state of affairs. A further indication in this direction is to be found in the evidence concerning the eponymous office of *prytanis*.[7] This evidence, which comes from the so-called 'Pergamene Chronicle', a tantalizingly fragmentary remnant of the city's history, inscribed in the second century AD on a now very worn block in the Pergamon Museum in Berlin, constitutes our only direct information concerning the political life of the pre-Attalid city.[8] The extant portion of the text begins as follows: [— ἔπεισεν Ἀ]ρχίας [πρυτάν]εις αἱ[ρεῖσθαι τῆς | πόλεως κατ'] ἔτος ἕκασ[τ]ον, καὶ πρῶτος ἐπρύτ[ά|νευεν Ἀρχί]ας, καὶ ἐξ ἐκείνου μέχρι νῦν πρυτα[νευόμενοι] διατελοῦσιν. This event, the introduction at Pergamon of the

---

[5] I am inclined, despite the ambiguous letter-forms (see above, 17 n. 29), to prefer a date before the rule of Philetairos, as the treaty seems to be an entirely independent enactment, and although Philetairos had less control over the city than Eumenes I, the omission of a reference to the dynast seems to me to be striking in a document concerned with the city's external relations. Naturally this point is tentative; it may be that the city was allowed a greater measure of freedom under Philetairos than is usually admitted. It is also possible that the decree was passed on the motion of the *strategoi* implementing the dynast's wishes (as Schmitt has pointed out, *StV* iii ad loc., p. 332), but in such cases it was still usual to refer personally to the dynast.

[6] *AM* xxxiii (1908), 407, no. 36; cf. *BSA* lxvi (1971), 10.

[7] On the *prytanis* at Pergamon, see G. Corradi, *Studi Ellenistici*, 349 ff.; Magie, *Roman Rule*, ii. 1005, n. 45.

[8] *IvP* ii. 613; *OGIS* 264. Cf. Ad. Wilhelm, *AM* xxxix (1914), 156–60.

eponymous office of *prytanis*, well known in other cities of western Asia Minor and elsewhere in the fourth and third centuries, and later,[9] can be dated from the Chronicle itself and from other evidence. The reform is listed in the inscription immediately before a reference to the revolt of Orontes against Artaxerxes II and his death, events which took place in the 350s; we may therefore date the reform at Pergamon to the early fourth century, most probably the 370s or 360s.[10]

The name Archias is traditionally associated with another event at Pergamon: the introduction of the cult of Asklepios from Epidauros. The circumstances are narrated in a well known passage of Pausanias,[11] and are corroborated by references in inscriptions. One of these is from the Asklepieion at Epidauros, is dated to 191 BC, and records a grant of *proxenia* and *enktesis* to a man whose name may safely be restored, for reasons which will shortly be apparent, as Archias:[12] ['Αρχίαν 'Ασκλαπι]|άδου Περγαμηνόν, ἱερ[ατεύοντα 'Ασκλαπιοῦ] | Περγαμοῖ, πρ[όξ]ενον ε[ἶμεν τῶν 'Επιδαυρίων] | καὶ θεαροδόκον τοῦ 'Απ[όλλωνος καὶ τοῦ 'Ασκλαπι]|οῦ διὰ τὰν ἀφ[ί]δρυσιν [τοῦ θεοῦ, ἂν ἐποίησαν αὐ]|τοῦ οἱ πρόγονοι ἀπὸ τᾶ[ς πόλεως ἁμῶν κτλ.]. A law of Pergamon passed shortly after the end of the monarchy confirmed the right of the family of Archias and Asklepiades to hold the priesthood:[13] τὴν μὲν ἱερωσύνην | τοῦ 'Ασκληπιοῦ καὶ τῶν ἄλλων θεῶν τῶν ἐν τῶι 'Ασκληπιείωι ἱδρυμένων εἶναι 'Ασκληπιάδου | τοῦ 'Α[ρχί]ου καὶ τῶν ἀπογόνων τῶν 'Ασκληπιάδου | εἰς ἄπα[ντ]α [τ]ὸν χρόνον.

[9] On the eponymous office of *prytanis* in the Greek cities, see H. Swoboda, *Griechische Volksbeschlüsse* (Leipzig, 1890), 88, n. 1; Busolt, *Griechische Staatskunde* (*Handbuch der klass. Altertumswissenschaft,* IV. I., ed. 3, Munich, 1920), 504–5, with his list, 505, n. 2; Magie, *Roman Rule,* ii. 835–6, n. 21. The following instances should be added to Magie's list: NASOS, *IG* xii. 2, 646 (accounts of the temple of Asklepios dated by successive *prytaneis*); KOLOPHON as attested by *IvPr* 57, line 4; PHOKAIA, *OGIS* ii. 489, line 12 (imperial). A good example of the administrative convenience of such an institution is provided by *IG* xii. 2, 74, = *Syll.*[3] 968 (Mytilene, third century), which records a list of agricultural produce, divided year by year according to the *prytanis* in office.

[10] Cf. Beloch, *Gr. Gesch.* iii.[2] 2, 240.

[11] ii. 26. 8: 'Αρχίας ὁ 'Αρισταίχμου τὸ συμβὰν σπάσμα θηρεύοντί οἱ περὶ τὸν Πίνδασον ἰαθεὶς ἐν τῇ 'Επιδαυρίᾳ τὸν θεὸν ἐπηγάγετο ἐς Πέργαμον. *IvP* 190 is a statue-base honouring a later member of the same family. See in general Ohlemutz, *Kulte,* 123–5.

[12] *IG* iv. 1.[2] 60.

[13] *IvP* ii. 251, = *Syll.*[3] 1007.

This evidence leaves the supplement in the text from Epidauros beyond doubt, and it emerges that the family of Archias and Asklepiades retained the priesthood from the fourth century to the reign of Eumenes II, in which the decree of Epidauros was passed, on to the end of the dynasty, when the city of Pergamon confirmed once more the family's hereditary rights.

That the Archias mentioned by Pausanias is the same man as the constitutional innovator at Pergamon seems beyond reasonable doubt, although some scholars have expressed reservations in this regard.[14] It will be seen, in particular, that there is a connection between the introduction of a cult and the innovation of an eponymous magistracy. The *prytanis*, at Pergamon as elsewhere in the fourth century and later, was an office of prestige but little executive power.[15] Its introduction may be seen as an administrative reform, enabling the more accurate and convenient recording and dating of public documents. It was also an office of religious significance, as is clear from evidence from Teos dating from the second century, when the city was tributary to the Attalids. Here the *prytanis* is listed in a sacral inscription, after the priest of the joint cult of Aphrodite and Apollonis and the priesthood of Eumenes' queen Stratonike, as taking part in sacrifices.[16] At Magnesia and Priene in the third century it appears at first sight that the principal eponymous magistrate was called *prytanis* and later *stephanephoros*; in fact, it is probable that the new name was simply a title added to the privileges and functions of the *prytanis*, thus supplanting the old name, which does however recur, at Priene at least.[17] At Chios, we find the title πρύτανις ὁ στεφανηφόρος specifically attested,[18] and it is clear from all this

[14] Ohlemutz, for example (*Kulte*, 125), seems to me too sceptical.

[15] As shown by Corradi, *Studi Ellenistici*, 349 ff.

[16] *OGIS* 309 as revised by L. Robert, *Ét. anat.* 9–20; see above, 150.

[17] Cf. Busolt, *Gr. Staatskunde*, 499. *IvM* 5, a decree of *c*.250 for the Macedonian Archelaos, is dated by the *prytanis*; a *stephanephoros* first appears in *IvM* 7D. At Priene, where dating by a *prytanis* was usual in the fourth century (cf. *IvPr* 139), the change can be dated to about 334: the well-known decree honouring Antigonos Monophthalmos (*IvPr* 2, = *Syll.*³ 278) refers to a *prytanis*, whereas *IvPr* 3, a decree for Megabyzos of Ephesos passed shortly afterwards, has *stephanephoros*. It is noteworthy, however, that the title *prytanis* probably reappears in a later decree of Priene: *IvPr* 73 (second century; dating-formula partly restored but probable).

[18] J. Vanseveren, *Rev. Phil.* xi (1937), 337, no. 10. Cf. Magie, *Roman Rule*, ii. 837, n. 23.

evidence that during the fourth and third centuries the office acquired a greatly increased importance, not least in religious life.

At Pergamon, the sacral significance of the office of *prytanis* is
again clear from prescripts of decrees of the late Attalid and early
Roman periods, which are sometimes dated ἐπὶ πρυτάνεως καὶ
ἱερέως [name].[19] There is then good reason to associate the introduction of the office of *prytanis,* and the introduction of the cult of
Asklepios, both implemented early in the fourth century by Archias, with each other. It is the first evidence we have of the
advancement of civic and religious life at Pergamon; this, and the
importance of the city in the cult of Meter at Mamurt-Kaleh,
referred to in a previous chapter (above, 15–16), show clearly that
Pergamon was already a city of cultural and political maturity
before the arrival of the dynasts.

Significantly, the position and prestige of the *prytanis,* as we
have so far defined them, do not seem to have been changed under
the Attalids. Few documents of the royal period refer to this office,
but there are enough to show that it survived in much the same
form. The treaty with Temnos has already been mentioned. To this
we may add a letter written by Eumenes II to the same city, extant
only in small and insubstantial fragments, but whose heading is
almost completely preserved:[20] ἐπὶ πρυτάνιος Ἡρακλείδου τοῦ
Ἑρμαγόρου, μη[νὸς - - -]| βασιλεὺς Εὐμένης Τημνιτῶν τῆι βουλῆι
καὶ [τῶι δήμωι χαίρειν]. At a later date, as we have noticed, the
style became, at least in civic decrees, ἐπὶ πρυτάνεως καὶ ἱερέως.
It is noteworthy that a royal letter should be dated by a civic
magistracy, a point which will be taken up later in this chapter.[21]
Here it is enough to demonstrate the survival of the office in the old
form.

The evidence concerning the *prytanis* shows, then, that this
office continued to function largely unchanged under the Attalids,

---

[19] *AM* xxxiii (1908), 375, no. 1 (Attalos III); *AM* xxv (1910), 401, no. 1 (early
Roman). An interesting parallel to this identification of priest and *prytanis* is to be
found in a late second-century decree of Bargylia, which provides that the
stephanephoros appointed shall be the priest of Apollo (Holleaux, *Études,* ii. 180 A,
lines 7–8, ὅπως καθ' ἕκαστον ἐνιαυτὸν καθίστη|ται στεφανηφόρος ὁ ἱερασόμενος
τοῦ Ἀπόλλωνος: cf. Holleaux, ad loc., 181–2).
[20] *IvP* 157, = Welles, *RC* 48.
[21] See below, 175–6.

and affords a clear indication that the civil processes of law-making were, at least as regards form, unaltered. Turning to the Pergamene *strategoi,* we see the same phenomenon, but with an important difference, which characterizes more sharply dynastic policy in regard to the city's administration.

The *strategos* was, of course, an office of greater substance and power.[22] We have already found reason to believe that it existed as such before the Attalid period, when its most important function was the submission of motions for discussion to the *ekklesia* and *boule.* Throughout the Attalid period this remained its cardinal power; all the extant decrees of the Attalid city are, with a single exception, introduced with the formula γνώμη στρατηγῶν, or an equivalent, and the body of surviving material is sufficiently copious and chronologically representative to render this fact of greater significance than the mere chance of survival.[23] The view, expressed with reservations by Cardinali, that individuals could put motions to the *ekklesia* through the formal mediation of the *strategoi,* was based on a doubtful restoration of a fragmentary decree which has since proved to be wrong.[24] It emerges clearly that the *strategoi,* as a body, alone had the right to introduce

[22] On the powers of the *strategoi* at Pergamon, see Cardinali, *RP* 244–65; G. Corradi, *Studi Ellenistici,* 347 ff.; Bengtson, *Strat.* ii. 232–40. Magie, *Roman Rule,* ii. 1006–7, n. 47 gives a list of other cities with the same office, to which should be added Smyrna (*OGIS* 229, line 1) and Priene (*OGIS* 11, = *IvPr* 14, line 2).

[23] A list of the extant decrees of Pergamon datable to the Attalid period may be useful at this point (texts which are too fragmentary to be fully of use are marked with asterisks): *IvP* 5 (*OGIS* 265; *StV* iii. 555, early third century); 18 (*OGIS* 267, II); 156; 161*; 162*; 166*; 167 (*OGIS* 299, Eumenes II); 224 (*OGIS* 323, Attalos II); 249 (*OGIS* 338, shortly after the death of Attalos III); *AM* xxxiii (1908), 375, no. 1 and 379, no. 2 (Attalos III). In the fragmentary decrees it is not always possible to identify the prescripts, despite the misfounded optimism of Hansen, *Attalids,* 188, n. 143: 'although the formula γνώμη στρατηγῶν is not extant in [*IvP*] nos. 156, 162, and 166, it can be restored with certainty in these decrees.' For the classification of Pergamene decrees, see H. Swoboda, *Rh. Mus.* xlvi (1891), 497–510; Cardinali, *RP* 244–58. On *IvP* 18, which does not have the formula γνώμη στρατηγῶν, see below, n. 25.

[24] *IvP* ii. 260, of the early Roman period, was restored by Cardinali, *RP* 256–8, to read: εἰσαγγειλάντω[ν τῶν δείνων· γνώμη στρατηγῶν· ἔδοξε τ]ῶι δήμωι κτλ. It is more likely, however, that the supplement required in this inscription is that suggested by Fränkel, attested by a decree published shortly after Cardinali wrote, *AM* xxii (1907), 257, no. 8 (a), col. ii, line 44: εἰσαγγειλάντων τῶν στρατηγῶν εἰς τὴν βουλ[ὴν] καὶ τὸν δῆμον, κτλ. See on this point G. Corradi, *Studi Ellenistici,* 364, n. 4.

business to the *boule* and *ekklesia,* a fact of special significance in that the dynast, at least from the time of Eumenes I, assumed the right of appointing the *strategoi,* as we learn from a much discussed inscription recording a letter of Eumenes to the people of Pergamon and the city's answering decree. In the letter the diplomatic forms of respect are maintained, but the dynast's effective control of the constitution is clear:[25]

[Eumenes son of Philetairos] sends greetings [to the people of Pergamon]. The *strategoi* [appointed in the year of N.'s priesthood, Palamandros, Skymnos, Metrodoros, Theotimos, Phil]iskos, have clearly [fulfilled all the obligations of] their office [with distinction], and their administration[26] has been a just one. For their own part[27] they have attended to the entire civil and sacred funds in a way beneficial to the people and the gods.[28] They have even looked into deficiencies left by their predecessors,[29] spared none of those guilty of misappropriation, and restored the money due to the city. They have also been responsible for the maintenance of the sacred offerings. Their organization has been so efficient that their successors will be able to take over affairs without difficulty if they follow their example.

We think it right, then, that due recognition should be given to such distinguished service,[30] in the hope that those next appointed[31] will try to give fitting leadership to the people in their turn. We have already arranged that they receive crowns at the Panathenaia, and have now decided

[25] *IvP* 18, = *OGIS* 267; Welles, *RC* 23 (Eumenes' letter only). The city's answering decree is the only extant example introduced by a private individual, but the explanation of Cardinali (*RP* 252–3; cf. Bengtson, *Strat.* ii. 233), that the special circumstances arising from honouring the *strategoi* necessitated an exceptional procedure, is usually followed and seems to me satisfactory. I cannot accept Swoboda's view (*Rh. Mus.* xlvi (1891), 498–9) that direct recourse to the *ekklesia* was possible as a regular procedure alternative to proposals of the *strategoi,* because this view is based on *IvP* 18 alone, which for reasons considered above hardly constitutes substantial evidence.

[26] This translates τῶν τε γὰ[ρ] . . . [μ]ὲν πεπολίτευνται δικαίως. The supplement required at the beginning of line 5 is not immediately clear. Fränkel's suggestion of a partitive genitive, e.g. τῶν τε γὰ[ρ | ἱερῶν καὶ τῶν πολιτικῶν πάντα μ]ὲν κτλ., is, as Dittenberger noted, hardly a satisfactory complement to the verb πολιτεύω.

[27] [ἐ]φ' αὐτῶν.

[28] I follow here the supplements of Ad. Wilhelm, *Neue Beitr.* v (1932), 5: [καὶ οὐ μόνον πάσας τὰς τ]ῆς πόλεως καὶ τὰς ἱερὰς προσόδους | [τὰς οὔσας ἐ]φ' αὐτῶν ᾠκονομήκασι συμφερόντως τῶι δήμωι καὶ | [το]ῖς θεοῖς κτλ.

[29] (continuing from previous note) ἀλλὰ καὶ τὰ παραλελειμμένα ὑπὸ τῶν πρότερον ἀρχείων ἀναζητήσαντες. For ἀρχεῖον in this sense, see Dittenberger, ad loc., n. 5.

[30] μὴ ὀλιγωρεῖν τῶν οὕτως ἐπιστατούντων.

[31] οἱ μετὰ ταῦτα δεικνύμενοι: a tactful way of referring to a further dynastic appointment. See Cardinali, cited above, n. 25.

to write to you on the matter, with the intention that you discuss it and bestow the honours you think appropriate.

This letter points directly to the key position held by the *strategoi* in the relations between the dynasts and the city at an early stage of their association. As important, surely, as the fact that the *strategoi* were appointed by the dynast, on which all commentators have dwelt,[32] is the place of the dynast in relation to the city as reflected in the services of the *strategoi* cited in the letter; most important is the consideration that Eumenes took a personal initiative, through his appointment of the *strategoi*, in implementing the necessary reforms and correction of abuses in the administration, and at the same time, that he was able to manipulate existing constitutional forms, without changing them, to his own advantage. This is surely a measure of the independence achieved by Eumenes after the battle at Sardis.

We see also that the dynasts (the same is true of Philetairos) stood outside and apart from the constitution. The full heading of Eumenes' letter is not preserved, but its restoration is certain: Eumenes was writing as any Hellenistic monarch would write to a Greek city. The *demos* replies with a decree of its own duly commending the board of *strategoi*. Thus the distinction between royal and civil decisions is clear, and the machinery is evidently allowed to operate as in any similarly constituted Greek city, once activated by the dynast's request.

We have seen that a corner-stone of the Attalids' policy in relation to their kingdom was their concern to keep a personal control, in one form or another, over finance, an issue that was always dear to their hearts.[33] At Pergamon, an important consequence of the situation just described was that the dynast, who appointed the *tamiai* and the *strategoi,* was able to maintain a very much firmer control over the financial administration of the city than would otherwise have been possible, given the separate constitutional status of the city's administration.[34] The importance of

[32] See Welles, *RC* 23, ad loc.; Bengtson, *Strat.* ii. 232–3.

[33] See above, 109.

[34] This important point was first emphasized by Cardinali, 'L' amministrazione finanziaria del comune di Pergamo', *Mem. Accad. Bologna,* x (1915–16) 181–93; cf. Bengtson, *Strat.* ii. 234–6. The *tamiai* were also royal appointments (*OGIS* 267, lines 33–4): οἱ ταμίαι οἱ κα|τιστάμενοι [sic] κατ' ἐνιαυτόν.

the *strategoi* in this aspect of the administration at Pergamon is well attested throughout the Attalid period. Eumenes' letter to the city refers, as we have seen, to specific financial responsibilities:[35]

[καὶ οὐ μόνον πάσας τὰς τ]ῆς πόλεως καὶ τὰς ἱερὰς προσόδους |
[τὰς οὔσας ἐ]φ᾽ αὐτῶν ὠικονομήκασι συμφερόντως τῶι δήμωι καὶ
| [το]ῖς θεοῖς, ἀλλὰ καὶ τὰ παραλελειμμένα ὑπὸ τῶν πρότερον |
ἀρχείων ἀναζητήσαντες καὶ οὐθενὸς τῶν κατεσχηκότων | τι
φεισάμενοι ἀποκατέστησαν τῆι πόλει. The fact that the *strategoi* were also presidents of the Pergamene *boule* and *ekklesia* (προΐ-στασθαι τοῦ δήμου) therefore corresponds, in this respect, with practice in other Greek cities, where finance was largely the responsibility of the *boule*.[36] The separation of secular and sacred funds is not an unusual feature of financial administration in the Hellenistic period,[37] and we will see later that a measure of reform was introduced at Pergamon in this regard, probably in or shortly after 188, whereby the increased burden carried by the *strategoi* was alleviated by the institution of new and important officials appointed by the king.

The decree answering Eumenes' letter provides evidence of another development in relations between the dynast and the city. Here, a city festival honouring the dynast, and a sacrifice on his behalf, are attested; among the honours voted to the *strategoi* is the provision: διδότωσαν δὲ αὐτοῖς ἀεὶ οἱ ταμίαι οἱ κα|τιστάμενοι κατ᾽ ἐνιαυτὸν ἐν τοῖς Εὐμενείοις πρόβατον, οἱ δὲ | λαμβάνοντες θυέτωσαν Εὐμένει εὐεργέτηι. Eumenes is accordingly honoured by the city as a benefactor, perhaps in part on account of his reform of the administration. No direct cult is implied, but the provisions indicate a firm and well-based relationship between city and dynast.

It is evident, then, that although no constitutional title is attested for either of the first two dynasts, Eumenes exercised a much tighter control over the Pergamene constitution than Philetairos had done, while allowing it, at least to outward appearances, to function as before. We can say, in fact, that the position evolved by

---

[35] *OGIS* 267, lines 6–10, as restored by Wilhelm (see above, n. 28).
[36] H. Francotte, *Les Finances des cités grecques* (1909), 131 ff., esp. 137–9; Jones, *Greek City*, 241.
[37] Cf. Cardinali, art. cit. (n. 34), 182, n. 4; G. Corradi, *Studi Ellenistici*, 383–4.

Eumenes remained the basis of dynastic relations with the city until the end of Attalid rule. There is little sign of any significant change in the position under Attalos I in constitutional terms, even after his assumption of the royal title, although the lack of any extant correspondence between Attalos and the city precludes certainty on the point.

There are however signs that after his assumption of the royal title, Attalos' relations with Pergamon developed in the context of the city's religious life. Significant in this respect is the form of Attalos' reply in *c.*206/5 to Magnesia accepting the city's request for recognition of its festival for Artemis Leukophryene, which we have discussed in a previous chapter.[38] Attalos replies for himself, as king, and, indirectly, for the cities under him (ὑπ' ἐμὲ πόλεις). This kind of directive to subject or dependent Greek cities in the matter of recognition of *asylia* is attested also for the Antigonids (Antigonos Gonatas, Philip V), and the Seleukids (Antiochos III).[39] In Attalos' letter, however, the city of Pergamon seems to be distinguished, in the last surviving line of the text, from the subject cities: καὶ[ὶ Πέργαμη?]|νοῖς δὲ καθ' ὅσον ὁ δῆμος [αἰτεῖται | συνα]υξήσω τὸν ἀγῶνα - - -. This restoration, although questioned by Welles, seems to me very plausible.[40] If it is correct, it indicates that the kingdom continued to consist of the three elements evolved under Eumenes I: the dynast, now king, the city of Pergamon, and the subject cities.[41] The allied cities such as Teos and Kolophon, and, in the Troad, Alexandria Troas, Ilion, and

---

[38] *IvM* 22, = *OGIS* 282; Welles, *RC* 34; see above, 45.

[39] Herzog and Klaffenbach, *Asylieurkunden aus Kos* (*Abh. Berlin*, 1952), no. 6 (Amphipolis replying to Kos, 242), 13–14: εἶναι δὲ καὶ τὸ ἱε[ρὸν ἄσυλον, καθάπερ καὶ ὁ βασιλεὺς Ἀντίγονος προαιρεῖται. *IvM* 47, = *Syll.*³ 561 (Chalkis replying to Magnesia, 206/5), 1–3: [περὶ ὧν ὁ β]ασιλεὺς Φίλι[π]πος | ἔγρα[ψε]ν τῆι βουλῆι κ[αὶ τῶι] δήμ[ωι] περὶ [M]αγνή|των τῶν ἐπὶ Μαιάνδρωι. *IvM* 18, = *OGIS* 231 (Antiochos III replying to Magnesia, 206/5), 25–8: γεγράφαμεν δὲ καὶ | τοῖς ἐπὶ τῶν πραγμάτων τεταγμένοις, | ὅπως καὶ αἱ πόλεις ἀκολούθως ἀπο|δέξωνται.

[40] Welles, *RC* ad loc., 150–1. Ad. Wilhelm, *ÖJh* iv (1901), Beiblatt, 27, n. 6, read a lambda at the beginning of line 22 and restored καὶ ἐν τοῖς ἄλλοις.

[41] On the question of the 'subject' cities, so-called, I ask the reader to bear in mind the qualifications expressed above in chapters 2 and 3, especially in relation to the reference in *OGIS* 266 (*StV* iii. 481), line 37: ἐάν τι παραλάβω παρ' αὐτοῦ, ἢ πόλιν ἢ φρού|[ριον] κτλ. Ghione's attempt (*Mem. Accad. Torino*, lv (1905), 67–149) to show that Pergamon shared the subject status of other cities is not indicated or borne out by the evidence, when examined thoroughly.

Lampsakos, lay outside the scope of Attalos' letter.

The advanced status of Pergamon under Attalos I is reflected also in the importance attached to the city's god, Athena, who was also Attalos' own patron goddess. The Pergamene Panathenaia are attested already under Eumenes I,[42] but it was under Attalos I that Athena was elevated to the sublime position which found its final fulfilment after the Treaty of Apameia. The temple of Athena in the city was enlarged and partly rebuilt to contain the spoils dedicated to the goddess after Attalos' succession of military victories.[43] On Attalos' coins Athena appears as the bringer of victory,[44] and an important festival, probably the forerunner of the later Nikephoria although not yet called by that name, was founded during the 220s as a further recognition of the special devotion of Attalos to Athena, his god, and the goddess of Pergamon.[45] In this evidence we have a clear sign of the development of a relationship between a king and his capital.

As a result of the Treaty of Apameia, which created the first true Attalid Kingdom, Pergamon became a royal residence of greatly enhanced fame and prestige, and it is interesting to examine firstly what changes, in practical terms, were made in the city's administration, which must obviously have had much more work to do after 188, and, secondly, the ways in which the relations between king and city were developed, and in which directions.

It causes no surprise that after 188 the evidence relating to civic institutions and administration becomes much more copious, and our conclusions become in many important respects more substantial. We find, in the first place, a range of new officials not encountered before 188, and these collectively point to a reform in the administration which we may reasonably relate to developments after the Treaty of Apameia. They also indicate a further measure of royal control over the city's affairs.

Of prime importance as evidence in this respect is the Astynomic Law, an inscription from Pergamon first published by W.

[42] In Eumenes' letter, and in the city's answering decree (*OGIS* 267, see above) it is provided (lines 17, 31–2) that the five *strategoi* receive their crowns ἐν ταῖς Παναθηναίοις. See further above, 122.

[43] See above, ch. 4 (iii).

[44] *MvP* ii. 6; Ohlemutz, *Kulte*, 34–5.   [45] See above, ch. 4 (iii).

Kolbe in 1902, and re-edited by G. Klaffenbach in 1954.[46] This law,
as we have it, is almost certainly a copy of the time of Trajan or
Hadrian of an Attalid law concerned with the upkeep on the part of
the relatively insignificant *astynomoi* of the streets and buildings of
the city.[47] Its reinscription is typical of the Roman imperial method
of adding weight to its laws by invoking precedents from the past,
in this case a royal law, a βασιλικὸς νόμος.[48] The original law dates
from a time when the city was fully developed, that is, during the
reign of Eumenes II or possibly Attalos II or III — in any event
after the Treaty of Apameia — and provides the best evidence we
have of the institutions and workings of the civil administration
after 188.

The office which emerges from this text as having the greatest
authority is, as we would expect, that of the *strategoi,* but some of
the powers that at an earlier date they enjoyed alone now appear to
be shared. For example, responsibility for enforcing the astynomic
law as a whole is shared with the νομοφύλακες and the ἀστυνόμοι,
and the ultimate responsibility in this carefully structured hierar-
chy rests with the *strategoi* and an official attested specifically for
Pergamon only by this inscription, ὁ ἐπὶ τῆς πόλεως. In a passage
dealing with certain duties of the ἀμφοδάρχαι, officials responsible for sections of the city, it is provided that these officials should
be fined by the *astynomoi* for any failure in their duties, and the
money be deposited monthly in a separate account supervised by
the *tamiai.* The text then continues: 'if they (the *astynomoi*) fail to
implement any of these provisions, they shall be fined fifty
drachmai for each infringement by the *strategoi* and the ἐπὶ τῆς
πόλεως.'[49] The expression used here puts the two offices on an
evidently equal footing: ζημιούσθωσαν ὑπὸ τῶν στρατη|γῶν καὶ

[46] W. Kolbe, *AM* xxvii (1902), 47, no. 71, = *OGIS* ii. 483, with addenda, pp.
551–2; G. Klaffenbach, *Die Astynomeninschrift von Pergamon.* All three editions
have extensive commentaries. The lineation given in the following notes follows
Klaffenbach's edition; I use the prefix 'Kla.'.

[47] For the office of *astynomos* see Busolt, *Gr. Staatskunde,* 492–3.

[48] On the date of the extant text of the astynomic law, and its relevance to Roman
rule, see the full treatment of Klaffenbach, 19–25; J. H. Oliver, *AJPh* lxxii (1951),
200 and *Hesperia,* xxiv (1955), 88–92; P. M. Fraser, *JHS* lxxvi (1956), 138–9.

[49] Kla. 67–70: [ἐὰ]ν δέ τι μὴ ποιήσωσιν οὗτοι τῶν γεγραμ|μένων, ζημιούσθωσαν
ὑπὸ τῶν στρατη|γῶν καὶ τοῦ ἐπὶ τῆς πόλεως καθ' ἕκαστον | ἀτάκτημα δραχμαῖς
πεντήκοντα.

τοῦ ἐπὶ τῆς πόλεως; the term ὁ ἐπὶ τῆς πόλεως is, furthermore,
attested elsewhere in the Hellenistic world, especially in Egypt, of
civic officials appointed by a king and, as the name suggests, it
represents a senior office, often the most senior in the administration.[50] Evidently then, at some time during the reign of Eumenes
II, and most probably after the Treaty of Apameia, the *strategoi*
were made to share some of their powers in the civil administration
with a royally appointed ἐπὶ τῆς πόλεως, who was at least their
equal.

The *tamiai* mentioned in the Astynomic Law call for no comment, being the usual financial officials; they are attested early in
the Attalid period as appointees of Eumenes I.[51] More noteworthy
is the appearance of another royal appointment, ὁ ἐπὶ τῶν ἱερῶν
προσόδων, again on terms of evident equality with the *strategoi*. A
section of the law dealing with the city's springs lays down that
their upkeep shall be the responsibility of the *astynomoi*, but 'in the
event of any necessary repairs, they shall report to the *strategoi*
and the ἐπὶ τῶν ἱερῶν προσόδων, who will make the necessary
arrangements.'[52] The involvement of sacred funds in the maintenance of springs may be explained by their religious significance,
as they were often dedicated to specific deities.[53] Of interest here
is the fact that the authority of the *strategoi* again appears to be
shared by an official holding a specific royal appointment, the ἐπὶ

[50] Most notable is the office of ὁ ἐπὶ τῆς πόλεως at Ptolemais and Alexandria (cf.
Bengtson, *Strat.* iii. 128–33; P. M. Fraser, *Ptol. Alex.* 106, with further discussion,
ii. 194, n. 99) and in Cyprus (*Strat.* iii. 148) and the cities of Cyrenaica (*Strat.* iii.
164). The evidence is exhaustively treated by Bengtson, and I need not cite it all in
detail here. The office is not found in a technical sense in the Seleukid and Antigonid
kingdoms, but it appears in a decree of the Cappadocian city of Anisa: Michel 546,
re-edited by F. Cumont, *REA* xxxiv (1932), 135 ff.; cf. Rostovtzeff, *SEHHW* iii.
1533, n. 120; Bengtson, *Strat.* ii. 253–4; although its date is uncertain, it seems
likely that the constitution implied in this decree, including royal appointment, is
essentially Hellenistic.

[51] See above, 167 and n. 34.

[52] Kla. 176–180: ἐὰν | δὲ τιν<ε>ς ἐπισκ[ε]υῆς προσδέωνται, προσαγ|γελ-
λέτωσαν τοῖς στρατηγοῖς καὶ τῶι ἐπὶ | τῶν ἱερῶν προσόδων, ὅπως διὰ τούτων
γεί|νωνται αἱ ἐκδόσεις.

[53] The separation of civic and sacred funds in Hellenistic cities is not uncommon;
we have met it in the decree from Bursa (post-Apameia) honouring Korrhagos
(above, 88–9; cf. Holleaux, *Études,* ii. 94), and we have seen that expenses for a
sacrifice to Attalos III were to be met [ἐξ ἱερῶν κα]ὶ πολιτικῶν προσόδων (*OGIS*
332, line 41, a sound supplement).

τῶν ἱερῶν προσόδων corresponding to the ἐπὶ τῆς πόλεως. It
seems clear that, in this respect too, work once done by the
strategoi alone was later made a joint responsibility with another
royal nominee.[54] In Eumenes' letter to Pergamon the *strategoi*
appear to have complete authority in respect of sacred finances;
the omission of a reference to another office would be understandable if it were a subordinate one, since the letter is concerned
with praising the *strategoi* and naturally dwells on their achievements; since, however, this consideration would not apply to an
office entitled ὁ ἐπὶ τῶν ἱερῶν προσόδων, we must conclude that
during the rule of Eumenes I it did not exist.

I may adduce also in this connection a rarely discussed Pergamene inscription recording a royal letter about the establishment
of a priesthood, probably of Zeus.[55] The sacred funds are, according to this letter, in the hands of the temple's priests, and no
mention is made of an ἐπὶ τῶν ἱερῶν προσόδων. Admittedly the
text deals with a specific priesthood, and not the sacred finances as
a whole, but the omission of an office of such importance is surely
significant. The dating of this inscription is problematical. The
text, which is now in the Pergamon Museum in Berlin (*vidi* August
1969), is invariably assigned, on the basis of the letter-forms, to the
reign of Attalos I;[56] this is very probably incorrect. Many of these
forms indicate the first half of the second century rather than the
third century. Alpha appears, as often at Pergamon, in a number of
forms and is therefore not a reliable guide. The omicron and theta
are fairly large, occupying most of the line, and all the other letters
are well developed, especially sigma and omega. Pi, with well
pronounced apices, is a clear second-century form; it is not found
again in this form in any Pergamene inscription attributable to the
reign of Attalos I. There seems to me, on this evidence, to be a
strong probability that the author of this letter is Eumenes II, and
that it was written in the early part of his reign. This dating
indicates that the reform of the sacred finances, and with it the

---

[54] See Cardinali, art. cit. (n. 34), 190–1.
[55] *IvP* 40, = *Syll.*[3] 1018 (Hiller); Welles, *RC* 24; Sokolowski, *Lois sacrées de l'Asie Mineure,* 11.
[56] So Fränkel, followed by Hiller and Welles; Paepcke, *de Perg. litt.* 13; Ohle-
mutz, *Kulte,* 65 ('aus dem Anfang der Regierungszeit Attalos I').

establishment of the office of ὁ ἐπὶ τῶν ἱερῶν προσόδων, as well perhaps as other new royal appointments, were implemented shortly after the Treaty of Apameia in 188. There can be little doubt that the *strategoi* remained officials of importance in all branches of the civil administration, but it is not surprising that with the dramatic advancement of the status of Pergamon in 188, additional appointments were required to carry the burden of increased business.

*

As is well known, Pergamon was transformed during the 180s to a city of monumental greatness, whose wealth, beauty, and culture might, it was hoped, recall the days of classical Athens, and rival the claims of contemporary Alexandria. It can be said of Eumenes that he was a builder of great buildings, while Attalos had been a builder of great monuments.[57] His aspirations for the city are best characterized by the introduction of Athena Parthenos to stand in the Library at Pergamon, and by his dedication of the rebuilt precinct of Athena:[58] Βασιλεὺς Εὐμένης ᾿Αθηνᾶι Νικηφόρωι.

The special status of the city of Pergamon in the kings' regard is reflected in a number of documents dating from the fifty years or so from the Treaty of Apameia to the death of Attalos III. Pergamon was, as we have seen, with Teos one of the two centres of the royal cult, and the worship at Pergamon of Dionysos Kathegemon was formally linked with the activities of the Dionysian *technitai* at Teos. This has already been discussed, and I need not repeat the evidence here.[59] It is enough to draw attention again to the fact that the strongest bond between dynast and city, especially after 188, was formed by these cult activities. Also important in this respect is a letter of Attalos III to the *demos* of Pergamon, informing it of his decision to appoint his cousin Athenaios to the priesthood of Sabazios.[60] The letter is dated 5 October 135, and was evidently written shortly after the death of Attalos' mother, Queen Stratonike, who had brought the cult of Sabazios to Pergamon

[57] Cf. Kähler, *Gr. Fries*, 142.
[58] *IvP* 149; cf. *AvP* ii. 52; Kähler, *Gr. Fries*, 137–8.
[59] See above, 148–52.
[60] *OGIS* 331, IV, = Welles, *RC* 67.

from Cappadocia.⁶¹ As a result of an epiphany of the god, as we learn from Attalos' letter, it was decided to enshrine Sabazios with Athena Nikephoros, and the request was formally made that the city 'register the *prostagmata* in its sacred laws':⁶² κρίνομεν διὰ ταῦ|τα, ὅπως ἂν εἰς τὸν ἄπαντα χρόνον ἀκίνητα καὶ ἀμετάθετα μένηι τά τε πρὸς | τὸν θεὸν τίμια καὶ τὰ πρὸς τὸν Ἀθήναιομ φιλάνθρωπα, τὰ γραφέντα ὑφ' ἡμῶμ | προστάγματα ἐν τοῖς ἱεροῖς νόμοις φέρεσθαι παρ' ὑμῖν. At the top of the stele recording this and other royal letters on the subject of Athenaios' priesthoods, is preserved the end of a decree of the city, which enacts this enrolment in the sacred laws:⁶³ [ἐγγρά]|ψαι *(sic: vidi)* δὲ καὶ εἰς [το]ὺ[ς ἱ]εροὺς νόμους [τοὺς τῆ]ς πόλεως [τ]όδ[ε τὸ]| ψήφισμα καὶ χρῆσθαι αὐτῶι νόμωι κυρίωι εἰς ἄπαντα τὸγ χρόνον. This legislative process, by which a royal wish became civic law (in this case sacred law), appears then to have consisted of three elements: the royal *prostagma*, the city's decree embodying the *prostagma*, and the enrolment in the city's laws. The last two elements are, of course, those of a nominally and apparently independent city, and we find them implemented at Pergamon also in respect of the city's own legislation. The decree referred to earlier in this chapter, concerning the priesthood of Asklepios, and passed shortly after the death of Attalos III, concludes with a corresponding provision:⁶⁴ ἐγγράψαι δὲ καὶ εἰς τοὺς νόμους | [τοὺς τ]ῆς πόλεως τὸ ψήφισμα τόδε, καὶ | [χρήσθω]σαν αὐτῶι νόμωι κυρίωι εἰς ἄπαντα τὸν χρόνον.

These examples suggest that, with or without the initiative of a royal *prostagma*, the legislative process remained the same, and that the independent constitutional functions of the city continued to be respected. The distinction between the city's laws, νόμοι τῆς πόλεως, and royal law, βασιλικὸς νόμος, is further emphasized by the evidence of the Astynomic Law, which is a clear example of the latter. Of interest also is the letter of Eumenes II to the city of Temnos (noticed briefly above), which is prefaced, unusually for a royal letter, with the date of the eponymous *prytanis*.⁶⁵ Other

---

⁶¹ *BSA* lxvi (1971), 9; cf. above, ch. 6, and below, Appendix iii.
⁶² *OGIS* 331 IV, lines 57–60.
⁶³ *OGIS* 331 I.
⁶⁴ *Syll.*³ 1007; see above, 162.
⁶⁵ *IvP* 157, = Welles, *RC* 48, quoted above, 164.

176 The City of Pergamon

Attalid letters are dated, when they are dated at all, by the month and year of the king's reign, differing in this respect from the Seleukid practice of dating by a Seleukid era. There is a good explanation that suggests itself of a copy of a royal letter bearing a civic date: that this copy is of the civic, and not the royal, archive. In fact an *archeion* is attested at Pergamon by the Astynomic Law, and it is most likely that it housed copies of royal letters and *prostagmata* as well as copies of its own civil legislation.[66] This fact is further evidence of a strongly maintained distinction between the royal and civil bureaucracies.

It remains, finally, to consider the territorial extent of the jurisdiction exercised by the civil administration. After the Treaty of Apameia the administration of the kingdom was, as we have seen, exclusively the concern of the royal administration, which was significantly developed to meet these new requirements.[67] The civil administration at Pergamon, which remained, according to the conclusions reached above, entirely separate from the concept of the kingdom, was confined to the city itself and the surrounding country. We have seen from the evidence of the ephebic lists that, apart from the citizens of Pergamon listed with patronymic and tribe, and the ξένοι listed with patronymic and ethnic, there are those designated as being ἀπὸ τόπων, which we have concluded to be villages in the territory of the city, and therefore presumably subject to the city's authority.[68] The fact that they are listed without tribal designation indicates that in the regal period they were not citizens of Pergamon; significantly, a group of *katoikoi*, villagers of the Pergamene *chora*, received citizenship after the death of Attalos III, according to the decree concerned with the extension of these rights:[69] τῶν στρατιωτῶν τοῖς κα[το]ικοῦσιν [τὴμ πό]|λιγ καὶ τὴγ χώραν, ὁμοίως δὲ καὶ Μακεδό[σι]ν καὶ

---

[66] Kla. 227–32: ὅσοι δ' ἂν τῶν ἀστυνόμων μὴ | θῶνται τὴν ἐφ᾽ ἑαυτῶν γραφὴν τῶν φρε|άτων εἰς τὸ ἀρχεῖον ἢ μὴ ποιήσωσιν, καθ᾽ ἃ | ὁ νόμος προστάσσει, πραξάτωσαν αὐτοὺς οἱ | νομοφύλακες δραχμὰς ἑκατὸν καὶ κατα|ταξάτωσαν εἰς τὰς αὐτὰς προσόδους. On this *archeion* cf. Bengtson, *Strat.* ii. 238; compare the *archeion* of the magistrates at Seleukeia in Piereia (Holleaux, *Études*, iii. 199–200, = Welles, *RC* 45 A, lines 22–5, with Holleaux's commentary ad loc., p. 246).

[67] On the royal administration see above, ch. 4 (i) and (iv).

[68] See above, ch. 4 (i).

[69] *IvP* 249, = *OGIS* 338; *IGR* iv. 289, lines 13–16.

Μυ[σοῖς]‖ καὶ τοῖς ἀναφερομένοις ἐν τῶι φρουρίωι καὶ [τῆι πόλει τῆι]‖ ἀρχαίαι κατοίκοις καὶ Μασδυηνοῖς κτλ. These *katoikoi* were surely not, as has been suggested, royal mercenaries in the usual sense,[70] but rather members of the village communities around Pergamon who served, as well as Pergamene citizens, in the army as reorganized by Attalos I. The distinction is clear, as we have seen, in the lists of names appended to the honorary decrees of Lilaia dating from the time of the First Macedonian War.[71] It is apparent from all this evidence that citizenship of Pergamon was closely confined, and that many communities were kept outside full civic life until the drastic reorganization of these rights after the death of Attalos III.

The Attalids, then, were concerned to promote the esteem of the city of Pergamon in the Greek world. Its political freedom was clearly limited, especially after 188, by the kings' powers of appointing important officials, especially the *strategoi* and later the *ἐπὶ τῆς πόλεως* and the *ἐπὶ τῶν ἱερῶν προσόδων*, and by their issue of royal *prostagmata*; but the fact that it retained its own legislative and executive functions, its own body of laws and its own archive, quite distinct from the royal chancery, shows, despite these restrictions, that it was regarded as a political entity in a class by itself, separate in concept from the Attalid Kingdom, and in practical terms from the royal administration, and constitutionally self-dependent. Of greater importance than these outward forms, however, is the undeniable special favour shown to the city by the kings, and nowhere more clearly than in religious life: its gods were ever more closely identified with theirs, and royal and divine cults were subtly blended, the physical glorification of the city being the clearest outward expression of this unique process of spiritual union.

---

[70] So Dittenberger ad loc., n. 12: *milites mercennarii regis.* In n. 13 they are explained as *quos maxime ex parte Graecos fuisse probabile est,* and are distinguished from the Macedonians, *coloni qui iam antiquitus in illis regionibus consederant.* I see no reason to regard the former category as mercenaries.

[71] Cf. above, 33.

APPENDICES

I

THE GENEALOGY OF THE ATTALIDS

The genealogy of the Attalids adopted in this study, and argued below, is
as follows:

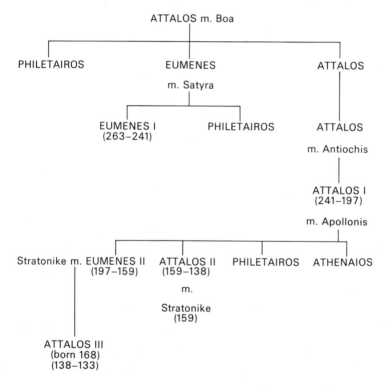

The basis of our knowledge of the Attalids' relationships to one another
is the narrative of Strabo, which also provides us with a framework of
Attalid chronology (see above, 9–11), xiii. 4. 1–2, 623–4. Here we are
given the following information (T[estimonia] 1–6):

1. ἦσαν δ' αὐτῷ (Philetairos the Founder) δύο ἀδελφοί, πρεσβύτερος μὲν
Εὐμένης, νεώτερος δ' Ἄτταλος.
2. ἐκ μὲν οὖν Εὐμένους ἐγένετο ὁμώνυμος τῷ πατρὶ Εὐμένης, ὅσπερ καὶ
διεδέξατο τὸ Πέργαμον κτλ. (= Eumenes I).
3. ἐκ δὲ Ἀττάλου καὶ Ἀντιοχίδος, τῆς Ἀχαιοῦ, γεγονὼς Ἄτταλος

διεδέξατο τὴν ἀρχήν, καὶ ἀνηγορεύθη βασιλεὺς πρῶτος κτλ. (= Attalos I).

4. (Attalos I) κατέλιπε δὲ τέτταρας υἱοὺς ἐξ Ἀπολλωνίδος Κυζικηνῆς γυναικός, Εὐμένη, Ἄτταλον, Φιλέταιρον, Ἀθήναιον. οἱ μὲν οὖν νεώτεροι διετέλεσαν ἰδιῶται, τῶν δ' ἄλλων ὁ πρεσβύτερος Εὐμένης ἐβασίλευσε (= Eumenes II).

5. (Eumenes II) ἀπέλιπεν υἱῷ τὴν ἀρχὴν Ἀττάλῳ, γεγονότι ἐκ Στρατονίκης τῆς Ἀριαράθου θυγατρὸς τοῦ Καππαδόκων βασιλέως. ἐπίτροπον δὲ κατέστησε καὶ τοῦ παιδὸς νέου τελέως ὄντος καὶ τῆς ἀρχῆς τὸν ἀδελφὸν Ἄτταλον (= Attalos II).

6. (Attalos II) κατέλιπε δὲ τὴν ἀρχὴν τῷ ἐπιτροπευθέντι Ἀττάλῳ (= Attalos III).

A genealogical tree based on this evidence appears as follows:

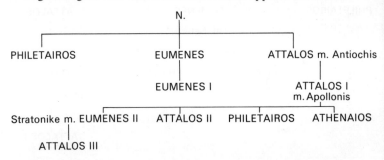

It has always been assumed in studies of Attalid genealogy that, when Strabo speaks of 'Attalos, the son of Attalos and Antiochis' (= T3 above), he means us to understand the elder Attalos, the father of Attalos I, as being the same man as the brother of Philetairos mentioned earlier (= T1).[1] This evidently was the inference made by Pausanias (i. 8.1): ὁ δὲ Ἄτταλος Ἀττάλου μὲν παῖς ὤν, ἀδελφιδοῦς δὲ Φιλεταίρου, τὴν ἀρχὴν Εὐμένους παραδόντος ἔσχεν ἀνεψιοῦ. I have reproduced this assumption here for convenience, but it should be realized that Strabo is not specific on the point, and that Pausanias' inference has no more validity than our own.

Strabo (xiii. 4. 1) has nothing to say of Philetairos' parentage beyond calling him ἀνὴρ Τιανός, θλιβίας ἐκ παιδός, but his Paphlagonian origin on his mother's side is attested elsewhere:

[1] The following abbreviations are used of frequently cited studies of Attalid genealogy:

Dörpfeld = W. Dörpfeld, *AM* xxxv (1910), 525–6.
Cardinali, *Mem.* = G. Cardinali, *Mem. della R. Accademia dell' Ist. di Bologna*, 1912–13, 177 ff.
Cardinali, *Rendiconto* = G. Cardinali, *Rendiconto dell' Accad. delle scienze di Bologna*, 1913–14, 37–41.
Preuner = E. Preuner, *Hermes*, lv (1920), 394 ff.
Meyer = Ernst Meyer, *Klio*, xix (1925), 462–71.

Pausanias i. 8.1: Δόκιμος . . . Φιλέταιρον Παφλαγόνα εἶχεν εὐνοῦχον.

Athenaeus xiii. 577B (from Karystios of Pergamon): Φιλέταιρον δὲ τὸν Περγά-
μου καὶ τῆς καινῆς ταύτης λεγομένης βασιλεύσαντα χώρας Βόας αὐλητρίδας
ἑταίρας τὸ γένος ἀπὸ Παφλαγονίας υἱόν φησι γενέσθαι Καρύστιος ἐν ἱστορικοῖς
ὑπομνήμασιν.

IvP ii. 613 (*OGIS* 264, 'Chronica Pergami').
The text is too fragmentary to
restore in full, but the Paphlagonian side of Philetairos' parentage is clear from lines
14–15: [αὕτη δὲ συνοικήσασα - - - -]νι, Παφλαγόνι [τὸ γένος, ἔτεκε - - - -].

The main problems concerning Attalid genealogy can be grouped together under two headings: I. the relationships of the early Attalids, down
to Attalos I; and II. the parentage of Attalos III. I list here the remaining
testimonia (T7–36) relating to each heading, with a discussion of each
group.

I. The Early Attalids.

7. P. M. Fraser, *REA* liv (1952), 233–45, nos. 1(a), 1(b), 2, 3; Appendix
iv, no. 1. Boiotian dedications of Philetairos: Φιλέτηρος 'Αττάλω Περγαμεύς.
8. *Mamurt-Kaleh*, p.10. Dedication of Philetairos at the temple of Meter:
Φιλέταιρος 'Αττάλου μητρὶ θεῶν.
9. Dedications of Philetairos at the temple of Apollo Chresterios near
Aigai: (a) *OGIS* 312: 'Απόλλωνι Χρηστηρίῳ | Φιλέταιρος 'Αττάλου.
 (b) G. E. Bean, *Belleten*, xxx (1966), 525–8, = J. and L. Robert,
Bull. 1968, no. 446: [Φιλέταιρος] | 'Αττάλω | 'Απόλλωνι |
Χρηστηρίῳ | τὰν χώραν | | ἀνέθηκε | ὡς αἱ στάλ\λαι ὁρίσζοισι.
10. *OGIS* 748. Record of Philetairos' donations to Kyzikos, headed: τάδε
ἔδωκεν Φιλέταιρος | 'Αττάλου τῶι δήμωι.
11. *AM* xxxv (1910), nos. 22–3. Dedication of the temple of Demeter at
Pergamon: Φιλέταιρος καὶ Εὐμένης ὑπὲρ τῆς μητρὸς Βόας Δήμητρι.
(Compare the beginning of a similar dedication of an altar, *AM* xxxvii
(1912), 282, no. 5: Φιλέτ[αιρος - - - -]. See Ohlemutz, *Kulte*, 204–5).
12. Petrakos, *Arch. Ephem. Chronika*, 1967, 11, no.11, = J. and L.
Robert, *Bull.* 1968, no. 282, = *SEG* xxiv. 356. Dedication from the Am-
phiareion at Oropos: Φιλέταιρον | 'Αττάλου | Εὐμένης | ἀδελφὸς | 'Αμφια-
ρά[ωι].
13. *IG* xi. 4. 1106 (on the restoration, see below): Εὐμένης [Εὐμένου]
Φιλέταιρον τ[ὸν ἀδελφόν].
14. Holleaux,*Études*, ii. 9–16 (from*REA* 1918), = *F. Delphes*, iii. 1. 432:

Δελφοὶ ἔδωκαν [Φιλεταίρωι καὶ τῶι υἱ]ῶι 'Αττάλωι,
καὶ τῶι ἀδελφῶι [Εὐμένει Περγα]μεῦσσι προξενίαν, κτλ.

15. *Mamurt-Kaleh*, p. 38. Dedication from the temple of Meter: ῎Ατταλος
Φιλεταίρου | 'Αντιοχίδα τὴν γυναῖκα.
16. *IG*. xi. 4. 1108, = *Choix*, 52. Dedication of Attalos I from Delos:
[Βασιλεὺς] ῎Ατταλος | ['Αττάλου τ]οῦ Φιλεταίρου | [καὶ 'Αντι]οχίδος.
17. *AM* xxxiii (1908), 405, no. 34. Dedication from Pergamon: Φιλέταιρος
'Αττάλου | Εὐμένη τὸν υἱόν.

18. *AM* xxxv (1910), 463–5, no. 45: Εὐμένης Φιλεταίρου | Ἄτταλον τὸν υἱόν.
19. *IG* xi. 4. 1107, = *Choix*, 33: Εὐμένης Εὐμένου | τοῦ Φιλεταίρου ἀδελφοῦ | καὶ Σατύρας τῆς Ποσειδωνίου.
20. Diog. Laert. iv. 6. 38: Εὐμένης ὁ τοῦ Φιλεταίρου.
21. *IvP* 13, = *OGIS* 266, = *StV* iii. 481. Treaty of Eumenes I with the mercenaries at Philetaireia and Attaleia, lines 1, 26, 27, 32, 36, 39, 43–4, 49: Εὐμένης Φιλεταίρου. (Restored in *IvP* 18, = *OGIS* 267, = *RC* 23, line 1.).
22. *IvP* 13 etc., lines 46–7: Εὐμένης ᾿Αττάλου.
23. P. M. Fraser, *REA* liv (1952), 235, no. 4 (a), = *OGIS* ii. 750; Appendix iv, no. 1(e): Φιλέταιρος Εὐμένου.

From this evidence, the information derived from Strabo can be supplemented as follows:

(i) The Founder Philetairos was the son of an Attalos. Holleaux reasoned conclusively (*Études,* ii. 1–16, two articles from *REG* 1902 and *REA* 1918) that the Philetairos of T7–10 is the Founder and not the younger brother of Eumenes II; this conclusion has been confirmed by further epigraphical evidence, especially T9 (b) and T12.
(ii) Philetairos at one time adopted Attalos, the father of the future Attalos I (T14–16) and later adopted his nephew Eumenes (T17–18, 20–1). In T20 Meyer amended the text to read Εὐμένης ὁ τοῦ Φιλεταίρου ἀδελφιδοῦς; the text was shown to be right, however, by the evidence of the adoption (cf. Cardinali *RP* 13, n. 3).
(iii) The mother of Eumenes I was Satyra, and her father was Poseidonios (T19).
(iv) Two names, otherwise unattested in their respective forms (see below on T13), are supplied by T22 and 23: Eumenes son of Attalos, and Philetairos son of Eumenes. In the case of T23 the absence of the royal title, and the letter-forms of the inscription, discount an association with the later king, Eumenes II.
(v) Eumenes I also adopted his successor, Attalos I (T18).

The first difficulty concerns the father of Attalos I. In their studies of Attalid genealogy (see n.1, above), Dörpfeld and Cardinali, following the assumption that in Strabo's passage the Attalos who is the father of Attalos I (=T3) is the same as the brother of Philetairos the Founder (=T1), posed the problem that according to the epigraphical evidence Philetairos adopted this Attalos (T15–16); Strabo was therefore in error unless we are to believe that Philetairos adopted his own brother.[2] Ernst Meyer advanced strong chronological arguments against this possibility.[3] Finally, the publication of T16, and then of T14, in which Attalos is designated the son and Eumenes the brother of Philetairos, confirmed, if confirmation were needed, that this Attalos could not be the brother of the Founder.[4]

[2] Cardinali, *Mem.* 181, n. 5; Holleaux, *Études,* ii. 11, n. 3; Meyer 467.
[3] Meyer 466. If Philetairos was born about 343, he will have been a little over sixty in 280, and not 'über 70 Jahre' as stated by Meyer.
[4] The most plausible restoration in line 3 of the inscription is τῶι ἀδελφῶι [Εὐμένει] κτλ. (Holleaux, *Études,* ii. 13–14). On T16 (a dedication of Attalos I on Delos), which supports Cardinali's original line of enquiry, see Cardinali, *Rendiconto,* 37 ff.

Cardinali's solution of the problem, later supported by T14, and followed by Ernst Meyer, was to distinguish the father of Attalos I from the brother of Philetairos, thus:

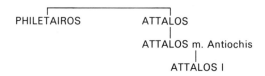

Strabo and Pausanias have therefore, according to Cardinali, confused the first two of the name Attalos as being one person.

Dörpfeld suggested, on the other hand, that the Attalos of T15–16 was not the adopted son of Philetairos the Founder, but the son κατὰ φύσιν of another Philetairos, brother of the Attalos who was the father of Philetairos the Founder:

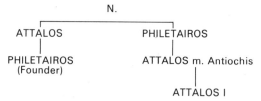

This system makes Attalos, the father of Attalos I, a cousin of Philetairos the Founder and not, as Strabo implies, a brother; thus, according to Dörpfeld, Strabo (xiii. 4. 2) mistook ἀδελφός for ἐξάδελφος. Needless to say, the postulation of a second Philetairos is quite arbitrary and cannot be taken as a sound basis for understanding Strabo's error, if there is an error. Cardinali's system has the virtue of doing the least possible violence to Strabo's evidence while explaining its evident ambiguity; nor does it at any point contradict Strabo's evidence since, as has been noted, Strabo only implies that Attalos the brother of Philetairos is the same as Attalos the father of Attalos I. What is more, in Dörpfeld's system Attalos I is a cousin of Eumenes I, a relationship that poses considerable chronological difficulties.[5] Cardinali's system also fits well with T14, while Dörpfeld's does not.[6]

From this beginning, the system can be built up to include other attested relations of Philetairos the Founder:

A. Eumenes, brother of Philetairos and father of the dynast Eumenes I. According to Strabo (T1), Eumenes was the elder and Attalos the younger of the two younger brothers of Philetairos, and yet it was Attalos' son who was adopted by Philetairos in the first instance, and Eumenes' son only later. A further difficulty arises from the fact that the dedication of the temple of Demeter at Pergamon (T11) bears only

[5] Cardinali, *Mem.* 179 ff.; Meyer 466 (with the proviso stated above, n. 3).
[6] Holleaux, *Études,* ii. 11 ff.

the names of Philetairos and Eumenes, not Attalos. Cardinali and Meyer, following a suggestion of Hepding,[7] concluded that the elder Attalos, Philetairos' brother, had died by the time of the dedication to Demeter, and that the younger Attalos, the father of Attalos I, who had been adopted by Philetairos and married to the Seleukid princess Antiochis, daughter of the elder Achaios, also died, some time before 263, necessitating Philetairos' adoption of Eumenes, son of his other brother Eumenes.[8] Meyer dated the marriage of Attalos to Antiochis to *c*. 280,[9] and concluded that since Attalos was adopted first, he had a prior claim, namely that his father Attalos was the elder of Philetairos' two brothers, while his uncle, Eumenes, was the younger: 'mit anderen Worten, sein Vater (= Attalos) war der ältere, Eumenes, der Vater Eumenes' I, der jüngere Bruder des Philetairos, ganz wie Cardinali wollte.' There are two major objections to this view:

1) the same presumption of death, for which there is no evidence in either case, has conveniently to cater for two members of the family; and 2) Strabo names Eumenes the elder, and Attalos the younger, of the brothers of Philetairos, as we have seen (T1). I reject it because an alternative explanation is apparent which conforms with Strabo's evidence. We know from an extract of Memnon (16 = *FGrHist* 434) that a Eumenes, very probably Philetairos' brother, held a position at Amastris similar to Philetairos' own at Pergamon, and that he came to Pergamon some time after the battle of Corupedion, having handed over Amastris in 279 to the rulers of Pontos, Mithridates II and Ariobarzanes.[10] It is likely from these facts that at the time when Philetairos wished to designate an heir (*c*.280), Eumenes was still at Amastris and not yet at Pergamon, while the younger brother, Attalos, was presumably resident at Pergamon. It was more reasonable, therefore, to adopt the son of Attalos than the son of Eumenes, and the choice signifies availability rather than seniority. The later adoption of Eumenes I may have been for any of a number of reasons besides death (such as ill health or fall from favour), and the same is true of the omission of the elder Attalos' name from the dedication to Demeter at Pergamon.

B. Εὐμένης 'Αττάλου (T22). In Cardinali's view he was the elder son of Philetairos' brother Attalos. This view was followed by Reinach (see below), but rejected by Ernst Meyer[11] for reasons which depended on dating the revolt at Philetaireia and Attaleia later than the end of the second Syrian War in 252, a chronology which I do not find acceptable (see 22–4, above). Meyer's own view, depending again on this chronology, was that Εὐμένης 'Αττάλου was a younger brother of Attalos I. Since I believe that the revolt of the mercenaries occurred in the years 263–261, I cannot subscribe to this view: Attalos I was only about six years old at this time,[12] and a younger brother could not therefore have been involved in events of this kind.

It is for positive reasons, however, that I return to the view of Smith and de Rustafjaell,[13] that this Εὐμένης 'Αττάλου was the brother of Philetairos the Founder, and the son of Attalos of Tios; that is, that the names headed A and B

[7] *AM* xxxv (1910), 437–8.

[8] Meyer 465 ff.

[9] Meyer 466. According to Seleukid chronology, Antiochos I was born about 323, his younger brother Achaios about 322, and his (Achaios') daughter about 300; she was therefore married to Attalos about 280. It should be noted that 280 marks the year of Antiochis' eligibility; she may have married Attalos somewhat later, although this is unlikely.

[10] Ed. Meyer, *Gesch. des Koenigreichs Pontos,* 41; cf. Rostovtzeff, *SEHHW* i. 577–8, and above, 14.

[11] Meyer 469 ff.

[12] Attalos I died in the autumn of 197 at the age of 72 (see above, 10 and n. 6); he was therefore born in 269 and was six years old at the time of Eumenes' accession in 263.

[13] *JHS* xxii (1902), 197; cf. Holleaux, *Études,* ii. 6, n.1.

above represent one and the same person. This view was rejected by Reinach, although he dated the revolt of the mercenaries to the late 260s, shortly after the accession of Eumenes I. His objection was mainly chronological: if Philetairos was aged eighty when he died in 263,[14] we cannot expect to find his brother at the centre of a conspiracy that took place a year or two later.[15] This argument clearly depends on the age-difference between the two brothers, a point on which we have no information, and it presents itself with no real cogency. Attalos II was young enough to succeed his brother in 159 and rule for twenty-one years, while the succession of four Hekatomnids of one generation in a previous century provides an even more forceful precedent.[16] Reinach's second objection, 's'il était encore en âge de jouer un rôle, pourquoi n'avait-il succédé à son frère comme Attalos II devrait succéder à Eumène II?', takes for granted the application of the stable dynastic succession of the later Attalids to the earlier period, an assumption which the treaty with the mercenaries disproves in itself; furthermore, it overlooks the principle, examined below, whereby Philetairos deliberately avoided the designation of his brothers as heirs.

Studies of Attalid genealogy have tended to rely on a schematized view of the succession in the early years of the dynasty, whereas it is all too clear that the issue was open and unsettled. It is evident that Philetairos' policy was to designate successors among his nephews, thereby passing over his own brothers. Since this is the only discernible principle involved, it should be the basis of our understanding of the events reflected in T21–2, the treaty with the mercenaries, and in particular of our identification of the rebellious Εὐμένης Ἀττάλου. It is possible that the right of Eumenes I to succeed Philetairos was contested by a cousin (Cardinali's view), but it is much more likely that the rival claimant was Eumenes' own father, the ex-ruler of Amastris who returned to Pergamon and was passed over in favour of the son.

C.Φιλέταιρος Εὐμένου (T23). Cardinali suggested that he might be the son of B above, where B is, according to Cardinali, the elder son of Philetairos' brother Attalos; thus C becomes a cousin of Attalos I. Cardinali's system can be presented as follows (1, 2, and 3 represent the order of succession of the dynasts):

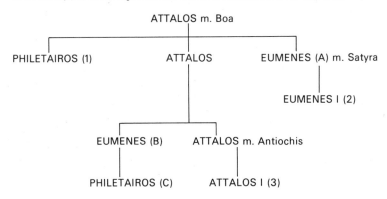

[14] Macrobius 12; cf. Meyer 466, n. 2.

[15] A. J. Reinach, *Rev. Arch.* xii (1908), 185 n. 3. This point naturally has greater force in the context of Ernst Meyer's chronology, in which the revolt of the mercenaries is dated later than 252.

[16] Judeich, *Kleinas. Studien* (Marburg, 1892), 226 ff.; Grampa, 'Nine Greek Inscriptions', in A. Westholm, *Labraunda,* i. 2. 121–33; G. Bockisch, *Klio,* li (1969), 117 ff.

If however, as I believe, A and B are the same person, the genealogy can be presented as follows (I invert the order of Philetairos' brothers in accordance with Strabo, for reasons already given):

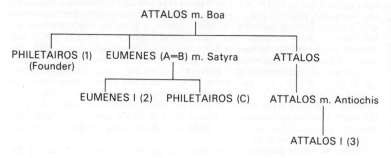

ATTALOS m. Boa

PHILETAIROS (1) (Founder) EUMENES (A=B) m. Satyra ATTALOS

EUMENES I (2) PHILETAIROS (C) ATTALOS m. Antiochis

ATTALOS I (3)

Ernst Meyer also made Φιλέταιρος Εὐμένου a brother of Eumenes I, but for reasons other than the equation of Eumenes A and Eumenes B proposed here.[17]

I should like now to draw attention to a base from Delos (T13), which bears the following inscription:

Εὐμένης - - - - - - - - - - - -
Φιλέταιρον τ[ὸν - - - - - - -

This text has been overlooked or discounted by all who have studied Attalid genealogy, including Ernst Meyer, who described it as 'zu verstümmelt'.[18] I believe that it has more to offer than has been realized.

The letters are of the mid-third century; we can therefore discount any association with the sons of Attalos I.[19] In identifying this Eumenes we are therefore left with three possibilities: (1) he is an unknown Eumenes, yet another mysterious member of the royal family; (2) he is the dynast Eumenes I; (3) he is the elder Eumenes, brother of Philetairos the Founder. The first may be put aside as long as others remain to be argued.

In the second case, it remains to identify the Philetairos who is the object of the dedication. Clearly he could be the Founder, Eumenes' father by adoption.[20] We then have Εὐμένης - - - - | Φιλέταιρον τ[ὸν πατέρα], with the option of restoring Εὐμένου or Φιλεταίρου in the first line. Either form would be extremely bizarre; we would expect surely

[17] Meyer 470, following Preuner 400 ff. Preuner rejected Cardinali's view on the grounds that the son of a rebel would hardly have been allowed to call himself Περγαμεύς beside Philetairos, the founder of the dynasty; this is not a valid objection, however, since the rebellion took place at a later date. There is greater cogency in Preuner's argument that, since the dedication T23 belongs to the same time as Philetairos' own, it can hardly have been the work of a son of his nephew, separated from him by two generations.

[18] Meyer 463, n. 2.

[19] The absence of the royal title in the case of Eumenes is not in itself decisive, since the dedication could have been made, on this criterion alone, by Eumenes II before he became king.

[20] As Magie evidently believed: *Roman Rule*, ii. 732, n.14.

Φιλέταιρον Ἀττάλου Εὐμένης ὁ υἱός. So this possibility can be discounted with confidence. There remains Eumenes I's own brother Philetairos. The restoration then suggested is far more plausible: Εὐμένης [Εὐμένου] | Φιλέταιρον τ[ὸν ἀδελφόν].

If, however, the third possibility is considered, the Philetairos concerned will be either the brother of Eumenes, that is Philetairos the Founder, or the son, that is the brother of Eumenes I, thus:

either Εὐμένης [Ἀττάλου] | Φιλέταιρον τ[ὸν ἀδελφόν]

or Εὐμένης [Ἀττάλου] | Φιλέταιρον τ[ὸν υἱόν].

This much is established from the evidence of Attalid genealogy. On other historical evidence we can perhaps hope to reach nearer the truth. Attalid contacts with Delos date from the end of the rule of Philetairos and, more firmly, from the reign of Eumenes I; as we would expect of Delos, this contact is represented personally and exclusively by the dynasts. The Delian Philetaireia were evidently founded by Eumenes I shortly after his accession (see above, 22 and n. 46), and Eumenes' statue was probably the first of an Attalid to be erected on the island.[21] I have suggested elsewhere that the base bearing an inscribed epigram celebrating the Galatian victories of Philetairos was erected on Delos by Attalos I at the time of his Galatian wars (see above, 31 n. 8), and in any event the letter-forms indicate a date after Philetairos' death. In view of the evident lack of firm contact with Delos under Philetairos, and since this contact, when established, was apparently made by the dynasts alone, it is unlikely that Philetairos' younger brother will have had the opportunity of making so monumental an offering. It appears surely to be the work of a dynast of Pergamon, namely Eumenes I. I believe then that the inscription under discussion should be completed as follows:

Εὐμένης [Εὐμένου]
Φιλέταιρον τ[ὸν ἀδελφόν].

II. The Chronology and Parentage of Attalos III.

24. Polyb. xxx. 2 (168/7): Stratios is sent to Rome by Eumenes II to dissuade his brother Attalos (II) from rebelling against him; he would shortly be king in any case (5–6), ἅτε τοῦ βασιλέως διὰ μὲν τὴν σωματικὴν ἀσθένειαν αἰεὶ προσδοκῶντος τὴν ἐκ τοῦ βίου μετάστασιν, διὰ δὲ τὴν ἀπαιδίαν οὐδ᾽ εἰ βουληθείη δυναμένου τὴν ἀρχὴν ἄλλῳ καταλιπεῖν· οὐδέπω γὰρ ἀναδεδειγμένος ἐτύγχανεν κατὰ φύσιν υἱὸς ὢν αὐτῷ ὁ μετὰ ταῦτα διαδεξάμενος τὴν ἀρχήν.

25. Polyb. xxxiii. 18. 1–4 (embassies in Rome in 152): ἡ σύγκλητος πρῶτον

---

[21] In the inscription on the base (=T19), Eumenes is called Εὐμένης Εὐμένου, not Εὐμένης Φιλεταίρου. I consider that this is because the Attalids' dedications and foundations at Delos were of a personal nature, and not because the base necessarily dates from before Philetairos' adoption of Eumenes. Eumenes is only called Εὐμένης Φιλεταίρου in documents of an official nature and in dedications from within the Attalid Kingdom.

190   Appendix I

μὲν εἰσεκαλέσατο τὸν Εὐμένους τοῦ βασιλέως υἱὸν Ἄτταλον· παραγεγόνει γὰρ ἔτι παῖς ὢν κατὰ τὸν καιρὸν τοῦτον εἰς Ῥώμην χάριν τοῦ τῇ τε συγκλήτῳ συσταθῆναι καὶ τὰς πατρικὰς ἀνανεώσασθαι φιλίας καὶ ξενίας. οὗτος μὲν οὖν... λαβὼν... τιμὰς ἁρμοζούσας τῇ καθ᾿ αὑτὸν ἡλικίᾳ κτλ.

26. Plutarch, *Moralia* 184B: Εὐμένης ἐπιβουλευθεὶς ὑπὸ Περσέως ἔδοξε τεθνάναι· τῆς δὲ φήμης εἰς Πέργαμον κομισθείσης, Ἄτταλος ὁ ἀδελφὸς αὐτοῦ περιθέμενος τὸ διάδημα καὶ τὴν γυναῖκα γήμας ἐβασίλευσε· πυθόμενος δὲ προσιόντα ζῶντα τὸν ἀδελφὸν ἀπήντησεν ὥσπερ εἰώθει μετὰ τῶν σωματοφυλάκων δοράτιον ἔχων· ὁ δὲ Εὐμένης φιλοφρόνως ἀσπασάμενος αὐτὸν καὶ πρὸς τὸ οὖς εἰπών, «μὴ σπεῦδε γῆμαι πρὶν τελευτήσαντ᾿ ἴδῃς», οὐδὲν ἄλλο παρὰ πάντα τὸν βίον οὔτ᾿ εἶπεν ὕποπτον οὔτε ἐποίησεν, ἀλλὰ καὶ τελευτῶν ἐκείνῳ τὴν γυναῖκα καὶ τὴν βασιλείαν ἀπέλιπεν. ἀνθ᾿ ὧν ἐκεῖνος οὐδὲν ἐξ ἑαυτοῦ τέκνον ἔθρεψε, πολλῶν γενομένων, ἀλλὰ τῷ Εὐμένους υἱῷ τὴν βασιλείαν ἔτι ζῶν ἐνηλίκῳ γενομένῳ παρέδωκε. Ibid. 489F: Ἄτταλος οὖν ὁ πρεσβύτατος αὐτοῦ τῶν ἀδελφῶν, ἀνὴρ ἐπιεικὴς καὶ περὶ τὸν Εὐμένη πάντων ἄριστος, οὐ μόνον βασιλεὺς ἀνηγορεύθη διαδησάμενος, ἀλλὰ καὶ τὴν γυναῖκα τἀδελφοῦ Στρατονίκην ἔγημε καὶ συνῆλθεν· (The same story then follows.) τί οὖν ἐκεῖνος (Attalos); ἀποθανόντος αὐτοῦ (Eumenes II) παιδίον οὐδὲ ἓν ἠθέλησεν ἐκ τῆς γυναικὸς ἀνελέσθαι, τεκούσης πολλάκις, ἀλλὰ τὸν ἐκείνου παῖδα θρέψας καὶ ἀνδρώσας ἔτι ζῶν ἐπέθηκε τὸ διάδημα καὶ βασιλέα προσηγόρευσεν. Cf. Livy, *Epit.* lviii: *Attalos, rex Pergami, Eumenis filius;* Florus i. 35. 2: *Attalus rex Pergamenorum, regis Eumenis filius.*

27. *IvP* 246, = *OGIS* 332. Decree, probably of Pergamon, honouring Attalos III, who is called (lines 21–2, 24–5, 44–5) βασιλεὺς Ἄτταλος Φιλομήτωρ καὶ Εὐεργέτης θεοῦ βασιλέως Εὐμένου Σωτῆρος.

28. *IvP* 248, = *OGIS* 331, = *RC* 65–7. Letters concerning the priesthood of Dionysos Kathegemon, line 18 (letter of Attalos II): κεκρίκαμεν κἀγὼ καὶ [Ἄτταλ]ος ὁ τἀδελφοῦ υἱός; lines 32, 39 (letter of Attalos III): Ἄτταλος ὁ θεῖός μου; lines 45–6 (the same): βασίλισσα Στρατονίκη ἡ μήτηρ μου.

29. Swoboda, Keil, and Kroll, *Denkmäler aus Lykaonien*, 33, no. 75. Letter of Attalos II to Amlada, lines 4–5: [Ἀττά]λωι τῶι τἀδελφοῦ [υἱῶι].

30. *AM* xxix (1904), 170 ff., no. 14. Decree of the Pergamene *epheboi* honouring Attalos (III), 147/6, line 9: Ἀττάλωι βασιλέως Εὐμένου.

31. *OGIS* 329 (decree of Aigina, Attalos II), line 40: Ἄτταλ[ον τὸν] βα[σιλέως] Ε[ὐμ]ένου.

32. Appendix iv, no. 15. Decree of Miletos honouring Eumenes II, his brothers, καὶ ὁ υἱὸς Ἄτταλος (line 40). On the date, see above, 116–118.

33. *IvM* 87, = *OGIS* 319 (honorary decree of Magnesia), line 16: Ἀττάλου τοῦ υἱοῦ τοῦ βασιλ[έω]ς Εὐμένου.

34. *IvP* ii. 613, = *OGIS* 264 ('Chronica Pergami'), lines 16 ff.:

Ε[ὐ]μέ[νης, διὰ βίου ἤδη τῆς ἀρχῆς κοινω-]
νήσας [᾿Ατ]τά[λωι τῶι ἀδελφῶι, ἀπέθανε κατα-]
λείπων τὴν [μὲν βασιλείαν τῶι ἑαυτοῦ υἱῶι]

Ἀττάλωι, κατ᾽ ἐ[πιτροπὴν δὲ ἐκείνωι. οὗτος δὲ]
20   ἀπέδωκεν τὴ[ν βασιλείαν ἀποθνήσκων Ἀττάλωι]
τῶι τοῦ Εὐμέν[ους - - - -

35. Appendix iv, no. 24, lines 2–3: ἄξιος . . . τῆς Ἀττάλου τἀδελ[φοῦ |μου παιδεί]ας.

36. Börker and Merkelbach, *Inschr. von Ephesos*, no. 200: Ἀττάλο[υ---] | θεοῦ Εὐμέ[νου(ς) Σωτῆ|ρο]ς ὑοῦ.

Apart from T24, which reveals the young Attalos as the still unrecognized heir of Eumenes II in 168/7, all the evidence, literary and epigraphical, emanating from Pergamon and elsewhere, indicates that Attalos III was the son κατὰ φύσιν of Eumenes II and his queen, Stratonike. T24, the statement of Eumenes' physician Stratios, quoted by Polybios, certainly throws an isolated but effective doubt on this conclusion, and since Köpp's argument, based on this passage, that Attalos III was the son of Stratonike and Attalos II, a considerable bibliography has grown up on this subject.[22] Köpp's argument was devised from the tradition found in Plutarch (=T26) that Attalos II took the throne and married Stratonike for a short time in 171 after Eumenes II had been attacked near Delphi and was for a while thought to be dead. Ferguson and others, following Köpp and noting the passage of Polybios (=T24) which shows Attalos III to be unrecognized by Eumenes II five years later, believed that he was the outcome of this temporary union of Attalos II and Stratonike.[23]

The objection usually adduced against this view is that if Attalos III was born in 171 or 170 he could hardly be described as ἔτι παῖς ὤν in 152 (Polybios in T25), for he would then have been eighteen, and maturity at Pergamon was reckoned from the age of fifteen,[24] but this reasoning seems

[22] F. Köpp, 'De gigantomachiae in poeseos artisque monumentis usu' (Diss. Bonn, 1883); *Rh. Mus.* xlviii (1893), 154–5. To the bibliography given by Hansen, *Attalids*, 471–4 should be added the works cited by Magie, *Roman Rule*, ii. 772, n. 76. For the view that Attalos III was the son of Eumenes II by a concubine, see Niese iii. 204, n. 4; Magie, loc. cit. This is clearly an arbitrary view designed to explain T24 in the simplest way; there is no evidence to support it, and it is discounted by the arguments presented here.

[23] On this incident see Livy xlii. 15–16, the only reliable account (see below). W. S. Ferguson, in *C. Phil.* i (1906), 231–4, explained in terms of these events an admittedly unusual dedication from Thrace honouring Eumenes II (*OGIS* 302) in the form ὑπὲρ βασιλέως Εὐμένου Φιλαδέλφου καὶ Εὐεργέτου. Two dedications to Attalos II were found with this one (*OGIS* 303–4). According to Ferguson, Eumenes was prematurely deified in 171; Attalos II married Stratonike, and Attalos III was born of this marriage. Eumenes returned and forgave Attalos, who duly abdicated, and the dedication *OGIS* 302 was erected in gratitude for the clemency and brotherly love of the restored king. This reasoning would be attractive if it did not rely on a late and clearly distorted tradition which Ferguson accepts at face value and does not examine (see below), and if there were not other historical contexts for the epithets used in the Thracian dedications: in chapter 6 it was shown that Eumenes II and Attalos II were called θεοὶ φιλάδελφοι at least after their deaths.

[24] *AM* xxix (1904), 170 ff, no. 4, line 7.

to me to have little force, since the evidence comes not from Pergamon but from Polybios, who uses the same term elsewhere of the seventeen-year-old Philip V of Macedon (see below, n. 30). On the other hand, the evidence on which Köpp's view rests is hardly reliable. Livy, who in following Polybios provides us with the nearest to a contemporary account, merely narrates that Attalos II took the opportunity provided by news of Eumenes' presumed death to court Stratonike (xlii. 16. 7–9):[25]

Attalus quoque celerius quam dignum concordia fraterna erat credidit; nam et cum uxore fratris et praefecto arcis tamquam iam haud dubius regni heres est locutus. Quae postea non fefellere Eumenen; et quamquam dissimulare et tacite habere et pati statuerat, tamen in primo congressu non temperavit, quin uxoris petendae immaturam festinationem fratri obiceret.

It is the later and therefore less reliable tradition, represented by Plutarch (=T26), that elaborates the story into one of marriage with Stratonike and assumption of the kingship. Furthermore, even this later tradition fails to meet the demands of Köpp and Ferguson. According to Plutarch, 'many children' were born of Attalos II and Stratonike, but none was raised by Attalos, and the crown was allowed to pass to *Eumenes'* son. Apart from the obvious objection that even in this tradition, on which Köpp and his followers, including Ferguson, rely, Attalos III is named a son of Eumenes II as distinct from the children of the alleged marriage of Attalos II and Stratonike, it is clear also that in this tradition the children of Attalos II were thought to have been born of the marriage eventually concluded after the death of Eumenes in 159. Finally, this later version can be discredited on another count. In *Mor.* 389F Attalos II is said to have 'shared the diadem (with Attalos III) and called him king'. This statement is true only to the extent that Attalos III appears to have shared in some decisions before his formal accession (see below); beyond that it is contradicted by contemporary records, and in particular by the letter written by Attalos II to his cousin Athenaios about the priesthood of Dionysos Kathegemon (=T28), in which Attalos III appears without the royal title, in the simple form Ἄτταλος ὁ τἀδελφοῦ υἱός. This document is dated to 142 BC, a year in which Attalos III was, on any chronological view, well beyond maturity and old enough to succeed in his own right; indeed, Köpp's view leads to the conclusion that he was nearly thirty years old in this year! It is clear, then, that the tradition on which Köpp and Ferguson have relied not merely fails to support their conclusion, but even contradicts it on a number of points, and is itself discredited on another.

Attempts have been made in this connection to estimate the year of the birth of Attalos III. Those who follow Köpp and the corrupt tradition of course date this to 171 or 170; the problems raised thereby have already been indicated. Eumenes was betrothed to Stratonike, the daughter of Ariarathes IV of Cappadocia, in 188 BC, and the marriage probably took place shortly thereafter, although the exact date is not known.[26] On the

[25] This point was rightly emphasized by Nissen, *Kritische Untersuchungen* (Berlin, 1863), 246.

[26] Livy xxxviii. 39. 6; see below, Appendix iii.

evidence of T25, Attalos III cannot have been much more than eighteen in 152, the year of the embassies in Rome, and therefore cannot have been born much earlier than 169: hence the objection raised by Magie and others, that 'even granting that Stratonike and Eumenes were not married for several years after their betrothal in 188, it is difficult to believe that their son was not born until after 167' (167 being Magie's *terminus post quem*, interpreting ἔτι παῖς ὤν in T25 as implying an upper age limit of fifteen in 152, but see above). This absurd generalization is admittedly less fanciful than the implied notion of Ferguson: 'Stratonike had been child-less for over sixteen years; she now (171) became pregnant, and, in due course, bore a son . . .'; but it should hardly be necessary to point out the irrelevance and historical worthlessness of this kind of argument, or to state the requirement of more cogent arguments in support of so loose a hypothesis.[27]

We remain, then, for the time being, with an estimate of *c.* 167 for the year of the birth of Attalos III. Further attempts have been made to reach a more exact date. In a decree dated 147/6 (=T30), Attalos was honoured by the newly promoted ephebes of that year, but there is no sound reason for supposing that he was one of their generation, that is, that he was fifteen in 147/6 and therefore born in 162/1,[28] and I do not believe that this piece of evidence can be expected to make any precise contribution to the problems of Attalos' chronology. There is, however, a line of enquiry which has not been attempted in studies of this problem, but is more secure than many others more usually followed. Attalos II continued to rule until his death in 138 although Attalos III, over whom he had been appointed *epitropos* (T5), had reached an age of majority well before then, and was associated with a decision of Attalos II in a document dated 142/1 (T28: κεκρίκαμεγ κἀγὼ καὶ [Ἄτταλ]ος ὁ τἀδελφοῦ υἱός). The younger Attalos was also involved in dealings with the Pisidian city of Amlada, according to one of the letters of Attalos II to the city (T29); these dealings should be dated to the late 150s or the early 140s rather than later, since they resulted from the Galatian war of Eumenes II, to which reference is made in another letter of the correspondence.[29] This evidence shows that Attalos III was participating fully in the administration of the kingdom at about the time of his visit to Rome in 152; clearly, then, we must interpret Polybios' designation ἔτι παῖς ὤν with reference to this year (T25) as implying an age more advanced than that of childhood, and 167 becomes a *terminus ante quem* of Attalos' birth.[30]

All the considerations so far discussed suggest the year 168 as the most likely date of the birth of Attalos III. He will then have been sixteen in 152, a conclusion consistent with Polybios' evidence, as we have seen. Stratios' words, as reported by Polybios in T24, now require some expla-

[27] Magie, *Roman Rule,* ii. 773; Ferguson, loc. cit. (n. 23), 233–4.

[28] In Hansen's view, *Attalids,* 474, this 'seems probable'. I do not think so.

[29] Appendix iv, no. 23; see above, 143–4.

[30] Note that Polybios at iv. 2. 5 uses the same expression ἔτι παῖς ὤν of Philip V of Macedon at the age of seventeen.

nation, and this will hinge ultimately on the interpretation drawn from the words οὐδέπω γὰρ ἀναδεδειγμένος ἐτύγχανεν κατὰ φύσιν υἱὸς ὢν αὐτῷ ὁ μετὰ ταῦτα διαδεξάμενος τὴν ἀρχήν. If my chronological conclusion is correct, Attalos was born at about the time of Stratios' visit to Rome in 168/7: so, while Cardinali's interpretation of the word ἀναδεδειγμένος as 'born' is clearly wrong,[31] it may be understood to mean 'recognized' in the sense 'made public knowledge', if the child was either born or expected shortly before Stratios' departure for Rome. Polybios' use of the word ἀπαιδία of Eumenes points to the second of these possibilities.

We may now usefully summarize the conclusions reached as follows:

168/7	Stratios' embassy to Rome (=T24)
168	Birth of Attalos III
Late 150s	Attalos III taking part in the royal administration, but not given the royal title before 138
152	Attalos, aged sixteen, visits Rome (=T25)
147/6	Attalos, aged twenty-one, is honoured by the ephebes of the year (=T30)

The earliest dated document referring to Attalos III as Eumenes' son is T32, a decree of Miletos passed about 159.[32] This means that recognition of Attalos was granted between 168 and 159, but no further precision of this point is possible, and it contributes little to a solution of the problems concerning Attalos' parentage.

[31] Cardinali, *RP* 137; cf. Magie, *Roman Rule*, ii. 772–3.

[32] This decree has been dated in the past to between 163 and 160, and has therefore been used as a *terminus ante quem* of the recognition of Attalos III that is conveniently close to the supposed *terminus post quem* of 168/7 (see Magie, *Roman Rule*, ii. 773); for the date adopted here, see above, 116–18.

II

THE GALATIAN WARS OF ATTALOS I AND HIS ASSUMPTION OF THE ROYAL TITLE

As we saw in chapter three, the chronology of Attalos' Galatian wars depends to a large extent on the dating of the dedicatory inscriptions and monuments celebrating his victories, and I have postponed to this point the detailed arguments whose conclusions are followed in the main body of the book. The monuments with which we are concerned may conveniently be divided into three groups:[1]

(1) The round base of a large monument which was evidently intended to be a show-piece in the precinct of Athena at Pergamon. The base bears the following inscription (*IvP* 20, = *OGIS* 269):

[Βασιλεὺς "Ατταλος, νικήσας μά]χηι Τολιστ[οαγίους Γαλάτα]ς π[ερὶ πηγὰς]
Καΐκ[ου ποταμοῦ, χα]ρι[στ]ή[ριον 'Αθ]η[νᾶι].

(2) A large *bathron* which probably originally carried reconstructions in bronze figures of battle scenes; the inscriptions are *IvP* 21–8, = *OGIS* 273–9. The first of these inscriptions (*IvP* 21, = *OGIS* 273) is the dedication to Athena of the whole monument, embracing all Attalos' recent victories:

Βασιλεὺς "Ατταλος τῶν κατὰ πόλεμον | ἀγώνων χαριστήρια 'Αθηνᾶι.

The other inscriptions associated with this monument refer to individual victories:
IvP 24, = *OGIS* 276 (victory over the Tolistoagian Galatians at the sources of the River Kaikos):

'Απὸ τῆς περὶ πηγ[ὰς] Καΐκου ποταμοῦ | πρὸς Τ[ολισ]τοαγίους Γαλάτας μάχης.
(Compare *IvP* 20 above, and *IvP* 51, discussed below.)
IvP 23, = *OGIS* 275 (victory over the Tolistoagian and Tektosagan Galatians and Antiochos Hierax at the Aphrodision):[2]

['Απὸ τῆς περὶ τὸ] 'Αφροδίσιον πρὸς Τολιστοαγίους | [καὶ Τεκτοσά](γ)ας
Γαλ<λ>άτας καὶ 'Αντίοχον μάχης.
IvP 22, = *OGIS* 274 (victory over Hierax in Phrygia):

['Απὸ τῆς ἐμ Φρ]υγίαι τῆι ἐφ' Ἑλλη]σ[πόντου πρὸς Α]ντίοχον μάχης.
IvP 27, = *OGIS* 278 (victory over Hierax at Koloe in Lydia):

['Απὸ τῆς περὶ Κολ]όην | [πρὸς 'Αντίοχον μ]άχης.
IvP 28, = *OGIS* 279 (victory over Hierax in Caria):

['Απὸ τῆς παρὰ τὸν "Αρπασον ἐν Κ]αρίαι | [πρὸς 'Αντίοχον μ]άχης.
We should also associate with this victory the fragment published by Th. Wiegand, *Berl. Abh.* 1928 (iii), 18, no. 1, = *SEG* iv. 688: - - - - καὶ 'Αθηνᾶι [ἀπ]ὸ τῆς παρὰ - - -. The preposition παρά invariably introduces the name of a river, as Holleaux has shown; in other cases we find περί.[3] We are therefore left with παρὰ [τὸν "Αρπασον], and we can restore the text with some confidence as follows: [Βασιλεὺς

---

[1] See in general on these monuments, Kähler, *Gr. Fries,* 131 ff.

[2] [ἀπὸ τῆς παρὰ] Fränkel, Dittenberger, followed by Hansen, *Attalids,* 34; [ἀπὸ τῆς περὶ] Holleaux, *Études,* iii. 60, n.1. Cf. Kähler, *Gr. Fries,* 185, n.17, and further, below.

[3] Holleaux, *Études,* iii. 60, n.1. Note also the battle attested by *IvP* 64, = *Syll.*[3] 606: ἡ ἐν Λυδίαι παρὰ τὸν Φρυγίον πόταμον μάχη.

"Ατταλος] | [Διι] καὶ 'Αθηνᾶι | [ἀπ]ὸ τῆς παρὰ [τὸν] | ['Άρπασον ἐγ Καρίαι | πρὸς 'Αντίοχον μάχης].

The victories over the Galatians and Antiochos Hierax were further celebrated by a dedication to Zeus and Athena made by the soldiers who had taken part in them (*IvP* 29, = *OGIS* 280, of *c*.227):[4]

Βασιλέα "Ατταλον | 'Επιγένης καὶ οἱ ἡγεμόνες καὶ στρατ[ιῶ]ται | οἱ συναγωνισάμενοι τὰς πρὸς τοὺς Γ[αλ]άτας | καὶ 'Αντίοχον μάχας χαρισ[τ]ήρια | Διι, 'Αθηνᾶι.

The large *bathron* also included the victories won by Attalos over Lysias and the *strategoi* of Seleukos III, and was therefore erected at a later date than *IvP* 29 (*IvP* 25 + 26, = *OGIS* 277): 'Απὸ τῆς παρ[ὰ - - - - πρ]ὸς Λ[υ]σίαν | καὶ τοὺς Σελ[εύκου στρατ]ηγο[ὺ]ς μάχης.

(3) A number of small bases inscribed with individual dedications for these same victories (*IvP* 33, 34, 35 (= *OGIS* 272), 36, 37, 51,[5] 53, 58 (= *OGIS* 271)). In some of these dedications Athena has the cult epithet *Nikephoros*, and the style and lettering of the inscriptions, quite different from those of the round base and the large *bathron*, show that they were rededications of the reign of Eumenes II, as we have seen in our discussion of Eumenes' development of the Pergamene Nikephoria.[6]

Of these inscriptions, it is those under headings (1) and (2) that contribute significantly towards a clarification of the chronology and implications of the wars of Attalos I. The victory over the Tolistoagian Galatians was clearly held to be of particular importance, since it was further commemorated by an exceptionally splendid and prominent monument, the large *bathron*, to be set up in the temple of Athena.[7] It can therefore be identified with a high degree of probability with the victory which, according to the literary sources, led to Attalos' assumption of the royal title:

Polyb. xviii. 41. 7–8: νικήσας γὰρ μάχῃ Γαλάτας . . . ταύτην ἀρχὴν ἐποιήσατο καὶ τότε πρῶτον αὑτὸν ἔδειξε βασιλέα. τύχων δὲ τῆς τιμῆς ταύτης καὶ βιώσας ἔτη δύο πρὸς τοῖς ἑβδομήκοντα, τούτων δὲ βασιλεύσας τετταράκοντα καὶ τέτταρα.

Strabo xiii. 4. 2, 624: "Ατταλος διεδέξατο τὴν ἀρχήν, καὶ ἀνηγορεύθη βασιλεὺς πρῶτος, νικήσας Γαλάτας μάχῃ μεγάλῃ.

Pausanias i. 25. 2: καὶ Γαλάτων τὴν ἐν Μυσίᾳ φθορὰν ἀνέθηκεν "Ατταλος ὅσον τε δύο πηχῶν ἕκαστον.

Pausanias is the only one of these writers to name the area in which the battle took place, ἐν Μυσίᾳ, a description which fits well with the designation of the dedicatory inscriptions, 'at the sources of the Kaikos'. We know from Livy that Attalos refused to pay the Galatians tribute, and it

[4] On the date see Kähler, *Gr. Fries*, 185, n.18.

[5] *IvP* 51 has been convincingly restored by Kähler, *Gr. Fries*, 191, n. 56, as follows (I give my readings taken from a study of the stone in Berlin): Βασιλεὺς "Α[ττ]αλος | Διι καὶ 'Αθηνᾶι Ν[ικηφ]όρωι | ἀπὸ τῆς περὶ π[ηγὰς Καΐκου] | [ποταμο]ῦ π[ρὸς Τολιστοαγίους] | [Γαλάτας μάχης].

[6] See above, ch. 4 (iii).

[7] The possibility that these monuments refer to two separate attacks of the Tolistoagians on Pergamene territory, the 'sources of the Kaikos' being a natural point of entry for such attacks, may be discounted. The large *bathron* includes a dedicatory inscription referring to the war with the *strategoi* of Seleukos and is therefore to be dated to the end of this series of wars: it would surely have referred to two victories over the Tolistoagians if there had been two. See Kähler, *Gr. Fries*, 182.

was doubtless this refusal that led to the battle, Attalos' victory, and his assumption of the royal title.[8]

It remains to determine dates for these events. The literary sources give little indication of date, but they do imply that the victory, and Attalos' consequent assumption of the royal title, occurred early in his reign. On the other hand, we have to allow enough time for Attalos to have achieved the reorganization of his army which, as we saw in chapter 3, in all probability inspired Attalos' decision to resist the Galatians.[9] It has been argued from Polybios' words βασιλεύσας τετταράκοντα καὶ τέτταρα that Attalos took the royal title in the first year of his rule, thus 'reigning as king' for the specified forty-four years (241–197). It is clear, however, that Polybios' statement is compressed, and that an exact distinction between *dynasteia* and *basileia* would be out of place in such a summary context.[10]

The only other literary source that gives an indication of date is the prologue to Book xxvii of Trogus, which places a Gallic victory won by Attalos after Antiochos Hierax's defeat of Seleukos II at Ankyra:

Seleuci bellum in Syria adversus Ptolemaeum Tryphonem. item in Asia adversus fratrem suum Antiochum Hieracem, quo bello Ancurae victus est a Gallis. utque Galli Pergamo victi ab Attalo Ziaelam Bithunum occiderint.

I do not believe, however, that the battle mentioned here is to be identified with the one in which Attalos defeated the Tolistoagian Galatians at the sources of the Kaikos.[11] It is true that Trogus does not refer to Antiochos Hierax in connection with this victory, and that this omission fits well with the rest of the tradition, in which Attalos' great Gallic victory is said to have been over Galatians and no one else, but the point has no force when account is taken of the natural brevity and summary nature of the prologues, in which points of detail (or lack of them) are neither here nor there. In my view Trogus' location of the battle 'at Pergamon' is decisive: the battle is not the one at the sources of the Kaikos, but the one which, according to our epigraphical evidence, took place at the Pergamene Aphrodision, the only one to fit with Trogus' description.

This conclusion receives some support, for what it is worth, from what little sense can be made of the corresponding passage in Justin's account:[12]

interea rex Bithyniae Eumenes sparsis consumptisque fratribus bello intestinae discordiae quasi vacantem Asiae possessionem invasurus victorem Antiochum Gallosque adgreditur.

This passage makes sense only if Justin is referring to Attalos I of Pergamon, and not to the bogus Eumenes of Bithynia, and an important victory over Antiochos Hierax and the Galatians such as Justin describes can only be identified with the one that is prominently commemorated on the great *bathron*: again, that is, the victory at the Aphrodision. I do not think, then,

---

[8] xxxviii. 16. 14; see above, 30–1.
[9] See above, 32–3.
[10] Wilcken, *RE*, s.v. Attalos (9), 2160; cf. Kähler, *Gr. Fries*, 181, n. 11.
[11] For this identification, see Kähler, *Gr. Fries*, 182–3.
[12] xxvii. 3.

that Trogus and Justin between them are referring to two battles, the one with the Galatians at the sources of the Kaikos and the one with the Galatians and Antiochos Hierax at the Aphrodision, both of which are consequently to be dated after the battle at Ankyra; I think that they are referring in corresponding contexts to the same battle, the one at the Aphrodision. Thus the battle at the Aphrodision is to be dated to the years after the battle at Ankyra, but Attalos' great Galatian victory is not necessarily to be dated to this period on the basis of the arguments so far presented.

These chronological problems are further aggravated by the fact that the battle fought between Antiochos Hierax and Seleukos II at Ankyra is itself of uncertain date. In Bickermann's chronology, which has found general acceptance, the battle is dated to 239, three years before the peace between the two brothers attested for 236, the one fixed chronological point of these years.[13] This chronology assumes a resumption of Hierax's war with Seleukos, and that with Attalos, after 236, and is largely dependent on the premisses that Attalos took the royal title before 236 and that his Galatian victory was part of the war with Hierax: the first premiss corresponds with the view adopted here, but the second does not. It is more likely that the entire series of battles involving Attalos, Antiochos Hierax, and Seleukos II, should be dated after the year of peace attested for 236. In this case Attalos' victory at the Aphrodision is also to be dated after 236.

We still have, then, to determine the date of Attalos' victory over the Galatians at the sources of the Kaikos and his assumption of the royal title. Those who regard this victory as connected with the status of the Galatians as mercenaries of Hierax naturally date this to the years of Hierax's war with Attalos, after 236 on the arguments discussed above. There are, however, two points to be emphasized. Firstly, Attalos' dedications for this victory make it quite clear that his opponents were the Galatians fighting alone; when Hierax is involved he too is mentioned in the relevant dedications. Secondly, the Galatians' attack on Attalos is not connected in any part of our tradition with the war with Hierax; it is far more plausibly to be associated with the marauding activities which enabled the Galatians to demand tribute from those who wanted to be safe from them. These considerations suggest that we should date Attalos' victory to the years before 236, and more precisely to 238 or 237, years which take account of the time required for Attalos to assume power in 241 and complete the reorganization of the army at his disposal. The defeated Tolistoagians, joined by the Tektosagans, later entered Hierax's service and reappeared as Attalos' enemies at the Aphrodision.

The chronology of the epigraphical evidence relevant to Attalos' titulature is also obscure. *OGIS* 268, a decree from Bakir, dated βασιλεύοντος Ἀττάλου, πρώτου ἔτους, is more probably to be dated to the reign of Attalos II or III, than to that of Attalos I.[14] Equally suspect in this context is a letter from Soma in the upper Kaikos valley concerning the remission

[13] See E. Bickermann, *Berytus*, viii. 2 (1944), 76 ff.; Kähler, *Gr. Fries*, 183.
[14] See above, 105.

of taxes paid by the *katoikoi* of Apollo Tarsenos, which is headed without the royal title: Ἄτταλος [- - - -] χαίρειν, and is dated to a twelfth regnal year: *IB Δύστρου* | [- - - -] | *M* [έ]νανδρος ἐκ Περγάμο[υ]. This document has now been shown to be a letter of Attalos II written during the reign of his brother, Eumenes II.[15] Finally, stamped tiles from Pergamon bearing the monogram *BA* and numbers from five to forty, have been adduced as evidence that Attalos assumed the royal title and antedated his regnal years in or before the fifth year of his accession, but the identity of these numbers as regnal years is extremely tenuous.[16]

More important is an Athenian decree of 229/8, which contains an obscure reference to a king whose initial letter is A: [ἐπειδὴ - - ..]ντος καὶ πρότερον ἐν παντὶ κ[αιρῶι - - - ....] φρό[ν]τιζεν οὐθὲν ἧττον ἤ - - - ....] τοῦ βασιλέως Ἀ[- - - - - ....] τοὺς Α[ἰ]τω[λοὺς - - - - -]. The two possibilities for restoration are, clearly, βασιλέως Ἀ[ντιγόνου] and βασιλέως Ἀ[ττάλου]. If it refers to Attalos, this decree constitutes the earliest documentary evidence of his use of the royal title. It would thus establish 229 as a *terminus ante quem* of Attalos' Gallic victory. It has been argued that the king referred to in this decree cannot be Attalos, on the grounds that Attalos' Gallic victory, after which he took the royal title, was the final event in his campaigns against Antiochos Hierax and necessarily later than the archonship of Heliodoros at Athens, the year in which the decree was passed.[17] This chronology is not supported by the evidence, however, and this objection therefore cannot stand.

[15] *AM* xxiv (1899), 212 ff. Cf. L. Robert, *BCH* liii (1929), 151 f., Welles, *RC* 47. Boehringer's attempt (*AvP* ix. 92) to ascribe this letter to Attalos I, and to argue that the absence of the royal title therefore establishes a *terminus post quem* for its assumption in 230/29 (= year 11), although followed by Schober (*Wien. Anz.* lxxviii (1941), 9–12), was convincingly refuted by Kähler, *Gr. Fries*, 182.

[16] Boehringer, *AvP* ix. 136. The monograms were identified as *B(ΑΣΙΛΕΩΣ) A(TTAΛOY)* by Bickermann, loc. cit. (n.13), 77–8.

[17] *IG* ii.² 833; A. C. Johnson, *AJPh* xxxiv (1913), 388–9, followed by A. Wilhelm, *Att. Urkunden*, iii (1925), 58.

III

QUEEN STRATONIKE

The publication in *Altertümer von Pergamon* viii. 3 of a statue-base of Queen Stratonike from the temple of Demeter in Pergamon, may serve to clarify a number of problems concerning her chronology and titulature.[1] The base is inscribed with the dedication, ὁ δῆμος | βασίλισσαν Στρατονίκην | βασιλέως Ἀριαράθου | ἀρετῆς ἕνεκεν καὶ εὐνοίας | τῆς εἰς ἑαυτόν.[2] This invites comparison with an Athenian dedication, now long known, of a statue on Delos: ὁ δῆμος ὁ Ἀθηνα[ίων] | βασίλισσαν Στρατον[ίκην] | βασιλέως Ἀριαρά[θου] | ἀρετῆς ἕνεκεν καὶ εὐνοίας | τῆς εἰς ἑαυτόν, | Ἀρτέμιδι, [Λητ]οῖ, Ἀ(π)ό[λλωνι].[3] The problem posed by this Delian dedication has been, that although Stratonike is given the title βασίλισσα, she is also called daughter of Ariarathes (IV of Cappadocia), thereby suggesting that the dedication was made before her marriage to Eumenes II of Pergamon, to whom she was betrothed in 188 BC.[4] Now, outside the Ptolemaic Kingdom the use of the title βασίλισσα of a princess,

[1] See now Hopp, *Untersuchungen*, 27–9, whose conclusion differs from that reached here. Very little has been written on Stratonike. Geyer's article, *RE*, s.v. (11), IV. A.1 (1931), 321–2, is inadequate, and dwells too much on the question of the parentage of Attalos III, at the expense of more important considerations. Niese's article, *RE*, s.v. Ariarathes (4), II. 1 (1895), 817–18, does not deal at length with the problems concerning Stratonike's marriage. For the importance of Stratonike to the cult of Sabazios at Pergamon, touched on below, see Ohlemutz, *Kulte*, 269–72.

[2] Habicht, *AvP* viii. 3, 'Die Inschriften des Asklepieions' (1969), pl. 2 (mentioned on p. 28, and dated as 'gesetzt nach 188'). The text is noticed by J. and L. Robert, *Bull.* 1971, no. 538. It is strange that this important inscription has hitherto remained in the dark; as long ago as 1940, Ohlemutz (*Kulte*, 222, n. 56) referred to it as 'noch unveröffentlicht'.

[3] *CIG* 2280; *OGIS* 350; Durrbach, *Choix*, 89; *Inscr. de Délos*, 1575.

[4] Livy (from Polybios) xxxviii. 39. 6: *et Ariarathes rex parte dimidia pecuniae imperatae beneficio Eumenis, cui desponderat per eos dies filiam, remissa in amicitiam est acceptus.* Cf. Polyb. xxi. 41. 7: τοῖς δὲ περὶ Ἀριαράθην εἶπεν (Cn. Manlius Vulso) ἑξακόσια τάλαντα δόντας τὴν εἰρήνην ἔχειν, and xxi. 45: Μάλιος ὁ ἀνθύπατος τριακόσια τάλαντα πραξάμενος παρ' Ἀριαράθου φίλον αὐτὸν ἐποιήσατο Ῥωμαίων. See also J. Seibert, *Hist. Beiträge zu den dynastischen Verbindungen in hellenistischer Zeit* (*Historia*, Einzelschriften, 10, 1967), 113–14. The initiative for this marriage alliance lay certainly with Ariarathes, as rightly noted by Seibert (114), and not with Eumenes (which would be incomprehensible), as wrongly deduced by McShane, *Foreign Policy*, 173, and Will, *Hist. pol.* ii. 193: 'Eumène lui demanda la main de sa fille.'

as distinct from a queen, is otherwise unknown.[5] In the case of an Athenian dedication, two explanations are apparent: either (1), the Athenians retained Stratonike's patronymic as a special mark of friendship to Ariarathes V, a benefactor at Athens[6] (in this case the base should perhaps be dated after 163, when this Ariarathes came to the throne), or (2), they designated Stratonike βασίλισσα as the bride betrothed to Eumenes, the queen very shortly to be (in this case the base is dated exactly to 188 BC). It was perhaps envisaged that by the time the base was completed and the statue ready for erection, Stratonike would have become, officially, queen.

An important point needs to be considered before we proceed. Although Stratonike was betrothed to Eumenes immediately after the Treaty of Apameia, we have no evidence as to the date of the actual marriage. In the circumstances, however, we may conclude that the interval will have been minimal. Prior to the Treaty of Apameia Ariarathes IV had been Eumenes' enemy in the Antiochic War, having married Antiochos' daughter Antiochis shortly before the war, probably in 195.[7] Ariarathes supported his father-in-law in the war with Rome, and gave help to the Galatians during the campaigns of Cn. Manlius Vulso.[8] Thus the Cap-

[5] As pointed out by Durrbach, *Choix*, p. 150, against Dittenberger, who dated the dedication *ante hiemen* 189/8 *a. Chr. n.* (ad loc., n.1). For the designation of a Ptolemaic princess as βασίλισσα, see especially *IG* ix.[2] 1. 56 (Thermos); cf. U. Wilcken. *Archiv für Papyrusforschung*, vi (1920), 453; W. Otto, *Zur Gesch. der Zeit des 6. Ptolemäers* (*Abh. München*, 1934), 14, 120, n. 9. The suggestion of Th. Reinach, *Trois royaumes de l'Asie Mineure* (Paris, 1889), 15 (cf. W. S. Ferguson, *Hellenistic Athens* (London, 1911), 301), that the statue of Stratonike was erected on Delos after the death of Attalos II, whom the widowed Stratonike married in 159, is implausible; she would not at this late date be called βασίλισσα Στρατονίκη βασιλέως Ἀριαράθου, on Delos or anywhere else. The base from Pergamon, as interpreted below, also rules out this theory. Durrbach's own suggestion, that the Delian base was originally one of a pair with a base of Eumenes II (or Attalos II), is ingenious, but again rendered unlikely by the fact of a parallel dedication at Pergamon.

[6] For the benefactions of Ariarathes V at Athens, see W. S. Ferguson, *Hellenistic Athens*, 300–1. This explanation is, however, unlikely. The patronymic designates Ariarathes IV; it is difficult to believe that he, as distinct from his son, will have been so specifically honoured even at a later date. It is surely more probable that the patronymic was included as a matter of form, and we should work on this basis.

[7] Appian, *Syr.* 5. Cf. Niese ii. 674; Seibert, *Beiträge*, 64–5. The date is implied by the context of Appian's narrative, where Antiochos makes a number of betrothal offers. The immediately preceding events in the narrative are the marriage of Antiochos' children Antiochos and Laodike at Seleukeia (winter 196/5: Schmitt, *Untersuchungen*, 13–14), and the meeting of Antiochos and Hannibal at Ephesos in autumn 195 (Holleaux, *Études*, v. 180–3). A later date (e.g. 192/1, O. Leuze, *Hermes*, lviii (1923), 211–12) would clearly strengthen the argument put below as to Stratonike's parentage, but is unlikely.

[8] Niese ii. 759; *RE* loc. cit. (n.1), 817.

202   *Appendix III*

padocian king remained Eumenes' opponent to the last moment, and his change of alliance was a political volte-face, designed, as the literary evidence explicitly states, to secure more favourable terms from Rome. In these circumstances we must surely reckon with the intention of an immediate marriage with Eumenes when Stratonike was betrothed in 188, as is clear from another instance of this kind of gesture at the end of a war. When the Egyptian princess Berenike was betrothed to Antiochos II by her father, Ptolemy II, in 253 BC, the motive was the same; Philadelphos wanted to end hostility and begin a period of friendship, as we see most clearly from the evidence of Hieronymos (*in Danielem* ii. 11. 6): *volens itaque Ptolemaeus Philadelphus post multos annos molestum finire certamen, filiam suam, nomine Bernicem, Antiocho uxorem dedit.*[9] We know from two important papyri of the Zenon Archive (*PCZ* 59242, 59251), that this marriage was negotiated in 253 and took place in spring 252 BC, after the shortest possible delay, and that for this purpose Berenike was escorted by Philadelphos' minister Apollonios to the Syrian border.[10] The prime concern seems to have been speed in completing the arrangements. It was obviously important in such circumstances that the marriage be completed without delay, and the same is true, we may believe, of the parallel situation in Asia Minor in 188. Two further points may be added: firstly, if a delay was envisaged between the betrothal and the marriage of Stratonike, the dedication of her statue in Pergamon, which must necessarily be dated before the marriage took place (see below), will have read Στρατονίκην θ. Ἀριαράθου and not, as it does, βασίλισσαν Στρατονίκην θ. Ἀριαράθου. Secondly, it is hardly credible that Eumenes, by accepting a child-bride (as has been suggested) in 188, will have been prepared so drastically to postpone his chances of obtaining a legitimate male heir to the royal house. This conclusion, that Stratonike was ready for marriage in 188, and that the marriage was expected to take place immediately, has an important bearing on our discussion.

In the first place, Stratonike cannot have been the daughter of Antiochis, as is often supposed.[11] Ariarathes married this daughter of Antiochos III in *c*.195, as we have seen, and an interesting passage of Diodoros (xxxi. 19. 7) suggests that for some years the marriage was childless:[12] ταύτην δὲ (= Antiochis) μὴ γινομένων τέκνων ὑποβαλέσθαι δύο παῖδας ἀγνοοῦντος τοῦ ἀνδρός, Ἀριαράθην καὶ Ὀλοφέρνην. μετὰ δέ τινα χρόνον τῆς φύσεως ἐπιδεξαμένης ἀνελπίστως τεκεῖν αὐτὴν δύο

[9] Niese ii. 139.
[10] *P. Cairo Zeno* 59251 (= Hunt and Edgar, *Select Papyri* (Loeb Classical Library, 1930), i. no. 93): a letter, dated *c*.15 April 252, to Zenon from Artemidoros the physician, who accompanied Apollonios on the mission, lines 2–3: ὅτε δέ σοι ἔγραφον, παρεγινόμεθα εἰς Σιδῶνα, συμπεπορευμένοι τῆι βασιλίσσηι | ἕως τῶν ὁρίων.
[11] e.g. by Welles, *RC*, p. 270, whose chronology is at fault (cf. Ohlemutz, *Kulte*, 270, n. 44). Antiochis is known only from this event: cf. Holleaux, *Études*, iii. 187, n. 3; Schmitt, *Untersuchungen*, 24–5.
[12] Cf. Niese, *RE* loc. cit.; Schmitt, *Untersuchungen*, 24–5.

μὲν θυγατέρας, υἱὸν δὲ ἕνα τὸν ὀνομασθέντα Μιθριδάτην. This Mithridates, as the only legitimate son of Ariarathes IV, was to succeed him in 163 as Ariarathes V.[13] Neither of the legitimate daughters, however, can be identified as Stratonike, since, for reasons discussed above, we must discount the possibility that Eumenes was betrothed to a child in 188.

We may conclude, then, that Ariarathes' marriage to Antiochis was his second, the first queen remaining unknown, and that Stratonike was the daughter of the former marriage.[14] On the evidence presented above, she must have been at least sixteen years old in 188, and was therefore born in 204 at the latest. On the other hand, a passage of Justin (xxxvi. 4. 5), if its chronology can be pressed, suggests a date for Stratonike's death shortly before that of her son, Attalos III, who was preparing her mausoleum when he died: *matri deinde sepulcrum facere instituit, cui operi intentus morbum ex solis fervore contraxit et septima die decessit.* This conclusion is supported by epigraphical evidence that is often overlooked. In a letter written by Attalos III to the city of Pergamon, dated 5 October 135,[15] the king refers to his mother's devotion to the gods, and to her goodwill towards his father and himself, in the past tense (1–4): ἐπεὶ βασίλισσα Στρατονίκη ἡ μήτηρ μου ―――― πρὸς ἅπαντας μὲν τοὺς θεοὺς εὐσεβῶς προσηνέχθη, κτλ. The omission of the word θέα in this context, where Attalos writes of his mother in a very personal way, is no objection to the natural conclusion that Stratonike was then already dead. In fact it is probable that she was recently dead, and that the enshrining of Sabazios, whose cult Stratonike had brought to Pergamon in 188, with Athena Nikephoros, as explained in the letter, was done in honour of her mem-

[13] Diod. xxxi. 17. 8. Cf. Niese, *RE*, s.v. Ariarathes (5), 818; Schmitt, loc. cit.

[14] This is mentioned as a possibility by Magie, *Roman Rule,* ii. 770–1, n. 72 (cf. Seibert, *Beiträge,* 113–14), but with a preference for the view that the marriage did not take place until a later date, because Stratonike was not ready for marriage in 188. He cites in support of this view three documents honouring members of the Attalid royal family between 188 and 175/4, in which the name of Stratonike does not appear (see also Hopp, *Untersuchungen,* 28–9): the decree of Telmessos dated 184 BC (Appendix iv, no. 7); the Aitolian decree of 182 BC accepting the Pergamene Nikephoria (Appendix iv, no. 9); and the Athenian decree of 175/4 passed after the accession of Antiochos IV (Holleaux, *Études,* ii. 127–47; *OGIS* 248). Of these, the first is not relevant, because it praises Eumenes specifically for his success in the war with Prusias I of Bithynia and the Galatians in the late 180s (on the chronology and circumstances see Habicht, *Hermes,* lxxxiv (1956), 99) and the same consideration applies to the musical ἀγῶνες honouring Eumenes (called Soter) mentioned in a decree of Tralles, which Hopp adduces (Appendix iv, no. 6; Hopp, *Untersuchungen,* 28, n. 68); nor do I think that the other two documents constitute a serious objection to the chronology argued here; documents of this time could be strangely selective in the matter of persons honoured, and there was no hard and fast rule. Thus the Amphiktyonic decree accepting the Pergamene Nikephoria, passed at the same time as the Aitolian mentioned above, unlike the latter honours Eumenes alone, apart from a formal reference to Attalos I in the second line (Appendix iv, no. 10).

[15] *OGIS* 331. IV; Welles, *RC* 67.

ory.[16] I propose then to date Stratonike's death to the year 135 BC, and the family tree of her parentage must be drawn as follows:

<pre>
                                              ANTIOCHOS III
                                                    |
     ARIARATHES IV m. (1) ?   (2) Antiochis
              |
        Stratonike (c.204–135)
        m. EUMENES II (188/7)
</pre>

To return to the base from the temple of Demeter in Pergamon: of the explanations suggested above for the wording of the Athenian base erected on Delos, only the second will fit the Pergamene dedication, and because it is Pergamene, that is, a dedication of Eumenes' capital, which was to receive the new bride, further consideration is required. Clearly, the dedication must be dated after the betrothal, since before that time, as we have seen, the two royal houses had been enemies. After the marriage of Stratonike had taken place, however, the addition βασιλέως Ἀριαράθου would disappear in a Pergamene dedication; the royal title alone would suffice, as in the dedications made by Stratonike's priestess Eurydike,[17] Βασίλισσα[ν] Σ[τρατονίκην] | Εὐρυδίκη Δη[μ]άρ[χου, ἱέρεια] | διὰ βίου, ἀ[ρ]ετῆ[ς ἕνεκεν] | καὶ εὐνοίας τῆ[ς εἰς ἑαυτήν], and by the royal official Menogenes,[18] [Βασίλισσαν] Στρατ[ονίκην | Μηνογένης] Μην[οφάντου, | ὁ ἐπὶ τῶν πραγμάτων, ἀρετῆς ἕνεκεν | καὶ εὐνοίας τῆς εἰς ἑαυτόν]. It follows, then, that the statue of Stratonike was erected in the temple of Demeter[19] after her betrothal to Eumenes in 188, but before the marriage, and this procedure makes sense, at Pergamon at least, only if the marriage was expected to take place after a short interval, thus confirming the conclusion reached earlier.

This conclusion, reached from historical considerations, is more positive than that to be deduced from the indications of the letter-forms of the inscription. The photograph was published by Habicht for purposes of comparison with a base from the Pergamene Asklepieion, inscribed with a dedication of the δῆμος of Pergamon for Athenaios, brother of Eumenes II and recently ἀγωνοθέτης of the festival called Σωτήρια καὶ Ἡράκλεια. This base is dated by Habicht to the 180s or even later, a chronology which is historically implausible in the case of the dedication of the statue of Stratonike. Nor do the letters of the base of Stratonike seem to me to point

[16] Cf. my remarks on this subject in *BSA* lxvi (1971), 9.

[17] *IvP* 178, = *OGIS* 313. The priesthood was rightly identified as that of Stratonike by Dittenberger (n. 2, ad loc.). Stratonike also had a priesthood at Teos during her lifetime: L. Robert, *Ét. anat.* 9–20; see above, 150.

[18] *IvP* 173, = *OGIS* 293.

[19] The choice of Demeter is interesting. Apollonis too had associated herself closely with the cult of Demeter by greatly extending the temple area in Pergamon, as attested by her dedication to the goddess from the Propylon (*AM* xxxv (1910), no. 24): Βασίλισσα Ἀπολλωνὶς Δήμητρι κ[α]ὶ Κόρηι Θεσμοφόροις χαριστήριον τὰς στοὰς καὶ τοὺς οἴκους. See the useful account of Ohlemutz, *Kulte*, 207–12.

to a date later, rather than earlier, in the reign of Eumenes II. Other documents relevant to Athenaios are cited by Habicht as having distinctly earlier letter forms (*AvP* viii. 3, p. 27, n.1; p. 28): 'mit Ausnahme des Dekrets von Kolophon scheiden sich an dieser Formfrage die jüngeren Steine von den älteren sehr klar. Tatsächlich ist jedoch auch der Text aus Kolophon keine Ausnahme, sondern von Holleaux zu hoch datiert.' The reference here is to the decree of Colophon Nova honouring Athenaios, dated by Holleaux (*Études,* ii. 51–60) before 197, because Eumenes is not specifically mentioned; a later date is probable, and the omission of a royal name in a civic decree is not necessarily of chronological significance (see above, n.14), but the letters are not directly comparable with those of the base from the Asklepieion, which are surely of an earlier date.[20] Of the other texts cited, *IvP* 219, a dedication made by Athenaios for his brother Attalos, is the most relevant, as a Pergamene dedication; it is to be dated very probably after 159, when Attalos was king, but the letters are more distinctly those of the second half of the second century than either the base from the Asklepieion or the base for Stratonike. The letters on the base for Stratonike are recognizable as the elegant type of lettering that recurs at Pergamon in the reigns of Attalos I, Eumenes II, and Attalos II alike; for a specific example it is enough to indicate *IvP* 62, of *c.* 192 BC, whose letters are very close in style to those of the base of Stratonike. But since these letters are to be found over a large part of the second century, a close dating on this criterion alone is not possible.

All things considered, then, we should retain the date argued above for the erection of statues of Stratonike on Delos and in Pergamon, i.e. 188 BC, as a result of the betrothal of Stratonike to Eumenes earlier in the year. It must be remembered, as was pointed out above, that a period of time will have been envisaged for the completion of the work of sculpting and inscribing, and it is almost certainly for this reason that we read the royal title on the bases: the decision to erect each statue was taken after the betrothal, but in anticipation of the marriage having taken place by the time the work was completed — a further reason for minimizing the interval in our chronology.

One can imagine that Stratonike had a difficult task ahead of her in succeeding to the position of Apollonis, the queen of Eumenes' father and predecessor, Attalos I. Apollonis, not herself of royal blood, became one of the very few ladies of the Hellenistic courts about whom our literary

---

[20] See above, 56. The base for Athenaios reads: ὁ δῆμος | Ἀθήναιον βασιλέως Ἀττάλου | ἀγ[ω]νοθετήσαντα τὰ δεύτερα | Σ[ω]τήρια καὶ Ἡράκλεια | καλῶς καὶ ἐνδόξως. The first celebration of the festival of Σωτήρια καὶ Ἡράκλεια is dated by Habicht, following H. Hepding (*AM* xxxv (1910), 412), to the reign of Eumenes II, to be associated with one of his local wars. Could it not have been founded earlier, e.g. after the Antiochic War? The letter-forms of this base, especially Ξ (cf. C. Paepcke, *de Perg. litt.* 8, 29), seem to me to have earlier characteristics, and are generally similar to those of *IvP* 47, which was probably reinscribed at the time of Eumenes' restoration of the precinct of Athena in the 180s; cf. Kähler, *Gr. Fries,* 185, n. 22.

sources have nothing but good to say.[21] Stratonike was to join a family which had always been proud of its close relationships. She was, furthermore, the centre of attraction in an alliance between two royal houses whose relations had up to the last moment been hostile. She had to provide an heir. Much clearly depended on her. In the event, as is well known, the alliance proved fruitful, and remained an important factor in the foreign policies of the two dynasties. Stratonike was highly honoured by the Attalids, who gave her, at Teos and at Pergamon, a special place in the royal cults of the newly enlarged Pergamene Kingdom.[22] In 188 the importance of the marriage was evidently well recognized, and Stratonike was not surprisingly hailed as queen at the earliest possible moment.

[21] See especially the warm encomium of Polybios (xxii. 20).
[22] See above, n.17, and, on the cults of Stratonike, ch. 6.

IV

SELECTED INSCRIPTIONS

An edition of all the non-Pergamene texts relating to the Attalids is a desideratum. This selection of the most important, which is additional to the texts given in the body of the book, includes those recently published, some of those not available in the standard epigraphical collections (such as *ISE*, *OGIS*, and *Syll.*³), and others which have been reproduced in these collections but have since received significant revision. Inscriptions from Pergamon itself, being regularly available in the reports of *Athenische Mitteilungen*, are not included.

The text followed is that of the most recent edition, except as noted in the apparatus. Variants superseded by the edition followed are not normally repeated.

1(a) Foucart, *BCH* viii (1884), 158; *SGDI* i, Addenda, p. 402, no. 805a; *IG* vii. 1788; *OGIS* 310; Fraser, *REA* liv (1952), 233–45, no. 1(*a*) (Karata, near Thespiai). Philetairos.

> Φιλέτηρος ᾿Ατ-
> τάλω Περγα-
> μεὺς ἀνέθει-
> κε τὰν γᾶν
> 5 τῆς Μωσῆς
> τῆς ῾Ελικω-
> νιάδεσσι ἱαρὰ-
> ν εἶμεν τὸν πάν-
> τα χρόνον

1(b) *BCH* viii (1884), 158; *IG* vii. 1789; *REA* liv (1952), 233–45, no. 1(*b*) (Karata). Philetairos.

> Φιλέτηρος ᾿Ατ-
> τάλω Περγ[α-]
> μεὺς ἀνέθεικ[ε]
> τὰν γᾶν τῆς Μω-
> 5 σῆς τῆς ῾Ελικω-
> νιάδεσσι ἱαρὰν
> εἶμεν ἐν τὸν
> πάντα χρόνον

1(c) Foucart, *BCH* ix (1885), 405, no. 16; *IG* vii. 1790; *OGIS* 311; *REA* liv (1952), 233–45, no. 2 (Karata). Philetairos.

> - - - - - - - - - *A* - - - - - *AΣ* - -
> [τὰ]ν [γ]ᾶν ἀνέθε[ικε]

[Φι]λέτηρος ᾿Ἀττάλω
[Π]εργαμεὺς τῆς Μ̣[ω-]
5　[σ]ῆς κὴ τῦς συνθύτης τοῖ(ς)
Φιλετηρείεσσι ἱαρὰν
[ε]ἶμεν τὸμ πάντα χρό-
νον.

1(d) Jamot, *BCH* xxvi (1902), 156, no. 6; *OGIS* 749; *REA* liv (1952),
233–45, no. 3 (Karata). Philetairos.

Φιλέτηρος ᾿Ατ-
τάλω Περγα-
μεὺς ἀνέθει-
κε τὰν γᾶν τοῖ
Ἑρμῇ ἐν τὸ ἐ-
ληοχρίστιον
ἱαρὰν εἶμεν
ἐν τὸν πάντα
χρόνον

1(e) *BCH* xxvi (1902), 155, no. 5; *OGIS* 750; *REA* liv (1952), 233–45,
no. 4 (*a*) (Thespiai). Philetairos.

[Φ]ιλέταιρος Εὐμένου
Περγαμεὺς Μούσαις
[Κ]αφισίας
ἐποίησε

2 *IG* ii.[2] 885; Allen, *BSA* lxvi (1971), 1–12 (Athens). Attalos I.

- - - - - ὁ βα[σιλεὺς - - - - - - - -
- - - - - πρὸς του - - - - - - - - - -
- - - - ν μὲν παρὰ | - - - - - - - - - -
- - - - ν τὰς ἐπεΣΑΝ∠ - - - - - - - - -
5　- - - οὐδὲ]ν ὑποστειλάμεν[ος - - - - - - -
- - - - τῶν Ἑλλήνων κα - - - - - - - - -
- - - - κατὰ τὰ ἔθνη τιμω | - - - - - - - -
- - τ]έμενη ἀνείθη vac. ἀπετ - - - - - - - -
- - - βασι]λέως ᾿Αττάλου ἐν αἷς οἱ κατ - - - - - - -
10　- - - ον καὶ τοὺς κατέχοντας θεο[ὺς - - - - - - -
- - - ποιήσουσιν δὲ καὶ σύνναον καὶ [σύμβωμον τῷ Αἰακῷ?]
[διὰ τὰ]ς γεγενημένας ὑπ᾿ αὐτοῦ πράξ[εις πρὸς τὴν σωτηρίαν?]
[τῶν Ἑ]λλήνων. vac. βουλόμενος δὲ καὶ εἰς - - - - - -
- - - - σ]αφεστέραν τήν τε εὐσέβειαν κα[ὶ - - - - - -
15　- - - πατ]ρίου αὐτῶι ὑπάρχοντος τὸ τιμᾶν - - - - - -
- - - - ον ὑπάρχοντα vac. καὶ νῦν δὲ παραλα[βὼν τὴν νῆσον (or τὴν
(ἡμετέραν) πόλιν)]
[διὰ τὴν Ἡρακ]λέους πρὸς Αἰακὸν συγγένειαν - - - - - -
- - - - οις ἐξεφθαρμένων τῶν τὴν ἀρχὴ[ν - - - - - -

- - - - πρότερον τιθέμενος τῆς π - - - - - - - -
20 - - - - ε]ὐνοίας ἠβουλήθη σύ - - - - - - - - -
- - - - ἀνθ]ρώπων ἀπεστ[αλ - - - - - - - - -
- - - - πα]ραγε[νόμενος - - - - - - - - -

Length of line and line divisions conjectural   22 ?πα]ραγε[νόμενος εἰς τὴν
νῆσον

3 Ducrey and van Effenterre, *Kret. Chron.* ii (1969), 277 ff.; Ducrey,
BCH xciv (1970), 637-59 (Malla, Crete). Attalos I.

A

[- - - - - - - - - - - - - - c. 26 - - - - - - - - - - - - - -] ΑΣΑΤ.Α.
[- - - - - - - - - - - - - c. 23 - - - - - - - - - - -] Σ εἶναι ΑΓΩ
[- - - - - - - - - - - - - c. 20 - - - - - -] ΙΕΑΕΣΕΙΝΤΑΚ
[- - - - - - - - - - - - - c. 17 - - - τὸ]ν ὑπογεγραυμένον
5 [ὅρκον - - - - ἐ]ὰν δέ τι τῶν γεγραυμέν-
[ων - - - - ἐν] τῆι ὁμολογίαι Μαλλαῖοι μὴ π-
[οιήσω]ντι ἔνοχοι ἔστωσαν τῶι παρησπ-
[ο]νδηκέναι καὶ λελύκεν τασυνθήκας. <κα>
κατὰ ταὐτὰ δὲ καὶ ἐὰν Μαλλαῖοι χρείαν ἔ[χ-]
10 οντες συνμαχίας πένπωσι πρὸς βασιλέα Ἄτταλον, ἀποστελλέτω βασιλεὺς Ἄτ[τ-]
αλος ἄνδρας τριακοσίους καὶ ἡγεμόνα[ς]
[ἐ]π' αὐ[τῶ]ν, ἐὰν δὲ μὴ ἐκποιῆι τὸ πλῆθος τοῦτ-
[ο] διὰ τινὰς καιροὺς, ὅσους ἂν ἐνδέχηται, ἐ-
15 [ὰ]ν μὴ ἐπ' Ἱεραπυτνίους ἢ Πριανσίους ἢ Ἀρκά-
δας παρκαλῶσιν · οὗτοι δὲ ὑπεξαιρήσθων ὑ-
πὸ βασιλέος Ἀττάλου. τοῖς δὲ πενπομένοις
πορεῖα μὲν παρεχέτω βασιλεὺς Ἄτταλος κ-
αὶ τὰ ὀψώνια καὶ τὰ δέοντα ἐν τῶ(ι) πλὸῶι. <οτα>
20 ὅταν δὲ παραγένωνται πρὸς Μαλλαίους, τ[ρ-]
ε[φ]έτωσαν τὴν συνμαχίαν αὐτοί, παρέχ[ο-]
οντες τῆς ἡμερᾶς ἑκάστωι ἀνδρὶ δραχμὰν
αἰγιναῖαν, τῶν δ' ἡγεμόνων ἑκάστωι δραχμὰς δύο καὶ κατὰ σῶμα χοίνικα ἀττ[ικ]ὴν, ἐὰν μ-
25 ὴ ἐν πολεμίαι ὦσιν, οὗ ἔσται σῖτον λαμβά-
νειν. παραμενέτωσαν δὲ οἱ ἀποσταλέν-
τες ἕως ἂν Μαλλαῖοι χρείαν ἔχωσι. ὅταν δὲ
ἀπολύωσιν τουσυνμάχος πρὸς βασιλέα Ἄ-
[τ]ταλον τὰ πορεῖα δότωσαν αὐτοὶ ΣΥΝΑ

B
[ό-]
30 [μο]λόγημ[εν - - - εἰ μὴ παραβ-]
[α]ίνοντας ὁμολογί[αν, ἤτω ἐξώλης τε καὶ]
πανώλης καὶ αὐ[τὸ]ς [καὶ γυνή καὶ τέκν-]
α καὶ πατρὶς καὶ οἱ βασι[λέως φίλοι. ἐὰ-]

35 ν δὲ καὶ ἐνμένοντι ἐν τ[ο]ῖς [ὡμολογημένοι-]
[ς], εἶναι καὶ βίον εὐδαίμονα [αὐτῶι καὶ]
γυναικὶ καὶ τέκνοις καὶ πατρίδι καὶ τοῖς [φ-]
ίλο(ι)ς. Ὅ[ρκ]ος βασιλέως Ἀττάλου· ὀμνύω Δί[α] ,
Γῆν, Ἥλιον, Ποσειδῶ, Δήμητρα, Ἄρη, Ἀθην-
40 ᾶν Ἄρειαν καὶ τὴν Ταυροπόλον καὶ τοὺ(ς) ἄ-
λλους θεοὺς πάντας καὶ πάσας· ἐνμέν-
ειν ἐν τῆι φιλίαι καὶ τῆι συνμαχίαι καὶ τ-
[οῖ]ς ὡμολογημένοις πρὸς Μαλλαίους ε-
ἰς τὸν πάντα χρόνον καὶ πρὸς αὐτοὺς καὶ τ-
45 οὺς ἐγγόνους καὶ οὐθὲν παραβήσεσθαι
τῶν ὡμολογημένων. εὐορκοῦντι μέν
μοι εὖ εἴη, ἐφιουρκοῦντι δὲ τἀναντία.

6–7 μή π[[οιήσω]]ντι Daux, *Rev. hist. de droit français et étranger*, xlix (1971), 374
(*N| - - - NII* eds.)

4 Wescher and Foucart, *Inscr. de Delphes*, 336; *Syll.* 447; *SGDI*
2001; *Syll.*² 846 (not reproduced in *Syll.*³) (Delphi). Attalos I.

Στραταγέοντος Φαινέα μηνὸς Πανάμου, ἐν Δελφοῖς δὲ ἄρχοντος
Ἐμμενίδα μηνὸς Βουκατίου, ἐπὶ τοῖσδε ἀπέδοτο Δαμέας
ὁ παρὰ τοῦ βασιλέως Ἀττάλου ὁ ἐπὶ τῶν ἔργων τῶν βασιλικῶν
Ἀρτεμιδώραν τὰν βασιλικὰν παιδίσκαν τῶι Ἀπόλλωνι τῶι Πυθίωι,
5 ἀργυρίου στατήρων τεσσαράκοντα τριῶν, καθὼς ἐπίστευσε
Ἀρτεμιδώρα τῶι θεῶι τὰν ὠνάν, ἐφ' ὧι αὐτὰν ἐλευθέραν εἶμεν,
                                                    ποιεῖν
ὅ κα θέληι, εἶμεν εἴ κα θέληι. βεβαιωτὴρ κατὸν νόμον· Ἐτυμώνδας
Δελφός. μάρτυρες· τοὶ ἱερεῖς καὶ ἰδιῶται Νι[κό]δαμος, Ὀρθαῖος,
Πολύκλειτος, Θεύτιμος Ἀμφισσεύς.

5 *SEG* iv. 632; *Sardis* vii. 1. 4 (Sardis). Eumenes II.

Ἔδοξεν τῆι βουλῆι καὶ τῶι δήμωι στρατηγῶν
γνώμη· ἐπεὶ Τίμαρχος Μενεδήμου, τεταγμένος πρότερον ὑπὸ τοῦ θεοῦ βασιλέως ῥισκοφύλαξ ἐν Περγάμωι
καὶ πίστεως οὐ μικρᾶς ἠξιωμένος, ἔν τε τοῖς κατὰ τὴν
5 χρείαν διεγενήθη ἀκολούθως τῆι τοῦ ἐγχειρίσαντος
προαιρέσει καὶ ἐν τοῖς ἄλλοις ἀνεστράφη ἀμέμπτως,
διόπερ ὁ βασιλεὺς ἐπιγνοὺς τὴν περὶ αὐτὸν ὑπάρχουσαν
καθαρειότητα καὶ τὴν κατὰ τὸν βίον εὐταξίαν τε
καὶ μετριότητα, καὶ νομίζων εὔθετον εἶναι πρὸς τὴν
10 θεραπείαν καὶ εὐκοσμίαν τῶν κατὰ τὸ ἱερὸν τῆς
παρ' ἡμῖν Ἀρτέμιδος κατέστησεν νεωκόρον τῆς θεοῦ,
γινόμενός τε πρὸς τοῖς ἐγκεχειρισμένοις καὶ ἀμέμπτως ἀναστρεφόμενος συντηρεῖ τὴν ὑπάρχουσαν
αὐτῶι παρὰ πᾶσιν εὐφημίαν, εὐσεβῶς δὲ διακείμενος
15 καὶ πρὸς τὸ θεῖον καὶ φιλαγάθως πειρᾶται κατὰ τὴν ἑαυτοῦ
δύναμιν καὶ ἐν τούτοις μηδενὸς λείπεσθαι μερίζων

παρ' ἑαυτοῦ καὶ εἰς τὰ τῆι θεῶι χρήσιμα· ἵνα οὖν καὶ ὁ δῆμος
φαίνηται τιμῶν τοὺς ἀγαθοὺς καὶ πολλοὶ ζηλωταὶ
γίνωνται τῶν ὁμοίων, δεδόχθαι τῆι βουλῆι καὶ τῶι δήμωι
20 ἐπαινέσαι Τίμαρχον ἐπί τε τῆι πρὸς τὸ θεῖον εὐσεβείαι
καὶ τῆι πρὸς τὴν πόλιν αἱρέσει, καὶ στεφανῶσαι αὐτὸν
ἐν τῶι θεάτρωι θαλλοῦ στεφάνωι ἐν τοῖς ἀχθησομένοις
Διονυσίοις προνοηθέντων τῆς ἀναγγελίας τοῦ τε
ἀγωνοθέτου καὶ τοῦ γραμματέως τοῦ δήμου, ἀναγράψαι
25 δὲ καὶ τὸ ψήφισμα εἰς στήλην καὶ ἀναθεῖναι
ἐν τῶι ἱερῶι, ὅπως οὗτός τε πολλῶι μᾶλλον ἐκκαλῆται
πρὸς εὐεργεσίαν τῆς πόλεως καὶ οἱ ἄλλοι βλέπον-
τες τὴν ἀπαντωμένην τοῖς ἀξίοις τῶν ἀνδρῶν
εὐφημίαν πολὺ προθυμότερον διατιθῶνται τῆι
30 πρὸς τὰ κοινὰ φιλαγαθίαι.

6 Papadopoulos Kerameus, *Ἑλλ. Φιλ. Συλλ.* (1884), 58–60; Robert,
Rev. Phil. viii (1934), 279 ff. (Tralles). Eumenes II.

. . . . Σ· τύχηι ἀγαθ[ῆι· δεδόχθαι· ἐπαινέσαι]
[μὲν τὸμ Φωκαιέων δῆμ]ον ἐπὶ τῆι εὐνοίαι χα[ὶ τῆι προαι-]
[ρέσει ἣν ἔχει πρὸς τὸ]ν δῆμον τὸν ἡμετέ[ρον] καὶ ἐ[πὶ τῶι]
[. . . . . ἐπιμεληθῆναι] τοῦ ἐξαποσταλῆναι ἄνδρας ἀ[γαθοὺς]
5 [καὶ δικαίους πρὸς ἡμᾶς] καὶ στεφανῶσαι αὐτὸν χρυσῶι στεφ[ά-]
[νωι· ἐπαινέσαι δὲ καὶ τὸ]ν δικαστὴν καὶ τὸν γραμματέα χ[α]λο-
[καγαθίας ἕνεκεν καὶ δικ]αιοσύνης ἧς ἔσχοσαν περὶ τὰς δίκας·
[στεφανῶσαι δὲ τὸν μὲ]ν δικαστὴν χρυσῶι στεφάνωι, τὸν δ[ὲ]
[γραμματέα θαλλοῦ στ]εφάνωι· ἵνα δὲ καὶ ἡ ἀναγγελία τῶν
10 [στεφάνων γένηται πα]ρ' ἡμῖν ἐν τοῖς μουσικοῖς ἀγῶσιν τοῖς
[συντελουμένοις ὑπὸ το]ῦ δήμου βασιλεῖ Εὐμένει Σωτῆρι ἐπι-
[μέλειαν ποιησάσθω ὁ γ]ραμματεὺς τοῦ δήμου μετὰ στεφα-
[νηφόρον . . . . ἐμ Φ]ωκαίαι δὲ ποιησάσθωσαν τὴν ἀναγγελ[ί]
[αν ἐν τῶι ἐχομένωι ἔτ]ει·

Lines 1–14 only reproduced here

7 Jacopi, *Cl. Rhodos* ii (1932), 172–4, no. 3; improved text by Segre,
Riv. di fil. lx (1932), 446–52 (Telmessos). 184/3.

[Βασιλεύοντος] Εὐμένου Σωτῆρος | ^ ιδ΄,
[ἐφ ἱερέως . . .]ώρου, μηνὸς Αὐδναίου ϛ΄, ἐ[κ-]
[κλησίας κυρί]ας γενομένης, ἔδοξεν Τελ-
[μεσσέων] τῆι πόλει καὶ τοῖς ἄρχουσι
5 [. . . . .]ώρωι Δαπάραι Ἑρμοφάντωι· ἐπει-
[δὴ βασι]λεὺς Εὐμένης ὁ σωτὴρ καὶ εὐεργέ-
[της ἡμ]ῶν, ἀναδεξάμενος τὸν πόλεμον οὐ μό-
[νον ὑπ]ὲρ τῶν ὑφ' αὐτὸν τασσομένων ἀλλὰ καὶ
[ὑπὲρ ἄ]λλων τῶν κατοικούντων τὴν Ἀσίαν, ὑ-
10 [πέστ]η τὸν κίνδυνον, καὶ παρακαλέσας τοὺς

[θεο]ὺς καὶ διαγωνισάμενος πρός τε Προυσίαν
[κα]ὶ Ὀρτιάγοντα καὶ τοὺς Γαλάτας καὶ τοὺς
[σ]υμμάχους αὐτῶν, vac. ἐνίκησεν ἐνδόξως καὶ
[κ]αλῶς καὶ ὡς ἡμεῖς εὐχόμεθα τοῖς θεοῖς· ἀγα-
15 θῆι τύχηι, δεδόχθαι τῆι πόλει καὶ τοῖς ἄρχου-
σιν· ἐπὶ τοῖς γεγενημένοις ἀγαθοῖς εὔχεσ-
θαι μὲν τοὺς ἱερεῖς καὶ τὰς ἱερείας ἀνεωιγ-
μένων τῶν ἱερῶν πάντων καὶ εἰς τὸ λοιπὸν δ[ι-]
δόναι βασιλεῖ Εὐμένει νίκην καὶ κράτος καὶ
20 κατὰ γῆν καὶ κατὰ θάλασσαν, καὶ τῆι μητρὶ
βασιλίσσηι Ἀπολλωνίδι, καὶ τοῖς ἀδελ[φο]ῖς
αὐτοῦ· στεφανηφορῆσαι δὲ τοὺς π[ο]λίτας
καὶ τοὺς ἄλλους ἅπαντας, καὶ θύσαντας
χαριστήρια τοῖς θεοῖς εὐωχεῖσθαι ἐν τῆι
25 [ἐκκλησί]αι (?)· εἰς τὸ λοιπὸν δὲ καθ' ἕκαστον μῆ-
[να θυόντω] οἱ ἄρχοντες τῆι προτέραι, ἐν ἧι νε-
[νίκηκεν ὁ βασιλ]εὺς Διὶ Γενεθλίωι καὶ Ἀθηνᾶι Ν[ι-]
[κηφόρωι, - - - -] ΩΣΑΝ^.ΣΥΝ.. ΥΙ

8 Kalinka, *ÖJh* xxiii (1926), 151–2, no. 87 (Panion, Thrace). Eumenes
II, ?180s.

ὑπὲρ βασιλέως
Εὐμένου σωτῆρος
καὶ εὐε[ργ]έτου κα[ὶ]
κτίστου· τῆς πόλε-
5 ως καὶ τῶν ἀδελ-
φῶν αὐτοῦ καὶ βα-
σιλίσσης Στρατονί-
κης Διόδωρο[ς]
Ἀρριδαίου Διὶ [Σω-]
10 τῆρι καὶ Ἀθην[ᾶι]
Νικηφόρωι κ[αὶ]
Ἀπόλλωνι Π[υθίωι].

9 Haussoullier, *BCH* v (1881), 372, nos. 2–3; *Syll.*³ 629; *IG* ix.² 1. 179;
Daux, *Delphes*, 299–301; *F. Delphes*, iii. 3. 240 (Delphi). 182/1.

[Θ   ε]   ὁ   ς   [Τ   ύ]   χ   α
[Ἔδοξε τοῖς] Αἰτωλοῖς· [ἐπ]εὶ βασιλεὺς Εὐμένης ὑπάρχων φίλος καὶ
σύμμαχος διὰ προγόνων τὰν οὖσα[ν ἐκ πα-]
[λαιῶν χρόνων ε]ὔνοιαν ἐμ παντὶ καιρῶι φανερὸς γίνεται συναύξων,
καὶ πολλὰς καὶ μεγάλας ἀποδείξε[ις]
[πεποίηται τ]ᾶς ἐν τὸ ἔθνος εὐνοίας καὶ τοὺς ἄλλους Ἕλλανας, ἀεὶ τὰ
συμφέροντα διαπρασσόμενο[ς],
5 [σπουδᾶς καὶ] φιλοτιμίας οὐθὲν ἐνλείπων, γεγονότων τε αὐτοῖ πολλῶν καὶ μεγάλων εὐαμερημά[των]

[κατὰ τοὺς π]ολέμους ἐπαυξηκὼς τὰμ βασιλείαν καὶ ἐν τὰν καλλί-
σταν διάθεσιν ἀγνηκὼς κέκρικε
[συντελεῖν] ἀγῶνας καὶ θυσίας τᾶι Ἀθάναι τᾶι Νικαφόρωι μετὰ τῶν
ἀδελφῶν καὶ τοῦ δάμου τῶν
[Περγαμηνῶ]ν, περὶ πλείστου ποιούμενος τὰν ποτὶ τοὺς θεοὺς εὐσέβειαν, παρακαλεῖ [δ]ὲ καὶ το[ὺς]
[Αἰτωλοὺς ἐ]ξαπ[ε]σταλκὼς θεωροὺς Πέρσαν, Θεόλυτον, Κτήσιππον ἀποδέξασθαι τοὺς ἀγῶνας
10 [τῶν Νικαφ]ορίων στεφανίτας, τὸμ μὲν μουσικὸν ἰσοπύθιον, τὸν δὲ
γυμνικὸν καὶ ἱππικὸν ἰσολύμπιον,
[καὶ ὡσαύτ]ως ἄσυλον τὸ τέμενος τᾶς Ἀθάνας τᾶς Νικαφόρου·
δεδόχθαι τοῖς Αἰτωλοῖς [ἐπ]αινέσαι
[μὲν βασιλέ]α Εὐμένη καὶ τοὺς ἀδελφοὺς αὐτοῦ Ἄτταλον, Φιλέταιρον, Ἀθήναιον καὶ βασίλισσαν
[Ἀπολλωνίδα] τὰμ ματέρα αὐτῶν καὶ τὸν δᾶμον τῶν Περγαμηνῶν
ἐπὶ τᾶι ποτὶ τοὺς [θεοὺ]ς εὐσεβεί[αι]
[καὶ στεφανῶ]σαι ἕκαστον αὐτῶν εἰκόνι χρυσέαι, τὸμ μὲν βασιλέα
ἐφ' ἵππου, τοὺς δὲ ἄ[λλους πεζικᾶι],
15 [ἀρετᾶς ἕνεκε]ν καὶ εὐνοίας τᾶς ἐ(ν τὸ ἔθνος), ἀποδεδέχθαι δὲ καὶ
τοὺς ἀγῶνας τῶ[ν Νικαφορίων οὓς]
[συντελεῖ βασ]ιλεὺς Εὐμένης [σ]τεφανίτας, τὸμ μὲν μουσικὸν ἰσοπύθιον, τὸν δὲ γυ[μνικὸν ⟨καὶ ἱππικὸν⟩ ἰσολύμπιο]ν,
[εἶμεν δὲ] κα[ὶ] τοῖς νικεόντοις τῶν Αἰτωλῶν τὰς τιμὰς καὶ τὰ λοιπὰ
πάντα τὰ ἐν τ[οῖς νόμοις περί τε τῶν]
[Πυθίων κ]αὶ Ὀλυμπίων ⟨τὰ⟩ κατακεχωρισμένα καὶ καθάπερ ὁ
βασιλεὺς Εὐμένης ἀνα[δεικνύει] τὸ τέμ[ενος]
[τᾶς Ἀθά]νας τᾶς Νικαφόρου τὸ ποτὶ Περγάμωι ἄσυλον, καθώς κα
ὁρίξη, συναποδεδέχθαι τοὺς Αἰτω[λοὺς]
20 [ἄσυλον] εἶμεν αὐτὸ τὰ ἀπ' Αἰτωλῶν καὶ τῶν ἐν Αἰτωλίαι κατοικεόν-
των καὶ μηθένα ἄγειν μηδὲ ῥυσι[ά-]
[άζειν ἐ]ντὸς τῶν ὁρίων· εἰ δέ τίς κα ἄγη ἢ ῥυσιάξη ἢ ἀποβιάξαιτο ἢ
διεγγυάσῃ, ὑπόδικον εἶμεν ἐν τοῖ[ς]
[συνέδρ]οις τῶι ἀδικηθέντι καὶ ἄλλωι τῶι θέλοντι ἐν ταῖς ἐκ ποτιστά-
σιος δίκαις· ἀποστέλλειν δ[ὲ]
[θεωρ]οὺς ἐν Πέργαμον, ἐπε[ί] κα ἁ θυσία καθήκηι τᾶι Ἀθάναι τᾶι
Νικαφόρωι· τᾶς δὲ ἐκπονπᾶς ἐπι-
[με]λεῖσθαι τὸν στραταγὸν ἀεὶ τὸν ἔναρχον· τοῖς δὲ θεωροῖς τοῖς
ἐπαγγελλόντοις τοὺς ἀγ[ῶνας]
25 [τῶν Ν]ικαφορίων καταστᾶσαι τὰς πόλεις ἑκάστας θεωροδόκους
τῶν ἰδίων πολιτᾶν καὶ ἀνενεγ-
[κεῖ]ν τοὺς ἄρχοντας τοὺς ἀπὸ τᾶν πολίων τῶι στραταγ[ῶ]ι Προξέ-
νωι ἐν τὰ Πύθια, διδόμεν δὲ
[ἐκέχει]ρον καὶ ξένια ὅσα καὶ τοῖς τὰ Ὀλύμπια ἐπαγγελλόντοις
θεωροῖς δίδοντι· ὅπως δὲ καὶ ἐ[ν]
[τοὺς ν]όμους καταχωρισθῇ ἅ τε ἀποδοχὰ τῶν ἀγώνων καὶ τοῦ ἱεροῦ
ἁ ἀσυλία καὶ ἁ τῶν θ[ε]ωροδόκων
[κατάστ]ασις καὶ τὰ ἄλλα τὰ ἐν τῶι ψαφίσματι κατακεχωρισμένα,

ἐπιμέλειαν ποιήσασθαι τὸν στραταγὸν
30 [Πρόξενον] καὶ τοὺς ἄλλους ἄρχοντας · ἐπαινέσαι δὲ καὶ τοὺς θεωροὺς Πέρσαν Δ[ιο]νυσίου Συρακόσιον,
[Θεόλυτον] Ἀρίστωνος Αἰγινάταν, Κτήσιππον Δαματρίου Περγα-
μηνὸν καὶ εἶμεν αὐτοὺς προξένους
[καὶ εὐεργέτ]ας τῶν Αἰτωλῶν · ἔγγυος τᾶν προξενιᾶ[ν ὁ γ]ρ[αμ-
ματ]εύς · ἀναγράψαι δὲ καὶ τὸ ψάφισ[μ]α
[τόδε ἐν στ]άλαις λιθίναις δύο καὶ ἀναθέμεν τὰν μίαν ἐν Θέρμο[ν],
τὰν δὲ ἐν Δελφοῖς · τὸ δὲ γενόμεν[ο]ν
[ἀνάλωμα] δόμεν τὸν ταμίαν τᾶς ΚΩΛ[. . .]Κ[.]Λ[.]Ι[.]ΡΙ[.]Ε
[. . . .]Σ[. . . .]Λ[. .]ΙΛΙ τὸν γραμματῆ τῶν
35 - - - - - - - c.13 IAN vac.

10 Holleaux, *Mélanges Havet* (1909), 187–96 (*Études*, ii. 63–72); *Syll.*[3]
630; Daux, *Delphes*, 293–5; F. *Delphes*, iii.3.261 (Delphi). 182/1.

[Ἄρχοντος ἐν Δελφοῖ]ς Δημοσθένου, δόγμα Ἀμφικ[τιόνων · ἐπειδὴ
βασιλεὺς]
[Εὐμένης παρειληφ]ὼς παρὰ τοῦ πατρὸς βασιλέως Ἀττάλο[υ τήν τε
πρὸς τοὺς θεοὺς]
εὐσ[έβειαν καὶ τὴ]ν πρὸς τοὺς Ἀμφικτίονας εὔνοιαν καὶ διατη[ρῶν
τὴν πρὸς Ῥωμαίους]
φιλίαν ἀεί [τινος ἀγ]αθοῦ παραίτιος γινόμενος διατελεῖ τοῖς Ἕλ-
λησ[ιν καὶ μετεσχηκὼς]
5 τῶν αὐτῶν κ[ινδύ]νων ὑπὲρ τῆς κοινῆς ἀσφαλείας πολλαῖς τῶ[ν
Ἑλληνίδων] πό[λεων]
δωρεὰς δέδ[ωκ]εν ἕνεκεν τοῦ διατηρεῖσθαι τὴν ὑπάρχουσ[αν αὐ-
τον]ομίαν δι' ἣν
αἰτίαν καὶ Ῥω[μαῖ]οι θεωροῦντες αὐτοῦ τὴν προαίρεσιν ἐπευξ[ήκα-
σιν τ]ὴμ βασιλείαν
νομίζοντες [δεῖ]ν καὶ τῶμ βασιλέων ὅσοι μὲν ἐπιβουλεύουσιν [τοῖς
Ἕλλ]ησιν τυγχάν[ειν]
τῆς καθηκού[σης] ἐπιπλήξεως, ὅσοι δὲ μηθενὸς γίνονται κακοῦ
[παραίτιο]ι τούτους τ[ῆς]
10 μεγ[ί]στης [ἀξιο]ῦσθαι παρ' ἑαυτοῖς πίστεως · ἀπέσταλκεν δὲ κ[αὶ
θε]ωροὺς τοὺς
παρακαλέσ[οντ]ας τοὺς Ἀμφικτίονας, ὅπως τὸ τῆς Ἀθηνᾶς τῆς
Ν[ικηφό]ρου τέμενος
συναναδε[ίξωσι]ν ἑαυτῶι ἄσυλον, καὶ τοὺς ἀγῶνας οὓς διέγ[νωκε
συντελεῖν
στεφανίτα[ς τό]ν τε μουσικὸν ἰσοπύθιον καὶ τὸν γυμνικὸν κα[ὶ ἱπ-
πι]κὸν ἰσολύμπιον
ἀποδέξων[ται · ἀ]πελογίσαντο δὲ καὶ οἱ θεωροὶ τὴν τοῦ βασιλέως
[εὔ]νοιαν ἣν ἔχων
15 δ[ια]τελεῖ κ[οινῆι τ]ε πρὸς ἅπαντας τοὺς Ἕλληνας καὶ καθ' ἰδίαν
π[ρὸ]ς τὰς πόλεις·
[ὅπως οὖν καὶ οἱ Ἀμ]φικτίονες φαίνωνται ἐπακολουθοῦντες το[ῖς
ἀξιουμένοις

[καὶ τιμῶντες τ]ῶν βασιλέων ὅσοι διατηροῦντες τὴν πρὸς
Ῥωμ[αί]ους τοὺς κοινοὺς
[εὐεργέτας φιλία]ν ἀεί τινος ἀγαθοῦ παραίτιοι γίνονται τ[οῖς] Ἑλ-
λησιν· τύχηι
[ἀγαθῆι· δεδόχθα]ι τοῖς Ἀμφικτίοσιν ἐπαινέσαι βασιλέα [Εὐ]μένη
βασιλέως
20 [Ἀττ]άλου καὶ σ[τε]φανῶσαι δάφνης στεφάνωι τῶι ἱερῶι τ[οῦ
Ἀ]πόλλωνος τοῦ
[Πυ]θίου ὧι πάτρι[όν] ἐστιν στεφανοῦν τοὺς ἑαυτῶν εὐεργέ[τ]ας,
ἀρετῆς ἕνεκεν
καὶ εὐνοίας τῆ[ς] εἰς τοὺς Ἕλληνας, στῆσαι δὲ αὐτοῦ καὶ εἰκ[ό]να
χαλκῆν ἐφ' ἵππου
ἐν [Δ]ελφ[ο]ῖς, ἀναδεδεῖχθαι δὲ καὶ τὸ ἱερὸν τῆς Ἀθηνᾶς τῆς
Ν[ικ]ηφόρου τὸ πρὸς
Περγάμ[ω]ι ἄσυλ[ο]ν εἰς ἅπαντα τὸν χρόνον καθ' ἃ ἂν ἀφορίσ[ηι]
βασιλεὺς Εὐμένης
25 καὶ μηθ[έ]να ἄγ[ει]ν ἐ[κ] τοῦ περιωρισμένου τόπου μήτε πολέμ[ου]
μήτε εἰρήνης
πρὸς [μηθὲ]ν [ἔγκλημα]· ἀποδεδέ[χθ]αι δὲ [κ]α[ὶ] τοὺς ἀγῶ[να]ς
[τοὺ]ς στεφανίτας
[τῶν Νικηφορίων οὓς συντελεῖ βασιλεὺς Εὐμένης, καὶ εἶνα]ι
καὶ τ[αῖς τιμαῖς καὶ τοῖς]
[λοιποῖς πᾶσι τοῖς ἐν τοῖς νόμοις γεγραμμένοις τὸμ μὲν μ]ουσικὸν
ἰσ[οπύθιον, τὸν δὲ]
[γυμνικὸ]ν καὶ ἱπ(π)ικὸν ἰσ[ολύμπιον· ἀναγράψαι δὲ τὸ ψήφ]ισμα ἐν
Δ[ελφοῖς εἰς τὴν]
30 [βάσιν το]ῦ ἀνδριάντος τ[οῦ πατρὸς βασιλέως Ἀττάλο]υ καὶ ἐμ
Π[εργάμωι ἐν τῶι]
[ἱερῶι τῆ]ς Ἀθηνᾶς τῆς Νικη[φόρου· κηρῦξαι δὲ τὸν στέ]φανον το[ῦ
βασιλέως κ]αὶ τὴν
[ἀσυλί]αν τοῦ ἱεροῦ ἐν τοῖς ἀγ[ῶσι τῶν Πυθίων καὶ Σωτηρί]ων.

26 init. πρὸς [ἰδίο]ν [σύμβολον] F. Delphes: πρὸς [ἔγκλημα μηθέν] Wilhelm, Gr.
Inschriften rechtlichen Inhalts, 48–51: πρὸς [μηθὲ]ν [ἔγκλημα] Daux, BCH lxxvii
(1954), 370–1, who reports N certain.

11 Lambrino, Rev. Arch. xxix (1929), 107–20; Welles, RC 49; cf. Segre
ap. Robert, Hellenica, v (1948), 102–28 (origin unknown: probably
Iasos). 182/1.

[Βουλόμενοι δὲ καὶ ὑμᾶς μ]ετ[έ]χειν τῶν θυσιῶν καὶ [τῶν ἀγώνων
πεπόμφα-]
[μεν θεωροὺς Μ]εγωνά τε τῶν φίλων Ἐφέσιον, ἐν τιμῆι [τῆι πρώτηι
παρ' ἡμῖν ὄντα, ὅ-]
[μοίως δ]ὲ καὶ Κάλαν Περγαμηνόν, κρινόμενον καὶ ὑφ' ἡ[μῶμ μὲν
ἄξιον, ὡς δὲ πολί-]
[την] τετευχότα κατὰ τὴν ἡλικίαν τῶν προσηκόντω[ν, καὶ προκεχει-
ρισμέ-]

5 [νον] ὑπὸ τῆς πόλεως διὰ τὸ καταγγέλλειν μεθ' ἡμῶν τ[αῦτα. καλῶς
οὖν]
[πο]ιήσετε πρῶτομ μὲν διὰ τὴν θεόν, ἔπειτα δὲ καὶ δι' ἡ[μᾶς τῶν
ἀνδρῶν τε φι-]
[λοφ]ρόνως διακούσαντες καὶ ἀποδεξάμενοι τά τε Ν[ικηφόρια καὶ
τὴν ἀσυλίαν·]
[τ]αῦτα γὰρ πράξαντες τὰ μὲν ἐκήνης τίμια φανεῖσ[θε συναύξοντες,
τὸ δὲ λοιπὸν]
[ἡμᾶς] ὡς ἐνδέχεται μάλιστα προθύμους ἕξετε κατὰ τ[ὸ δυνατὸν εἰς
πάν-]
10 τα τὰ συμφέροντα τῶι δήμωι. τὰ δὲ πλείονα περὶ τούτων ἀκο[ύσετε
παρ' αὐτῶν.]
ἔρρωσθε. ἀπέδωκεν Μέγων Ἀνθεστηριῶνος ἕκτηι.
Ἐπὶ στεφανηφόρου Ἀπολλωνίου τοῦ Διογένου, Ἀνθεστηριῶν[ος
ἕκτηι ἱσταμένου·]
[ἔ]δοξεν τῆι βουλῆι καὶ τῶι δήμωι· πρυτάνεων γνώμη· ἐπει[δὴ βασιλεὺς Εὐμένης]
[βασιλ]έως Ἀττάλ[ου] καὶ βασιλίσσης Ἀπολλωνίδος φίλος κ[αὶ εὔνους καὶ εὐεργέτης]
15 [διὰ προ]γόνων ὑπάρχων τοῦ δήμου γέγραφεν πρὸς τὴν βουλὴ[ν καὶ
τὸν δῆμον ὅτι]
[τιμᾶι μὲν τὴν] Ἀθηνᾶν μάλιστα τῶν ἄλλων θεῶν διὰ τὸ πολλὰς κ[αὶ
μεγάλας ἐν παν-]
[τοδαπαῖς περιστάσε]σιν καιρῶν εὐημερίας αὐτῶ[ι] περι[τ]ε-
θεικ[έναι, Νικηφόρον τε]
[προσηγόρευκε]ν καλλίστην νομίζων εἶναι καὶ οἰκειοτάτην τ[ὴν
προσωνυμίαν]
[ταύτην, νῦν δ]ε αὔξειν τε βουλόμενος τὰς τιμὰς αὐτῆς καὶ μ[είζω
χαριστήρια]
20 [τῶν κατὰ πόλεμον ἀ]γώνων ἀπο[διδ]ό[ναι] καὶ διεγνωκὼς
σ[υ]ν[τ]ελ[εῖν - - - -]

15–20 Segre, after text 12

12 Herzog, *Hermes*, lxv (1930), 455–63; Welles, *RC* 50; (with new fragment) Segre *ap*. Robert, *Hellenica*, v (1948), 102–28 (Kos). 182/1.

[Β]ασιλεὺς Εὐμένης Κ[ώιων τῆι βουλῆι καὶ]
τῶι δήμωι χαίρειν· τὴν Ἀ[θηνᾶν μὲν τιμῶμεν]
μάλιστα τῶν ἄλλων θε[ῶν διὰ τὸ πολλὰς καὶ]
μεγάλας ἡμῖν περιτεθε[ικέναι εὐημερίας ἐν]
5 παντοδαπαῖς περιστάσ[εσιν καιρῶν, Νικηφόρον]
τε προσηγορεύκαμεν, [καλλίστην νομίζον-]
τες εἶναι καὶ οἰκειοτάτη[ν τὴν προσω-]
νυμίαν ταύτην καθάπερ [καὶ πρότερον ἐγράψαμεν·]
δὶς γὰρ ἤδη παρακληθέ[ντες ὑφ' ἡμῶν τάς τε]
10 πανηγύρεις ἃς τότ[ε κατηγγείλαμεν ἀπεδέξασθε]

φιλοφρόνως, καὶ πέμψ[αντες θεωροὺς ἐκοινω-]
[ν]ήσατε τῶν ἱερῶν ὁ[σίως καὶ εὐσεβῶς · καὶ νῦν]
[ἐ]παύξειν δὲ βουλόμ[ενοι τὰς τιμὰς αὐτῆς]
[κ]αὶ μείζω χαριστή[ρια τῶν κατὰ πόλεμον ἀγώνων]
15 [ἀ]ποδιδόναι, διεγχ[ωκότες δὲ συντελεῖν αὐτῆι πα-]
[ν]ήγυριν τε διὰ πεν[ταετηρίδος καὶ μουσι-]
[κο]ὺς καὶ γυμνικοὺς [καὶ ἱππικοὺς ἀγῶνας, ἀνα-]
[δεδ]ειχότες καὶ τὸ π[ρὸς Περγάμωι τέμενος ἄσυλον]
[καθ'] ὧι θήσομεν αὐ[τοῦ τὰ ὅρια, καλῶς δὲ ἔχον κε-]
20 [κρικότες ταῦτα] ὑπὸ [θεωρῶν καταγγέλλεσθαι,]
[ὥστε τ]οὺς ἀγῶνα[ς τούτους συντελεῖσθαι σὺν]
[ἅπα]σι τοῖς ἐκτενεσ[τάτοις ἡμῖν τῶν Ἑλλήνων, ἐπι-]
[τε]υγμάτων μεγάλω[ν χαριστήρια τῆι Ἀθηνᾶι,]
πεπόμφαμεν θεωρ[οὺς πρὸς ὑμᾶς - - - -]
25 ῥέα, τυγχάνοντα παρ' [ἡμῖν τιμῆς τε τῆς πρώτης καὶ προ-]
εδρίας δι(ὰ) τὴν καλοκ[αγαθίαν, καὶ - - -]
Μυριναῖον καὶ Μέγων[α Ἐφέσιον, τῶν φίλων τῶν προ(?)-]
τιμωμένων παρ' ἡμῖν [καὶ - - - - καὶ Κάλαν Περγα-]
μηνούς, καὶ ὑφ' ἡμῶν μὲ[ν κρινομένους ἀξίους, ὡς]
30 δὲ πολίτας τετευχ[ότας κατὰ τὴν ἡλικίαν τῶν προση-]
κόντων, προκεχιρισ[μένους δὲ καὶ ὑπὸ τῆς πόλεως]
διὰ τὸ καταγγέλλε[ιν μεθ' ἡμῶν τὰ Νικηφόρια · καλῶς]
οὖν ποιήσετε π[ρῶτον μὲν διὰ θεόν, ἔπειτα δὲ]
καὶ δι' ἡμᾶς τῶν ἀνδ[ρῶν τε φιλοφρόνως διακούσαν-]
35 τες καὶ ἀποδεξάμεν[οι τά τε Νικηφόρια καὶ τὴν ἀσυλίαν ὥσ-]
περ ὑμῖν ἁρμόζει · ταῦτ[α γὰρ πράξαντες τὰ μὲν ἐκείνης τί-]
μια φανεῖσθε συναύξ[οντες, ἡμᾶς δὲ ἀκολούθως τῆι]
παρ' ἡμῶν ὑπαρχούση[ι πρὸς τὸν δῆμον ὑμῶν εὐνοίαι]
ὡς ἐνδέχεται μάλισ[τα προθύμους ἕξετε τὸ λοιπὸν κατὰ]
40 πάντα καιρὸν πρὸς τ[ὰ συμφέροντα ὑμῖν · τὰ δὲ πλείονα]
περὶ τῶν κατὰ μέρος [ἀκούσετε παρ' αὐτῶν τῶν θεω-]
ρῶν. ἔρρωσθε. [ἔδοξε τᾶι βουλᾶι καὶ τῶι δάμωι ·]
γνώμα προστατᾶν · [ἐπειδὴ βασιλεὺς Εὐμένης ἀποστέλλων]
θεωροὺς [παρ' αὐτοῦ τε καὶ παρὰ πόλιος τᾶς Περγαμηνῶν]
45 ἐπαγ[γέλλει - - - - - - - -]

8–12 καθάπερ [καὶ ὁ πατὴρ ἡμῶν.] | δὶς γὰρ ἤδη παρακληθέ[ντες ὑπ' αὐτοῦ τάς τε]
| πανηγύρεις, ἃς τότ[ε κατήγγειλε, ἀποδέξασθε] | φιλοφρόνως καὶ πέμψ[αντες
θεωροὺς ἐκοινω|ν]ήσατε τῶν ἱερῶν ὁ[σίως καὶ εὐσεβῶς πάντων ·] Klaffenbach,
MDAI iii (1950), 99–106   16–19 διὰ πένθ' ἡμέρων καὶ στεφανίτας μουσι|-
κ]οὺς καὶ γυμνικοὺς [καὶ ἱππικοὺς ἀγῶνας, ἀνα|δεδ]ειχότες καὶ τὸ π[ρὸς Περγά-
μωι ἱερὸν αὐτῆς ἀσυ|λον], ὧι θήσομεν αὐ[τοὶ τὰ ὅρια] Klaffenbach: διὰ πεν[ταετη-
ρίδος καὶ μουσικο|ὺς καὶ γυμνικοὺς [ἀγῶνας, καὶ τὸ ἱερὸν ἀνα|δεδ]ειχότες καὶ
τὸ π[ερὶ αὐτὸ τέμενος ἄσυλα, | καθ'] ὧι θήσομεν αὐ[τῶν τὰ ὅρια] Segre   τὸ
πρὸς Περγάμωι τέμενος cf. text 9, lines 18–19.

218   *Appendix IV*

13 Wiegand, *Abh. Berlin*, 1904, 86; *OGIS* 763; Rehm, *Milet*, i. 9,
    no. 306; Welles, *RC* 52 (Miletos). Eumenes II.

Βασιλεὺς Εὐ[μένης Ἰώνων τῶι κοινῶι χαίρειν·]
τῶν παρ᾽ ὑμῶν πρεσβευτῶν Μενεκλῆς [μὲ]ν
οὐ συνέμειξέ μοι, Εἰρηνίας δὲ καὶ Ἀρχέλαος
ἀπαντήσαντες ἐν Δήλωι ἀπέδωκαν
5 ψήφισμα καλὸν καὶ φιλάνθρωπον, ἐν ὧι
καταρξάμενοι διότι τὰς καλλίστας ἀπὸ τῆς
ἀρχῆς ἑλόμενος πράξεις καὶ κοινὸν ἀναδείξας
ἐμαυτὸν εὐεργέτην τῶν Ἑλλήνων πολλοὺς μὲν
καὶ μεγάλους ἀγῶνας ὑπέστην πρὸς τοὺ[ς]
10 βαρβάρους, ἅπασαν σπουδὴν καὶ πρόνοιαν ποιού[με-]
νος ὅπως οἱ τὰς Ἑλληνίδας κατοικοῦντες πόλε[ις]
διὰ παντὸς ἐν εἰρήνηι καὶ τῆι βελτίστηι καταστάσ[ει]
ὑπάρχωσιν, ἀντικαταλλασ(σ)όμενός [τε πρὸς] τὸ[ν]
ἐπ[α]κ[ολουθ]οῦντα κίνδυνον καὶ [πόνον τὴν εὔκλειαν, ἐμμε-]
15 [νειν δὲ ἑ]λόμεν[ος ἐν τ]οῖς [πρὸς τὸ κ]οινὸν ἀκολούθως τῆ τοῦ πατρὸς προ[α]ιρέσει ἐν πολλοῖς φανερὰς
πεποίημαι τὰς ὑπὲρ τούτων ἀποδείξεις κοινῆ τε
καὶ κατ᾽ ἰδίαν πρὸς ἑκάστην τῶν πόλεων εὐνοϊκῶς
διακείμενος καὶ πολλὰ τῶν πρὸς ἐπιφάνειαν
20 καὶ δόξαν ἀνηκόντων συνκατασκευάζων
ἑκάστῃ, ἅπερ διὰ τῶν ἔργων τὴν ἐμήν τε φιλοδο-
ξίαν .[.].. εν καὶ τὴν εὐχαριστίαν τοῦ κοινοῦ·
διόπερ ἔ[δο]ξεν ὑμ<ε>ῖν, ὅπως ἀεὶ φαίνησθε τὰς
καταξίας τιμὰς τοῖς εὐεργέταις ἀπονέ-
25 μοντες, στεφανῶσαι μὲν ἡμᾶς χρυσῷ στεφάνωι ἀριστείωι, στῆσαι δὲ εἰκόνα χρυσῆν ἐν ὧι ἂμ
βούλωμαι τόπωι τῆς Ἰωνίας, ἀναγγεῖλαί τε τὰς τιμὰς
ἔν τε τοῖς ὑφ᾽ [ὑ]μῶν συντελουμένοις ἀγῶσιν
καὶ κατὰ τὰς πόλεις ἐν τοῖς τιθεμένοις ἐν ἑκάστηι,
30 [καὶ ἀσπάσασθαι δέ μ]ε παρὰ τοῦ κοινοῦ [καὶ συνησθῆναι]
[ἐπὶ τ]ῶι κἀμὲ κ[αὶ τ]οὺς ἀναγκαίους ἐρρῶ[σθαι εἶναί τε]
τὰ πράγματα κατὰ λόγον, παρακαλεῖν τ[έ με θεωροῦντα]
τὴν εὐχαριστίαν τοῦ πλήθους τὴν κ[αθήκουσαν πρό-]
νοιαν ποιεῖσθαι δι᾽ ὧν τὸ κοινὸν τῶν Ἰ[ώνων ἐπαυξηθή-]
35 σεταί τε καὶ διὰ παντὸς ἐν τῆι ἀρί[στηι καταστάσει ὑπ] ἄρ-
ξει· οὕτω γὰρ καὶ μετὰ ταῦτά με πάν[των τεύξεσθαι τ] ῶν
εἰς τιμὴν καὶ δόξαν ἀνηκόντων. ἀ[κολούθως δὲ πᾶσιν]
τοῖς κατακεχωρισμένοις καὶ οἱ πρ[εσβευταὶ μετὰ π] λεί-
ονος σπουδῆς διελέχθησαν ἐξηγο[ύμενοι σύμπα] ν-
40 τος τοῦ πλήθους πρὸς ἡμᾶς ἐκτενε[στάτην τε καὶ]
εἰλικρινῆ τὴν εὔνοιαν. τά τε τίμια φιλο[φρόνως ἀποδέ-]
χομαι κ(α)ὶ οὐδέποτ᾽ ἐλλελοιπὼς κατά [γε τὴν ἐμὴν]
δύναμιν εἰς τὸ περιποιεῖν ἀεί τι καὶ κ[οινῆι πᾶσιν]
καὶ κατὰ πόλιν ἑκάστοις τῶν πρὸς [τιμὴν καὶ δόξαν]
45 ἀ[ν]ηκόντων πειράσομαι καὶ νῦν τῆς

τοιαύτης προθέσεως μὴ ἀφίστασθαι.
γίνοιτο δὲ τῆι βουλήσει μου καὶ τὰ πράγματα
συνεξακολουθεῖν. οὕτω γὰρ ὁμολογουμέ-
νην λήψεσθε μᾶλλον δι' αὐτῶν τῶν ἔργων
50 τῆς ἐμῆς προαιρέσεως τὴν ἀπόδειξιν.
ὅπως δὲ καὶ εἰς τὸ λοιπὸν ἐν τῆι πανηγύρει
τῶν Πανιωνίων ἡμέραν ἐπώνυμον ἄγοντες
ἡμῖν ἐπιφανέστερον τὴν ὅλην ἑορτὴν συν-
τελῆτε, προσόδους ὑμῖν τὰς ἱκανὰς ἀνα-
55 [θήσ]ω ἀφ' ὧν ἕξετε τὴν καθήκουσαν ἡμῖν
[ἀνατιθ]έναι μνήμην. τὸν δὲ χρυσοῦν ἀνδρι-
[άντα ποιή]σω μὲν ἐγὼ προαιρούμενος ἀδά-
[πανον πάν]τως [τὴν] χάριν εἶναι τῶι κο[ινῶι.]
ἀνατεθῆναι δ' αὐτὴ[ν βούλομαι ἐν τῶι ἐψη-]
60 φισμένωι ἡμῖν ὑπὸ Μιλησ[ίων τε]μένε[ι· ὅ-]
τε γὰρ ἐν ταύτηι τῆι πόλει συντελοῦντε[ς]
τὴν πανήγυριν ἐψήφισθε τὴν τιμὴν ἡμῖν,
τῆς πόλεως μόνης τῶν Ἰάδων μέχρι τοῦ
παρόντος τέμενος ἀναδεδειχοίας ἡμῖν
65 καὶ συγγενοῦς κρινομένης διὰ Κυζικηνούς,
ἔνδοξα δὲ πολλὰ καὶ ἄξια μνήμης ὑπὲρ τῶν
Ἰώνων πεπραχυίας, οἰκειοτάτην ἐλογιζόμη[ν]
τὴν ἀνάθεσιν ἔσεσθαι ἐν ταύτηι. τὰ δὲ κατὰ
μέρος ὑπὲρ τῆς ἐμῆς εὐνοίας κοινῆι τε
70 πρὸς πάντας ὑμᾶς καὶ καθ' ἑκάστην πόλιν
ἀκηκοότες οἱ πρεσβευταὶ δηλώσουσιν
ὑμῖν. ἔρρωσθε.

13–16 follow Wilhelm, *Klio*, Beiheft xlviii (1943), 43–6: ἀντικαταλλασ<σ>όμε-
νος [δὲ πρὸς] τὸ[ν] | ἐπ[α]χ[ολουθ]οῦντα κίνδυνον καὶ [ἐκτενὴς καὶ φιλόδο|ξος
εἶναι προε]λόμεν[ος ἐν τ]οῖς [πρὸς τὸ κ]οινὸν ἀκολού[θως τῇ τοῦ πατρὸς
προ[α]ιρέσει κτλ. Welles

14 Wiegand, *Abh. Berlin*, 1911, 26–7; Rehm, *Milet*, i. 9. no. 307;
Herrmann, *Ist. Mitt.* xv (1965), 104. II (Miletos). Eumenes II (160s).

Ἔδοξε τῶι δήμωι· οἱ πρυτάνεις καὶ οἱ εἰρημένοι ἐπὶ τῆ[ι φυλακῆι]
[ε]ἶπαν· ἐπειδὴ βασιλεὺς Εὐμένης συγγενὴς κ[αὶ φί-]
λος καὶ εὔνους καὶ εὐεργέτης ὑπάρχων τῆς πό[λ-]
εως διὰ προγόνων καὶ πρὸς ἅπαντας μὲν τοὺς Ἕλλη-
5 νας φιλοδόξω(ς) ἀπὸ τῆς ἀρχῆς διακείμενος καὶ
τὰς περὶ τούτων ἀποδείξεις φανερὰς διὰ (πάν-)
των πεποημένος τῶν ἔργων καθ' ὅτι αἵ τε κα-
θ' ἑκάστους τῶν καιρῶν σ(υν)τετελεσμέναι<ς> καὶ
αἱ παρὰ τῶ(ν) εὐε(ρ)γετημένων ἀπηντ(η)κυῖαι τι-
10 μαὶ τῶι βασιλεῖ τὴν περὶ τῶν προειρημένων βεβ-
αιοῦσι πίστιν, βουλόμενος δὲ καὶ τὰ προϋπάρχ-
οντα διὰ προγόνων αὐτῶι πρὸς τὴν ἡμετέραν πόλ-

[ι]ν οἰκεῖα καὶ φιλάνθρωπα ἐπαυξῆσαι καὶ τῆς ἑα[υ-]
τοῦ πρὸς τὸ πλῆθος αἱρέσεως καλὸν ὑπόμ[νη-]
15 μα<ι> ἄξιον τῆς ἰδίας ἀρετῆς καὶ τοῖς ἐπιγινομ̣[έ-]
νοις ὑπολιπέσθαι, γράμ(μ)ατα ἀπέσταλκεν πρός [τ-]
ε τὴν βουλὴν καὶ τὸν δῆμον, δι᾽ ὧν τά τε ὑπὸ Εἰρ[η-]
νίου ἐμφανισθέντα αὐτῶι ἐχθέμενος καὶ τὴν π̣ . . .
πρὸς τὸν δῆμον αἵρεσιν διὰ τῶν κατὰ μέρο[ς . . . . . .].

15 Wiegand, *Abh. Berlin*, 1911, 27–9; Laum, *Stiftungen*, ii., p. 159, no. 129b; Rehm, *Milet*, i. 9. 151; *Didyma*, ii. 488 (Didyma, originally of Miletos). Eumenes II (160s).

- - *19–20* - - α[τ]ὴν κ . . . . το - - *8–9* - -
[- - *9–10* - Λη]ναιῶνος τῆι ἕκτη ἀπὸ [τῆς πρ]οσό[δου]
[τῆς ἐκ τῶν εἰρ]ημένων χρημάτων. vac. δεδόχθα[ι]
[τῆι δ]ρ[υ]λῆι ἑλέσθαι ἐν τῆι ἐκκλησίαι ἄνδρας
5 [δύο,] τοὺς δὲ αἱρεθέντας προνοῆσαι, ὅπως κατα-
[γο]ρασθῆι σῖτος ὁ ἱκανὸς ἢ μισθωθῆι ἡ παροχὴ
[το]ῦ ἱκανοῦ πλήθους εἰς τὴν διαμέτρησιν, ἵνα
[δ]ῶσιν ἑκάστωι τῶμ πολιτῶν ἡμιεκτῆ ἓξ ἐν τῶ[ι]
μηνὶ τῶι Ληναιῶνι τῆι ἕκτη(ι), ἐν ἧι ἐγένετο ὁ βασ[ι-]
10 λεὺς Εὐμένης, καὶ ἡ θυσία καὶ ἡ ἑστίασις συντελε[σθῆι]
[δ]ιευκ[ρ]ινουμένων τῶν τε κατὰ τὰς πομπὰς χ[αὶ]
τὰς θυσίας καὶ τὸν καθοπλισμὸν τῶν ἐφήβων
[κ]αὶ τῶν ἄλλων τῶν διατεταγμένων κατά
[τ]ε τὸν στεφανηφορικὸν νόμον καὶ τὴν περὶ
15 [τ]ῆς ἱερεωσύνης διαγραφήν. αἱρεῖσθαι δὲ κα[ὶ]
εἰς τὸν ἑξῆς χρόνον τοῦ μηνὸς τοῦ Ταυρεῶνο[ς]
τῆι δωδεκάτηι τοὺς καταγοράσοντας σῖτο[ν]
ἢ μισθώσοντας τὴν παροχὴν τοῦ ἱκανοῦ πλήθους. vac. ἵνα δὲ τύχηι τὰ προειρημένα τῆς προσ[η-]
20 [κ]ούσης οἰκονομίας, τοὺς εἰρημένους ἄνδρας
[ἐ]πὶ τῆς κατασκευῆς τοῦ γυμνασίου Εἰρηνίαν Εἰρη-
[ν]ίου, Ζώπυρον Ἀσκληπιοδώρου ἀποσυστῆ-
[σ]αι ἐμ μηνὶ Ἀρτεμισιῶνι τῶι ἐν τῶι ἐνεστῶτ[ι]
[ἐ]νιαυτῶι ἀπὸ τῶν ὀφειλομένων ἐμπορικῶν
25 δανείων τάλαντα τριάκοντα τοῖς αἱρεθησομέ-
νοις ἐπὶ τῆς δημοσίας τραπέζης εἰς τὸν ἐνιαυτὸν τὸμ μετὰ τὸν δεύτερον θεὸν τὸμ μετὰ Μενε-
κράτην, τοὺς δὲ χορηγεῖν τοῖς αἱρουμένοις ἀνδρά-
[σ]ιν ἀπὸ τῆς προσόδου εἰς τὸν καταγορασμὸν τοῦ
30 σίτου, ἐξιόντας δὲ παρ[αδ]ιδόναι τοῖς με-
θ᾽ ἑαυτοὺς τραπεζ[ίταις - - c. 10 - -] συ[μ-]
βόλαια εὐαρκ[ετὰ - - - - - - - αἱ-]
τῆσαι τοὺς α[ἱρουμένους? - - - - - - -]
v. v. v. v. π̣[οιε]ῖ̣ν̣ [δὲ - c. 7 - εὐθὺς τὸν] καταγο[ρασμὸν]
35 [ἢ τ]ὴν μίσθω[σιν τοῦ σίτου κα]ὶ ἐγγρά(φ)εσθαι εἰς τ[ὸν]

[λ]όγον. ν. ν. ὅπω[ς δὲ τῆς ἁρ]μοζούσης τηρήσεω[ς]
τυγχάνηι τὰ ἐ[ψηφισμένα κ]αὶ ἡ εἰς τὸμ βασιλέα
μνήμη διαφυλά[σσητ]αι εἰς τὸν ἀεὶ χρόνον, ἐπ[ι-]
γνῶσι δὲ καὶ οἱ ἀ[δε]λφοὶ αὐτοῦ βασιλεύς τε Ἄτ-
40 ταλος καὶ Ἀθήναιος καὶ ὁ υἱὸς Ἄτταλος τὴν τοῦ
δήμου καὶ ἐν τούτοις προαίρεσιν, vac. μὴ εἶναι μη-
θενὶ μήτε εἰπεῖν μήτε ἀναγνῶναι μήτε προθεῖ-
ναι μήτε προγράψαι μήτε ἐπιψηφίσαι, ὡς δεῖ με-
τατεθῆναι τὰ χρήματα εἰς ἄλλο τι καὶ μὴ ὑπάρχει[ν]
45 εἰς τὰ ἐν τῶι ψηφίσμ[ατι] κατακεχωρισμένα. ἐὰν δ[έ]
τις παρὰ ταῦτα π[ράξηι] τρόπωι (ὅτωι)οῦν, τό τε γρ[α-]
φὲν ἄκυρον ἔσ[τω, ὁ δὲ π]ράξας τι τῶν ἀπειρη-
μένων [ἀποτεισάτω στατῆρας] δισχιλίους ἱεροὺς
το[ῦ Ἀπόλλωνος τοῦ Διδυμ]έως· ὁμοίως δὲ
50 [- - - - - - - πρ]όστιμον καὶ τοῦ
- - - - - - - - - ὦσιν, τὰ διάφορα
- - - - - - - - - μένα. ν. ν. τὸ δὲ ψή-
[φισμα τόδε ἀναγράψαι εἰς στήλ]ην λιθίνην καὶ στ[ῆ-]
[σαι ἐν τῶι ἱερῶι τοῦ Ἀπόλλωνος το]ῦ Διδυμέως π[ρὸ]
55 [τοῦ ναοῦ - - - - - -]μένους· τοὺς [δὲ]
[- - - - - - - - - - - κα]τασκευῆ[ς τῆς]
[στήλης   vac.?   ]

16 Herrmann, *Ist. Mitt.* xv (1965), 71–117, no. 1A (Miletos). Eumenes
II (160s).

Ἔδοξε τῶι δήμωι· οἱ πρυτάνεις καὶ οἱ εἰρημένοι ἐπὶ τῆς φυλακῆς
εἶπαν· ἐπει-
δὴ Εἰρηνίας Εἰρηνίου τὴν καλλίστην διὰ παντὸς ὑπὲρ τῶν συμφερόντων τῆι
πόλει ποιούμενος ἐκτένειαν καὶ ἀεί τι τῶν πρὸς ἐπιφάνειαν καὶ
δόξαν ἀνηκόν-
των συγκατασκευάζων τῆι πατ(ρ)ίδι, ἐντυχὼν δὲ καὶ βασιλεῖ Εὐμένει κατὰ τὴν δο-
5 θεῖσαν ὑπὸ τοῦ πλήθους αὐτῶι συνχώρησιν καὶ διὰ τῆς ἰδίας συστά-
σεως
προτρεψάμενος αὐτὸν δοῦναι τῆι πόλει δωρεὰν πυρῶν μεδίμνων
μυριά-
δας δεκαὲξ εἰς κατασκευὴν γυμνασίου καὶ ξύλωσιν εἰς τὰ δεδηλωμένα
τὴν ἱκανήν, τοῦ δὲ δήμου ψηφισαμένου τὰς ἁρμοζούσας ἐπὶ τοῖς
προειρη-
μένοις τιμὰς τῷ βασιλεῖ καὶ πρεσβευτὴν ἐξαποστείλαντος Εἰρηνίαν
δια-
10 λεγεὶς μετὰ πάσης φιλοτιμίας καὶ παραστησάμενος αὐτὸν προσεπαυ-
ξῆσαί τε τὰ κατὰ τὴν ἐπαγγελίαν καὶ τὰς δαπάνας τὰς εἰς τὴν συν-
τέλειαν τῶν τιμῶν ἀναδέξασθαι παρ᾽ αὐτοῦ ὥστε τὴν μὲν τοῦ πλή-

θους εἰς τοὺς εὐεργέτας εὐχαριστίαν φανερὰν πᾶσιν καταστῆσαι, τὰς
δὲ εἰς τὰ δεδηλωμένα χορηγίας ἐκ τῶν τοῦ βασιλέως ὑπηρετηθῆ-
15 ναι, καλὴν καὶ συνφέρουσαν οὐ μόνον ἐπὶ τοῦ καθήκοντος, ἀλλὰ
- - - - - - - c. 7 lines -

17 Herrmann, *Ist. Mitt.* xv (1965), 71–117, no. 2 (b) (Miletos, originally of
Myus). Eumenes II (160s).

[. . .] *ΔΗΜΟ* [5–6] *ΕΣ*.[.] *ΑΕ*. [c. 6] *ΟΝΕΧ*. . *ΣΑ* [- - - - - -

φιλοδοξίαν· τὸ δὲ συναχθὲν π[λ]ῆθος ἐγδανείσουσιν, ὅπως ἡ πί-
πτουσ[α ἀπ’ αὐτοῦ]
πρόσοδος ὑπάρχῃ εἰς τὰ διὰ τοῦ ψηφίσματος ἀποτεταγμένα· τὸν δὲ
[- - - - -
τὸν γραμματέα προνοιῆσαι ἐν ἀρχαιρεσίαις ὅπως ἱερωσύνη πραθ[ῇ ἡ
- - - -
5 Εὐμένους θεοῦ, αἱρεθῶσι δὲ καὶ ἄνδρες οἵτινες διαγραφήν τε εἰσοί-
σου[σιν περὶ τῆς]
ἱερωσύνης καὶ τὰ ἐψηφισμένα εἰς τοὺς νόμους κατατάξουσιν τοὺς
[- - - - - -
ὑπάρχοντας Μυησίοις, ἀναγραφῇ δὲ καὶ τόδε τὸ ψήφισμα εἴς τε τὸ
βῆ[μα ἐφ’ οὗ]
σταθήσεται ἡ τοῦ βασιλέως εἰκὼν καὶ εἰς τὴν παραστάδα τοῦ ναοῦ
[τοῦ Ἀπόλλω-]
νος το[ῦ Τ]ερμινθέως· τὸ δὲ ἐσόμενον εἰς ταῦτα ἀνήλωμα ὑπ-
ηρετῆσ[αι τὸν τα-]
10 μίαν ἀ[πὸ ἁ]πάσης τῆς προσόδου καὶ ἐγγράψασθαι εἰς τὸν λόγον·
ἐλέ[σθαι δὲ δύο]
πρεσβ[ευτ]άς, τοὺς δὲ αἱρεθέντας ἀφικομένους πρὸς τὸν[βασιλέα τό
τε ψήφισ-]
[μα] ἀποδοῦναι καὶ παρακαλεῖν τὸν βασιλέα ὅπως προν[οιησάμενος
τῶν ἑαυ-]
[τοῦ] τιμῶν καὶ τῶν τοῦ δήμου ἐνδόξων ἀεί τινος ἀγαθοῦ [παραίτι-
ος γένηται ἡ-]
[μῖν·] προνοιῆσαι δὲ καὶ ὅπως ἀνασταθῇ ὑπ’ αὐτοῦ ὁ περὶ τ[- - - -
15–18 - - -
15 [καθ]ότι καὶ διὰ τοῦ πρότερον ψηφίσματος ὁ δῆμος τὴμ π[- - - - - - - -
[. . . .]ο καὶ Εἰρηνίας δὲ τοὺς καθήκοντας λόγους πράσσει[ν ὑπέ-
σχετο, καὶ ποιεῖν]
[ὅτι ἂν] ἀγαθὸν δύνωνται τῶι δήμωι. Ἡρέθησαν Εἰρηνίας Εἰ[ρη-
νίου, - - - 10 -
[. . . . . . .]ίδου.

Appendix IV 223

18 *CIA* ii. 436; *IG* ii.² 953 (Athens). 160/59.

['E]πὶ Τυχάνδρου ἄρχοντος ἐπὶ τῆς Ἀκαμ[αντίδος ἔκτης πρυ-]
[τ]ανείας, ἧι Σωσιγ[έ]νης Μενεκράτου Μαρ[αθώνιος ἐγραμμάτευ-]
[εν·] Ποσιδεῶνος δευτέραι μετ' εἰκάδας, ἐ[νάτηι τῆς πρυτανεί-]
[ας· ἐ]κκλησία κυρία ἐν τῶι θεάτρωι· τῶν πρ[οέδρων ἐπεψήφιζεν - -
-]
5 - - - - Διοζότου Οἰναῖος καὶ συμπροέδρο[ι· ἔδοξεν τῆι βουλῆι καὶ]
[τῶι δή]μωι· Νικόστρατος Φιλίσκου Θοραι[εὺς εἶπεν· ἐπειδὴ - - -]
[- - οἰκ]εῖος ὢν τοῦ βασιλέως Εὐμένους [ἐν τῶι ἔμπροσθεν χρό-]
[νωι εὔνο]υς ὑπῆρξεν καὶ παρεχόμενο[ς χρείας κοινῆι τε τῶι δήμ-]
[ωι καὶ κα]θ' ἰδίαν τοῖς ἀφικνουμένοις τ[ῶν πολιτῶν εἰς Πέργαμον]
10 [διετέλεσε] καὶ νῦν Εὐμένο[υς] τὴν ἀρχ[ὴν παραδόντος (or ἐπιτρε-
ψάντος) τῶι ἀδελφῶι Ἀττάλωι, κτλ.]

10 from squeeze

19 Keramopoullos, *Arch. Delt.* iii (1917), 366; Robert, *Ét. anat.* 84, n. 4; Fraser, *REA* liv (1952), 233-45, no. 5 (Thebes). Eumenes II.

ἱερὰ ἡ γῆ Διονύσου
Λυσείου, ἀφ' ὧν ἀνέθη-
κε βασιλεὺς Εὐμένης

20 Macridy, *ÖJh* viii (1905), 161–3, no. 1; Holleaux, *BCH* xxx (1906), 349–58 (with revisions, *Études*, ii. 51–60) (Colophon Nova). Eumenes II or Attalos II.

. . . . [Ἀπόλλωνος] (?) Κλαρί-
[ου . . . . σταθῆναι δὲ] τὴν εἰκόνα
[ἐν τῶι ἐπιτηδειοτάτωι τόπωι (?)] τοῦ ἱεροῦ πλησίον
[τῶν εἰκόνων τῶν ἀδελφῶν Ἀθηναί]ου καὶ τῆς μητρὸς
5 [αὐτῶν βασιλίσσης Ἀπολλωνίδο]ς· καὶ ἐπειδὴ οἱ με-
[- - - - - - - - - - - - τῶν τε νέων] καὶ τῶν ἐφήβων ψήφισ-
[μα προγράψαντες ἀξιοῦσι] τιμῆσαι Ἀθήναιον ὄντα
[εὐεργέτην καὶ τῶν καλλ]ίστων ὀρεγόμενον ταῖς
[ἄλλαις τιμαῖς, ἀποδιδ]όντες ἐπιφανῆ καὶ μνήμης
10 [ἀξίαν - - - - - - - - - - -]αι χάριν· δεδόχθαι περὶ τού-
[των τῆι βουλῆι καὶ τῶι] δήμωι· τὸν γυμνασίαρχον
[τὸν ἑκάστοτε γινόμε]νον, ἐν ἧι ἡμέραι Ἀθήναιος ἐ-
[γένετο, θυσίαν συντ]ελεῖν καὶ διαδρομὴν τῶν νέων
[καὶ τῶν ἐφήβων Ἀθη]ναίωι, συντελεῖν δὲ ἐν τῆι αὐ-
15 [τῆι ἡμέρα καὶ τ]ὸν παιδονόμον ἀγῶνα παίδων, δίδοσ-
[θαι δὲ αὐτοῖ]ς ὑπὸ τοῦ οἰκονόμου εἴς τε τὴν θυσίαν
καὶ τὴν διαδρομὴν καὶ τὸν ἀγῶνα ὃ ἂν ὁ δῆμος τάξηι
ἐγ Κρονιῶνι μηνί. τῶν δὲ ἱερείων τῶν τεθέντων, ἀ-
φαιρεθέντων εἰς τὰ ἆθλα τοῖς τε νέοις καὶ τοῖς ἐφή-

224   Appendix IV

20 βοις καὶ τοῖς παισίν, ἐὰμ μή τι καὶ ἄλλο βούλωνται
τιθέναι τοῖς νικῶσι, τὰ λοιπὰ διανεμέτω ὁ γυμνα-
[σ]ίαρχος τοῖς ἀλει[ψ]αμένοις καὶ τῆι βουλῆι καὶ
[τοῖ]ς ἄλλοις ἄρχουσι καὶ τοῖς ἱερεῦσι καὶ πρυτά-
[νει κα]ὶ προφήτη (sic) καὶ ἱερῶι<ι> συνεδρίωι καὶ τοῖς
25 [νικήσα]σι τοὺς στεφανίτας ἀγῶνας καὶ ἱεροκή[ρυ-]
[ξι καὶ γρα]μματεῦσιν. τὴν δὲ διαδρομὴν συντελ[εῖσ-]
[θαι ὑπὸ τοῦ γ]υμνασιάρχου ἐν τῶι Ὁμηρείωι. τ[οὺς]
[δὲ νικήσαντας ἀ]ναγγέλλεσθαι ὑπὸ τῶν ἀρχόντων
[αὐθήμερον (?). τὸν δὲ] παιδονόμον τὸν ἀγῶνα συντε-
30 [λεῖν τῶν παίδων ἐν τῶι Ὁ]μη[ρ]ε[ί]ωι, μέχρι π[α]ιδικὴ
[τούτοις οἰκοδομηθῆι. ἀναγορ]εύεσθαι δὲ τὴν ἡμέ-
[ραν, ἐν ἧι ἥ τε θυσία καὶ ἡ διαδρομ]ὴ καὶ ὁ ἀγὼν συντε-
[λεσθήσεται ὑπὸ τῶν ἱεροκηρύκων. ἐξ]εῖναι δὲ καὶ
[- α]ὐτῆι καὶ . .

5–6 οἱ [π]ε|[ρὶ τὸ γυμνάσιον τῶν τε νέων] Holleaux in *BCH*: OIME Robert,
Ét. anat. 153, n. 6   6–7 or ψήφισ|[μα προεγράψαντο περὶ τοῦ] Holleaux,
REG xxv (1923), 194, n. 3 (*Études*, ii. 56, n. 1)

21 Saucıuc, *Andros*, 133–7, no. 4; *IG* xii Suppl. p. 124, no. 250. See also
Robert, *BCH* xl (1926), 493, n. 8; *Hellenica*, xi-xii (1960), 116-25
(Andros). Eumenes II or Attalos II.

- - - - - - - - - - - - - - - ἀποδείξεις πεποίηται τῆς - - - - - - - - - - - - - - - -
- - - - - - - - - - - ἀρχὴν καλῶς καὶ ἐνδόξως καὶ μεγαλομερῶς
ἀνέ[στραπται (?) - - - γυμνασίαρχος δὲ αἱ-]
[ρεθε]ὶς εἰς τὸν ἐπ᾿ Ἀρτεμιδώρου ἄρχοντος ἐνιαυτὸν ἔν τε τοῖς κατὰ
τὴν ἀρχήν ΛΙΙΛ.ΙΙΙΛ [- - - - - - - - - - - - - - - - τὴν]
[ἀ]ναστροφὴν πεποίηται [πρ]όνοι[α]ν ποιούμενος πάντων τῶν εἰς τὸ
γυμνάσιον παραγινομένων ΜΛΙΙΥ [- - - προ-]
5 [στα]τῶν τῆς τῶν νέων εὐκοσμίας προσκαρτερῶν διὰ παντὸς καὶ ἐν
τοῖς κατὰ τὴν χορηγίαν μεγαλ[ομερῶς - - - -]
[- - -ω]ς τὸ γυμνάσιον κεκόσμηκεν κατασκευάσας, πυλῶνα λίθου
λευκοῦ καὶ ἐξέδραν ἀναθεὶς καὶ τοῦ βασ[ιλέ-]
[ως ἄγα]λμα λίθου λυχνέως· ἔν τε τῆι γενεθλίωι τοῦ βασιλέως
ἡμέρα συντελουμένης πομπῆς καὶ θυσίας ὑπὸ τοῦ δήμ[ου]
- - - - - ΙΛΥΛΗ..Η..ΕΙ. ὑπὲρ τοῦ βασιλέως συνεπόμπευσεν ἄγων
ἴδιον βοῦν καὶ [ἔθυ]σεν παραχ[ρ]ῆμα τὰ πο[μπευθέντα ἱερεῖα]
[- - - - - - παρ]εχόμεν[ος μετ᾿ ἐκτεν]ίας [τὰς χρ]είας τῶι βασιλεῖ καὶ
τῶι πατρὶ αὐτοῦ ὅσα πρ[άττων]
10 - - - - - - - - - - αὐτῶν ἐ[κ] τῶν νόμων, ὁμοίως δὲ καὶ ταῖς
βασιλίσσαις· θύσας δὲ καὶ τοῖ[ς -]
[- - - - - - - - Ἀσκληπι]ῶι καὶ Ὑγιείαι καὶ Ἑρμεῖ καὶ Ἡρακλεῖ καὶ
καλλιερήσας ὑπέρ τε τῆς τοῦ βασιλέως ὑγιείας καὶ σωτηρίας [προσ-]
[ηνέγκατο ἐκτε]νίαν (?) σπουδῆς καὶ φιλοτιμίας οὐθὲν ἐλλείπων
ἀπόδειξιν ποιούμενος τῆς πρὸς τὸν βασιλέα [εὐνοίας - - - - -]

Appendix IV   225

- - - - - - - - - - εὐεργετήματα πλείονα τὰ μὲν ἴδια λυσιτελῆ
                                        παραπέμπων - - - - -
- - - - - - - - - - - - - - ουν -

22 Swoboda, Keil, and Kroll, *Denkmäler aus Lykaonien* (1935), 33, no. 74 I (Amlada). Eumenes II.

- σ - - - - - ιε - - - - - - -
[εἰς τὸν ἔπειτ]α χρόν[ον] τὴν εὔνοιαν, οὐδ[ε-]
[νὸς ὑστ]ερήσετε τῶν παρ' ἡμῶν φιλανθρώπω[ν·]
[περὶ] δὲ τῶν αὐτῶν καὶ τῆς εὐνοίας ἣν ἔχο[μεν]
5 [πρὸ]ς ὑμᾶς ἀκούσεσθε παρὰ τῶν πρεσβευτῶν.
[ἐγ]ράφη   ἐμ Μιστίαι, ὅτε ὁ βασιλεὺς κατεῖχεν
Ὀά[σ]α[δ]α. ἔρρωσθε.

23 Jüthner et al., *Vorläufiger Bericht über eine archäologische Expedition nach Kleinasien* (1903), 22; *OGIS* 751; Welles, *RC* 54; Swoboda et al., *Denkmäler aus Lykaonien*, 33, no. 74 II (Amlada). Eumenes II.

Ἄτταλος Ἀμλαδέων τῆι πόλει καὶ τοῖς γεραιοῖς χαίρει[ν·]
οἱ παρ' ὑμῶν πρεσβευταὶ Ὀπρασάτης Κιλαρ[ίου, Βο . . . .]
νου Ναλαγλόας Κιλαρίου Μεννέας συνμείξαντες ἡμῖν
καὶ διαλεγέντες περὶ ὧν ἐνετετάλθειτε αὐτοῖς ἠξίουσαν
5 ὅμηρά τε ὑμῶν ἀπολυθῆναι [κ]αὶ ἐν τῶι Γαλατικῶι πολέμωι
ἃς προσωφείλετε δραχμὰς ἐνακισχιλίας ἐπισκευ[ῆ]ς [ἔνε-]
[κ]ε καὶ ἀπὸ τῶν δύο ταλάντων ἃ τελεῖτε κατ' ἐνιαυτὸν [κου-]
φίσαι ὑμᾶς, ἐπεὶ θλιβέντες ἐμ πλείοσιν ἀσθενῶς [σχή-]
σετε· θεωρῶν οὖν ὑμᾶς μετανενοηκότας τε ἐπὶ τοῖ[ς]
10 προημαρτημένοις καὶ τὰ ἐπιστελλόμενα ὑφ' ἡμῶν
προθύμως ἐπιτελοῦντας πρόνοιαν ὑμῶν ἔ[σχον καὶ]
χαρισάμενος τῶι τε Ὀπρασάτηι καὶ τῆι πόλει ἐπι-]
τέταχα ἀφελεῖν ἀπὸ τοῦ φόρου καὶ τε[λέ]σ[ματ]ος
[δραχ]μὰς τρισχιλίας καὶ ἄλλας δραχμὰς ἐνακισχιλίας [ἃς]
15 [προσ]ωφείλετε ἡμῖν· ἀπέλυσα δὲ καὶ ὅμ[η]ρα ὑμῶν.
[ἐγράφη] ἐν [- - - - - - - - vac.? - - - - - - ἔρρω]σ[θε.]

24 Knibbe, *ÖJh* xlvii (1964–5), Beiblatt, 1–5, no. 1; Börker and Merkelbach, *Die Inschr. von Ephesos* (*Inschr. griech. Städte aus Kleinasien*, XII. 2, 1979), no. 202. (Ephesos). Attalos II.

[Βασιλεὺς Ἄτταλος Ἐ]φεσίων τῆι βουλῆι καὶ τῶι δήμωι χαίρειν·
                                                               Ἀριστο [- - -
- - - -] πολίτης θ' ὑμῶν κριθεὶς ἄξιος ὑφ' ἡμῶν εἶναι τῆς Ἀττάλου
                                                               τἀδελ[φοῦ]

226   Appendix IV

[υἱοῦ ἐπιμε]λείας μετεπέμφθη, καὶ συσταθεὶς αὐτῶι τῆς καθηκού-
                                    σης παιδείας
[προενόη]σε · πολὺ δὲ μᾶλλον ὑφ' ἡμῶν ἀπεδέχθη διὰ τὸ μὴ μόνον ἐν
                                    τῆι τῶν λόγων ἐνπει-
5 [ρίαι καὶ π]αραδόσει προέχειν πολλῶν, ἀλλ' ὅτι καὶ τῶι ἤθει τοῦ
                                    παντὸς ἐφαίνετ' ἄξιος
.... ου καὶ ἐπιτηδειότατος νέωι συναναστρέφεσθαι · ὅτι γὰρ
                                    ζηλοῦσι τὰς ἀγωγὰς
[τῶν ἐ]πιστατῶν οἱ ἐκ φύσεως καλοκαγαθικοὶ τῶν νέων παντὶ πρό-
                                    δηλόν ἐστιν · δι' ὃ
[δὴ] οὗτος οὐ μόνον ὑφ' ἡμῶν, ἀλλὰ καὶ ὑπ' αὐτοῦ τοῦ Ἀττάλου
                                    σφόδρα προσηνῶς
[ἀ]ποδεχθεὶς δικαίας παρ' ἡμῖν καὶ παρὰ τούτωι ἐτύγχανεν ἐπιση-
                                    μασίας

2-3 τῆς Ἀττάλου τἀδελ[φοῦ | υἱοῦ ἐπιμε]λείας (from new squeeze) Herrmann,
Zeitschr. Pap. Epigr. xxii (1976), 233–4: τῆς Ἀττάλου<υ> ἀδελ[φι|δοῦ μου
παιδεί]ας Knibbe   4 init. [προενόη]σε Herrmann: [προέστη] J. and L.
Robert: [ἔνεκα,] Knibbe.   4–5 ἐνπει|[ρίαι καὶ π]αραδόσει J. and L.
Robert, Bull. 1968, no. 464: ἐνπει|[ρίας π]αραδόσει Knibbe   6 init. [τοῦ
Ἀττάλ]ου Knibbe, questioned by J. and L. Robert (an attribute is required after
ἄξιος): [ἐπαίν]ου Engelmann, Zeitschr. Pap. Epigr. xix (1975), 224

25 Knibbe, ÖJh 1 (1976), Beiblatt, 12–14, no 4; Börker and Merkelbach,
    Inschr. von Ephesos, no. 201. ?Attalos II.

            [Δημ]ήτριον Ἀπολλων[ίο]υ
            [τὸν] γενόμενον ἐπὶ τῆς
            [σφρα]γῖδος τοῦ βασιλέως θεοῦ
            [Εὐμέ]νου Σωτῆρος καὶ στρατη-
5   [γὸν ἐ]πί τε Ἐφέσου καὶ τῶν κατ' Ἔ-
            [φεσο]ν τόπων καὶ Καΰστρου πε-
            [δίου] καὶ τὸ Κιλβιανὸν Δημη-
            ... ς

2–3 J. and L. Robert, Bull. 1972, no 388.   7 τὸ Κιλβιανόν: cf. Pliny, Nat. Hist.
v. 120 Cilbiani inferiores et superiores.

26 Petzl and Pleket, *Chiron*, ix (1979), 73–81 (Kyme). Attalos I or II.

Γνώμα στραταγῶν· ἐπειδὴ Ἐπίγονος Δαμοκράτευς Ταραντῖνος
διατρίβων παρὰ τῷ βασιλεῖ Ἀττάλῳ περί τε τῶν κοινᾷ συμφερόντων
τᾷ πόλει τὰμ παῖσαν σπουδὰν καὶ πρόνοιαν ποιῆται καὶ εἰς τὰ ἴδια
ἑκάστῳ τῶμ πολιτᾶν χρήσιμα πρόθυμον ἑαυτὸν παρέχεται
5 ἀκόλουθα πράσσων τᾷ τῶ βασιλέος αἱρέσει καὶ θέλων ἀπόδειξιν
ποιῆσθαι τᾶς πρὸς τὸν δᾶμον φιλίας· vac. δεδόχθαι τῷ δάμῳ
ἐπαινέσαι τε ἐπὶ τούτοισι Ἐπίγονον καὶ στεφανῶσαι χρυσέῳ
στεφάνῳ, τὰν δὲ ἀναγγελίαν ποιήσασθαι τὸν ἀγωνοθέταν
ἐν τοῖς πρώτοις Διονυσίοισι καὶ Ἀτταλείοισι· δεδόσθαι δὲ καὶ
10 προξενίαν αὐτῷ καὶ τοῖς ἐκγόνοισι καὶ ἀποδεῖξαι ἄνδρα
τὸν ἐπιμελησόμενον, ἵνα τοῦτό τε τὸ ψάφισμα καὶ τὸ ὑπὲρ τᾶς
προξενίας δόγμα καταχωρισθέντα εἰς στάλλαν καθ' ὅγ κε
θέλῃ τῶμ πινάκων τῶν ἐν τῷ ἱρῷ τᾶς Ἀθάνας ἀνατεθῇ εἰς τὸ
ἱρὸν τᾶς Ἀθάνας· τὸ δὲ εἰς ταῦτα ἐσσόμενον ἀνάλωμα προχρῆσαι
15 τοῖς στραταγοῖς, κομίσσασθαι δὲ ἐκ πόρω, ὧ κε ὁ δᾶμος ψαφίσση-
ται··
ἀνενεγκάτωσαν δὲ τὸ ψάφισμα τοῦτο καὶ πρὸς Ἐπίγονον οἱ πρῶτ[οι]
ἀποσταλησόμενοι πρεσβευταὶ πρὸς τὸμ βασιλέα καὶ παρακαλήτ[ω-
σαν]
αὐτὸν καθότι καὶ νῦν καὶ εἰς τὰ μετὰ ταῦτα διαφυλάσσην τὰν ε[ὔ-
νοιαν]
πρὸς τὰμ πόλιν. ἀπεδείχθη Νικίας Ἑρμογένεος· τᾷ ἐκκ[λησίᾳ]
20 στραταγὸς ἐπήστακε Ξενότιμος Λυσανία, μη[νὸς ....]
ἑκκαιδεκάτᾳ, ἐπὶ πρυτάνιος Ἀπολλωνίῳ [τῷ (name)].

SELECT BIBLIOGRAPHY

Allen, R. E., 'Attalos I and Aigina', *BSA* lxvi (1971), 1–12.
Altertümer von Pergamon (Berlin, 1885–   ). The following volumes are of
   particular importance to the subjects treated in this study:
   II. *Das Heiligtum der Athena Polias Nikephoros* (R. Bohn, 1885).
   III. 1. *Der grosse Altar, der Obere Markt* (J. Schrammen, 1906).
       2. *Die Friese des grossen Altars* (H. Winnefeld, 1910).
   VIII. *Die Inschriften von Pergamon*
       i. Bis zum Ende der Königszeit.
       ii. Römische Zeit. Inschriften auf Thon (ed. M. Fränkel, with E. Fabri-
         cius and C. Schuchhardt, 1890 and 1895).
       iii. Die Inschriften des Asklepieions (ed. Chr. Habicht, 1969).
   IX. *Das Temenos für den Herrscherkult* (E. Boehringer, F. Krauss, 1937).
Beloch, K. J., *Griechische Geschichte,* iv. 1 and 2 (ed. 2, Berlin and
   Leipzig. 1925–7).
Bengtson, H., *Die Strategie in der hellenistischen Zeit*, I - III (*Münchener
   Beiträge zur Papyrusforschung und antiken Rechtsgeschichte*, 26, 32,
   and 36), Munich, 1937–52, reprinted with corrections and additions,
   1964–7.
—— *Die Inschriften von Labranda und die Politik des Antigonos Doson,*
   SB München 1971, 3.
Bickermann (or Bi(c)kerman), E., 'Bellum Antiochicum', *Hermes,* lxvii
   (1932), 47–76.
—— 'La cité grecque dans les monarchies hellénistiques', *Rev. Phil.* lxv
   (1939), 335–49.
—— 'Notes on Seleucid and Parthian Chronology', *Berytus,* viii (1944),
   73–83.
—— 'Notes sur Polybe. I. Le Statut des villes d'Asie après la paix
   d'Apamée', *REG* 1 (1937), 217–39.
(Bickermann's name is variously spelt in different publications. For con-
   sistency in this book the form *Bickermann* is always used.)
Broughton, T.R.S., 'New Evidence on Temple-Estates in Asia Minor',
   *Studies in Roman Economic and Social History in honor of Allan
   Chester Johnson* (1951), 236–50.
Cardinali, G., 'L'amministrazione finanziaria del comune di Pergamo',
   Mem. Accad. Bologna, x (1915–16), 181–93.
—— 'Ancora sull' albero genealogico degli Attalidi', *Rend. Accad.
   Bologna,* vii (1913–14), 37–41.
—— 'La Genealogia degli Attalidi', *Mem. Accad. Bologna,* vii (1912–13),
   177–85.
—— 'La morte di Attalo III e la rivolta di Aristonico', *Saggi di storia
   antica e di archeologia offerti a G. Beloch* (1910), 269–320.
—— *Il regno di Pergamo* (Rome, 1906).

Conze, A., and P. Schazmann, *Mamurt-Kaleh: Ein Tempel der Götter-mutter unweit Pergamon* (*JDAI Ergänzungsheft*, ix, 1911).

Crampa, J., 'Some Remarks on Welles, Royal Correspondence 29', *Op. Athen.* viii (1968), 171–8.

Daux, G., 'Craton, Eumène II et Attale II', *BCH* lix (1935), 210–30.

—— *Delphes au deuxième et au premier siècle*, (Paris, 1936).

—— 'Sur une clause du Traité conclu entre le roi Attale Iᵉʳ de Pergame et la cité de Malla (Crète)', *Rev. hist. de droit français et étranger*, xlix (1971), 373–85.

De Sanctis, G., 'Eumene II e le città greche d'Asia', *Riv. di fil.* liii (1925), 68–78.

Droysen, J. G., *Geschichte des Hellenismus*, iii. *Geschichte der Epigonen* (ed. 2, Gotha, 1877–8).

Ducrey, P., 'Nouvelles remarques sur deux traités Attalides avec des cités crétoises', *BCH* xciv (1970), 637–59.

—— and H. van Effenterre, 'Traités Attalides avec des cités crétoises', *Kretika Chronika*, xxi (1969), 277–300.

Ferguson, W. S., 'The Premature Deification of Eumenes II', *C. Phil.* i (1906), 231–4.

Fraser, P. M., 'Dédicaces Attalides en Béotie', *REA* liv (1952), 233–45.

von Fritze, H., 'Zur Chronologie der autonomen Prägung von Pergamon', *Corolla Numismatica*, (1906), 47–62.

—— *Die Münzen von Pergamon* (*Abh. Berlin*, 1910).

Ghione, P., 'I comuni del regno di Pergamo', *Mem. Accad. Torino*, lv (1905), 67–149.

Giovannini, A., *Rome et la circulation monetaire en Grèce au IIe siècle av. Jésus-Christ* (*Schweiz. Beitr. zur Altertumswissenschaft*, xv, Basel, 1978).

Habicht, Chr., *Gottmenschentum und griechische Städte* (*Zetemata*, xiv, revised ed., Munich, 1970).

—— 'Prusias (1)', *RE* 1086–1107.

—— 'Prusias (2)', *RE* 1107–27.

—— 'Über die Kriege zwischen Pergamon und Bithynien', *Hermes*, lxxxiv (1956), 90–110.

Hansen, E. V., *The Attalids of Pergamon* (ed. 2, Cornell, 1972).

Herrmann, P., 'Antiochos der Grosse und Teos', *Anadolu*, ix (1965), 29–159.

—— 'Neue Urkunden zur Geschichte von Milet im 2. Jahrhundert v. Chr.', *Ist. Mitt.* xv (1965), 71–117.

Holleaux, M., 'Le Décret de Bargylia en l'honneur de Poseidonios', *REA* xxi (1919), 1–19; *Études*, ii. 179–98.

—— 'Décret des Amphictions de Delphes relatif à la fête des Niképhoria', *Mélanges Havet* (1909), 187–96; *Etudes*, ii. 63–72.

—— *Études d'épigraphie et d'histoire grecques* (ed. L. Robert, 6 vols. with index and bibliography, Paris, 1938–68).

—— 'L'expédition d'Attale Iᵉʳ en 218', *Revue des univ. du Midi*, 1897, 409–34; *Études*, ii. 17–42.

—— 'L'expédition de Philippe V en Asie (201 av. J. C.)', *REA* xxii (1920),

230   *Select Bibliography*

237–8; xxiii (1921), 181–212; xxv (1923), 330–66; *Études*, iv. 211–335.
—— 'Inscription de Pergame', *REG* xi (1898), 251–8; *Études*, ii. 43–9.
—— 'Inscription trouvée à Brousse', BCH xlviii (1924), 1–37; *Études*, ii. 73–125.
—— 'Note sur une inscription de Kolophon Nova', *BCH* xxx (1906), 349–58; *Études*, ii. 51–60.
—— ΦΙΛΕΤΑΙΡΟΣ ΑΤΤΑΛΟΥ, *REG* xv (1902), 302–10; *Études*, ii. 1–8.
—— 'Sur la date de fondation des Niképhoria', *REA* xviii (1916), 170–1; *Études*, ii. 61–2.
—— 'Sur la lettre d'Attale aux 'Αμλαδεῖς, *REA* xx (1918), 17–19; *Études*, ii. 149–51.
—— 'Un nouveau document relatif aux premiers Attalides', *REA* xx (1918), 9–16; *Études*, ii. 9–16.
—— 'Un prétendu décret d'Antioche sur l'Oronte', *REG* xiii (1900), 258–80; *Études*, ii. 127–47.
Hopp, J., *Untersuchungen zur Geschichte der letzten Attaliden* (*Vestigia*, xxv, Munich, 1977).
Imhoof-Blumer, F., *Die Münzen der Dynastie von Pergamon* (*Abh. Berlin*, 1884).
Inschriften von Pergamon, see *Altertümer von Pergamon*.
Jones, C. P., 'Diodoros Pasparos and the Nikephoria of Pergamon', *Chiron*, iv (1974), 183–205.
Kähler, H., *Der grosse Fries von Pergamon. Untersuchungen zur Kunstgeschichte und Geschichte Pergamons* (Berlin, 1948).
Keil, J., and A. von Premerstein, *Bericht über eine Reise in Lydien und der südlichen Aeolis ausgeführt 1906* (*Denkschr. Wien. Akad.* liii (1908)).
—— *Bericht über eine zweite Reise in Lydien ausgeführt 1908* (*Denkschr. Wien. Akad.* liv (1911)).
Kienast, D., 'Cistophoren', *Jahrb. für Numismatik und Geldgeschichte*, xi (1961), 159–88.
Klaffenbach, G., *Die Astynomeninschrift von Pergamon* (*Abh. Berlin*, 1953, 6).
—— 'Die Nikephorien von Pergamon', *MDAI* iii (1950), 99–106.
Kleiner, F. S., 'The Dated Cistophoroi of Ephesos', *American Numismatic Society Museum Notes*, xviii (1972), 17–32.
—— and S. P. Noe, *The Early Cistophoric Coinage* (American Numismatic Society, *Numismatic Studies*, xiv, New York, 1977).
Köpp, F., 'Ueber die Galaterkriege der Attaliden', *Rh. Mus.* xl (1885), 114–32.
Launey, M., 'Un episode oublié de l'invasion Galate en Asie Mineure (278/7 av. J. C.)', *REA* xlvi (1944), 217–36.
—— *Recherches sur les armées hellénistiques* (2 vols., Paris, 1949–50).
Leuze, R., 'Die Feldzüge Antiochos' des Grossen nach Kleinasien und Thrakien', *Hermes*, lviii (1923), 187–287.
McShane, R. B., *The Foreign Policy of the Attalids of Pergamon* (*Illinois Studies in the Social Sciences*, liii, Urbana, 1964).
Magie, D., *Roman Rule in Asia Minor* (2 vols., Princeton, 1950).

—— 'Rome and the City-States of Asia Minor from 200 to 133 B. C.', *Anatolian Studies presented to W.H. Buckler*, (1939), 161–85.

Meischke, K., *Symbolae ad Eumenis II Pergamenorum regis historiam* (Leipzig, 1892).

Meyer, Eduard, *Geschichte des Koenigreichs Pontos* (Leipzig, 1879).

Meyer, Ernst, *Die Grenzen der hellenistischen Staaten in Kleinasien* (Zürich and Leipzig, 1925).

—— 'Zum Stammbaum der Attaliden', *Klio*, xix (1925), 462–71.

Niese, B., *Geschichte der griechischen und makedonischen Staaten seit der Schlacht bei Chaeronea* (3 vols., Gotha, 1903).

Nock, A. D., ΣΥΝΝΑΟΣ ΘΕΟΣ, *Harv. Stud.* xli (1930), 1–62; *Essays on Religion and the Ancient World* (Oxford, 1972), i. 202–51.

Noe, S. P., 'Beginnings of the Cistophoric Coinage', *American Numismatic Society Museum Notes*, iv (1950), 29–41. See also Kleiner, F. S.

Ohlemutz, E., *Die Kulte und Heiligtümer der Götter in Pergamon* (Würzburg, 1940).

Oliver, J. H., 'The Date of the Pergamene Astynomic Law', *Hesperia*, xxiv (1955), 88–92.

Paepcke, C., *de Pergamenorum litteratura* (Rostock, 1906).

Petzl, G., and H. W. Pleket, 'Ein hellenistisches Ehrendekret aus Kyme', *Chiron*, ix (1979), 73–81.

Picard, C., 'Un oracle d'Apollon Clarios à Pergame', *BCH* lxvi (1922), 190–7.

Préaux, C., *Le Monde hellénistique* (*Nouvelle Clio*, vi, 2 vols., Paris, 1978).

von Prott, H., 'Dionysos Kathegemon', *AM* xxvii (1902), 161–88.

Radet, G., 'Eumeneia', *Anatolian Studies presented to W. M. Ramsay* (1923), 315–21.

Reinach, A. J., 'Les mercenaires et les colonies militaires de Pergame', *Rev. Arch.* xii (1908), 174–218, 364–89; xiii (1909), 102–19, 363–77.

Robert, L., *Études anatoliennes* (Paris, 1937).

—— *Hellenica, Recueil d'épigraphie, de numismatique, et d'antiquités grecques*, i–xiii (Paris, 1940–65).

—— *Opera Minora Selecta. Épigraphie et antiquités grecques*, i–iv (Amsterdam, 1969–74).

—— *Villes d'Asie Mineure* (ed. 2, Paris, 1962).

Robinson, E. S. G., 'Cistophori in the Name of King Eumenes', *Num. Chron.* xiv (1954), 1–7.

Rostovtzeff, M., 'Notes on the Economic Policy of the Pergamene Kings', *Anatolian Studies presented to W. M. Ramsay* (1923), 359–90.

—— 'Pergamum', in *Cambridge Ancient History*, viii (1930), 590–618.

—— 'Some Remarks on the Monetary and Commercial Policy of the Seleucids and the Attalids', *Anatolian Studies presented to W. H. Buckler* (1939), 277–98.

Schmitt, H. H., *Untersuchungen zur Geschichte Antiochos' des Grossen und seiner Zeit* (*Historia*, Einzelschriften, vi, Wiesbaden, 1964).

Schober, A., 'Zur Datierung Eumenischer Bauten', *ÖJh* xxxii (1940), 151–68.

Segre, M., 'Due nuovi testi storici', *Riv. di fil.* lx (1932), 446–53.
—— 'L'Institution des Niképhoria de Pergame', in Robert, *Hellenica,* v (1948), 102–28.
Seyrig, H., 'Le Traité d'Apamée et le monnayage des villes d'Asie', *Rev. Num.* v (1963), 19–22; 'Questions Cistophoriques', ibid. 22–31.
Starr, C. G., 'Rhodes and Pergamum, 201–200 B.C.', *C. Phil.* xxxiii (1938), 63-8.
Swoboda, H., 'Zu den Urkunden von Pergamon', *Rh. Mus.* xlvi (1891), 497–510.
—— Keil, J., and F. Kroll, *Denkmäler aus Lykaonien, Pamphylien und Isaurien* (Prague, 1935).
Tscherikower, V., *Die hellenistischen Städtegründungen von Alexander dem Grossen bis auf die Römerzeit* (*Philologus,* Suppl. xix, Heft 1, Leipzig, 1927).
Westermark, U., *Das Bildnis des Philetairos von Pergamon* (Stockholm, 1960).
Wilhelm, Ad., *Akademieschriften zur griechischen Inschriftenkunde* (ed. W. Peek, 3 vols., Leipzig, 1974).
—— *Griechische Inschriften rechtlichen Inhalts* (Athens, 1951).
—— 'Kleinasiatische Dynasten', *Neue Beiträge zur griechischen Inschriftenkunde* (*SB Wien,* clxvi (1911), i. 11, 48–63).
Will, E., *Histoire politique du monde hellénistique (323-30 av. J.-C.)* (2 vols., Nancy, 1966–7; ed. 2, 1979–81).
Wörrle, M., 'Antiochos I, Achaios der Ältere und die Galater', *Chiron,* v (1975), 59–87.

INDEX OF INSCRIPTIONS

Readers are referred in this index to the most recent reliable edition of each text, but a corpus reference (e.g. *F. Delphes, Syll.*³) is generally preferred to a journal reference. The index is not intended to serve as a concordance of references, but to assist readers who may be expected to approach a text from any of several editions: a text cited from *OGIS* may be known also from its inclusion in *IvP*, and so on. The edition referred to in the index is not necessarily that cited on every occasion in the text, as there may be particular reasons for citing a different edition. Cross-reference by bold number (e.g. see **23**) is to the list of inscriptions given in Appendix iv, which is put first in this index.

GENERAL INDEX

I. NAMES AND SUBJECTS

Galatians (*continued*)
  defeated by Attalos I, 28n., 29-35,
    122, 136-41, 195-9
  as mercenaries of Attalos I, 40, 57,
    138, 141
  campaign against by Cn. Manlius
    Vulso, 80, 90, 107, 201
  and Eumenes II, 78, 79, 80, 90,
    101, 107, 128, 151
  and Attalos II, 82, 133, 143-4
Gambreion, 16
garrisons, 109
  on Aigina, 75
genealogy, Attalid, 181-94
Greek cities, of Asia Minor, 4, 39-58,
    80-1, 85, 114
Gryneion, 21n., 24n.
gymnasium, Attalid interest in, 118,
    120, 155

Hadrian, 171
Hekatomnids, 187
Helikonian muses (at Thespiai), 15
Hellespont, 72
  Galatians settled there by Attalos I
    in 218, 40, 57
Hellespontine Phrygia, 30, 38, 41,
    45-6, 55, 57-8, 62, 148n.
  Attalos I defeats Galatians in, 35
  awarded to Eumenes II in 188, 87
  administration of, 87-91, 93
Herakleia (by Latmos), 98, 99, 110
Herakleia (Pontic), 84n.
Herakles, 137n.
Hierapytna (Crete), 47n., 72n.
Hierapolis, 105, 149, 150, 152
Hierocaesarea, 104n.
Hikesios (of Ephesos), 106, 120, 135
Hydra, Cape, 25

Iasos, 127, 133-4
Ilion, 3, 20n., 40, 49n., 58, 61, 110,
    111n., 138, 139, 169
Ionia, 40, 45-6, 57, 62, 65
Ionian *koinon*, 115-16
Ipsos, battle at, 9
Istron (Crete), 47n.
Itanos (Crete), 91n.
Izmir, 95, 140

Kaikos, River, 31, 34, 38, 122, 140,
    141, 195, 196-9
Kalynda, 46
Kardakes, 95
Karseai, 40
Karystios (of Pergamon), 183
Karystos (Euboia), 74n.
Kassandros, 61n.
katoikoi, 94-8, 114
Kaunos, 46
Kephisodoros (gymnasiarch at
    Apameia), 154
Ketschi-Agyl, 25
Kibyra, 110
Kiddioukome, 140
Kios, 84n.
Kleon (*epistates* at Aigina), 105
Knossos (Crete), 47n.
Koile Syria, 22
Koloe, battle at, 195
Kolophon, 49, 56, 57-8, 110n., 162n.,
    169
  see also Colophon Nova
Korrhagos (Attalid *strategos*), 6, 55,
    88-91, 94, 95, 107, 111n.
Korris (priest at Labraunda), 143
Kos, 57, 110, 127, 133-4, 146, 149n.,
    155, 169n.
Krates (of Mallos), 142n.
Kraton, 150-2, 153
Kybele, 142
Kydonia (Crete), 47n.
Kyme, 17, 41, 99, 110, 134, 147
Kyzikos, 3, 14-15, 16, 26, 58, 104,
    110, 131, 137-8, 139, 146,
    151n., 183

Labraunda, 39, 91n., 143
Lachares (official of elder Achaios),
    140
Lade, battle at, 73
Lampsakos, 40, 58, 61, 110, 170
Laodike (queen of Mithridates II),
    138
Laodike (queen of Antiochos III), 48
Laodikeia, 37
Lato (Crete), 47n.
Lebedos, 111
Leonnarios, 137n., 139
Leschides (biographer of Attalids), 3

246 General Index

Leukophryena (at Magnesia), 127
Licinius Crassus, P. (cos. 171), 142
Lilaia, 33, 45, 107, 177
Loutarios, 137n.
Lycaonia, 87
Lycia, 100
Lydia, 38, 41
  Attalos I defeats Galatians in, 35
  awarded to Eumenes II in 188, 87
Lykos, River, 40, 43
Lysias (dynast), 13, 35-6, 196
Lysimacheia, 11, 87, 88, 100, 101
Lysimachos, 9-14, 121, 122
Lysimachos (biographer of Attalids), 3

Macedon, 66, 73
Macedonian foundations, 94
Macedonian war, first, 26, 33, 45, 49,
  62, 66-71, 75
  second, 49, 59, 72-5
Magnesia ad Maeandrum, 45, 56, 62,
  99, 104, 105, 110, 115, 127,
  163, 169, 190
Magnesia ad Sipylum, 13n., 24n.,
  100, 105, 110
  battle at, 44n., 59, 77, 87, 98
Makestos, River, 40
Mallos, 142n.
Mamurt-Kaleh, 16, 164, 183
Manisa, 18
Manlius Vulso, Cn., 80, 83n., 90,
  107, 201
Masdue, 93
Mastya, 73n.
Megara, 106
Megon (of Ephesos), 120, 133, 135
Mektepini (Phrygia), 112n.
Menogenes (ὁ ἐπὶ τῶν πραγμάτων),
  129-30, 133, 134
mercenaries, 23, 29, 30, 63, 115
  revolt of, at Philetaireia and
    Attaleia, 23-5, 187
Meter, 15, 19, 164, 183
Methymna, 99
Metris (priestess of 9th Nikephoria),
  127, 128
Metrodoros (strategos at Pergamon),
  166
Miletos, 7, 57, 98, 99n. 100, 104n.,
  111, 113n., 114-21, 139, 145,
  155, 157, 190, 194

Milyas, 87
mints, royal, 109-14, 135
Mithridates I, 138
Mithridates II, 138, 140-1, 186
Mithridates (= Ariarathes V), 202-3
Mylasa, 91n., 99n.
Myndos, 111
Myrina, 17, 21n., 24n., 41, 111
Mysia, 25, 39-45, 55, 62-5, 68, 96
  Attalos I defeats Galatians in, 31
  'Mysiam, quam Prusia rex
    ademerat', 63-5, 87
  Olympene, 63
Mytilene, 19, 21, 24n., 111
Myus, 115, 118-19

Nabis (of Sparta), 77, 125n., 126
Nakrasa, 26, 101n., 106, 129, 133
Nasos, 162n.
Neanthes of Kyzikos (biographer of
  Attalids), 3
neokoros, 96
Neonteichos, 140
neos ktistes (designation of
  Philetairos), 161
Nikephoria, 79, 123-9, 133-4, 170
Nikephorion, at Pergamon, 44n.,
  123-5
  destroyed by Prusias II, 82
Nikephoros, see Athena
Nikomedes I, 15, 84n., 137n., 141
Nikomedes IV, 84-5
'Northern League', 15
Notion, 56
Nysa (queen of Pharnakes I), 117n.

Olus (Crete), 72n.
Oreos (Euboia), 74n.
Orontes (satrap of Artaxerxes II),
  162
Oropos, 183
Ortiagon, 79

palace, royal, at Teos, 153
  at Tralles, 153
Palamandros (strategos at
  Pergamon), 166
Pamphylia, 83
Panathenaia, at Pergamon, 122, 123,
  166, 170

Panionion, Eumenes II honoured at,
116
Paramonos, 107n.
Parion, 111
Pelekas, Mount, 40
Pella, 159
Peloponnese, Eumenes II honoured
in, 76-7
Pergamon, 159-77
Strabo on, 2
monumental and architectural
remains, 7-8
wealth at, 13-14, 77
source of Attalid inscriptions, 4, 6
ephebic lists from, 91-6, 176
pre-Attalid status, 15-16, 159-64
participates in cult of Meter, 16, 19
treaty of *isopoliteia* with Temmos,
16-17, 160
Philetairos at, from 302, 9
constitution at, 85, 108, 159-69,
170-6
ὁ ἐπὶ τῆς πόλεως at, 108, 171-3, 177
ὁ ἐπὶ τῶν ἱερῶν προσόδων at,
172-4, 177
strategoi at, see *strategos*
finance of, 109, 114, 167-8
mint at, 110
building programme in 180s at, 76,
126
gymnasial cult at, 154-5
Asklepieion at, 204
walls at, 126
and Apollonis, 205-6
and Aristonikos, 85
and Athena, 122, 126, 170 (see also
Nikephoria)
and Dionysos Kathegemon, 104
and royal cults, 120, 151-7
and Stratonike, 200-6
and *topoi* 93-4
and Zeus, 173
Perseus (of Macedon), 4, 80, 142
Pessinous, 82, 130, 142-4
Pharnakes of Pontos, 3, 4n., 79, 81,
100, 117n., 141
Phaselis, 111
Phialeia, 46
Philetaireia (Lydia), 23-6, 32, 107,
122, 184, 186

two of same name distinguished,
23n.
Philetaireia, at Delos, 22n., 146, 189
at Kyzikos, 15n., 138, 146
Philetairos, 9-20
literary tradition on, 2-3
parentage, 182-3
allegiance to Lysimachos, 13-14,
122
allegiance to Seleukids, 9, 12,
13-19, 160
beginning of rule, 9
length of reign, 10-11
financial independence, 14
befriends neighbours, 14-15
nature of authority, 14, 20
head on later dynastic coinage, 24,
32n., 112n., 113
and coinage, 14
and Delphi, 15
and Galatians, 31n., 136-9
and Kyzikos, 14-15, 58, 137, 146
and Meter, 15-16
and Pergamon, 14, 154, 159-60
and Pitane, 19
and succession, 187
and Thespiai, 15
Philetairos son of Eumenes (=
brother of Eumenes I), 184,
187-8
Philetairos (son of Attalos I), 116n.,
156, 181
Philip V, 4n., 44, 66-9, 72-4, 86, 147,
169, 192, 193n.
defeated at Chios in 202, 28n.,
72-3, 124
invasion of Asia Minor in 201, 49,
115, 123
defeated by Roman alliance in 197,
126, 128
and Antiochos III, 60, 73n.
and Cretan communities, 47-8
and Teos, 47-8
Philiskos (*strategos* at Pergamon),
166
Philomelids, 13, 19-20
Philomelos, 13, 20n.
Philopoimen (ὁ ἐπὶ τῆς σφραγῖδος),
107n., 132, 134
Phoinike, Peace of, 49, 55, 69, 71

Phokaia, 41-2, 86, 91, 101, 104,
	111n., 162n.
Phrygia, Greater, 87
	Epiktetos, 63-5
pirates, Cretan, 72
Pisidia, 37, 41, 83
Pitane, 16, 19, 21, 26, 41-2, 45, 91n.,
	104
Pleuratus, 68
Polemon (of Ilion), 3
Polyrrhenia (Crete), 47n.
Pontos, 3, 78, 138, 141, 186
Porphyrius, 35n.
Poseidonios (grandfather of Eume-
	nes I), 184
praefectus (= *strategos*), 90
Priapos, 101n., 111
Priene, 99n., 104n., 105n., 136n.,
	139, 163, 165n.
prostagma, 104, 109, 175, 176, 177
Prusa, 88
Prusias I, 3, 49, 63-4, 67, 69, 71, 79,
	101, 122-3, 128, 141, 151
Prusias II, 3-4, 82, 83, 99, 124, 128,
	131, 132, 143, 144
prytanis, 161, 163-5
Ptolemais (Egypt), 172n.
Ptolemies, 83, 114
Ptolemy II, 22, 202
Ptolemy Makron, 91n.
Ptolemy Physkon, 84

Rhaukos (Crete), 47n.
Rhodes, 4, 37, 46, 60n., 72-3, 80,
	98n., 99n., 100, 105n., 111,
	113n., 122
Roman settlement of 188 BC, 4, 8,
	25, 52-3, 54, 55, 57, 62, 63,
	78, 86-7, 88, 90, 91, 98, 126,
	128. *See also* Apameia
Rome, Attalos I's alliance with, 27-8,
	65-75, 146
	treaty with Aitolia, 67-8
	Eumenes II and, 4, 76, 80, 86-7
	alliance after death of Attalos I,
		78, 86
	envoys of Eumenes II and
		Pharnakes at (183/2), 79
	war with Perseus, 80
	Attalos II and, 143

assisted by Attalid forces in 149
	and 146, 83
Attalid dependence on, 84
Attalos III bequeaths kingdom to,
	84
royal title, taken by Attalos I, 29n.,
	31, 140, 159, 169, 198-9

Sabazios, 130-1, 174-5, 203
Samos, 120n., 132
Sardis, 16, 96, 103, 105, 110, 111,
	112, 142n., 158
	battle at (*c.* 262), 20-1, 24, 160
satrapal system, Seleukid, 78, 87, 97
Satyra (mother of Eumenes I), 181,
	184
Scerdilaidas, 68
Scipio, *see* Cornelius
Seleukeia, 78n.
Seleukeia in Piereia, 176n.
Seleukos I, 9, 11-14, 241
Seleukos II, 30, 34, 105n., 138, 197
Seleukos III, 29, 30, 35-6
Seleukos (son of Antiochos III), 113,
	123
Selge, 37, 83, 102n., 144
Senate (at Rome), 4, 27, 49, 53, 55,
	78, 79, 82, 84, 143
Sestos, 87, 94, 155
settlements, military, 93-4, 95-7
Sikyon, 77n., 147, 149
Skepsis, 3, 101n., 111, 138
Skymnos (*strategos* at Pergamon),
	166
slaves, 85
Smyrna, 13n., 18, 24n., 41n., 46,
	110nn., 111, 142, 165n.
Soli, 120n.
soma, 96-7, 198-9
Sosandros, 130-1
Sotas, 139
Soteria (of Prusias I), 123
sources, 1-8
Sparta, 125n., 126
Strabo, sources of, 2-3, 13-14
strategia, 107n.
strategos, kinds of office of this
	name in the kingdom, 107-8
	Attalid regional official, 6, 55,
		87-91

II. NOTABLE GREEK WORDS AND PHRASES